THE OUTSIDERS

THE OUTSIDERS

Refugees in Europe since 1492

PHILIPP THER

TRANSLATED BY JEREMIAH RIEMER

PRINCETON UNIVERSITY PRESS
PRINCETON AND OXFORD

Requests for permission to reproduce material from this work should be sent to permissions@press.princeton.edu

Published by Princeton University Press

41 William Street, Princeton, New Jersey 08540

6 Oxford Street, Woodstock, Oxfordshire OX20 1TR

press.princeton.edu

Library of Congress Control Number: 2019936643

ISBN: 978-0-691-1-7952-0

British Library Cataloging-in-Publication Data is available

The translation of this work was funded by Geisteswissenschaften International— Translation Funding for Work in the Humanities and Social Sciences from Germany, a joint initiative of the Fritz Thyssen Foundation, the German Federal Foreign Office, the collecting society VG WORT and the Börsenverein des Deutschen Buchhandels (German Publishers & Booksellers Association).

Editorial: Eric Crahan and Pamela Weidman

Production Editorial: Ellen Foos

Text Design: Carmina Alvarez

Production: Merli Guerra

Publicity: James Snyder and Caroline Priday

Jacket and text illustrations: Pauline Altmann / Suhrkamp Verlag

Maps: Peter Palm

This book has been composed in Minion Pro

Printed on acid-free paper. ∞

Printed in the United States of America

1 3 5 7 9 10 8 6 4 2

CONTENTS

DRAMATIS PERSONAE

(in alphabetical order)

Manuel Alarcón Navarro (1898–1939/40)

Madeleine Albright (1937-)

Hannah Arendt (1906–1975)

Lord George Curzon (1859–1925)

The Dublon family (extinguished 1944)

Jerzy Giedroyc (1906–2000)

Ruth Klüger (1931-)

Tadeusz Kościuszko (1746–1817)

Alan Kurdi (2012–2015)

Giuseppe Mazzini (1805–1872)

Talaat Pasha (1874–1921)

Queen Rania of Jordan (1970-)

The Robillard family (1687-)

Conrad Schumann (1942–1998)

Manès Sperber (1906–1985)

Erika Steinbach (1943-)

THE OUTSIDERS

INTRODUCTION

Flight and Refugees in Historical Perspective

The sight that presented itself to the members of the international commission in the refugee camps on the Greek islands and on the mainland was evidently hard to put into words:

> On the humanitarian side, imagination cannot encompass the event. Only those can attempt to understand who have seen destitution, misery, disease and death in all their possible forms, and the scale of disaster is so unprecedented as to demand a new vision even from such persons.[1]

A reporter for *Foreign Affairs* made do with comparisons from the animal kingdom: "[The] refugees . . . maintained a fox-like existence in tents, wooden barracks, shelters of twigs, or of turf, even in caves."[2]

In Germany it was too cold for these kinds of accommodations, but a report in the *Neue Berliner Zeitung* about the Scheunenviertel (the Berlin neighborhood that was home to Jews and other poor immigrants from Eastern Europe) depicted a situation just as desperate:

> That boardinghouse is currently home to 120 Jewish refugees from the East. Many of the men arrived straight from Russian POW camps. Their ragged garments were a weird and wonderful hodgepodge of internationalist working class uniforms. In their eyes I saw millennial sorrow. There were women there too. They carried their children on their backs like bundles of dirty washing. Other children, who went scrabbling through a rickety world on crooked legs, gnawed on dry crusts.[3]

In Viennese emergency centers circumstances were not much better; according to contemporary reports, twenty-five refugees on average were housed in a single dwelling, eight to ten people to a room.[4] The close confinement and terrible hygienic conditions were an ideal breeding ground for flees, bedbugs, and lice that, in turn, transmitted typhus, today an almost forgotten disease but one that at the time was often fatal. In addition, there were repeated outbreaks of dysentery, smallpox, tuberculosis, and influenza. Death was an ever-present companion to the homeless; in the Greek refugee camps up to 70,000 people died from malnutrition and diseases, some of them epidemic.[5]

The author of this moving report about the Scheunenviertel was the writer Joseph Roth, who himself was forced to take flight several times during his life. His last escape in 1933 and the reasons that made him leave Germany were so unbearable for him that he drank himself to death in his Parisian exile. The two other passages cited above also come from 1923; they recount the misery of Greeks from Asia Minor following the "exchange of populations" agreed to internationally at the conference of Lausanne. In Europe and its near neighborhood in the Middle East, a genuine "refugee crisis" was unfolding at that time, in part along the same "Mediterranean" and "Balkan route" that the refugees of 2015 would take. The scale of the mass flight nearly a hundred years ago was, however, incomparably greater. In the early 1920s, about seven million people were in flight: nearly three million fleeing the revolution and civil war in Russia, two million fleeing the Greco-Turkish war that erupted in 1919, and more than one and a half million attempting to escape various wars and local conflicts toward the end of the "long" First World War, a war that did not really come to a close in Eastern and Southeastern Europe until around 1923.

Yet these streams of refugees (metaphors invoking a force of nature became current at the time) were a mere trickle compared with the deluge that followed from National Socialism and the Second World War. In the 1940s at least thirty million people were on the run in Europe, a number that does not even include displaced forced laborers and prisoners of war. Two to three million people wandered the streets of occupied Germany in 1945, along with several hundred thousand each in Poland, Hungary, Czechoslovakia, Austria, Yugoslavia, Bulgaria, Romania, Greece, Finland, and the Soviet Union. Old people and children especially were often no match for the hardships they faced.

The humanitarian disasters that followed both world wars did produce at least one positive outcome, however: the international community took up the challenge of refugees. In 1921 the recently established League of Nations, in reaction to the mass flight from the Bolsheviks, appointed the well-known Norwegian naturalist and explorer Fridtjof Nansen as "High Commissioner for Russian Refugees."[6] Soon the adjective "Russian" was dropped, since Nansen also had to deal with Greece, which took in more than half a million refugees from Asia Minor within a few months of its catastrophic defeat at the hands of the Turkish army.[7] After the Treaty of Lausanne, which authorized the first ethnic cleansing of two entire countries (the only exceptions being Western Thrace in Greece and Istanbul in Turkey), the number of refugees again increased dramatically.[8]

Later in the 1920s there was a brief pause in this history of massive refugee movements. Owing to an improved economic situation, those who had recently fled their home countries were able to strike roots in their countries of exile. Some countries, like France, even took in refugees willingly in order to compensate for their demographic losses from the war. But as early as 1933, the next mass exodus was under way, at first from Germany. Almost 60,000 people fled the National Socialists, and by the end of the decade they were followed by 370,000 more, most of them Jews. The League of Nations reacted to this new challenge in 1933 with a convention for refugees from Germany, which was followed in 1938 by a similar convention for refugees from Austria. Unlike the situation in the early 1920s, the immediate plight of the refugees was no longer the major problem; instead, it was the reluctance of countries to admit them. At the infamous Conference of Évian, all attempts at the admission and international resettlement of Jewish refugees failed. Hundreds of thousands of Jews who were no longer able to flee from Germany and German-annexed Austria in time died in German concentration camps.

After the Second World War, the international community drew far-reaching conclusions from this experience. In 1946, under the umbrella of the United Nations, the International Refugee Organization (IRO) was founded, an institution that initially attended to displaced persons (DPs) in Germany, Austria, Italy, and other countries. Four years later, after tough negotiations, the UNHCR (United Nations High Commissioner for Refugees) emerged from out of the IRO, and to date this organization has been charged with the welfare of refugee groups all over the world. The British historian Peter Gatrell records the growth of international refugee assistance and the expanded scope of the tasks it has been assigned,[9] though often after serious delays, and—to this day—without adequate financial resources.

The desperate plight of refugees following both world wars forced the international community to define the term "refugee" with greater precision. This is obviously a matter of importance for this book as well, since distinguishing refugees from other groups of migrants was controversial already in the nineteenth century and remains so today.[10] The concept itself is of French derivation, dating to the era of the Huguenots, and that period will in consequence receive comprehensive treatment in the book's first chapter. It is striking that the way states and societies dealt with refugees was often more imaginative and accommodating in early modern Europe than in later periods. The same is true for the Cold War era, when the international community reacted quickly, effectively, and in a spirit of solidarity to a variety of crises (such as the Red Army's invasion of Hungary in 1956 and the "boat people" fleeing Vietnam in the late 1970s). One cannot derive any political prescriptions for contemporary challenges from these historical observations and comparisons, but the deeper temporal dimensions of history do undoubtedly open up new horizons for those facing these issues today.

In the 1920s the League of Nations was still handling refugees on a case-by-case basis; at issue were Russians, Greeks, Armenians, and Assyrian

Christians, who were viewed as "refugees" because they were stranded outside their countries of origin and did not enjoy "the legal protection of their government."[11] It was indeed fatal to be "stateless," as Hannah Arendt later termed it, in a world of nation-states. The precarious legal status of refugees was a major problem as it excluded them from the official labor market and from social services in their countries of arrival and was an obstacle at every border crossing. The League of Nations attempted to facilitate stateless people's onward journeys by issuing identification documents, so-called Nansen passports. This measure was, apart from the emergency assistance provided in numerous reception camps, the twentieth century's first venture into international refugee policy and the first test for the concept of international resettlement.

The Geneva Refugee Convention of 1951 rested not on any case-by-case but on a common definition of refugees that identified political, national, racial, social, and religious persecution as grounds for fleeing a country.[12] The convention was however initially confined to Europe and applicable only to those refugees who had had to leave their homeland before 1951. These geographic and temporal limitations were necessary in order to wrest approval of this UN convention from Communist countries. Alongside various sections about the humane treatment of refugees, the convention contained a prohibition against forcible return (non-refoulement): refugees were not supposed to be repatriated to their countries of origin against their will. Immediately after the Second World War, the leading Western allies, Great Britain and the United States, had violated this principle in the case of several hundred thousands of Soviet citizens fleeing the USSR, with fatal consequences. Hence, this book will also look into cases of flight that failed—and into the consequences for those affected by this failure.

The signatories to the Geneva Refugee Convention (including the numerous relief organizations that took part in drawing it up) undertook to open access to the labor market for refugees, recognize their educational degrees, and put them on an equal footing with respect to social welfare benefits.[13] These stipulations evolved historically and that fact needs to be recalled because, among other reasons, they have been called into question by various European countries reacting to the massive exodus from the Near East in 2015/16. At the same time, the signatory powers to the Geneva Convention restricted refugee status to specific groups. Owing to their experience of National Socialism, and in the context of the Cold War, victims of political persecution had priority. Wars or civil wars were not mentioned as reasons for flight. Domestic refugees, who today are a majority among all displaced persons, were left out entirely. The twelve million German refugees and the more than two million Poles from the eastern regions of Poland that had been annexed to the USSR in 1945 (these being the two largest groups that lost their homelands in postwar Europe) were thus not recognized as refugees, but they are treated as such in this book.

A call for legal and social equality entails an imperative to integrate, even if the Geneva Refugee Convention does not use the term "integration." But the convention turned "refugees" into a finite quantity: anyone naturalized in a host state would no longer be regarded as a refugee according to UN statutes. This is the point of departure for this book: integration has proven to be a better means for solving refugee crises, real and imagined, than the mostly futile attempts to build walls and fences or the resort to violent measures like the imposition of the Iron Curtain.

Is integration an appropriate telos for a historiography that deals with refugees and individual histories of flight? The Geneva Refugee Convention seems to suggest as much, since in international law (as we have seen) "refugee" status expires once a person obtains citizenship in the host country. Yet integration is no linear and irreversible process, despite what much of the sociological literature seems to suggest. (Additional details on the term "integration" and the rather new field of "integration history" will be explored in the next section.)[14] As a glance at the history of refugees and other migrants shows—and flight is, in the end, only another variant of migration[15]—integration has frequently been accompanied by conflicts and in rare cases by reversals.

For a number of years now, there has been a growing fear in Europe that the integration of past migrants has failed. This anxiety alters attitudes toward refugees, who are increasingly perceived as a threat, and not as objects for care and compassion. Alarmism of this kind is especially prevalent in the United States, where President Trump ordered a ban on admitting refugees immediately upon assuming office. His decision received much less attention than it deserved, because the media was preoccupied with his simultaneous "Muslim Country Ban." Nevertheless, it is the refugee ban, parts of which he was forced to rescind half a year later (although the ban was then reestablished for selected countries targeted by the original order), that may prove more damaging for international conflict resolution, especially for the UN and UNHCR. In addition to issuing restrictions on international resettlement, now fallen to levels lower than those that prevailed immediately after the terror attacks on September 11, 2001, the Trump administration has rolled back refugee rights and hindered asylum seekers from entering the United States. In Europe, right-wing politicians are demanding and, to the extent they have the power to do so, implementing similar policies.

In historical perspective, the closure of borders and suspicions against refugees are nothing new. This is also true for American history; in the 1920s and again in the 1950s era of Senator Joseph McCarthy, refugees from Russia and the Soviet Union were suspected of being crypto-communists and spies. The 300,000 displaced persons who were eventually admitted to the US in the late 1940s as the first major refugee movement ran up against deeply ingrained mistrust in 1945 and 1946. Although most of them were Holocaust survivors, it took years of political lobbying, above all by Jewish organizations, before they were granted entry visas. Humanitarian concerns prevailed only in the 1970s, as a legacy of the civil rights movement in the US and of the 68ers in Europe. Nevertheless, as Carl Bon Tempo has shown, this consensus on humanitarian principles was always shaky, and it became even less stable after 2001.[16] Since 2015 it seems to be on the retreat almost everywhere in the Western world. This book aims to explore why attitudes toward refugees have changed and why the doors to their admission have alternately opened and closed, both recently and in more distant times.

Throughout European or American history, refugees have repeatedly been misused as objects of demarcation. The reason for this is quite simply that refugees usually arrive as strangers and have-nots. Flight almost always involves both a loss of property, jobs, and social standing. Since the days of Emile Durkheim and Georg Simmel, two of modern sociology's founding fathers, we have known that strangers and the poor regularly incur prejudice and condescension. Simmel offered an explanation for this in his famous essay "The Stranger," in which he also portrayed the alien as "the *potential* wanderer."[17] Simmel takes on added relevance here due to his theory of power. In contrast with Max Weber's focus on charismatic leaders or Antonio Gramsci's attention to structural and discursive hegemony, Simmel's concern is the scope of action available to those confronted with power and hierarchy in state and society. Using both biographical case studies and a structural analysis of the longue durée, this book will ask how much latitude refugees had during their departure, along their flight routes, and in their countries of arrival.[18]

Although their own scope of action was usually very limited, refugees did bring change to the countries that received them. This was true, for example, of the "Indochina" refugees admitted to the US in the late seventies, whose resettlement signaled that "white only" immigration had ended once and for all. The admission of more than 400,000 Southeast Asians was a powerful message and a measure against racism. A limited comparison may be ventured between post-Vietnam America and (with a time delay) post-Holocaust Germany, which by 2015 was also keeping its doors open as proof that it had become a truly liberal country untainted by its National Socialist past. Whether concerns about refugees are projected in a negative or positive way, however, they have this in common: they are much more often about the host countries and societies than about the refugees themselves.

This book, by contrast, understands refugees not primarily as the objects of history, but rather as subjects and independent actors. As such, refugees should not remain nameless. To this end I have included biographical case studies, "analytical portraits" that take a look at individual refugees, some of them famous or at least familiar personages, others completely unknown. Flight, uprooting, the attempt (typically arduous) at starting over, and permanent exile abroad—all these things are better understood when viewed from a biographical perspective.

Refugees as a field of research

Modern European history is filled with refugees. This is also true of American history, for religious and political dissenters were among the founding fathers of the United States. Thomas Paine, one of them, wrote forcefully about refugees in 1776: "Every spot of the Old World is overrun with oppression. Freedom hath been hunted round the globe. Asia, and Africa, have long expelled her, Europe regards her like a stranger, and England hath given her warning to depart. O! receive the fugitive, and prepare in time an asylum for mankind."[19]

Because of their relevance to European and American history, there are dozens of books dealing with refugees. It would be impossible to provide even a rudimentary list of that secondary literature. Suffice it that over the past decade historians, including Peter Gatrell and Daniel Cohen, have written important general works on refugees and displaced persons.[20] Carl Bon Tempo, María Cristina Garcia, and Stephen R. Porter published fundamental works on refugee politics in the US.[21] There is even more literature covering specific periods of mass flight, such as the interwar and postwar years, and on individual countries in Europe. (Readers less interested in these reflections on research fundamentals can skip ahead to Chapter One.)[22] A common limitation of much of the older literature is that it deals mainly with the causes of flight, with the act of fleeing itself, and with the hardship and misery associated with flight, or with the policy of the receiving states, but devotes little attention to the agency of the refugees.

What happens to refugees after they flee home is mostly cut off, as if their lives had ended in the countries from which they departed or in the many refugee camps that were usually only a provisional (not their final) destination.[23] This book, by contrast, will take into account the history of refugees *after* their arrival in their respective host countries.[24] This widened focus rests on the aforementioned "analytical portraits" and on group studies of refugees (proffered here in full awareness of the problems posed by group-based approaches[25]), and by drawing on the insights of historical sociology and social science research (both past and present) on the integration of refugees.

Expanding the historian's horizons to include the afterlives of refugees, the years after their arrival, does have one major drawback: it makes the topic even more unwieldy. The simplest approach to structuring this book would have been to put everything in chronological order, starting (in principle) with the biblical exodus of the Israelites out of Egypt and ending with the Syrian civil war. But simply stringing together all the major instances of flight in human history (including prehistoric and ancient examples) would be too great a task for one single book. Moreover, a purely chronological approach would implicitly confirm a simplistic understanding of history in which a single and linear flow of time—what the language of high modernity once designated as "progress"—would permeate the entire world with equal intensity. In order to avoid these traps of traditional historiography, this monograph and its individual chapters are structured topologically: first the book deals with religious refugees, then with the escape from radical nationalism and ethnic cleansing, and finally with politically motivated flight.

The oldest reason for flight in modern European history is religious intolerance. At the end of the fifteenth century, which is where most historians set the beginning of the modern era, Spain experienced the first pervasive persecution of religious minorities. It was almost impossible for individual Muslims or Jews to escape the Inquisition. Even converts, including those of the second and third generations, were targeted. While local acts of collective expulsion had taken place as early as the Middle Ages (especially in German cities), the earthly purgatory that descended on Christian Spain was especially radical and wide-ranging; and the refugee movements it sparked were correspondingly harsh. Something like half a million Muslims and Jews were forced to leave Spain, an unprecedented number measured against the population of Spain and Europe at that time. The very term "religious refugee" in today's understanding was coined during the religious wars of the sixteenth and seventeenth centuries.[26] They are the focus of this book's first chapter, which includes as well later examples of religious persecutions, since differences of faith and denomination were also misused in later eras, most recently in the former Yugoslavia, in order to exclude and expel minorities.

Modern nationalism, which began to emerge in the late eighteenth century, was the cause of an increasingly rigid process of both exclusion and inclusion, and it triggered the most massive incidents of flight in history. In the twentieth century alone, around thirty million people lost their homelands in Europe owing to a radical, ethnic, and in part racist nationalism. These kinds of flight from nationalism will be treated in the second chapter of this book.[27] There was a reverse side to the coin of nationalist intolerance and persecution in the form of national solidarity, which helped countries cope with massive influxes of refugees. The absorption and integration of refugees under nationalist auspices, however, came at a price: it raised the general level of nationalism, which was often the catalyst for additional conflicts and violence.

The third variety of flight is less weighty in purely quantitative terms, but to this day it continues to shape international law and perceptions about refugees in the Western world. In the course of the American and the French Revolutions, for the first time, massive numbers of people were forced into exile on ideological grounds. This history of political and ideological flight (for the sake of brevity, we shall confine ourselves to the first attribute in the following pages, although nationalism is of course also a modern ideology) shaped the entire nineteenth century. In this era, following the revolutions of 1830–31 and 1848–49, the political exile was born as a historical figure and, in several Western European countries as well as in the United States, a right to asylum was established and secured.[28]

In the twentieth century, three periods of political flight may be distinguished: the early interwar period, when the League of Nations and international NGOs developed enduring principles and instruments to handle large-scale humanitarian crises; the 1930s, when Western states failed to meet the challenges triggered by fascism and National Socialism; and the era of the Cold War, when refugees experienced what Daniel Gerard Cohen has called their "Golden Age."[29] This is true inasmuch as this was the period when the Geneva Refugee Convention and other crucial rules were created and implemented. Most recently, Donald Trump's measures against the admission of refugees, the actions of likeminded presidents and prime ministers in Europe, and the disunity this has sown within the EU have ushered in bad times for refugees.

Looking back to the early postwar years, is "golden" really the right adjective? To answer that, one would in principle have to ask the refugees themselves, and this is what the analytical portraits in this book are intended to accomplish. On the one hand, there were periods over the last five hundred years when flight was relatively easy. On the other, there were times when refugees were turned away and only able to find a place where they could start life over again after arduous detours. One of the central concerns of this book is to identify those factors that determine when either favorable or unfavorable conditions tend to prevail for refugees, and to explain the causes for these vicissitudes. Ideally, there was a close geographical link between a refugee's departure and destination, as in the case of Eastern Bloc escapees. Once they had crossed the Iron Curtain, they were admitted into Western countries immediately and for good. But most flights were not structured so advantageously, and refugees had to overcome great distances until, often after many years, they found permanent accommodations. In addition to structural factors like these, normative attitudes are also decisive for determining the kind of reception refugees were likely to receive.

As a consequence of arranging the presentation according to these three major reasons for flight, the book's timelines run in parallel to some extent. Each of the following three chapters begins anew in terms of time and then follows its own chronology. At first glance this may be confusing, since certain periods and sometimes individual events are treated more than once. But this cannot be avoided, since specific historical watersheds, the two world wars for instance, saw every variety of flight. The advantage of this topological breakdown is that it makes it easier to understand how refugees are absorbed (or not) and under what conditions they might be able to start a new life. Questions about legal history are not the center of attention here, though one could fill many books with the details of international refugee conventions or of individual countries' asylum laws and practices.[30] Nevertheless, the most important changes in international and asylum law are a recurrent topic in all three major chapters, insofar as these changes shaped the way refugees were absorbed and integrated.

When it comes to differentiating among the major causes of flight—religious, nationalist, and political-ideological—we are dealing with ideal types in Max Weber's sense. Various minorities were forced to leave their homeland owing to their religious denomination *and* their nationality. Nationalism, moreover—like religion and denomination—was always also a very political issue. The motives refugees had were likewise diverse. For example, while people from the Eastern Bloc, regarded with so much sympathy in the context of the Cold War, emigrated out of political conviction, economic hardship also played a role. As the French historian Stéphane Dufoix has pointed out, a multitude of micro-decisions and micro-constraints are at work in every kind of flight.[31] Finally, there is the question as to whether this topological breakdown draws dividing lines artificially, and whether these "grand" categories are workable for the purposes of historical research and writing. It speaks for this approach that these three major causes of flight influenced both attitudes in the countries that absorbed refugees and the progress of their integration. Religious, national, and political forms of solidarity proved crucial when it came to taking in refugees and legitimizing an "open door" policy toward them.

The openness of the receiving society is also a crucial factor affecting long-term integration. This book will analyze historical integration processes in four areas. The first concerns refugees' legal status, whether they receive equal status, rights, and citizenship in their adopted country.[32] The spectrum is quite broad here, ranging from immediate legal equality—as in the case of German expellees after 1945—all the way to deliberate exclusion.

A second area of integration, one frequently examined by sociologists and taken up in this book time and again with respect to refugees, is the labor market. The issue at stake in this second and perhaps most important dimension of integration is whether refugees can find a job, to what extent that job fits their previous skills and qualifications, and whether employment facilitates upward mobility—at least for successive generations. Earlier refugees often succeeded in moving up the social ladder, sometimes even rising to form a new elite, as did the Huguenots in Prussia and as also happened with refugees from Southeastern Europe in the Turkish Republic.

Professional integration and social mobility are frequently based on geographical mobility, which is why housing, the third area, becomes so important. To what extent do refugees and other immigrants reside in mixed neighborhoods, to what extent do they live isolated, or even in camps? The issue of integration (or disintegration) in the living environment has given rise to such catchphrases as "ghettoization" and "parallel society." And, as so often, it is a problem that goes beyond debates about refugees and pertains also to other migrants.

The fourth and final area, which is sometimes viewed as the highest stage of integration, is marriage behavior. It certainly is a strong indicator of integration when people marry across cultural, social, and racial divides. Yet, historians specializing in Yugoslavia and the Soviet Union know that even states and societies with high rates of intermarriage can fall apart. One should also warn against viewing integration too literally in terms of "stages," since that term implies a modernist model of linear integration.

There was a time in the United States when the prevalent model was the "melting pot," a term invented by a second-generation descendant of Eastern European Jews who had fled from pogroms in Czarist Russia (see Chapter 1.4). In recent years, many politicians in Europe also seem to have had some process like the melting pot in mind when they talked about "integration" but seemed to mean "assimilation." Independently of how integration is envisioned (which depends on political and cultural preferences), both the term and the process are usually regarded as positive. This goes back to Durkheim, who used "integration" in a normative sense and warned against the disintegration of modern industrial societies. More recent sociologists follow a more neutral, functionalist approach, which this book shares.[33]

The philosopher Elizabeth Anderson has set standards in the American debates on integration, and also distinguishes it clearly from assimilation.[34] Both terms have in common that they are an issue discussed more intensively when integration (or in earlier times assimilation) *no longer* seems to work, and when increasing frictions in society arouse the worries of social scientists and (the rare) historian who chooses to work with sociological concepts.

The closest American equivalent to European discussions about integration are debates on multiculturalism. It is impossible to differentiate all the phases and details of these debates in the inevitably slim introduction to a book like this; nevertheless, the contours of this controversy merit at least a brief mention. In the United States, the debate has become both more settled and more contentious. In the 1960s, books like *Beyond the Melting Pot* and *The Rise of the Unmeltable Ethnics* raised the question of whether a "salad bowl" was perhaps a more apt metaphor for America as a "nation of immigrants."[35] In 1965, the restrictive quota system of the 1920s was reformed and a widely accepted consensus favoring the concept of "ethnic pluralism" emerged. One day a consensus like this might also inspire Europe, where multiculturalism has become more of a bugbear than a stimulus to constructive intellectual and political debates. But there is ongoing controversy in the US about which version of that consensus should prevail: the right wing's (assimilation) or the left wing's (now known as "multiculturalism").[36] In addition, anxiety about illegal immigration (especially from Latin America) and an American future that is non-white and "majority minority" helped propel Donald Trump into power.

Historians dealing with integration must confront an additional research problem: few sources convey sufficient information about what kind of identity individuals or social groups had, and whether (or to what degree) they felt integrated into receiving societies. Therefore, this book focuses more on social behavior. Although this may contradict the "linguistic turn" and other postmodern paradigms, I think that it is often more fruitful to focus on what people did than what they said or might have thought about their "identity." This approach seems especially conducive to moving the discussion forward to consider long-term processes like integration, which often occurs only in the second or third generation.

As far as historical sources are concerned, these four dimensions of integration—legal status, access to the labor market, everyday social contacts, and familial integration—can rarely be studied based on hard data (of the kind collected by social scientists today). The further back a period is, the harder it becomes to find precise information—about population groups, occupations, social mobility, and residential or living environments. Statistics on naturalization or marriages, by contrast, are easier to find, though here (as with other dimensions of integration) it is important to pay attention to gender differences.[37] To be sure, historical research on integration processes cannot be conducted as systematically as in the social sciences, yet it is possible to reach some conclusions derived from the deeper temporal dimensions of history. The preconditions for integration vary from one period to another, starting with a given country's type of statehood and its political system, and extending to its basic economic conditions.[38]

It may be of some consolation to historians studying past integration processes to learn that the data available for present-day studies of refugees are not much better. Most data are still gathered by state agencies or the subcontractors working for them. Moreover, government surveys, such as the microcensus of the German Federal Statistical Office, do not distinguish between refugees and other migrants, but record only their country of origin, evidence that the experience of flight plays at best a minor role from the perspective of government administrations. Refugees, in any event, have other worries and employ a different vocabulary; soon after they arrive sheer survival takes precedence, having a roof over one's head, and finding an opportunity to earn money. That was not so simple, as again Joseph Roth testified: "Of course: their papers! Half a Jewish life slips by in a fruitless struggle over papers. . . ."[39] What Roth meant by this was the residence and work permit that he, as a Galician refugee in Berlin and then later in Paris, was able to receive only after several tries. His voice and those of other refugees are heard in the final chapter of this book on experiences of flight. By narrating their own experiences in public and in writing, refugees inscribed themselves into the history of the receiving countries. Very often they presented themselves as industrious workers, skilled laborers, and carriers of modernization processes. Such success stories call for critical scrutiny, but it will be shown in various subchapters that the receiving countries almost always profit by taking in refugees. This message is even more relevant in times (past and present) when refugees are increasingly portrayed as a danger, a security risk, and (last but not least) as illegal migrants.

Flight and migration

How can we differentiate between flight and other forms of migration? It is almost self-evident that flight takes place under duress and under force or the threat of force. Two variations should be distinguished here: direct coercion, such as armed force or some other form of physical attack, and indirect coercion. In the latter case people flee because they fear violence and living conditions that threaten to become seriously worse.[40] In contrast to the mostly well-organized journeys undertaken by trans-Atlantic and intra-European economic migrants, these escape routes often pose serious threats to life and limb. Many refugees find themselves spending years on an odyssey through different countries, whereas labor migrants usually have clear ideas about what countries they are going to and head directly for these destinations. In general it can be said that "push factors" play a stronger role in the case of refugees, while "pull factors," such as the attractiveness of a (often idealized) new homeland, are more important for other migrants. The juxtaposition of "push" and "pull" is an old topos of migration research, but it is a schema that does not quite suit the history of flight because, in many cases, refugees are kept wandering from one country and even continent to another until they finally feel safe enough to start a new life. This is true, for example, of the Syrians who migrated from Turkey to the EU in 2015. Turkey was an intermediate stop; but they remained refugees, even if politicians like Hungarian prime minister Viktor Orbán dispute this. (It is astonishing how oblivious Orbán is to the history of his own nation and region. If one were to follow his notion of legality, then none of the 200,000 Hungarian refugees who crossed the border to Austria in 1956–57 would have had a hope of moving on to the countries of exile that later admitted them as permanent residents. The current Austrian government seems to have forgotten this as well. The international resettlement of refugees, at least in the form of an EU-wide distribution quota, is something Vienna's recent conservative–far right ruling coalition consistently rejected. Yet it is just this kind of cross-national burden sharing that saved Austria from a major humanitarian crisis in 1956–57, 1968, and 1992.)

All in all, the difference between labor migration and flight migration (I am aware that this term sounds a bit awkward in English, but the original

German distinction between *Arbeitsmigration* and *Fluchtmigration* has proven useful in scholarly debates) can be summarized quite simply: Refugees leave their homes in order to save their lives, while labor migrants do so in order to improve their living conditions. A second distinction is the prevalence or absence of violence and traumatization. There is, finally, a third difference that relates to the migrant's homeland, which is often cut off from the refugee but still accessible to the labor migrant. Many in the latter category send home remittances and even build retirement houses in the old country, while refugees often can only dream of returning to the homes they were forced to leave due to war and destruction.

An alternative concept circulating in the research literature is that of "forced migration." Here, however, it should be kept in mind that migration movements are seldom completely voluntary. Even labor migration is frequently a consequence of pressure and distress. When natural catastrophes trigger migration, people are also not leaving voluntarily. The same is true for environmental migration (which will be considered briefly in Chapter 4.2 on the Syrian and European "refugee crisis"). The boundaries between what is forced and what is voluntary are thus blurred, causing specialists in the history of migration, such as Leo Lucassen, to express well-founded doubts about the concept of forced migration.[41]

Refugees are welded together by their common experience of flight, no matter how different the details of their histories may be. Self-declared exiles tended to remain politically more active in the countries of arrival and attempted to have an impact on their countries of origin. Their ultimate goal was to overturn the political order that had compelled them to leave. Sometimes exiles labeled themselves also as émigrés, which suggests a more passive stance, and a coming to terms with the fact that the exile would be permanent.

Although there is a close linguistic identity between the two terms, it should not be taken for granted that refugees identify with their refuge. Some groups have even perceived the term "refugee" as pejorative and rejected the designation—among them the Germans who came from Eastern Europe to postwar Germany and the French who arrived in mainland France from Algeria. Moreover, collective labeling may obscure internal differences. On closer inspection (to offer just two examples), the Sudeten Germans from industrialized northern Bohemia and the Protestant agricultural workers from Masuria (formerly a part of East Prussia, today northeastern Poland) who arrived in West Germany in 1945 had just as little in common with each other as a Christian merchant from Aleppo with a Kurdish peasant from the Euphrates valley who both reached Germany, Austria, or Sweden in 2015. But by seeking refuge and being accorded the corresponding status in the countries that took them in, these groups had to grapple with that term and sometimes they chose to self-identify as refugees. Since the 1980s, when the public mood turned against immigration, and to some extent also against refugees, a number of pejorative terms emerged in the languages of every Western country. There was and still is talk of "pseudo asylum seekers" (in German *Scheinasylanten*), "economic refugees" (an awkward term that casts suspicion on the motives for flight), and more recently (in the US) "fake refugees." These terms served to delegitimize refugees by imputing primarily material motives to them.

Even in earlier historical eras, the way refugees were treated depended less on their previous history and the vicissitudes of their persecution, and much more on the attitudes and political elites of the society taking them in. In any country wanting to distinguish itself from Communist dictatorships during the Cold War, Eastern European or Cuban refugees were welcome as living proof of human rights violations and of the dark or even criminal sides of Stalinism and state socialism. If flight took place in times of economic crisis, the doors were shut, both in the national discourse and along national boundaries. One thing is new, however, in our era of postmodern mass democracies. Refugees are now increasingly used to stir up the public for campaign purposes and to foment blatant nationalism. The semantic details of these public discourses are just as important as the differences between individual instances of flight and different refugee groups, which a work of history must also, of course, bear in mind.

One thing that the "guest workers" of postwar-era Germany, Austria, France, and other European countries have in common with the refugees of earlier periods is that they, like the societies that took them in, were initially expecting only to stay provisionally. The first generation of refugees in particular kept a "packed suitcase," even though there was usually no option of return in the wake of ethnic cleansings and religious conflicts. Political refugees, by contrast, were more frequently able to return home from exile, since the great dictatorships of the twentieth century proved in the end to have unexpectedly short lifespans. In some cases former refugees rose to high positions in public office, as in the case of Willy Brandt and Bruno Kreisky, who had spent the formative years of their lives in exile, or in the case of various presidents of the Baltic states in the 1990s. Yet, unlike the situation of labor migrants, remigration back into the old (and imagined) homeland remained a rare exception; in most cases, refugees stayed put in the countries that had absorbed them. Almost always, this was to the advantage of the societies and economies of those countries.

There has been little discussion of these advantages recently. Since the autumn of 2015 debates about refugees in both the public and the media have centered almost exclusively on the ways in which societies are encumbered, overburdened, and threatened by refugees. The 1920s and the period after the Second World War, however, witnessed movements of refugees in much greater numbers relative to the size of the global population.[42] This is especially applicable to Europe, which through 1947 was affected more severely by mass flight than any other continent.

Reflections on space: A larger Europe

But what do we really mean here by "Europe," and how can we apply this geographical and political concept to history? Since the collapse of the Soviet Union, Europe has increasingly been equated with the EU. Although many Europeans and non-Europeans of course do realize that the continent ends at the Ural mountains in the East, European integration within the framework of the EU has reinforced the perception of the Bosporus and the Aegean in the southeast as a fixed geographical and almost natural boundary (the vision of the Caucasus is much less clear in this regard). Each of these boundaries is, as Norman Davies pointed out in his great synthesis of European history, a political construction. He highlighted the issue of the continent's changing visions and borders by employing the term "tidal Europe."[43] Indeed, in the east and southeast of the continent, geographic, political, and cultural borders were by no means as clear as they may appear today. A good hundred years ago, the conflicts over the European territories of the Ottoman Empire, which in 1912 still extended as far as the Adriatic and today's Serbia, were treated as an "Oriental question." Clearly, Westerners did not necessarily locate the Orient in the Near East, but from time to time, instead, in Southeastern Europe.[44] At the same time, until the Balkan Wars of 1912–13, the Ottoman Empire was part and parcel of the European balance of powers and state system. The Republic of Turkey was founded in the context of European nation-state building following the First World War. These substantive points make a powerful case for treating the Ottoman Empire and Turkey—despite all of today's political conflicts—as just as much a part of European history as the Russian Empire and the Soviet Union.[45]

Indeed, the Middle Eastern successor states of the Ottoman Empire—Egypt, Palestine, Syria, Lebanon, Jordan, and Iraq—also have ties to Europe, not least because they came into being as a result of French and British colonial rule. Israel was founded by refugees and emigrants from Europe who after World War II wanted to establish a nation-state on the European model, which led to massive refugee flows in this part of the world. It has already happened once, barely a hundred years ago (1922–23, as a result of the Greco-Turkish War), that about a million people fled across the Aegean in a way that affected public order and values in Europe, albeit under different and far more unfavorable circumstances.

All these and any number of other contexts can be better understood if we broaden our view of European history to include *neighboring regions* beyond the Mediterranean and the Asian territories of the Russian Empire or Soviet Union. It is almost a banality to state that the history of Europe has always been deeply connected with the Americas and the United States, but this is particularly true for refugee movements and the development of international refugee institutions, such as the UNHCR. Expanding our perspective to the east, south, and west is justified on empirical grounds, since Novosibirsk and faraway Vladivostok, Buenos Aires, and Boston have all been shaped by people and cultures coming from Europe; Beirut was once called the "Paris of the Middle East," and Istanbul's population had a Christian majority well into the late nineteenth century. This opening up of European history should not be read as an attempt to play down European colonialism, but rather to better take into consideration Europe's political, social, and cultural relations with neighboring world regions. It also helps complement global history, which usually looks at Europe by focusing on its overseas relations and colonies (subjects that also come up here, especially in Chapter 2.4, which deals with postcolonial flight and remigration). Global history and postcolonial studies have proved fruitful approaches, but they are influenced by colonial perceptions of space and an Occidentalist view of global relations.

The vision of a wider Europe and terms like "the West" (as presented here) also have their drawbacks and limits. Both can provoke accusations of "Eurocentrism." My main reply to this kind of knockout argument is that my own perspective rests on a different, above all more eastern conception of Europe, and not exclusively on the continent's occidental half. (What is criticized as "Eurocentrism" could often more accurately be labeled Occidentalism.) A strong focus on Europe is also inevitable, because the history of refuge and refugees has European origins. The Reconquista in Spain was the first case of an entire country purged of unwanted minorities. The trans-Atlantic caesura of 1492 needs also to be remembered in this regard. In the seventeenth century, the concept of the *réfugié* spread, owing of the persecution of the Huguenots. In the "long" nineteenth century, the Ottoman Empire took first place as a "refugee country," receiving about four million people from territories lost in Southeastern Europe.

Then, in the era of the "long" First World War (1912–23)—a conflict overwhelmingly fought in Europe—refugees became a global problem. Thus, well into the 1950s, it was in Europe that saw the most, and the most extensive, movements of refugees. It should be acknowledged, however, that today the vast majority of refugees have been uprooted from zones of conflict in the Global South. Hence, any book on recent or present-day refugee movements and policy challenges would require a different and wider geographic focus.[46] But as regards the first half of the twentieth century and earlier periods, much can be learned by focusing on Europe.

That is also true of the idea of human rights, which was constitutive for the UN Refugee Convention of 1951 and its predecessors in the interwar period. Many key ideas about that convention and of the interwar refugee regime originated on the old continent, not because "European civilization" was superior, but because Europe was so successful in developing radical nationalism, racism, and almost destroying itself in two world wars. As a negative example of actual Eurocentrism we might point to the geographical restriction of the 1951 Geneva Convention to Europe, as if there were at that time no acute refugee problems in other parts of the world.[47] In fact about thirty million people were uprooted in China during the Second World War, and in 1947, as a consequence of India's partition, more than twelve million people lost their homeland (a catastrophe in which Europeans, and more specifically Great Britain as a colonial power, played an inglorious part). India, Pakistan, and other newly independent states, however, did not ratify the Geneva Refugee Convention, since they feared that this would put them again under the influence of the European colonial powers.

A protocol added in 1967 finally removed this birth defect of the Geneva Refugee Convention; its legal validity and radius of action were extended worldwide. This process of universalization also had its beginnings in the immediate proximity of Europe. Between 1954 and 1962 about 200,000 Algerians fled that country's war of independence for Tunisia and Morocco, where they were looked after by the UNHCR. The globalization of the Geneva Refugee Convention was thus merely the next logical step.

More knowledge about the near neighborhood of Europe is also necessary in order that refugees from the Middle East who have arrived since 2015 can be better integrated. So long as our basic information about refugees' countries of origin—in the case of Syria about the Alawites, Assyrians, the members of different Sunni religious persuasions, or about nationalities like the Kurds—remains seriously limited, integration will be hard, at least harder than necessary. Here, too, a historical example is relevant: When, after the Conference of Lausanne barely a hundred years ago, Asia Minor's Christians were forcibly resettled, officials from the great powers and even people in Greece were astonished to learn that many of these Christians did not know much Greek but spoke Turkish instead. The "Karamanlides" from Anatolia were stigmatized as foreigners in Greece, which delayed their integration by decades. This drove many refugees into the arms of the Communists and contributed to the outbreak of the Greek civil war in 1945.[48]

This expanded view of Europe and its history is informed in particular by the geographical mobility of refugees, who even in earlier eras walked thousands of kilometers along land routes, headed across the Mediterranean along different trajectories, and even, of course, across the Atlantic. Mobility has recently been on the rise once again, thanks to new communications media. It is hard to prove or disprove that the selfies that refugees took with German chancellor Angela Merkel and sent around the world via Facebook, Whatsapp, and other social media acted all that strongly as a pull factor on the one million Syrians, Iraqis, and Afghanis who came to Europe in that year. Most of these "selfies" were, in fact, professional press photos of the German chancellor taken in a Berlin refugee home. What is unquestionable is that communication has brought the world closer together, especially between the countries of Europe and those across the Mediterranean.

Between the old and the new homeland, if that is what it will become, there lies a long and dangerous crossing. According to information from the Inter-

Alan Kurdi drowned together with his older brother and his mother when a boat overladen with refugees capsized on the way from the Turkish coast to the Greek island of Kos. The family had entrusted themselves to smugglers because they did not have the visas needed for regulated emigration to join an aunt living in Canada. Alan's body washed up onto the beach of the seaside resort of Bodrum on September 2, 2015. There the toddler lay like a piece of flotsam, clothed quite normally in a T-shirt, shorts, and a young child's shoes. The body appeared unscathed, but Alan's head was halfway under water. The photos reverberated powerfully in the media and politics: Swedish foreign minister Margot Wallström broke into tears while the television cameras were running, British prime minister David Cameron pledged to take in 20,000 refugees from Syria annually, and the Austrian and German governments announced three days later an opening of their borders to thousands of refugees who had made it through to Hungary and were stranded at the eastern train station in Budapest as well as in provisional camps. The pictures of Alan Kurdi unleashed such rage because they were not staged or—in postmodern parlance—"constructed." A child's innocence apparently stirs poignant responses across cultural boundaries, while grown-up refugees have all manner of possible motives imputed to them. On September 4, 2015, Alan Kurdi was buried along with his brother and his mother in his hometown of Kobane, a city in northern Syria besieged for months by ISIS.

national Organization for Migration (IOM), the most important NGO in this field, in 2015 alone 3,770 people lost their lives fleeing over the Mediterranean, and in 2016 the number of those drowned rose to over 4,500.[49] The number of unreported cases surely is far higher, since many nameless victims disappear without a trace, their corpses sinking into the sea. It was different, and momentously so, in the case of the toddler Alan Kurdi. The pictures taken of this three-year-old boy, who drowned in September 2015 while crossing the Aegean, stunned the world and contributed to Austria and Germany deciding against closing their borders to refugees from the Middle East. As will be discussed in Chapter 4.2, the borders were never opened in the literal sense; they were just not closed when masses of refugees arrived in Austria in September 2015.

In spite of so many deaths in the Mediterranean, movements of refugees over wide areas are easier today than in earlier eras of history, when tens and sometimes hundreds of thousands died in flight. By contrast—and this is an additional thesis of this book—the preconditions for social integration have been worsening since the 1970s.[50] The reasons for this are varied but are linked above all to changes in the labor market, declining social mobility, and media developments, as well as to a vicious circle of negative attitudes and anxieties.

Are today's anxieties about integration of refugees and other migrants justified? Here it needs to be said that Germany and other European states have managed to cope with much larger movements of refugees in their history. There can be no question that integrating the 890,000 refugees who arrived in the Federal Republic in 2015 (some 280,000 refugees were recorded for 2016) poses a major challenge. This also applies to Austria and Sweden, two countries that have taken in a similar or even greater number of refugees in relation to their overall populations. Yet in history various countries have successfully dealt with much larger numbers of refugees, and under more difficult economic and political circumstances. History also shows how to achieve the kind of solidarity that every society, and especially every democracy, needs.

Historical examples of integration will be discussed one refugee group at a time following an account of each group's flight and admittance to a new country. It should be noted in advance that it is not feasible to discuss every group this way, and certainly not every country of destination for refugees. A comparative history of integration along these lines would have to follow very precise parameters, and it would be a large-scale project taking several years. Yet it is possible to derive a few insights from the findings concerning the historical processes of integration presented in this book. To this end, I have not limited myself to contemporary history but have deliberately gone back to include a longer period of time, since many current studies about the so-called refugee crisis are, with all due respect, rather cursory. It is open to dispute how much one can really learn from history, especially from its deeper chronological layers, but certainly enough would be gained if one were to avoid repeating the mistakes of the past.

One mistake that should most especially be avoided is the outright rejection of refugees, such as happened in the 1930s and immediately following the Second World War, a dismissal that cost hundreds of thousands of people their lives. Failed flight is therefore another recurrent theme of this book. Refusing admission to refugees had, moreover, an impact on the integration of those migrants and refugees who had arrived earlier. Outward exclusion always brought with it domestic exclusion. Hence, at issue here is more than the fate of some "outsiders" who have lost their homes as a result of war and other violent conflicts. What is at stake is the normative order of the West, whether we still respect human rights at our borders and abroad, and the answer to this question affects how those same rights are respected at home, and impacts nothing less than the social peace of our societies. A small and very homogenous country like Hungary can be ruled by an authoritarian leader bent on exclusionary nationalism and an anti-immigrant stance, apparently without major disruptions (though the Roma minority will suffer as a consequence, and so will Hungarian Jews in the long run). But if countries like Germany, France, the United Kingdom, or the United States, with their greater ethnic diversity, follow the ideological recipes of right-wing nationalism, the risks are much higher. A blatant ethno-nationalism is likely to alienate some part of their immigrant populations, causing heightened inter-ethnic and racial tensions. The physical wall that President Trump intends to erect at the Mexican border is likely to create mental walls between ethnic groups already living in the US, as well as mental barriers against the whole of the outside world. Moreover, the media's preoccupation with covering and sometimes condemning Trump's border wall agenda may be diverting attention from simple geographic and material facts. It would be impossible to build a wall in the Gulf of Mexico or the Pacific Ocean (as the Europeans have already found out in the Mediterranean), so, in the end, the United States (and Europe) may end up paying drastically higher costs for border protection on both land and on the sea, which could well see new waves of "boat people" arriving in makeshift watercraft. Historians should, however, refrain from advertising such dystopias. There are numerous positive examples of managing refugee movements in constructive ways. These hopeful precedents—along with the refugees' own actions and agendas—are the central topic of this book.

1

THE ROOTS OF INTOLERANCE: RELIGIOUS CONFLICTS AND RELIGIOUS REFUGEES

Narratives of flight and refugees were common as early as the Hebrew Bible. Abraham's migration out of Canaan, the exodus of the Israelites from out of Egypt, the Babylonian exile, and numerous other episodes center on this theme. The New Testament is not far behind with its story of Mary and Joseph fleeing Herod's henchmen and able to return to their home in the Galilee only after the king's death.

The biblical texts already contain all the important motifs of flight and refuge: existential dangers and distress, ethnic conflicts, religious and political persecution. The reception of refugees described in the Bible is, on the one hand, underpinned by an ethical imperative to help the needy stranger. On the other, the Bible describes empty, sparsely inhabited swaths of land as the settlement places available to refugees. These conditions persist into much later history. Owing to the invasion of the Mongols in the thirteenth century, epidemics of plague, and the ravages of the Thirty Years' War, large sections of Europe were repeatedly depopulated. Increasing the number of residents and cultivating the land by settling it were therefore among the key elements of any government's development policy. Imagining the "New World" as a presumably empty space also played a major role in the legends European settler colonies told about the Americas. As a rule, medieval and early modern Absolutist monarchs saw refugees and other immigrants as an asset. Far from being a burden or a threat, they were a potential source of economic power. Jewish, Protestant, and other refugees were even solicited.

1.1 The Spanish Muslims and Jews

The year 1492 is commonly regarded as the dawn of modern history. It also marks a deep caesura in the history of mass flight, because it began with an unprecedented persecution and cleansing of unwanted minorities. Just as Christopher Columbus was first setting foot on American soil, the Spanish troops of the Reconquista were vanquishing the last Muslim-governed kingdom on the Iberian peninsula. Although the terms of surrender, negotiated in a treaty, guaranteed free exercise of religion to the Muslims in Grenada, the new sovereigns violated these agreements and exerted massive pressure on their conquered subjects to convert. In 1499 the hard-pressed Muslims staged a rebellion that could only be brought under control after two years of ruthless warfare. Resistance, guerilla-like fighting, and retribution proved especially fierce in the mountains of the Sierra Nevada. Whereupon the government, and especially the Inquisition, cracked down even harder on the Muslim minority, issuing instructions for collective and compulsory baptism. Thousands of Muslims fled to Morocco to avoid conversion or settled in the coastal region around Valencia, where less severe laws were initially in force.[1] Emperor Charles V closed this gap in the laws and, between 1523 and 1526, extended compulsory baptism to every region of Spain. This anti-Islamic policy is attributable above all to the bigotry of the House of Castile and the Habsburgs, as well as to the Inquisition's self-radicalization. There was, moreover, a foreign policy connection, since during those same years the Ottoman Empire conquered Hungary and expanded into the western Mediterranean as far as Algeria. Hence, throughout the sixteenth century, fear of a fifth column and an Ottoman intervention in Spain was not entirely unfounded.

Even conversion was not enough to guarantee peace for the descendants of the Spanish Moors, the so-called Moriscos. After another uprising in 1568–70 they were forced to leave the former Kingdom of Granada—all of them, without exception.[2] Once again, the uprising was suppressed with extreme brutality; after the siege and surrender of the Andalusian city of Galera, Don Juan de Austria (soon to be the victor in the 1571 naval battle of Lepanto, the decisive victory of the Christian Holy League over the Ottoman fleet), had around four hundred women and children killed. King Philip II did not even allow economic considerations to get in the way of persecuting Muslims. Although their massive flight led to the collapse of an irrigation system that had been built up over centuries and to a weakening of trade and commerce, the king nonetheless proceeded with the persecution of Muslims and Moriscos. In 1609/10, his successor Philip III issued deportation decrees against all Moriscos still in Spain. We cannot know with any precision how many fled between 1492 and 1614, because their departure took place largely in stages and over several generations.[3] Leonard Harvey has put the number of those driven out of the Kingdom of Granada and the numerous Muslim communities on the Valencian coast at 300,000.

As so often happens in the history of flight and expulsion, the state cracked down not just on one minority but on several of them simultaneously. Spanish Jews had no ties to any great power threatening Christian Europe, and they had never been military adversaries, but the Church viewed them as a domestic threat. Shortly before the conquest of Granada, the Inquisition staged a ritual murder trial in Andalusia in which the chief defendant, a converted Jewish merchant, confessed under torture to desecrating the host and murdering Christian children. He was burned at the stake, and the aroused masses committed pogroms in several cities. The Spanish state and clergy thereupon gave the Jews a choice between forced baptism or exile. In 1492, and then after a second great wave of persecution in 1513, around 200,000 Jews fled Spain for North Africa, Italy, the Netherlands, and especially the Ottoman Empire.[4] The fate of the Portuguese Jews ran a similar course; they had to leave their homeland in 1497, because the Spanish royal house had agreed to a dynastic tie with Portugal but insisted that the marriage, between Princess Isabella and King Manuel, could take place only under the condition that all Jews were thrown out of the country.

Like the Muslims, Iberian Jews found that not even conversion to Catholicism offered them durable protection, because, according to the principle of "limpieza di sangre" (purity of blood), the religious affiliation of the converted Marranos (the name is etymologically derived from the Spanish word for "pigs" and was meant to be an insult) was often traced back several generations, much as it had been with the Moriscos. Here, in principle, the Inquisition was obeying a logic similar to that followed by radical nationalists in the late nineteenth century, who introduced ethnically and racially defined criteria of ancestry to determine membership in a nation.

Little is known of the fate of the Muslim refugees (most of whom settled in what is today Morocco and Algeria), but we know a great deal about what happened to the Sephardic Jews. The Spanish and Portuguese Jews forced out of Iberia scattered all over Europe and adjoining regions along the Mediterranean (see Map 1). Some of them, as merchants, already had ties to Genoa, Pisa, Livorno, Venice, and Amsterdam, but most accepted an invitation from the Ottoman sultan and settled in Istanbul, Salonika, Sarajevo, Izmir, and other cities of the Ottoman Empire. As in early modern Poland and Prussia, the interest of the Ottomans lay in increasing the number of their subjects after population losses incurred in the costly conquest of Constantinople and the Balkans.[5] Compared with this grave concern, the new subjects' religion was of only secondary significance, which explains why Istanbul remained a majority Christian city even after 1453.

In the Ottoman Empire, the Sephardim were allowed to continue practicing their faith and operating their own schools and courts. This was the core principle of the so-called millet.[6] This system of far-reaching autonomy for groups (rather than territories) was possible because the government did not intervene as closely in the lives of its citizens as a modern state does. The Ottomans demanded only that the Sephardim—and, analogously, their Christian subjects—pay their taxes and behave loyally. The system functioned well from the fifteenth through the eighteenth centuries, but in the long run this

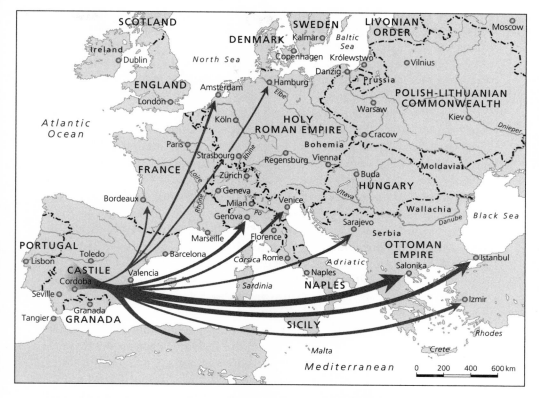

MAP 1. Flight routes of Sephardic Jews leaving Spain and Portugal after 1492

rather radical grant of group autonomy weakened the state, because it could not be run as effectively as the Absolutist monarchies in Western and Central Europe. Russia, France, England, and the Habsburg Empire used the presence of Christian minorities (which in some regions were a majority) to claim authority as their protectors and intervene in the internal affairs of the Ottoman Empire.

Moreover, the Ottoman Empire was increasingly subjected to economic and great-power competition. Owing to Europe's overseas expansion, the center of world economy had shifted to the West and the Atlantic world, while nineteenth-century colonialism had England and France impinging on the Ottoman Empire in Egypt and Algeria, much as the Russian Empire was doing from the north. Western Europe also gained the upper hand because of administrative reforms that centralized public administration, enabled each emerging nation-state to collect taxes throughout its territory, and strengthened the economy through mercantilism. Owing not least to the devastating defeats it suffered at the hand of Russia, the Ottoman Empire tried to join in this development. But the modernization of its administration, in the Tanzimat reforms in the middle third of the nineteenth century, was only partly successful because the highest offices of state continued to be sold, and the governors of individual provinces (vilâyets) then attempted to extract as much as they could out of their subjects. The social feudal order in the countryside was no less oppressive; a small stratum of large landowners and notables confronted a mass of poor peasants.

The conservative sultan Abdülhamid II, who began his reign in 1876, reacted to this external threat and to the domestic weakness of the Ottoman Empire (a few years before it had to declare a state bankruptcy) by calling off the Western-style reforms, suspending the imperial constitution that had just been drafted, and stressing the role of Islam as a state religion. After the revolution of the Young Turks in 1908 and alongside similar developments in the Russian and German empires, a phase of nationalization or Turkification paved the way for the formation of an ethnically defined nation-state. Up to this point, the Sephardim had lived largely undisturbed and free to preserve not only their religion, but also Ladino, their language based on medieval Spanish. Yiddish, which migrating Jews brought to Poland from the Holy Roman Empire, also survived as a widely spoken language until the Holocaust.

Multilingualism and the coexistence of multiple religions are frequently touted as admirable features of Ottoman and Eastern European history, but the special status accorded different minorities also made them easy to identify and attack. This kind of vulnerability should be kept in mind when cultural diversity is celebrated (or its loss mourned) in postmodern models of society. The multicultural character of some early modern societies was premised on different groups having their social and economic niches assigned to them, on their fulfilling these prescribed roles successfully, and on the groups not mixing with each other. Religion played an essential role in isolating different faith communities and ethnic groups, since marriages between the adherents of the three great monotheistic world religions were impossible unless one of the marriage partners agreed to convert. Hence Jews remained Jews; and, analogously, Christians and Muslims kept to themselves. Only the advent of secularization and civil marriage could break the hold of these rigid differences. Moreover, the societies of the early modern states were built upon social inequality. Perhaps the current trend in today's global metropolises is heading in this direction; it would not be the first time that history proceeds in cycles and not in the progressive manner that has shaped Western thinking since the Enlightenment.

At the same time, the case of the Sephardim helps illustrate the difference between integration and assimilation. The Jews who came from Spain were undoubtedly well integrated into the Ottoman Empire, although this was an integration that rested on the primacy of the state, its dynasty, and the ruling religion. There was a hierarchical relationship that one should not idealize, ex post facto, any more than one should romanticize the way cultures actually coexisted. Jews and Christians were exempt from military service, but also did not have the same rights as Muslims and had to pay higher taxes. If they fell too much out of favor with any sultan or governor, heads quickly rolled, and not just metaphorically. Yet the Sephardim did not have to assimilate; as late as the twentieth century, they were still clearly identifiable as a social group, especially in their stronghold of Salonika.[7]

This made them into obvious targets for modern nationalism and antisemitism, which existed in what became an independent Greece just as they did in other European countries. During the Second World War, the history of the northern Greek and Macedonian Jews came to an end in the gas chambers of Auschwitz. In 1943, the National Socialists deported the descendants of these Jewish refugees from Spain; some survived in hiding or in the Italian-occupied parts of Greece and Yugoslavia, and larger groups in Bulgaria and Turkey.

Early modern Poland's stance toward Jewish refugees may be compared to that of the Ottoman Empire. When Casimir the Great (1310–70) took in the Jews who had been expelled from German cities, he had in mind enhancing his country's economic power. He promised the Jews group autonomy, which was expanded further under the Jagiellonian dynasty in the sixteenth century. Polish Jews did not participate in political decision-making processes, such as electing the king, and they were not represented in the bodies representing the feudal estates, the pan-Polish Sejm and the regional Sejmiki. Accordingly, one may (as in the cases discussed earlier) speak of a specific kind of integration, or more precisely of an incorporation that did not include legal and political equality. Professionally, too, integration was limited, since the Jewish immigrants were only allowed to occupy or work in specific niches; and their living environments were also largely separated from those of Christian inhabitants. In the cities and especially on the land, where many Jews were employed as estate managers, major social conflicts arose. This was the source of the antisemitic stereotype of the Jews as exploiters, which was then spread to the masses by a variety of national movements.

In the nineteenth century, this early modern group autonomy proved barely sustainable as the modern state began to make new demands on its citizens, from compulsory school education through military service, all the way to an expectation of undivided loyalty. In exchange, citizens could make new demands of their state, and possibly even vote governments out of office. From these beginnings there arose the contentious question debated to this day in modern democracies: in every demos, who should belong and who should not?

A second, although disputable difference between early modern and later eras lies in the existence of sparsely populated areas. As we have seen, the Polish kings and Ottoman sultans summoned Jewish refugees into their kingdoms not least because they wanted to increase the size of the population and their economic power. Economic thinking also played an important role for subsequent rulers who welcomed refugees, including Elector Frederick William of Brandenburg and the Russian czarina Catherine the Great. A state's national homogeneity, something that would begin to define European politics in the late nineteenth century, remained a lower priority. The early modern rulers were in the right in this assessment. Cities like Istanbul, Salonika, Warsaw, Berlin, and Königsberg, as well as rural regions profited from immigration that, in the cases mentioned, came as a by-product of flight.

1.2 The refuge of the Huguenots

Over the last three centuries, the flight of the Huguenots out of France has developed into a German and European myth. This is due above all to the potent themes that are associated with the history of the Huguenots: the sometimes fatal consequences of Absolutist power, religious intolerance and persecution, the travails of flight initially replete with deprivation but ends in eager acceptance and successful integration.[8] In French and English, the term *refuge*, as well as the term *réfugiés* or refugees, goes back to the Huguenots.[9]

The part of their history that most intrigues the European public began in 1562, when the Huguenot Wars, which lasted for more than thirty years, erupted. These wars were not only about religious conflict, but also about competition between the centralizing power of the king and the nobility, many of whom had converted to Protestantism (as aristocrats had also done in Austria, Bohemia, Hungary, and Poland).

Like all religious wars, the Huguenot Wars were especially ruthless. The low point was the massacre of the Protestant elite on the night of Saint Bartholomew's Day in 1572, which became the subject of numerous paintings, dramas, and operas. In 1598 the wars were provisionally settled with a compromise. The Edict of Nantes granted the Protestants quite a number of special rights, including protective zones where they could practice their religion freely, easier access to universities and government posts, and, as well, a general freedom of conscience.

The peace held only for one generation, however, and by 1620–29 there was a series of smaller wars that ended with a victory of the crown against the predominantly Protestant nobility. Louis XIV, who began his reign in 1654, wanted to continue centralizing power in the state and therefore rescinded the Edict of Nantes. The "Sun King" replaced it with the Edict of Fontainebleau, which provided for the shutdown of the Protestant churches and aimed to eliminate French Calvinism within a generation. Henceforth marriages could only be contracted by Catholic priests, and children had to be baptized Catholic.

Given the draconian nature of these measures, a massive wave of emigration was to be expected. Louis XIV, who thought in mercantile terms, worried about the economic damage the flight of the Huguenots might occasion and tried to nip the problem in the bud. The government imposed severe penalties for illegal emigration and introduced controls at the national borders with Switzerland, the Holy Roman Empire, the Netherlands, at ocean harbors, and around Paris. This effort at deterrence worked only to a limited extent, because the early modern state had no machinery of surveillance anything like that of twentieth-century dictatorships.[10] Flight was nonetheless highly risky, and travel was expensive. It was not a decision that a Huguenot family could take lightly. How many children or sick and old people fell by the proverbial wayside is something far less studied than the Huguenot success stories.

In light of all these hardships of flight, conversion represented a plausible alternative. Besides, re-Catholicization was Louis XIV's actual objective, along with the elimination of opposition from the nobility. Hence, in contrast to the situation facing the Moriscos and Marranos in Spain, conversion did not lead to any professional discrimination or subsequent persecution. Ultimately, therefore, only 170,000 Huguenots, out of a total of around 800,000, emigrated.

Measured against the size of the population, the Protestant emigration out of the Spanish Netherlands to Holland was more extensive. Almost half the residents from what had been the flourishing city of Antwerp, from Ghent, and from Bruges emigrated following re-Catholicization at the end of the sixteenth century.[11] They settled in Holland, which owed much of its Golden Age to these Calvinist refugees; in Amsterdam and Leiden, for example, the population doubled. Mass flight from today's Belgium to today's Netherlands was favored because of their geographical and linguistic proximity, and (according to the current state of historical research) integration proceeded quickly due to the threat posed by Spain and the Counter-Reformation as well as to the economic boom.

By contrast, the Austrian Protestants, who were expelled or emigrated on their own initiative in the course of the Counter-Reformation, had longer distances to overcome. Moreover, due to the turmoil of the Thirty Years' War, almost all trace was lost of those who had fled and emigrated out of Austria, refugees that the Viennese historian Thomas Winkelbauer has estimated at 350,000. This invites a counterfactual thought: Between 1618 and 1648 there were actually many hundreds of thousands of minority Protestants and Catholics who would have had reason to flee because of their religious beliefs. Yet they lacked, apparently, a well-founded hope of arriving in a country where their religion was practiced, and saw no prospect of a durable exile. When no refuge loomed on the horizon and the flight routes were deemed or seemed too risky, these potential refugees stayed home out of necessity. One precondition for flight is the opportunity to flee, which history does not always grant.[12]

The kind of risk that going into exile could entail is illustrated by the experience of the eight thousand Hutterites who left Moravia in 1621–22 and

In order not to be caught at border controls, many family members moved abroad separately and remained scattered over months and years. The kinds of privations this entailed are known to us from a rather unique body of sources in which a mother and her eldest daughter tell the story of their flight from France, each from her own perspective.[13] In 1687 and 1688, the wealthy **Robillard de Champagne** family emigrated to England and the Netherlands via an escape route that passed through no less than ten stations. The seventeen year-old daughter Suzanna had been sent on ahead with her three sisters and two little brothers.[14] She had to take care of her siblings, who were between four and ten years old, lead them to a ship in La Rochelle, make sure they kept quiet in a dark cargo hold when the royal inspectors came by, and also pay the ship's captain and smuggler a thousand livres to convey the six children to England. On top of that, after the seven-day crossing, the smuggler refused to bring the children (today they would be classified as "unaccompanied refugee minors") to the harbor agreed upon. Instead, they were dropped off along another section of the coast. Here the six siblings were lucky enough to be taken in by a kind-hearted parson who cared for them until they were able to walk to their originally negotiated destination. From the perspective of the teenager Suzanne, the anxious waiting for her mother was another terrible experience.

The devout Marie Robillard (née Rochefoucauld), who had apparently pushed for her family's emigration harder than her husband, only arrived three months later, after missing the first ship she had hoped to board for her escape to England. Moreover, she had had to leave an infant child behind in France, something she did not mention in her flight memoirs, perhaps because of the pain of this loss. The emotional deprivations of the rest of the family became manifest after it was reunited in England. According to both narratives, the one kept in a sober tone by the mother and the more emotional one maintained by the daughter, the family spent the entire first night together crying tears of joy. Even at this moment of reunion, however, there was already an indication of the conflict to come between the mother and her eldest daughter, who did not feel sufficiently appreciated for her role as involuntary head of the family (the oldest brother having traveled with the mother) and organizer of the flight.[15]

The family's odyssey did not end in England. Fearing renewed persecution from the Catholic king James II (who was toppled shortly thereafter in the Glorious Revolution), the family emigrated to Holland. There the mother focused all her energy on obtaining positions for her sons at court, in the civil service, or in the army. That happened rather quickly, since French culture and language were highly prized by the European elites of the period; one ten-year-old son found a job as page at the court of the Prince of Anhalt-Dessau. A year later the father arrived. The change of regime in England brought him professional opportunities. He entered into service for William of Orange (through a contact to the court that the mother had engineered in Den Haag), assembled a regiment at his own expense for the new English king, and was then sent as an officer to Ireland. There catastrophe struck the family. Its enterprising father died suddenly from a serious illness. Grief at this loss prompted the mother to compose her memoirs of flight, which were quite dry in tone, not yet influenced by the more florid style of the later refugee genre. The eldest son was able to take over his father's position and pursued a career in the English army.

The rest of daughter Suzanne's life journey was less fortunate. In 1692 she was married off to a sixty-seven-year-old friend of her father from Champagne, who had lost a major part of his fortune fleeing France and died a few years after the birth of her children. The impoverished widow had to ask several times for support from the Estates of the Netherlands and later moved to Celle, in what is today Lower Saxony, where she apparently had personal contacts. Her bitterness about this social reversal and the lack of recognition from her family motivated Suzanne de la Motte Fouqué (she was the great-grandmother of the famous Romantic writer Friedrich de la Motte Fouqué) to write her memoir about her family's flight, in which she emphasized her role as substitute mother and temporary head of the family. Although later Huguenot narratives heroizing the experience of exodus often asserted that it welded families together, this certainly did not hold for the Robillards. There were disputes about inheritance involving at least one brother and the mother, and there was probably little direct contact with the other siblings owing to the distances between their homes in various German principalities, the Netherlands, and Ireland. So widely scattered was the Robillard family.

ended up in the United States more than two hundred years later. They were expelled from what is today the southeastern region of the Czech Republic because they stuck to their beliefs. Due to wartime violence and harsh living conditions en route to Transylvania, the first stop in their exile, about one third of the group lost their lives.[16] This high mortality is emphasized in the fragmentary historical record. Unlike the Huguenots, the Hutterites have left only sparse testimony about their flight and absorption, in part because only a few of them were able to report on their disastrous emigration and also because, on the subsequent legs of their exodus, to Catherine the Great's Russia and then (at the end of the nineteenth century) onward to the US, they carried only a few documents along with them.

The most important escape route taken by the Huguenots and Waldenses (another Protestant denomination) out of France and into the Holy Roman Empire led via Switzerland to Frankfurt am Main. Swiss cantons, responding to the massive onrush, put in place an allocation formula for the distribution of the refugees and established relief funds to secure food and accommodations for them. In addition, at the flight stations in Geneva, Lausanne, and other sites, so-called chambres des réfugiés and church-based relief funds were created that, as precursors of modern NGOs, collected donations in money and in kind.

Between 1685 and 1705 almost 100,000 refugees passed through Frankfurt am Main, which at the time had only about 30,000 inhabitants.[17] From Frankfurt the Huguenots were moved on to small principalities nearby, and to Hessen-Kassel, Württemberg, Brandenburg-Bayreuth, Brandenburg-Ansbach, and in larger numbers to Prussia. Denominational solidarity played a decisive role here; most of the German states willing to absorb the refugees were governed by Calvinist princes. They emphasized their religious solidarity with the refugees, but above all they were hoping to strengthen their economies.

One thing the Huguenots had in their favor was that, for the most part, they belonged to a social and political elite. From out of Switzerland, Frankfurt, and Cologne, the refugees sent emissaries to various countries to collect donations and negotiate terms for their settlement. When receptivity to the refugees eventually abated in the Netherlands and England, the countries that were initially among their preferred destinations, a regular competition for Huguenot artisans and tradesmen developed among the German states mentioned above. This found expression in the granting of special privileges that included citizenship, tax abatements, even start-up loans in some states, exemption from compulsory guild membership, and, in rural Prussia, release from the feudal burdens imposed on the peasantry.[18] In some cases the native population was obligated to provide assistance in absorbing the refugees, as in the principality of Brandenburg-Bayreuth, where in 1687 the ruling margrave forced the burghers of Erlangen to provide accommodations for arriving Huguenots, while his peasant subjects had to cart stones and building materials from the surrounding countryside to the Huguenot settlement in Neustadt.[19] There were protests against these burdens, but eventually the indigenous populace had to give in.

One especially striking thing about these privileges and the entire process of absorption is that they can be traced back to negotiations between the rulers and the refugees. Prussia, which took in a goodly 20,000 refugees, granted them special rights such as an autonomous judiciary and their own clerical organization; they were thus incorporated as a collective into state and society. In addition, they were placed under the authority of their own public office (the Commissariat Français) and clerical organization (the French-Reformed Church). The Commissariat Français, founded in 1685 immediately after the arrival of the Huguenots, was responsible for dealing with every issue in the French *Kolonien* (colonies), as the French settlements were called in a German term derived from the French. In 1718 the Commissariat was dissolved and replaced by the Grand Directoire Française, whose leader, just like the former "colony ministers," was a member of the Royal Privy Council, the government cabinet of the time. As a result, the highest representative of the Huguenots had direct access to the court and king.[20] This advocacy group was better acquainted with the needs and problems of the refugees than other administrative bodies, was at the disposal of both the refugees and the government as a channel of communication, and was able to cushion conflicts with the host society's majority, tensions that inevitably arose over the years. This was a great help, above all in economically difficult times and when there were new burdensome obligations, as in the case of war.

This special status does, however, suggest that, like the position of the Jews in early modern Poland, the Huguenots' arrangement was nothing like what later came to be known as integration (strictly speaking); rather, it was something more like incorporation. It is a matter of controversy among historians whether the privileges of the Huguenots in Prussia and other German states promoted or inhibited integration. Susanne Lachenicht, who has written a methodologically and empirically pioneering comparative study about the most important destination countries in Europe and North America,[21] inclines more toward a critical verdict. In her view, the special status of the Huguenots, their settlement in separate, frequently newly built city districts, and the autonomy of the French-Reformed Church cemented social separation. In today's Berlin this is something any tourist can see: On the city's Gendarmenmarkt, a major public square, there is both a German and a French cathedral, and the imposing towers of both churches are exactly the same height.

The privileging of the Huguenots and their high level of social and cultural prestige did, however, generate a kind of social integration that ran in the reverse direction. For old-established Prussian citizens it was attractive to settle in city neighborhoods dominated by the Huguenots, like Friedrichstadt in Berlin, and to marry into the families of refugees. As a result, the original islands of Huguenot settlement lost their ethnic cohesion, and gradually use of the French language diminished, first on the street and in everyday usage, later inside families. This embrace of refugees is, however, a rare exception in the history of integration processes. Refugees, like other immigrants, usually have to work their way up in order to acquire this kind of social prestige. That there was not more vehement protest against the privileging of the Huguenots had to do with the authoritarian character of Prussia and the other German states that hosted the refugees. As already mentioned, these states' rulers even ordered that relief services be delivered and work obligations be performed for the refugees. This would not have been feasible in a democratic society, or could at best be accomplished only indirectly, using taxes and levies whose revenues could then be steered toward refugees.

In spite of this unusual framework of political, social, and cultural conditions, it took two to three generations, as a rule, for the integration of the Huguenots to be completed. Only then was more German than French spoken in Huguenot households as the number of mixed marriages rose steadily.[22] Perhaps this kind of patience is something worth summoning up again today. But such a long-term perspective does not fit comfortably into the electoral cycles of Western democracies or into the narrower time horizons for political action they dictate.

In the older literature, the contribution made by the Huguenots to Prussia's economic development is constantly emphasized. These economic success stories, however, are as much a part of the Huguenots' self-presentation as is the myth of their rapid integration. By underscoring their contributions to the Prussian and then German fatherland, the Huguenots strengthened arguments for the retention of their privileges.[23] Although their prominent political and social position was quite literally set in stone between 1780 and 1785 by the construction of the French Cathedral in Berlin,[24] shortly after the building was completed the successor of the Francophile Frederick II had their privileges rescinded. In the Prussian Civil Code of 1794, all of Prussia's citizens were put on a broadly equal legal footing. For the Huguenots this meant the loss of their special status, but at the same time their permanent integration as citizens. Prussia now finally conformed to the prevailing practice in the Netherlands, England, and the USA, where refugees were accorded equality from the start.

In all those countries, their common religion made for an important bridge. The different Protestant denominations competed with each other to be sure, but there were no high hurdles blocking joint religious services and mixed marriages. In smaller communities where the number of Huguenots was too small to offer communion in French, adjustment proceeded at a fast pace; in major cities, French-Reformed Church congregations lasted into the twentieth century. But there was no need of conversion or even forced baptism to facilitate relationships and marriages between natives and refugees or their descendants. Mixing between adherents of the great monotheistic world religions, by contrast, has always been a great deal harder; in some Muslim countries, as is well known, it is a punishable offense. This has the consequence that integration can take place at best one-sidedly—as assimilation.

The two-sided and negotiated character of the Huguenots' acceptance and subsequent integration is also worth recalling, because Germany's current legislation on asylum and its massive absorption of Syrian and other refugees since 2015 has nothing of the same quality. While today's refugees, depending on their legal status, are entitled to social services provided by the German government, they are not asked with what goals they have arrived and how they want to shape their future. This absence of two-way negotiation has gone unnoticed by the media, nor are there recognized representatives of the refugees who could speak for them. That being the case, one cannot expect refugees to exhibit a particularly high degree of identification with the state that is taking them in, but perhaps more is achievable through daily communication with the Germans who are assisting them in starting a new life. Welfare state services, no matter how well-meaning, are also inevitably based on an asymmetry of power that was not exercised in the same way vis-à-vis the Huguenots. Their acceptance was additionally favored by the fact that their massive flight was drawn out over several decades. Not infrequently, therefore, they had established personal contacts abroad and could fall back on well-established networks.

An indisputable and lasting benefit conferred by the French religious refugees on the countries that absorbed them is that religious intolerance became discredited among the European public. This shift in opinion prevented additional religiously motivated instances of flight and expulsion. A good illustration comes from Silesia, a denominationally mixed region where Protestants had been subjected to enormous pressure after the Thirty Years' War came to an end. This pressure was applied not only to Lutherans persecuted by Catholics; members of Reformed (usually Calvinist) churches living in Lutheran principalities and regions did not always have it easy either. An intervention of the Protestant protecting powers Sweden and Prussia achieved a compromise in the form of the Altranstädt Convention of 1707. This put a brake on the Counter-Reformation and enabled Protestants to continue practicing their faith in certain principalities and peace churches.

In neighboring Saxony, the birthplace of the Reformation, coexistence between denominations became a governing principle when the ruling Wettin kings converted to Catholicism at the end of the seventeenth century in order to attain the Polish crown. August the Strong could not and would not impose a change of religion on his subjects, so from then on an overwhelmingly Protestant population had to live under a ruling Catholic dynasty. Power politics, consequently, counted for more than religious loyalty, and this calculation, in addition to triggering memories of the Thirty Years' War, was an important factor explaining why, at the beginning of the eighteenth century, the era of religious wars and religiously motivated mass flight in Western and Central Europe came to an end.

In October 1731, when Leopold Firmian, the prince-archbishop of Salzburg, issued an "emigration patent" for all the Protestants in his principality, his Edict of Expulsion seemed almost anachronistic. The expulsion made Prussia's king, Frederick William I, appear even more like the tolerant ruler he styled himself when he generously offered asylum to the "Salzburg exiles" (the *Salzburger Exulanten*, as they called themselves). As Mack Walker has shown in his study on the Salzburg Protestants, this mass expulsion raised a powerful media echo in the Holy Roman Empire and beyond. About 20,000 refugees (that is, almost as many as in the case of the Huguenots) moved to Prussia, where they were allotted land and admitted to the guilds in the cities; an additional 10,000 Salzburgers migrated to other German states.[25]

Only in remote regions and mountain valleys did scattered remnants of these persecuted religious communities stay put. Some examples are the Protestant communities on the Styrian side of the Dachstein mountain range and in Carinthia, the Bohemian Brethren in northern Czech Valteřice, and the Marranos in the Portuguese town of Belmonte who lived completely isolated from the outside world for centuries and were first rediscovered in 1917 by a Polish Jew. This kind of marginal existence was only possible, of course, to those willing to live furtively; converting to the majority or official religion was the path most frequently taken. Here we see the difference between interdenominational (usually intra-Christian) and interreligious (usually between Christians and those of other faiths) conflicts like those in early modern Spain, where in the long run not even conversion provided protection against persecution.

There were also so-called exiles in early modern Poland, in this case Catholic nobles who did not want to live under the rule of the Orthodox czar who, since the middle of the seventeenth century, had been extending his empire gradually westward. The Muscovite government had confiscated the lands of Polish aristocrats because they did not fit into the political system of Russian autocracy. So, beginning in 1667, the *egzulanci* started emigrating westward, more or less parallel to the movement of Poland's borders in the same direction.[26] Another group that fled from east to west somewhat earlier, between the fifteenth and seventeenth centuries, was the Tatars, who came from Crimea and the steppes north of the Black Sea. Smaller tribes of Tatars had sided with the Poles in several wars and for this reason suffered persecution from their fellow countrymen or, later, from the Ukrainian rebels under Bohdan Khmelnytsky. The Tatars who fled usually settled in newly founded villages, some of which exist to this day and are places where the Tatars have preserved certain culinary specialties and, to some extent, have retained their Muslim religion.[27] The Polish-Lithuanian Commonwealth thus succeeded in fully integrating Muslims with a minimum of conflict, an achievement few European states have managed since. But this feat has apparently been forgotten. For, otherwise, Warsaw's national-conservative Law and Justice party (the PiS, which has been the governing party since 2015) might not act as if fending off refugees from the Near East is Poland's only option.

But let us return to the Salzburgers. Partly owing to its serious economic repercussions, this was the last religiously motivated mass expulsion in Central Europe. Thereafter the German princes recoiled from similar acts of deportation. Toward the end of the eighteenth century, a variety of tolerance edicts further relaxed interdenominational conflicts, although these edicts also curbed older privileges, such as those of the Huguenots in Prussia. Legal equality did turn the practice of privileged incorporation used in the old estates systems into integration along modern lines. Yet the kind of tolerance practiced by the Absolutist monarchs applied only conditionally to the Jews, and not at all externally, that is, to the Muslims.

1.3 The Reconquista of Southeastern Europe

When, at the end of the seventeenth century, the Habsburgs pushed the Ottomans out of Hungary after the failed siege of Vienna, this was accompanied by a massive rout. Initially the flight comprised the gigantic army, which numbered around 200,000 and had been largely vanquished. Fleeing along with the army were the civil servants who had come into the country in the wake of the soldiers, and a large share of those Hungarians who had converted to Islam during the roughly one and a half centuries of Ottoman rule. The least harsh treatment afforded the Muslims was so-called safe conduct, meaning that they could withdraw without suffering force or violent attacks; this happened, for example, in 1716 in Temesvár, one of the few instances in which the reconquest was well-documented.[28] There are no exact figures on the number of refugees produced by the Habsburg Turkish wars, but it is clear that no Muslims remained behind in the conquered territories.

The only way to avoid death or expulsion into the shrinking Ottoman Empire was (re-)conversion back to Christianity. However, a political and social dynamic developed along the Habsburg military border similar to what happened in Andalusia following the Reconquista. The new rulers and the local population continued to discriminate against and persecute the New Christians well into the second generation. Therefore, most (re-)converts did finally emigrate after a delay of some decades to the Ottoman Empire.[29] As a rule this entailed yet another change of religion, something that apparently troubled the Ottoman authorities in Bosnia and Serbia less than it did the Christians on the other side of the border.

Religious intolerance also affected the rest of the Reconquista in nineteenth-century Southeastern Europe. Applying the term to this part of Europe may seem unusual, since it is usually reserved for the Iberian peninsula, whereas the Balkan nations and European philhellenes promoted the concept of liberation to characterize their region's recapture. Initially, however, the struggle against the Ottoman Empire was motivated above all by religion—as a liberation of Christians from the Turkish yoke. The adjective "Turkish" and the collectivizing noun "the Turks" lumped Southeastern European Muslims into a single aggregate independent of their ethnicity; in reality, however, depending on the region, these were predominantly Albanians, Bosniaks (Muslim residents of Bosnia, Herzegovina, and Sandžak—the term is a self-designation), or Pomaks (Bulgarian-speaking Muslims), and not ethnic Turks. A contributing factor to this collective designation, in addition to religiously motivated hatred, was a colonialist contempt for the rest of mankind that Europeans had acquired during the nineteenth century as they made contact with the Orient. The struggle was always further legitimated by historic or current atrocities committed by "the Turks" and the sultan. The result of this mixture was malicious violence against civilians, something that shaped all of the liberation movements in Southeastern Europe.

In Greece the liberation began in 1821 with an uprising in the Peloponnesus. Greek troops successfully laid siege to the city of Tripolis and followed up on their victory with an orgy of violence. The rebels killed up to 8,000 of the city's Muslim inhabitants, and about 15,000 people fell victim to the subsequent conquest of the peninsula.[30] The signal this massacre was meant to convey was clear: Muslims remaining in Greece should know what awaited them if they did not flee in time.

Western newspapers took note of the extreme violence used to expel the Turks with a certain amount of shuddering, but hardly anyone protested publicly against the massacre. On the contrary: in Lord Byron, the poet and military leader who died in 1824 at Missolunghi, philhellenes found a martyr to champion in this clash of civilizations. Their idealization of ancient (and contemporary) Greece rested at bottom on a contempt for the Ottoman culture that was to be deliberately eradicated in the "liberated territories." Just a few years after Greece gained independence, the mosques had disappeared, as had most Ottoman cemeteries and old inscriptions on public buildings.

In Serbia the violence directed against the Muslims and their material legacies was less sweeping, even though the national mythology there was even more highly charged with Christian narratives of victimization.[31] The less radical cleansing of Muslims was attributable to the compromising character of the autonomy conceded in 1817, and also to the fact that here there was no equivalent to Western philhellenism.[32] The rulers of the principality of Serbia, founded in 1833, were able to control most domestic affairs on their own and needed only to come to terms with an Ottoman garrison remaining in Belgrade. This coexistence of Serbs and Turks (most of whom were ethnic southern Slavs whose forebears had converted) lasted almost thirty years. In 1862, however, disturbances broke out between Serbs and Muslims; in reaction to the escalating violence, the European great powers resolved to expand Serbian autonomy and relocate all the Muslims remaining in Serbia.[33]

The decision on Serbia took place in the context of another, more comprehensive ethnic and religious cleansing. Following the Russian Caucasus campaign of 1860–64, at least half a million people were forced to leave what is today the Russian Black Sea Riviera around Sochi and the northern Caucasus. That was so far the worst incident of mass flight in European history. Those affected were mostly Circassians and Abkhazians, but included also Chechens, Tatars, and members of smaller nationalities, all of the Muslim faith. The estimate of 500,000 is based on Russian sources and the number of ship passengers registered in Russian Black Sea ports. If one takes into consideration land-based flight and non-registered refugees, one arrives at an even higher figure: as many as two million people likely fled to territories that remained part of the Ottoman Empire between 1860 and 1914.[34]

In the Crimea, too, where the Tatars had lived largely undisturbed alongside Russian and Ukrainian settlers until the Crimean War (1853–56), there was significant pressure to migrate. From the late eighteenth century to the end of the 1860s, up to 200,000 Tatars were forced to leave the peninsula.[35] Fleeing cost many people their lives, especially when it happened in the course of combat operations along shifting frontlines. Contemporary reports from the ports of arrival on the Black Sea also attest to the deaths of countless people. There around 20 percent of the new arrivals died from such epidemics as typhus, dysentery, and cholera, or from malnutrition. Behind this abstract number many concrete traumas are concealed, mental wounds that would be passed along from one generation to another in numerous families.[36]

The Crimean War was soon followed by the Russo-Turkish War of 1877–78, which had begun a year earlier as a regional conflict between Serbia and the Ottoman Empire. Initially, the war went favorably for Sultan Abdülhamid II, whose army vanquished a Serbian armed force backed up by many inexperienced volunteers. Then, as so often in the nineteenth century, the European great powers intervened: Russia declared war on the Ottoman Empire and sandwiched it from two sides, from the southern Caucasus and eastern Anatolia and along the lower reaches of the Danube.

This war's combat operations resulted in several waves of refugees. As early as 1876, the Ottoman authorities registered 276,000 new arrivals, then a total of 274,000 for the years 1877 and 1878.[37] In light of all the turmoil (the Ottoman Empire was on the verge of collapse) and the brutal nature of the warfare, which involved numerous local massacres, the actual number of refugees was certainly much higher. In San Stefano, the Ottoman Empire was forced to sign a humiliating peace treaty, one so favorable to Russia and its allies, Serbia and Bulgaria, that Great Britain and Austria demanded a revision. Through the mediation of Bismarck the great powers met at the Congress of Berlin, where they created a new order for the Balkans based on nation-states. This plan was problematic from the start, as the region's motley settlement structures did not fit in with the mandated order. Following the First World War, Central and Eastern Europe would confront the same insoluble challenge (more on this in Chapter Two).

In every one of the region's nation-states internationally recognized by the settlements of 1878 (Romania, Bulgaria, Montenegro, and semi-independent Bulgaria) there were significant minorities. The Balkan states were formally obligated to tolerate them, although what mattered most to the signatory powers were the Jewish or Christian-denominational minorities, not the Muslims. The large Ottoman landowners and other elites were expropriated or expelled if they had not already fled. The remaining Muslim peasants were therefore often unemployed and without future prospects. Everyday discrimination, attacks, and open violence on the streets and in market squares intensified the pressure to migrate, so that the flood of refugees—here the metaphor is no exaggeration—did not stop even after the conclusion of the peace treaties. Until 1896, according to serious calculations, 1,015,000 Muslims from the Balkans arrived in what was left of the Ottoman Empire, adding to the aforementioned refugees from the Caucasus.[38]

In reaction to his empire's devastating defeat and the challenge posed by these homeless masses, the pious Ottoman sultan Abdülhamid II made religious solidarity a part of his government's policy. He welcomed refugees from the Balkans and the Caucasus as *muhacir*, "brothers in faith," and thereby enhanced their status. The refugees also used the term *hijrah*, which in their case can be roughly translated as a religious homecoming and would later encompass more voluntary resettlement to the Ottoman Empire. The shared focus on religion was not in line with the contemporary trend in other European states to separate state and ecclesiastic powers. Nevertheless, Ottoman refugee policy can be compared with previous attempts by the Netherlands, England, and Prussia to facilitate the absorption of incoming Protestants from France, the Spanish Netherlands, and other Catholic states through appeals for religious solidarity.

As in other European states, there was also a broad administrative response. In 1860, reacting to the Russian campaign in the Caucasus and the resulting mass flight, the sultan appointed a refugee commission (the Muhacirin Komisyonu), which after 1876 grew into a sizable administrative tool planted in every province of the Ottoman Empire to manage the settlement of the refugees.[39] We know about this because of an excellent dissertation by Vladimir Hamed-Troyansky, who shows how the late Ottoman Empire became a refugee state. It should be noted that the refugees received Ottoman citizenship upon arrival, if they did not already have it. This response was another refugee policy in line with a broader European pattern.

However, the Ottoman Empire had great difficulties supporting the refugees when it came to every other aspect of integration. They needed food, firewood for cooking, and a roof over their heads, as well as arable land and pastures if they were to sustain themselves. The empire's large landowners were not much inclined to give up any of their land, just as homeowners were reluctant to offer living space. As a result, the refugees often took by force what they needed. The situation was especially tense in the regions near the new borders, where refugees were present in especially high numbers. In Kosovo, for example, which had remained Ottoman after the 1876–77 war, 800,000 natives confronted 200,000 refugees. One organized group among the refugees even murdered the governor there, who was actually trying to mediate between the needy and the local notables.[40] Chaos and hardship prevailed in the European parts of the empire, which further undermined the legitimacy of Ottoman rule. The situation was better in the Levant, where many refugees could settle on the relatively fertile areas in the west and, later, benefited from the Hejaz Railway going through several of their villages. According to Hamed-Troyansky, refugees from the Caucasus "founded three of the four largest cities in modern Jordan, including the capital city of Amman."[41] Space was also plentiful for settlements in Anatolia, but these regions were more difficult to reach, and most of them stagnated economically. The seemly unending hardships that followed on the suffering during the flight were a constant source of protest, and sometimes riots.

Especially notorious for their inclination to violence were the Circassians, although this cannot be explained by the kind of supposedly ethnic or cultural peculiarities that Pushkin, Lermontov, Tolstoy, and other Russian writers ascribed to the "wild" peoples of the Caucasus. The Circassians were doubly traumatized. Between 1860 and 1864 they had been forced to leave their Caucasian homeland and settled in different regions of the Ottoman Empire, partly in the Balkans.[42] After the Congress of Berlin, many of the Circassians resettled to the Balkans had to flee a second time and were, accordingly, outraged.

Often, the arrival of refugees would launch a new spiral of violence, and not infrequently refugees would become perpetrators and persecute Greek, Bulgarian, and Armenian Christians.

Up until the outbreak of the Balkan Wars, nearly 300,000 Christians fled Macedonia and Thrace alone. There also was a series of local uprisings, some of them spontaneous, some also intended to provoke renewed Russian intervention in favor of the Ottoman Christians. This strategy worked repeatedly, as in Eastern Rumelia, a region disputed between Bulgaria and the Ottoman Empire that the great powers had initially left under Ottoman rule in 1878, but which was ultimately annexed to Bulgaria (seven years later) in the wake of uprisings and disturbances.[43]

In light of this outside intervention and the local escalation of violence, one cannot paint the history of Southeastern Europe during the long nineteenth century in black and white, with Ottoman Muslims as the chief culprits and Southeastern European Christians as the sole victims, the view that most

Western media and publics took at the time. No party in all these conflicts was without its sinister shadow side. But one finding does stand out: disputes between Christians and Muslims were waged with excessive violence and inhumanity, resulting in a volume of mass flight unprecedented in European history.

The conflicts did not, however, lead to a removal of all Muslims, as happened on the Iberian peninsula three centuries earlier. This was due in part to the fact that it was impossible, as a matter of sheer practicality, to expel all the Muslims in the Balkans in either 1878 or 1912. It is also attributable to the regional imperialism of the Southeastern European nation-states. Their push into ever more territories where the patterns of settlement were ethnically and religiously mixed, especially after the two Balkan Wars, necessitated compromises with the local population. So long as the remaining Turks, Albanians, and other Muslims did not question the hegemony of the new nation-states, they were to a degree tolerated. Once the Ottoman Empire was almost completely driven out of Europe in 1912–13 and no longer posed a threat, Serbian and Bulgarian nation-building elites began to view the Slavic-speaking Muslims as lost sheep who could be assimilated to the national majority. A common language ultimately counted for more than religious differences, at least until the Greek-Turkish War of 1919–22 and the Second World War, when inter-ethnic conflicts in Southeastern Europe intensified once again.

As a result of modern nation-building, ethno-national criteria were superimposed on older religious criteria of exclusion and inclusion from the late nineteenth century onward. Yet this development was not universal, since in the 1923 Treaty of Lausanne regulating a Greek-Turkish "population exchange" (see Chapter 2.1), religious affiliation again became the decisive criterion for determining who would be allowed to stay and who would not.

Occasioned by the wars following the breakup of Yugoslavia in the 1990s, a controversy erupted among historians of Southeastern Europe over whether in the nineteenth century the Balkan Muslims had really been expelled or whether their migration should rather be attributed to the religiously motivated policies of Sultan Abdulhamid II, who on various occasions urged pious Muslims to return home.[44] Assessing the relative weight of push and pull factors is standard practice among historians of migration; in the case of the Southeastern European Muslims, "push" would trivialize the actions taken by the refugees' countries of origin. The pressure to flee was immense, while the attractiveness or "pull" of Anatolia, underdeveloped and arid in comparison with Macedonia or Thrace, was small.

In the case of most massive refugee movements, moreover, there was a mechanism at work that has influenced the entire history of migration: as soon as some members of a family or village community had left their home, those left behind acquired an additional motive and—through contact with earlier emigrants—better opportunities to follow in their turn. Over the course of time, this meant that war-induced flight segued into other forms of migration, though religiously motivated and (increasingly) nationalism-driven violence and discrimination remained the primary causes of flight. In the twentieth century, finally, chain migration (the term is used here as a neutral description, not with the negative connotation of recent anti-immigration polemic) acquired a new dimension thanks to new communication technologies— telegrams, and telephone lines, and for the last one or two decades E-mail, SMS, Facebook, and other social media.

1.4 Flight from pogroms

Improving communication also played an important role in the emigration of Russian and Polish Jews, who suffered from increasingly frequent and widespread pogroms. When it comes to the history of their persecution, it is hard to distinguish clearly between religious and nationalist motives; on the whole, the former predominated, since what triggered individual pogroms was almost always a rumor about the ritual murder of a Christian child or a desecration of the host.[45] This is true of the well-known pogroms in Odessa and Kishinev, and in other cities of the Russian Empire as well. Initially, most Russian Jews fled within the boundaries of their own city or country. But by 1881–82, during the first wave of pogroms, they began to arrive in neighboring states. About 25,000 refugees attempted to reach Galicia and Austria, most of them by way of the important border crossing in Brody.[46] In the face of this onslaught, customs officers, passport officials, and the military sometimes lost control of the border, which was not secured as frontiers would be in the twentieth century. In the hinterland, therefore, reception camps were hurriedly constructed. Feeding the refugees was largely left in the hands of Jewish organizations that collected donations throughout the Austro-Hungarian monarchy, in the German Empire, and internationally. This tradition of refugee welfare was later adopted by non-Jewish NGOs and, especially after the First World War, saved tens of thousands of refugees from starvation. (On the support provided by Jewish NGOs, see also the analytical portrait of Manès Sperber in Chapter 2.1).

Neither the Habsburg Empire nor any other European state was willing to accept permanently the Jews who had fled Russia. Only the larger Jewish communities in the Ottoman Empire—Salonika, Istanbul, and Izmir—declared their willingness. But reaching those destinations was a long haul for Russian Jews, and the escape route to the sultanate would have landed them in an empire denigrated in Russia and elsewhere as the "sick man of Europe." The best option was moving on to the United States, which at this time had an open immigration policy. But the American immigration authorities nevertheless paid close attention to those seeking entry into the country. Refugees had to be in good health, prove they had assets and cash, and be able to pay for their transit. Here they were helped by the aforementioned Jewish aid organizations, though ultimately about half of the refugees remained stranded in the reception camps and in the end had to return to the Russian Empire. The circumstances of this remigration (curiously there is neither a colloquial nor a scholarly term for an aborted flight) were certainly almost as devastating as the earlier pogroms, and yet we know little about them. Refugees prevented from fleeing have left behind few historical records.

News of the New World nonetheless spread via those refugees who did make it to the Americas. By the outbreak of the First World War, around 2.4 million East European Jews had left their homeland. This emigration, which can be viewed in large part as a flight from religious and ethno-national discrimination, reached a new peak following the pogroms of 1905 (the year of the first Russian Revolution), just as immigration to the United States reached its all-time high two years later. Apart from persecution and violence, however, there were also economic reasons for East European Jews to emigrate to the US.[47] In what was an increasingly prosperous society based on a rising industrial economy, they could start a new life, often working their way to great prosperity; and once integrated into American society, they could take up the work of assisting other refugees.[48]

1.5 Victims and perpetrators: The late Ottoman Empire

The Muslim refugees from the Balkans and the Caucasus, by contrast, found the Ottoman Empire to be an overwhelmingly agrarian country, poor to begin with and even more impoverished after its numerous wars. Frequently the flight routes of 1912–13 ran along much the same pathways as those traversed a century later in 2015, both across the Aegean and overland. (One of these passed through the Vardar valley in Macedonia, where we find the border town Idomeni which made headlines again in 2015–16 because of the Middle Eastern refugees trying to reach Austria and Germany who were blocked there after New Year's.) In contrast to later periods and to the well-organized flight of the Huguenots, the refugees from Southeastern Europe found no well-organized NGOs dedicated to assisting them. There were only the previously mentioned Jewish organizations and, in the Ottoman Empire, traditional Islamic social welfare institutions such as the soup kitchens of mosques to provide rudimentary assistance.[49] This hardly sufficed to counteract the general misery of the refugees who now faced new terrors in the form of rampant epidemics and the widespread deaths these caused.

Many ultimately ran aground in the big cities; at least 200,000 Southeastern European Muslims who were forced to flee in 1877–78 migrated to Istanbul. A large part of the population growth in the Ottoman capital, which went from 722,000 inhabitants in 1877 to 1.6 million at the outbreak of the First World War, can be traced back to these refugees and not, as elsewhere in

Europe, to the pull-effects of industrialization.[50] In the 1880s Muslims became a majority of the city's population for the first time, and old Constantinople was transformed into a predominantly Turkish Istanbul. Though most of the refugees arrived penniless, the educated elite among them were able to attain high positions in the army and administration following the Young Turk Revolution of 1908. One of the Turks who came out of Southeastern Europe was Kemal Pasha, the founder of the Turkish Republic later known as Atatürk, though at this time he was not yet playing any central role.

Most refugees at first led a life of bitter poverty, but there was an excellent vehicle of integration available to them: nationalism. After a brief attempt to establish a balance among the nationalities of the Ottoman Empire, the Young Turks opted for ethnic nationalism—in their own state and beyond its borders (via Pan-Turkism, which was in turn inspired by Pan-Slavism). Although Russia and its neighboring Balkan states were viewed historically as the Ottoman Empire's most dangerous opponents (excepting Bulgaria, where the sultan had concluded a peace treaty in 1913 that even included generous protection of the Muslim minority), propaganda and pent-up hate were largely directed against the empire's weaker domestic adversaries, the Christian minorities still under Turkish rule. Religion also played a role among the ostensibly secular Young Turks, as they came overwhelmingly from Muslim (though not necessarily Turkish) families.

The Young Turks had little they could blame in any specific way on the Greeks who lived along the Aegean and in Eastern Thrace (the European panhandle west of Istanbul that remained Ottoman in 1913 and remains part of Turkey today), but the series of defeats suffered by Turkey meant there was a backlog of anxieties, hatred, and desire for revenge. As a result of the Balkan Wars, moreover, more than 400,000 refugees had entered the country.[51] Especially among the educated and in an army pommelled by repeated defeats, nationalism acted as an outlet and a promise for the future. Finally there was an explanation for all the evil in the world and a vague yet attractive goal in sight, the founding of a nation-state or, in this case, the nationalization of a faltering empire. And, as with all ideologies, milieu- and group-specific mechanisms of integration took hold: in nationalist circles, once more, the voices that prevailed were those that advanced the most radical demands.

The outbreak of the First World War and Russia's initial successes in Eastern Anatolia further intensified this mood. There were numerous Armenians fighting in the Russian army (partly as volunteers, though mostly as recruits), and when Armenian nationalists inside the Ottoman Empire demanded first autonomy and then a nation-state of their own, the Young Turkish elites made the fateful decision to deport all Armenians from Central and Eastern Anatolia. This persecution was directed also against other Christian minorities, such as the Assyrians and the Anatolian Greeks. Once again religious motives had taken hold. That the deportation of the Armenians, by foot, across

Talaat Pasha (1874–1921), the longtime Ottoman interior minister, was one of the Balkan Turks who became a war criminal and a mastermind of the Armenian genocide.[52] During the First World War he issued the key orders and decrees deporting Anatolian Armenians to the Syrian desert, which led to the deaths of about a million people in 1915–16. Talaat's radical, murderous nationalism was shaped by his own family history. He was born in 1874 in the Eastern Rumelian district capital of Kırcaali (Bulgarian Kardzhali).[53] In this district Christian Bulgarians, Vlachs, and Roma lived alongside Turks and Pomaks. In addition to epitomizing centuries of multicultural coexistence, Kırcaali offers a prime example of the territorial conflicts and nationalist turmoil in Southeastern Europe. At the Congress of Berlin, the European great powers left Eastern Rumelia under the sovereignty of the Ottoman Empire, although it was supposed to be administered by a Christian governor. Only seven years later this compromise was broken by an uprising, and Eastern Rumelia was annexed by Bulgaria. Just two districts, including Kırcaali, remained Ottoman and, owing to their location close to the border and to the permanent danger of war, developed into hotspots of Turkish nationalism. During the First Balkan War in 1912, however, Talaat's hometown also fell to Bulgaria. Numerous Muslims, including a large part of his family, which presumably descended from the Bektashi religious order that had been persecuted in sixteenth-century Anatolia and forcibly resettled in Southeastern Europe, had to flee Rumelia.

Talaat chose a career in the postal service, which was ideally suited to disseminating nationalist and revolutionary propaganda. By 1907 he was among the founders of the Ottoman Freedom Society (Osmanlı Hürriyet Cemiyeti) in Salonika (Selanik), a circle of Young Turk conspirators who had joined forces with exiled activists to form the Committee for Unity and Progress (İttihad ve Terakki Fırkası). The Young Turks (on this designation, see also the portrait of Giuseppe Mazzini in Chapter Three of this book) initiated the Revolution of 1908 that led to the overthrow of Sultan Abdulhamid II. All of the Young Turks were fervent Ottoman patriots and Turkish nationalists, but they could not prevent their country's catastrophic defeat in the First Balkan War. Even the city of Edirne, where Talaat had spent most of his youth, fell to Bulgaria, forcing around 50,000 people, including some of his close relatives, to flee to Istanbul. There a cholera epidemic broke out, aggravating the suffering of the refugees. During the Second Balkan War, Turkish forces managed to recapture Edirne from Bulgaria, an important symbolic success as the city had served as the Ottoman capital before the conquest of Constantinople. Apart from Edirne, however, the Ottoman Empire did lose almost all of its European territories. For that reason the Young Turks clung even more fiercely to Anatolia, which was meant to serve as a bastion of Turkishness. During the World War, Talaat then issued the fatal orders for the deportation of the Armenians from Anatolia.[54] Some of the confiscated Armenian estates and homes were awarded to refugees from the Balkans and the Caucasus. Following the defeat of the Ottoman Empire, a search warrant for Talaat was issued and he was sentenced to death in absentia for his participation in the Armenian genocide. He fled to Berlin, where he was eventually tracked down and shot on the street by an Armenian nationalist.

the Anatolian highlands into the Syrian desert would lead to death on a massive scale was clear to those responsible for the genocide. In retrospect, it is difficult to distinguish the actual military threat posed by Russia and the Armenians (a pretext raised by the Young Turks and used to this day) from war propaganda. But at that time the Ottoman Empire was inhabited by several million people and partly governed by politicians and military officers who came from refugee families and had been traumatized themselves.[55]

Members of the Young Turks' governing elite had often experienced at firsthand (or learned from stories their parents told them) what had happened to Muslims in the Balkans and the Caucasus since 1876 (or since 1860); and, in addition, they had fresh memories of the lost Balkan War of 1912–13.[56]

As Erik Jan Zürcher has shown, 41 percent of the highest-ranking state officials in the Republic of Turkey came from the lost European territories of the Ottoman Empire.[57] Zürcher also provides biographical evidence showing how traumas they or their families suffered shaped genocidal policy toward the Armenians. The experience of violence is easily exploited as an incitement to counter-violence.

1.6 The long legacy of religious violence

Narratives of violence and victimhood passed on from generation to generation also played a fatal role in later periods of European history. In the 1980s, it was an easy game to play for the Serbian-Orthodox clergy, Slobodan Milošević, and leaders of the Serbian minority in Croatia and Bosnia to arouse painful memories of the genocidal civil war in occupied Yugoslavia between 1941 and 1944 (see the remarks on flight and expulsion during the Second

World War in Chapter 2.2) and depict Serbs as once again victims of genocide. In the 1990s violence against the Muslim Bosniaks, too, was justified by
invoking the supposed threat coming from "the Turks" and Islam. Serbian
propaganda used stereotypes about the enemy that went back to earlier eras.
In the summer of 1980 Milošević staged a gigantic celebration commemorating the six-hundredth anniversary of the Battle of Kosovo (at the Kosovo Polje
[Field of Blackbirds]) in 1389; he and other Serbian nationalists demonized
Ottoman rule, and various publishers reprinted anti-Turkish hate screeds from
the nineteenth century.

The examples of the former Yugoslavia in the 1990s, the Northern Ireland
conflict in the 1980s, the Cyprus War of 1974, and the Serbian-Croatian,
Serbian-Bosnian, and Polish-Ukrainian conflicts during the Second World
War all demonstrate that religiously motivated violence did not end with modernity and its concomitant secularization. Religion—or, to put it more accurately, the pretext of religious arguments—continued to play an essential
role in Europe's conflicts and wars, hostilities in which violence between population groups escalated and individual perpetrators got out of control.

One can hardly maintain, then, that Western Europe learned its lesson in
the Thirty Years' War, or from the Huguenots, or that it has been a haven of
religious tolerance since the Enlightenment. Efforts to paint a European
identity based on tolerance are well-intentioned, but about as sound as the
assertion that Europe has overcome radical nationalism because of the twentieth century's two world wars. The violent dissolution of Yugoslavia in the
1990s demonstrated once again the virulence of religiously charged nationalism and the tenacity of (pseudo-)religious arguments. Here we should also
point out that the infamous declaration issued by the Serbian Academy of
Arts and Sciences in 1986—which asserted that the Serbs had always been
disadvantaged in Yugoslavia, were victims of genocide (especially in Kosovo),
and should finally fight back—was preceded by an analogous declaration by
the Serbian-Orthodox Church. The terrible violence of the 1990s thus had
clerical backing. Muslims in the war in Bosnia and Herzegovina (a war to be
discussed in greater detail in this book's section on flight from nationalism)
once again became the primary victims, regardless of whether they were religious or not.

Serbian aggression did, however, miss one essential war aim: Bosnia and
Herzegovina were not reconverted; Muslims and Bosniaks continued to form
the majority of the population. Since the Dayton Accords of 1995, the share
of Bosniaks in the total population has even increased. In Southeastern Europe
there are today at least sixteen million Muslims, forming a bare absolute majority in Bosnia and a large majority in Albania and Kosovo. There is also an
overwhelming Muslim majority in the European parts of Turkey.[58] Europe,
predominantly Christian, needs to find common ground with these societies,
precisely because of the threat posed by militant Islamism. To this end, it is

impossible to avoid confronting European history's interreligious and interdenominational conflicts and the massive incidences of flight associated with them.

This also applies to the eastern Mediterranean, where Christians have for several years now been subjected to persecution, just as they were at the beginning of the twentieth century. The immense exodus of Syrian and Iraqi Christians makes it abundantly clear that religious persecution is not, unfortunately, an exclusively historical phenomenon; it is also a very current evil. To be sure, these Christians are not being accepted in the EU on account of their denominational or religious identities, but rather as war refugees. And this now brings us to some concluding observations about religious and denominational forms of solidarity and paths of integration.

In order to understand the history of mass flight, one needs to think about several things at once: about the starting points and thus the causes of displacement, about the escape routes, and about the refugees' admission into the countries and societies that were ready to help them.

The starting point was always religious intolerance, the persecution of one faith by another, but how this played out depended on whether the conflicts were interdenominational or interreligious. As early as the sixteenth century, the flight and expulsion of Protestants, especially in the Netherlands, assumed vast proportions. In the seventeenth-century conflicts between Christian denominations further escalated. The rivalry between Protestant and Catholic states and elites made religion even more of a political issue than it had been, and ultimately led to the outbreak of the Thirty Years' War.

Wars have always caused and accelerated flight on a massive scale. Yet, as the Thirty Years' War also demonstrates, that flight depends on structures that facilitate it, on escape routes that are somewhat secure, and on accessible destinations. The flight of the Huguenots stands out because it actually took place in peacetime. This facilitated a relatively smooth organization for this emigration in spite of the French prohibition against it, and in part because the forces of "push" and "pull" dovetailed.

The other side of the coin of religious persecution is religious solidarity. Many refugees reported witnessing welcoming scenes along their escape routes and upon arrival in their host countries. Of course, some of these stories and memoirs may have been intended to arouse or strengthen this kind of solidarity between refugees and their hosts. But very often both sides invoked biblical traditions and a moral impetus. In the case of the Huguenots, the chambres des réfugiés, clerical organizations, and other forerunners of modern NGOs did much to make flight possible in the first place and then to reduce the risk to life and limb. Religious currents also reinforced what were primarily economic expectations. The governments of the receiving countries hoped, above all, that refugees would increase local production and strengthen the tax base.

In Prussia and other Calvinist German states, a common faith went a long way toward legitimating the absorption of refugees and the burdens associated with taking them in. In the case of the Huguenots and other exiles, there was a virtual assumption that these were religious refugees, even though some of them (like those Salzburgers, who came from inhospitable mountain valleys) were also impelled by economic motives. The refugees' motives for fleeing were in fact rarely scrutinized. Religious persecution in their countries of origin provided them with a moral boost that helped justify the costs of their initial accommodations, the provision of land and other resources, the construction of their own churches, and many other investments in their permanent integration. Needless to say, the natives grumbled when they were enlisted to provide transportation, do construction work, and offer other services, but in the end they had to accept these burdens because the princely states in the Holy Roman Empire were run in an authoritarian manner.

Initially, this kind of integration as decreed from above, which strictly speaking made it more a form of incorporation, rested on a special status accorded refugees (an aspect avoided in the Netherlands and England). By the second or third generation, the newcomers usually had acquired the local language and increasingly intermingled and intermarried with the native population. This presumably model case of successful integration thus directs our attention, indirectly, to the importance of time horizons, a factor with which today's societies may also need to reckon. Without a doubt, the Huguenots had an advantage in that they brought with them French culture and language, which at the time stood in high regard. Moreover, most Huguenots who managed to leave France belonged to an elite class and therefore enjoyed high social and cultural prestige. An out-and-out competition for refugees ensued, especially for the manufacturers and tradesmen among them. The refugees were able to negotiate the conditions of their acceptance and to attain a variety of privileges. In Prussia, these negotiations even changed the direction of subsequent integration: the native population was now adjusting as much to the Huguenots as the other way around.

At the beginning of the eighteenth century, the countries that had taken in refugees experienced an economic upturn (though it was at times disappointing and disrupted by wars). By contrast, the countries from which they had fled began to notice the drawbacks to their policy. Taken together, both trends encouraged a change of mind in the direction of greater tolerance. Ultimately, too, Absolutist rulers like August the Strong in Saxony, Maria Theresa in Austria, and Frederick II in Prussia realized that it was in their interest to place power politics and economics above religion and the goal of denominational unity. Utilitarian thinking eventually prevailed over religious intolerance. Of course, much depended on the country and group in question: Jews were treated badly for a longer time in Central Europe. In 1731 the Salzburgers were sent along to and accepted by host countries like Prussia in a manner that had already become almost routine. It would take more than two centuries before the Cold War re-created such favorable circumstances for refugees.

Escaping from the cross in Spain and Southeastern Europe took place, from the very outset, under worse conditions. Spanish Muslims frequently looked back on an odyssey that lasted several generations and passed through many regions before their last remnant was expelled at the beginning of the seventeenth century. This persecution resulted in such heavy losses that the number of refugees, at around 300,000, remained lower than one might have suspected given the longtime presence of the Moors in Spain.

The Inquisition's religious intolerance, which extended even to converts and their descendants, also led to the expulsion of the Jews from Spain and Portugal. They were fortunate in that the Ottoman Empire was experiencing a long-lasting economic boom just as they began to arrive in Istanbul, Izmir, Salonika, Sarajevo, and other cities after 1492 or 1513. In these prosperous circumstances, Jewish refugees were able quickly to establish livelihoods and fill economic niches, for instance in textile production. The Spanish Muslims who found accommodations and employment in neighboring Morocco and in Ottoman-ruled northern Africa also encountered favorable conditions. Unfortunately there are hardly any studies about the extent to which religious solidarity played a role in their acceptance. But there was at least enough land available, as well as other resources, and this is precisely why all traces of these refugees have been lost; they simply merged into the majority of their co-religionists.

The refugees escaping from the Reconquista in Southeastern Europe arrived to much worse economic conditions. Having survived massive persecution and perilous escape routes, they found themselves in an Ottoman Empire weakened to the point of collapse. As already mentioned, we need to think about three elements in tandem—departure, itinerary, and reception—if we are to understand the structure of flight. The Ottoman Empire had been in decline since the eighteenth century, owing to the systemic corruption and the arbitrariness of its public administration. The arrival of more and more refugees as a consequence of lost wars overwhelmed the government and pushed the empire even deeper into chaos. The price for this disorder was paid by the refugees. Those who were lucky enough just to survive in good health still had to face great difficulties starting over again in a new occupation. There were masses of them, and they were not members of a social or professional elite like the Huguenots and Sephardim.

Religious solidarity undoubtedly contributed to better emergency care, but this assistance did not go beyond donations and soup kitchens at mosques, which were no substitute for a functioning state. Countless refugees died from epidemics and out of sheer weakness after their arrival. This continuous traumatization placed a heavy burden on all sides. The only possible advantage in their situation was the fact that Anatolia was sparsely settled; there was enough room for new arrivals both in the highlands, suitable for livestock breeding, and in the fertile coastal regions.

Following the lost Balkan Wars, the task of absorbing Muslim refugees acquired a strategic dimension: They were deliberately settled in Eastern Thrace and along the Aegean coast in order to form a bulwark against the expansion of Greece. Anatolia was to become the home of the hard-pressed Turks. This nationalist vision did not mean, however, that religious motives and criteria played no role at all. In the 1923 Treaty of Lausanne, for example, the minorities picked for resettlement were defined primarily by religion.

Denominational differences also caused or influenced the "wars within the war" fought between 1941 and 1945, and they are an important factor explaining why these conflicts acquired a genocidal dimension in Yugoslavia and eastern Poland. In fascist Croatia, there were about as many Serbs who lost their lives as were expelled to Serbia (for more on this, see Chapter 2.2). Finally, one might draw attention to the late twentieth century, to countries and regions as different as Cyprus and Northern Ireland, as well as to the wars in the former Yugoslavia, which saw societies breaking down along denominational dividing lines. Here, admittedly, religion served primarily to supercharge nationalist propaganda. Whether people were actually devout or practiced their faith was less important.

Just how subordinate a role was played by religion becomes especially apparent when we look at the reception accorded refugees from Bosnia and Herzegovina. Turkey was the only predominantly Muslim country that opened its doors to expelled Bosniaks. Yet, at rates higher than 95 percent, they preferred EU states and Switzerland as countries of refuge. This was attributable, on the one hand, to networks of refugees who already had numerous contacts in the European countries of destination owing to earlier labor migration by guest workers. But, on the other hand, a general, humanitarian kind of solidarity on the side of the receiving societies also had its impact.

When it comes to the exodus from Syria and Iraq, it is striking how those countries' next door neighbors, Lebanon, Turkey, and Jordan, have accepted many refugees, while other Islamic countries have hardly at all shared the burden. Poor countries like Egypt and Pakistan, which have a hard time just feeding their own populations, can hardly be blamed. But it remains an open question why wealthy countries like Saudi Arabia, the other Gulf states, and Iran, which use Islam as the foundation for their legal order, are not willing to express greater religious solidarity.

The same question could be addressed to the European host countries. Owing to the pervasive fear of Islamist terrorists, it has largely escaped notice that quite a number of refugees from the Near East are not Muslims at all. This oversight means that religious solidarity, for example with Syrian Christians, has largely ceased to be a vehicle for acceptance (with the notable exception of Armenia). It might be objected that greater solidarity among Christians might turn into favoritism toward them, shutting out exponents of other religions. But this need not be the case if one takes Christian ethics seriously. Promoting a solidarity based on Christian principles, instead of simply asking EU countries to accept the kind of top-down distribution quotient that Brussels attempted to issue in 2015, might have persuaded Eastern European countries, in particular Poland, to take in refugees from the Near East. To the extent that it promotes such goodwill, religion remains a factor that can facilitate the acceptance and integration of refugees. This holds true also in the United States, where since the postwar period members of local churches and other religious communities have helped resettled refugees find accommodations, schools for their children, and new jobs, as well as learn English. One should not underestimate the conflicts that could arise if such support were to become too missionary,[59] but well-meant help is usually recognized as such by the people who receive it.

2

THE TWO FACES OF NATIONALISM: ETHNIC CLEANSING AND NATIONAL SOLIDARITY

2.1 The rise of modern nationalism and the "long" First World War

The idea of the nation emerged in the early modern era and began to spread out as a mass movement beginning in the late eighteenth century.[1] In Western Europe the French Revolution provided the initial spark, while in Eastern Europe the impulse came from the partitions of Poland, which obliterated one of the oldest states and larger nations from the map of Europe. Initially the Jacobins, like the American revolutionaries of 1776, stood for a universal definition of the nation, primarily based on political values and convictions, and not on language or culture. Refugees accordingly were welcomed to France as long as they adhered to the values of the revolution. The second, republican Constitution of June 1793 established a right of asylum, basing it on a very simple principle: "It [the French Republic] serves as a place of refuge for all who, on account of liberty, are banished from their native country. These it refuses to deliver up to tyrants."[2] Based on this paragraph (120) in the constitution, all persons who were politically persecuted could find refuge in France, the sanctuary of freedom and democracy.

This openness toward newcomers from other nations did not last. Owing to military intervention by the ancien régime, French nationalism became more exclusive. Reacting to the external threat posed during the Coalition Wars, the Jacobins mobilized the population and the army by promoting a kind of nationalism that was now linguistic and, in a rudimentary way, already ethnic. Bertrand Barère, a member of the Committee of Public Safety and thus of the government's executive board, declared in 1794:

> Federalism and superstition speak Breton; emigration and hatred of the Republic speak German; [the] counter-revolution speaks Italian and fanaticism speaks Basque. . . . We must smash these instruments of harm and error. . . . [L]eaving citizens in ignorance of the national language . . .

is to betray the fatherland. . . . Among a free people language must be one and the same for everyone. . . .[3]

What stands out in this statement is the ideal of a linguistically and culturally homogenous nation. The growing xenophobia it represented had an immediate impact on the large number of political refugees from the Netherlands and Germany. In 1793, at Barère's instigation, the Committee on Public Safety promulgated a decree deporting all those refugees collectively under suspicion of supporting the counterrevolution.[4]

In the German states and Eastern Europe, from the very outset, nationalism had struck a sharper tone, setting what was foreign against what was native, foe against friend. This had to do with the Napoleonic Wars and the long era of foreign imperial rule. At the end of the Wars of Liberation, the famous Prussian reformer Freiherr vom Stein advocated a radical "purge" of the French from his Rhenish homeland:

> Every people that wants to be genuinely national will not place trust in foreigners so as to mingle indifferently in civic community with them. . . .
> It is our duty toward the German fatherland to purge the Rhineland of everything that has made it un-German and keeps it in this condition.[5]

The formula "genuinely national" and the rejection of any kind of mingling testify to an ethnic definition of the nation that would become prevalent among all Central and East European national movements in the course of the nineteenth century.

Holm Sundhaussen has pointedly summarized modern nation-state formation in the Balkans as a pattern combining the French model of a centralized and unitary state with the German model of a nation based on ancestry. Much the same may be said of East Central Europe, even if that region always had exceptions and saw attempts at forming a more supra-ethnic kind of nation-state, as in the case of interwar Czechoslovakia or (more recently) Ukraine. Each of these models, the French and the German, involved the narrowest possible conception of a state and nation—in contrast to federalism and to politically defined nations made up of citizens, as in the case of the US. Combining the two European models made for a highly conflict-ridden mixture, since the areas of settlement for nations in Central and Eastern Europe overlapped and because, over time, almost every national movement demanded a state of its own.

This demand was not compatible with the presence of national minorities, something that became apparent in Central Europe right after the Franco-German War of 1870–71. When the German Empire annexed Alsace and Lorraine, its inhabitants faced two alternatives: they could either become citizens of the German Empire or opt for France, in which case they would then have to leave their homeland. The existence of national minorities was not recognized. This was attributable, on the one hand, to the structures of modern administrative states, which invariably closed the distance between the state and individual citizens by means of compulsory education, the military draft, and an expanded bureaucracy, demanding unambiguous loyalty. On the other hand, the urge toward unambiguity was also a product of contemporary nationalism, which was growing in intensity.

Attitudes toward national minorities and relations among nations deteriorated even further under the impact of imperialism and Social Darwinism. Beginning in the late nineteenth century, relations among nations came to be interpreted as part of an eternal struggle for survival. According to the conventional biologistic and increasingly racist thinking of the time, minorities were a foreign body in the fabric of one's own nation, inhibiting national development and posing a threat.

This was also when the term "race" came up in public discourse. It was not used not only in our present-day understanding of "race" as referring to skin color and descent, but as the stand-in also for an inflexible and unalterable conception of what constituted a "nation." When, for example, Western observers wrote about the Bulgarian, Greek, or Albanian "race," they implied that these were fundamentally different and potentially conflicting nations. The possible confusion between these two meanings of "race" is one of the reasons why I prefer not to utilize the term as one of the main analytical categories in this book. I am of course aware how omnipresent race is in US academic discourse, and I agree that it is important, especially in studies of societal integration. Nor should one deny the relevance of race or racism for modern nationalism.

The radical ethnic nationalism that came up in late-nineteenth-century Europe was reflected above all in the concept of "minority problems," a term whose meaning branded minorities as the cause of troubles, whereas in fact the major cause was a too narrow concept of the modern nation-state. The fact that an international order based on nation-states did not provide peace and stability became evident first in Southeastern Europe after 1878. The reason was not "ancient hatred" of others, sometimes stereotyped as a specifically Balkan trait. (In the 1990s, this unfortunate cliché caused the West to commit serious blunders in its dealings with the war in the former Yugoslavia.[6]) The problem, rather, was the incompatibility between the newly founded nation-states and their national minorities. This was a structural problem, one that would catch up with Europe in its entirety after the First World War and one that remains virulent to this day. All modern European nation-states pursued a strategy of assimilation, but that approach succeeded only in relatively rich countries with a very long tradition of statehood. When assimilation failed, the nation-states in Central and Eastern Europe resorted to more brutal measures, to the suppression of minorities, and ultimately (in some cases) to their violent removal.

Flight during the First World War

Radical nationalism and Social Darwinist thinking contributed fundamentally to the outbreak of the First World War. For a very long time, historians concentrated on the mostly static warfare on the Western Front, the terrible human loss of 9.5 million fallen soldiers, and the substantial physical destruction of the war. Because of these horrors, much less attention was paid to the roughly 13 million war refugees.[7] The fact that more than four fifths of them were uprooted in Eastern Europe was also a factor. Research by Peter Gatrell, Włodzimierz Borodziej, and Maciej Górny has corrected the Occidentalism of the older historiography and increased awareness of the enormous numbers of refugees and their plight.[8] There were so many of them in Eastern Europe because fronts there so often shifted, and because combat was at least as ruthless as in the West. The country most affected by far was the Russian Empire, where about six million people were forced to flee in the course of the war.[9] Russia was followed by France with 1.8 million refugees, Austria-Hungary with 1.5 million, the German Empire with 850,000, Belgium with 650,000, Italy with 500,000, the Ottoman Empire with at least 400,000, Greece with about 400,000, and Serbia with at least 250,000 people.[10] Around one quarter of these refugees were able to return to their homes during or toward the end of the war. This was another factor contributing to the quick disappearance of the war refugees from public consciousness.

Nevertheless, the many facets of flight—impoverishment, hardship, hunger, unemployment—brought immediacy to the plight of European refugees, not only for those directly affected, but also for the societies that took them in. In the years following 1914, the notion of the refugee became established as an object of public discourse and a screen onto which other concerns were projected. Because of the pervasive hardships brought about by the war, refugees were rarely welcome. Solidarity was practiced mostly toward members of one's own nation. Who counted as belonging to a nation was decided more than before by ethnic factors, a way of thinking that would later contribute to the outbreak of new conflicts and wars. There were, however, a few examples of international assistance. The 650,000 Belgians who fled before the German army, which had illegally occupied their neutral country, were readily admitted into France, England, and the Netherlands. This had to do with human compassion, and above all with the consideration that solidarity with the Belgians would demonstrate the moral superiority of the receiving countries over Germany.

The internationalism propagated by Socialists and Communists was prevalent among the first victims of the world war, which brought into being throughout Europe a new, radicalized nationalism. Beginning in the final third of the nineteenth century, war and nationalism were commonly twinned. There was never one without the other, and they mutually reinforced each other. But

Among the First World War's numerous refugees was the future psychologist and writer **Manès Sperber** (1906–1985). After the Second World War he became famous above all for his settling of accounts with Communism and his autobiographically tinged trilogy, *Like a Tear in the Ocean*. There are few twentieth-century writers who depicted the fate of refugees as movingly and in a manner so true to life as did Sperber. His family came from the small Galician town of Zabłotów, which was located along a heavily contested section of the front in the First World War. The Sperbers fled four times from the Russian army under perilous circumstances before they finally packed their suitcases on the fifth try and moved to Vienna. There the family found accommodations in a small, bug-ridden apartment in Leopoldstadt, the Jewish and refugee district, where they quickly became impoverished. Hunger was as much a part of everyday life as freezing during the winter; the parents and their three sons tried desperately to keep their heads above water with piecework, specifically by rolling cigarettes for a living. In the first volume of his memoirs, Sperber offers this succinct summary of his difficult youth: ". . . between 1916 and 1918, sinking from level to level, I was to find out in endless detail, that every fall can trigger a further, deeper fall, and that the abyss has no bottom."[11] Only belatedly could he begin school at the local gymnasium, where he remained an outsider and was tormented by an antisemitic teacher. He was unable to finish school, in part because of a case of tuberculosis that only healed after many years and a long stay in a sanatorium. The Joint Distribution Committee (JDC), a Jewish-American NGO that pioneered aid for refugees worldwide, paid for his convalescence.

The experience of being uprooted shaped Sperber's political career. After a brief flirtation with Zionism and an active membership in the socialist Zionist youth group Hashomer Hatzair, he turned to Communism, hoping to find an intellectual home and friends within the movement.[12] After the Palace of Justice in Vienna was burned in 1927 (following clashes between Social Democratic defenders of the Republic and a right-wing anti-democratic veterans' group, which Sperber astutely recognized as an omen signaling the end of the Austrian Republic), he left Vienna and moved to Berlin. There he lived by lecturing and giving presentations on individual psychology, which was emerging as an important field at just that time. Sperber had received his training from Alfred Adler, one of the founders of this field. But he spent most of his time as an activist for the German Communist Party (KPD) and the Comintern. In 1931 Sperber traveled to the Soviet Union, where he found a poor and brutalized society instead of the workers' and peasants' paradise he expected. His experiences in Moscow led to a first estrangement from Communism and led Sperber to regard the KPD's fight against the Social Democrats as a failed strategy that contributed to the rise of Hitler. In March 1933 SA men tracked him down to a safe house where he was hiding and arrested him. Thanks to an intervention by the Polish embassy (Sperber was a Polish citizen), he was released from jail after five and a half weeks.[13] After a short stay in Prague he traveled on to Vienna, where he no longer felt at home, then moved for a time to Zagreb, where he quickly learned Serbo-Croatian and once again was able to earn a sporadic living by lecturing. From there he made his way to Paris, where he spent most of the 1930s.

Thanks to his work for exile newspapers and (with increasing frequency) for French publishing houses, Sperber managed to make ends meet, though he lived very modestly. One visitor once noted that his accommodations, a dark and confining hotel room in the Quartier Latin, were furnished with a table, a radio, and a hotplate.[14] Owing to his facility for languages and his charismatic personality, Sperber made connections with the Parisian intellectual scene and befriended André Malraux, who would, a few years later, save his life. In spite of this successful professional integration, Sperber remained critical of his environment: "The radical indifference of Parisians and their decided disinclination to be drawn into the life of foreigners or let such persons into their lives guarantees every individual a personal freedom that is hardly known elsewhere. This freedom benefited the exiles, but it also allowed the poorest and the loneliest among them to perish, 'to drown on the cobblestones out in the open, in the presence of many people, without a single passer-by as much as turning around.'"[15]

After the Hitler-Stalin Pact, Sperber renounced Communism, and in December 1939 he volunteered for the French army. Conceivably he was hoping to obtain French citizenship by serving in the Foreign Legion; his parents and two brothers escaped at the last minute to England. Following demobilization Sperber hid out for almost two years in the south of France, where his wife, a Latvian Jew, bore him a son in June 1942. Three months later, following a warning from his friend André Malraux, he entrusted himself to a smuggler who was supposed to smuggle him across the mountains into Switzerland. But the smuggler abandoned the refugee toward evening at a fork in the trail. Disoriented from exhaustion, Sperber fell asleep on the side of the trail, and at daybreak he found his way into Switzerland. After his arrival he was interned in a prison-like camp, while his wife and small son, who managed to escape two weeks later, lived in another camp for over a year.[16] Sperber became ill from a

(cont.)

(cont.)

duodenal ulcer and was taken in by a pastor's family in Zurich. In 1944 the family, finally reunited, was able to move into a small house. One year later the war was over, and the Sperbers moved back to Paris.

Although the eternal refugee was now finally able to settle permanently, he never got over the loss of so many friends who died during the Second World War. His writings—such as his fictional trilogy and his three-part autobiography, less well-known but equally well worth reading—have an eloquence and vividness that recall Stefan Zweig. Understandably, both books are permeated by a profound melancholy. After the first volume of the trilogy came out, Albert Camus wrote to Sperber: "It is one of the books of this time: beautiful, dark, and necessary. I have liked above all what some of the greatest books of this time actually lack: compassion and a certain trembling of humanity, which it seems to me I would be able to recognize from hell."[17]

there are other reasons why we should treat the war refugees of the twentieth century within the broader context of nationalistically motivated flight as defined by international law and the statutes of the UNHCR. Refugees from both world wars and the wars in the former Yugoslavia in the 1990s were victims, above all, of massive and nationalistically motivated violence. Hence, they deserve the same kind of protection and the same prospects for permanent integration as any other group of refugees.

This insight, moreover, makes it easier to understand why refugee flows did not cease with the official end of the two world wars, but actually increased. Although the weapons were officially silent as of November 1918 or May 1945, the victors of the wars thereafter attempted to broaden their territorial gains and to change population structures in their favor. Mass flight was thus no longer a result or symptom of war; it was turning into an aim of war. This first became apparent during the Balkan Wars of 1912–13, when national minorities were chased out of disputed regions in order to justify subsequent territorial claims. Waves of refugees also had military side-effects: they upset resupply lines to the front, sowed chaos, undermined the moral of the enemy, and distracted the adversary from military priorities. In the 1940 Blitzkrieg against France, the Wehrmacht deliberately used refugees to achieve these purposes. Toward the end of the "long" First World War—"long" because military actions did not stop in 1918—more than a dozen nations were affected by numerous follow-up conflicts. In Eastern Europe between 1919 and 1923 there were probably even more refugees than there had been earlier, during the grueling war years.[18]

One of the largest groups, alongside the Russian Civil War refugees and Greeks from Asia Minor, were again East European Jews fleeing from a myriad of pogroms that caused thousands of deaths. There was also a massive post-imperial flight by members of imperial nations leaving newly founded nation-states and lost territories. The losers of the First World War in Central Europe—the German Empire, Hungary, which had been reduced to a third of its former territory, and Austria, which shrank even more—had to cope with an influx of about two million people in total.[19] The Ottoman Empire was less affected, because so many Turks and Muslims had already been driven out of Southeastern Europe after 1876 and after 1912, but the Ottomans nevertheless took in around 350,000 Muslims from Greece who had been removed under the terms of the Treaty of Lausanne. Bulgaria, another loser in the war, had to cope with an influx of more than 200,000 people.

We know little about the integration of these post-imperial refugees; if they had relatives and contacts in their host countries, this was obviously an advantage. Compensation was only a promise received on paper (this was provided for in the Treaties of Neuilly and Lausanne, for example, which is why they fit so well into a world order of liberal nation-states); most of them had lost their property and were impoverished, but never received any compensation. The refugee communities were therefore soon rife with nationalism and its variants of revisionism and revanchism.

The images of massive suffering and dying cited in the introduction to this book mobilized international NGOs like the Carnegie Foundation, which had already documented war crimes in the Balkan Wars. Jewish aid organizations, like the Berlin-based Hilfsverein der Deutschen Juden (Relief Organization of German Jews), the aforementioned JDC, and the Hebrew Sheltering and Immigrant Aid Society in New York sent food and financial aid and tried to facilitate immigration. The International and the American Red Cross, and British and American Quakers maintained numerous refugee camps. Tens of thousands of people would have died without that support, which stands as a first fine hour for international humanitarianism.

The protection and diminution of minorities
after the Paris Peace Treaties

The international community reacted by attempting to use international law as a way of stopping minorities from being subjected to discrimination and persecution. According to estimates by Carole Fink, up to twenty-five million members of minority groups lived in the eastern half of Europe.[20] Hence there was an irrefutable need for measures to protect them, which the victorious powers undertook to so do under the influence of the aforementioned NGOs and made into law in all of the Parisian Peace Treaties, from St. Germain to Sèvres. Fink calls this the "little Versailles" next to the "big Versailles" (the peace treaties between the former adversaries of the war).

Minority protection in the interwar period had a bad press even at the time, and to this day it hardly enjoys a good reputation. The safeguards for minorities were indeed only second-rank in terms of international law. Their legal force could not be evoked without difficulty, and in the final analysis they did little to improve everyday life for Europe's many minorities. We can nevertheless view efforts toward minority protection as an attempt at preventing more nationalist-inspired mass flight—and in this respect it functioned passably well. A majority of national minorities remained in the areas where they had settled; this was true for Germans and Ukrainians in Poland, for Hungarians in Romania, and for numerous other population groups.

A fundamental design flaw in "little Versailles" was that the Western nation-states ruled out minority protection within their own borders, clinging to the ideal of a homogenous nation-state. Moreover, minorities subjected to discrimination could only initiate proceedings against treaty violations if they first succeeded in securing assistance from League of Nation members. They were dependent on external support, and as a rule it was the neighboring nation-state that all too willingly put itself in the limelight, as Germany did when it came to the German-speaking population in Poland.[21]

Other minorities, like the Jews, the Armenians, and the Ukrainians, had no nation-state of their own to advocate for their interests or serve as a refuge (although the Ukrainian Soviet Republic did attract a number of Ukrainian intellectuals from Poland in the 1920s). They fell between the cracks of the nation-state order. In concrete terms, this affected such groups as the approximately 20,000 Galician Jews who had fled to Vienna during World War I and stayed there until the end of the war, among other reasons because of the pogroms in their homeland. In 1920 the government of the Republic of Austria refused to grant Jewish refugees the right of residence and citizenship using ethno-nationalist arguments. At first the Interior Ministry pointed to the Jews' foreign language and then, since most of them spoke German only too well, to their "race" in order to justify deporting them to Poland.

If one interprets minority protection following the First World War in the context of the nation-state order created at the time, it becomes easier to understand why these safeguards went hand in hand almost everywhere with a deliberate reduction in the numbers of national minorities. The first Paris Peace Treaty, which linked both principles in a seemingly paradoxical manner, was the Treaty of Neuilly. It dealt with Bulgaria and imposed tough sanctions on this world war loser, comparable to the provisions imposed on Germany. In addition to paying sizable reparations, Bulgaria had to accept painful territorial losses; the Bulgarian part of Thrace was lost, and thus access to the Aegean. Although this allowed Greece to annex a region with a substantial Bulgarian minority, that minority's protection remained very limited. In the midst of all its many regulations about minority rights, the Treaty of Neuilly contains a collection of paragraphs about the "reciprocal and voluntary emigration of persons belonging to racial minorities."[22] In these passages the great powers and the two former military adversaries that were parties to this arrangement specified that Bulgarians should emigrate out of northern Greece and, in return, Greeks out of Bulgaria. The principle of voluntariness still applied, so that in the following two years only a few hundred families volunteered for emigration to "their" nation-state.

With the arrival of the Greek refugees from Asia Minor, whom Athens deliberately settled in the north of the country in order to form an ethnic bulwark there against Bulgaria, the local dynamics changed. The refugees clashed with the native population over their land and their houses, and a spiral of violence was quickly set in motion. The League of Nations dispatched an investigative commission, which in 1924 decided that emigration should in the future be obligatory for minorities.[23] That of course had an impact on local practice; emigration turned more and more into forcible expulsion. Overall, 103,000 Bulgarians had to leave Greece, and 53,000 Bulgarian Greeks moved in the opposite direction toward Greece. Today these figures might seem small but, especially for Bulgaria, this influx on top of all the refugees it took in from the Ottoman Empire, Romania, and Serbia, amounted to a burden that was almost impossible to manage. In the mid-1920s, Bulgarian authorities put the number of refugees at about 200,000, most of whom lived in abject misery and were only partly integrated.[24]

Although one can certainly categorize these refugees as victims of nationalist persecution, they created a breeding ground for an even more radical nationalism. In the 1920s and 1930s, the Internal Macedonian Revolutionary Organization (IMRO) launched suicidal terror attacks similar to those of the later Islamist group Al-Qaida. In 1934, in what was the organization's most spectacular assassination, a Bulgarian terrorist shot to death King Alexander I of Yugoslavia and the French foreign minister in Marseille. The IMRO recruited numerous adherents and activists, above all from the ranks of embittered refugees from Serbia and Greece.[25]

The 1920 Treaty of Sèvres, which dealt primarily with the Ottoman Empire, contained regulations similar to those in the Treaty of Neuilly. Minorities were supposed to be "exchanged" along a new Greco-Turkish borderline in western Asia Minor. The exchange never took place, however, because one part of the Turkish elite rejected this humiliating and colonialist agreement. Since Greece also marched into Asia Minor, Kemal Pasha, later known as Atatürk, formed a new Turkish army that in 1921 achieved a decisive victory west of Ankara at the Sakarya River. The Greek troops and the Greeks from Asia Minor were then driven into the sea, and by the end of 1922 some 600,000 to 700,000 refugees were already en route to Greece.

In 1923 the Treaty of Lausanne certified this mass flight as a matter of international law and expanded the population shifts to include all of Asia Minor and Greece. It was determined that all Christians had to leave the territory of

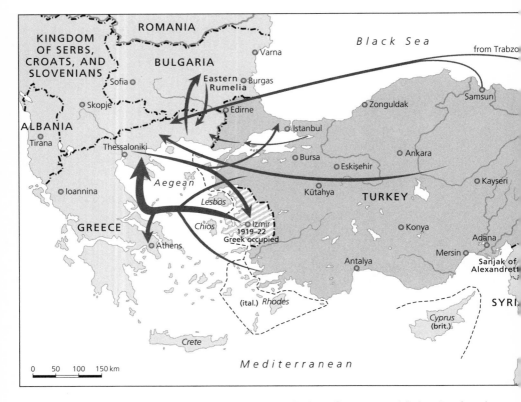

MAP 2. Flight and population shifts between Turkey, Greece, and Bulgaria after the Treaties of Neuilly (1919) and Lausanne (1923)

Turkey, with the exception of Istanbul and Western Thrace (which belonged to Greece according to the provisions of the Treaty of Neuilly), and all Muslims (or, as they were viewed at the time, Turks) had to leave Greece. This "exchange of minorities" was obligatory and comprehensive and led to massive population removals. In addition to the roughly 700,000 refugees of 1922, there were an additional 500,000 Greeks from Anatolia, Eastern Thrace, and the Black Sea coast, along with 350,000 Turks and other Northern Greek Muslims. Contemporaries commenting on the Treaty of Lausanne would often cite the cruelty of "the Turks," a theme widely disseminated in the nineteenth century owing to that era's numerous wars, uprisings, and acts of retaliation, and only confirmed by the genocide perpetrated on the Armenians.

The proposed contrast between a civilized Europe and a violence-prone Orient (or Balkans) does not stand up to closer scrutiny. After 1918 there were also massive expulsions of minorities in Central Europe; characteristically, these happened after the armistice. The expulsions initially affected around 150,000 Alsatians and Lorrainers whom France, after marching back into the

These accusations against Turkey had already begun at the Conference of Lausanne and were seriously pushed by the chief negotiator, British foreign minister **Lord George Curzon** (1859–1925). He is frequently quoted as stating that the comprehensive removal of minorities without exception—something the treaty prettified as an "exchange of minorities"—was "a thoroughly bad and vicious solution, for which the world will pay a heavy penalty for a hundred years to come."[26] Although he was right about that, the minutes of the negotiations clearly show that the British chair of the conference, who had already put his stamp on the Treaty of Neuilly, had himself added the "exchange of minorities" to the agenda. It was Curzon who insisted that there could be no exceptions to this population exchange and that it was obligatory. The conference chair also set aside any moral objections since, like Fridtjof Nansen, the High Commissioner for Refugees for the League of Nations, he was convinced that it was entirely possible to transplant millions of people quickly and integrate them into jobs at their new places of residence. This technocratic way of thinking shows that the flight from nationalism was not based solely on hatred, violence, and wars, but also on rational thinking and a ruthless kind of social engineering characteristic of European ultra-modernity.

Curzon developed his model of a territorial partition followed by population shifts when he was an Indian viceroy at the beginning of the twentieth century. The occasion was provided by the persistent conflicts between Hindus and Muslims in colonial India. In 1905, following the governing principle of "divide and conquer," Curzon initiated the division of Bengal (which was basically made up of today's Bangladesh and the Indian federal state of West Bengal) into two regions—one Hindu-dominated and the other preponderantly Muslim. Owing to protests on both sides, this partition was rescinded in 1911, yet in 1949 the border between an independent India and (East) Pakistan largely followed the line laid down by Curzon. The next "Curzon Line" that looked as if it could have been drawn on a map with a ruler was sketched in 1920 in Galicia, as part of an effort by the British foreign minister to mediate in the Polish-Soviet War. With some local deviations that line continued to serve as the new border between Poland and the Soviet Ukraine after September 1944. To be sure, one cannot make Curzon, who died in 1925, morally liable for the massive flight and expulsions that took place in India and Galicia during the second half of the 1940s. (In India there were about twelve million refugees, in Galicia more than a million.) But the populations shifts he recommended did go back to the principle of territorial partition that, apart from India, was also applied in the upper Adriatic region around Trieste as well as in the UN partition plan for Palestine.

region, defined as Germans. In 1918–19 the French Commissions de Triage (literally "Selection Commissions") divided the population in Alsace and Lorraine into four categories: descendants of French citizens, citizens who were products of mixed marriages with at least one parent of verifiable French ancestry, citizens from third states, and Alsatians classified as Germans. About one third of the Alsatians belonging to the fourth category were deported, while the others had to put up with serious disadvantages, for example when it came to exchanging their reichsmarks for the new currency of the franc.

The expulsion of 1919–20 undertaken by the French did not, however, solve the minority problem, since numerous Alsatians were not satisfied with the new government and its policy of linguistic assimilation. They founded an autonomy movement that was suppressed by Paris with police action, censorship and deportations. In turn, Alsatian refugees in the German Reich formed an influential lobby that agitated incessantly against France, supported the separatist wing of the Alsatian autonomy movement, and during the 1930s spread National Socialist ideas. After the Second World War this lobby was neutralized in the context of the Cold War; now, however, there were new lobbies of expellees within the context of the Cold War, agitating above all against Poland and Czechoslovakia.

The handling of the German minority in Alsace and Lorraine established a precedent for Central Europe. The Geneva Convention on Upper Silesia negotiated in 1922 between Germany and Poland was based on the model of a two-sided emigration (again, comparable to the Treaties of Neuilly and Sèvres). This region, the most important industrial district in East Central Europe, was partitioned, and minorities on both sides of the newly drawn border obtained a "right of choice," meaning an opportunity to emigrate to their external nation-state. Whether one can legitimately speak of a "right" here is another question. Ultimately, this was a choice between two evils. Overall, at least 170,000 Silesians opted for Germany or Poland and emigrated.[27] An unknown number had already fled from the violence and unrest (the so-called Silesian uprisings) that preceded the plebiscite in which they were asked to choose their postwar home.

Germany managed to cope reasonably well with the absorption of about one million post-imperial refugees and re-migrants, while much the same challenge overwhelmed the Southeastern European states. As mentioned earlier, up to 70,000 Greeks died from illness and conditions of scarcity on their way and *after* their arrival. In Bulgaria international NGOs did not have a very strong presence, so little is known about the refugees there. The regions along the coast and the major river valleys were, however, malaria-infested and not well suited to taking in more than two hundred thousand people.

While the suffering of the refugees was soon forgotten, politicians all over Europe praised the Treaty of Lausanne as a model for settling conflicts between hostile nations. From 1937 to 1947 the catchword "Lausanne" served as a reference point for almost a dozen international treaties in which massive population shifts were negotiated and regulated. A closer look at the Turkish-Greek relationship shows that conflicts were by no means successfully "solved" along Lausanne lines. In 1955 about 125,000 Greeks left Istanbul after the pogrom-like riots of the so-called Septembrianá (the Treaty of Lausanne applied a special regulation to the old capital of the Ottoman Empire and of Greek Orthodoxy). After the military putsch of 1974, the ethnically mixed island of Cyprus was partitioned, so that 210,000 people had to flee (on Cyprus, see Chapter 2.4 below).

If the Greeks of Asia Minor had had a stronger voice in the Western media and politics, perhaps this assessment of Lausanne would have turned out differently. Even years after arriving in their host countries, the refugees were still being ostracized, attacked, and chased out of the very fields they were meant to be cultivating. In 1924, in the Macedonian prefecture of Serres, there was even a small-scale pogrom. Twelve houses and a refugee settlement were destroyed, and fifty people were hospitalized. One Greek politician thereupon suggested identifying the refugees with yellow armbands.[28] The professional and day-to-day integration of Greeks from Asia Minor proceeded only slowly; as late as the 1970s and 1980s, certain villages and city neighborhoods were still clearly recognizable as former refugee settlements.

This intolerable situation ultimately came to an end because many refugees traveled on from Greece to other countries, including the US, Australia, France, and countries beyond the Mediterranean. One may speak here of a secondary flight—comparable to what has been happening to the Syrians who came to Germany in 2015 from Turkey or Lebanon. In Egypt during the 1920s the Greek community grew to about 50,000. The story of this diaspora ended a generation later when Egyptian president Gamal Abdel Nasser banished most Europeans, including the Greeks, following the Suez crisis of 1956.

This cross-generational and multi-stage flight was, as in the case of many groups of refugees, also economically motivated. The Egyptian and Australian Greeks—and the very concept of "diaspora," after all, comes from the Greek—show that dire situations such as that of the 1920s could be solved, among other ways, by the affected parties seizing the initiative and settling in third countries on their own.

Flight migration in stages was also a common experience for refugees from the Russian Civil War. Initially they fled mostly to neighboring states (more about this in Chapter Three). But Poland, Lithuania, and parts of Romania, were unable to feed, house, or even permanently take in such numbers. Moreover, Russia's despotic rule over Poland had ended a few years earlier, and the Polish-Soviet War of 1920 reactivated anti-Russian feelings. Since Poland's right-wing parties put Jews and Communists into the same pigeonhole, antisemitism increased as well. Eventually, at the start of 1923, the Polish government issued a decree requiring all refugees who did not have Polish citizenship to leave the country.[29] Many Russians, especially Russian Jews, tried to get to the Free City of Danzig, where there had been a shipping link to New York City since 1919. Until 1924 more than 120,000 people emigrated from Danzig to the US, 83,000 of them Jewish.

The Russian Jews who had found refuge in Romania at the beginning of the 1920s (depending on which estimate one uses, this was between 40,000 and 100,000 people) also attempted to get through to the West.[30] And in this case again, territorial conflicts (including the dispute over Bessarabia) and negative experiences with Russian supremacy played a role. Romanian animosity toward Russian domination admittedly went back further than more recent ill feelings in Poland (the Russian protectorate over Romania had ended with the Crimean War), yet the strongest imperial power in Southeastern Europe was still unpopular.

Oppressive poverty and terrible living conditions in Poland, Romania, Hungary, Austria, and other eastern central and southeastern countries increased migration pressures on Germany. Berlin was on the route to North Sea harbors where, prior to 1914, most East European migrants had boarded ships for overseas destinations. On top of that, the German capital was itself a magnet for Jewish and East European migrants, and there were still the remnants of a rudimentary welfare state in Germany so that, in spite of the hyperinflation and all its social costs, living conditions were somewhat better than in Poland or Romania.

When the refugees from Russia arrived by the hundreds of thousands, however, they soon began to sense that they were unwanted.[31] As a rule, government officials refused to grant them labor or residency permits, which excluded them from social welfare services. This forced the new arrivals into the shadow economy and into accepting very low paid jobs, which landed them in competition with the native lower classes. In November 1923, growing social tensions in the Scheunenviertel, the neighborhood in Berlin that was a mecca for Jews from Eastern Europe, erupted into a pogrom. Unlike pogroms in numerous Russian, Ukrainian, Polish, and Romanian cities, in Berlin the police got the violence under control, and there were no fatalities. Yet the looting and violence on the streets worked like a push factor, impelling forward migration to other countries. According to official French statistics, 72,000 Russians went to France, especially to Paris. Traces of other places where migrants eventually landed largely disappeared on the way overseas and en route to other European countries. About 100,000 Russian refugees remained in Germany, most of whom then had to pack their suitcases one more time after the National Socialists seized power.

The US, however, was largely closed to refugees after 1924. The Immigration Act enacted that year effectively sealed off, for more than two decades, what had until then been the most important destination admitting East European Jews. The quota rule issued earlier, in 1921, was already directed against immigrants from Eastern and Southern Europe. In Danzig there was often a backlog of Jewish refugees; several thousand people were at times housed under miserable conditions in provisional camps and tents.[32] They did, however, receive support from the aforementioned Jewish aid organizations, which also helped defuse acute distress in places like Bucharest, Berlin, or Vienna.

Yet Jewish NGOs could not prevent government discrimination in most of the Eastern European states or prevent the United States from passing the Immigration Act. As a rule, Jews integrated fairly quickly, even changing their names in many cases and, in a number of instances, amassing fortunes. (The very term "Melting Pot" was in fact the invention of a Jewish writer with East European roots.) In the end, though, positive experiences with integration often counted for little. Eagerness to integrate could not blunt the sharp edge of American isolationism, the matrix of immigration policy in the interwar era. Workers feared competition from immigrants and wage dumping, and antisemitism was also on the rise on the Western side of the Atlantic.

A fundamental problem faced by Polish and Romanian Jews was that, unlike Russian Civil War refugees, they were not viewed as victims of violence and persecution on the international stage. To be sure, most East European Jews emigrated in order to improve their living situation, yet very many of them had also experienced antisemitism and violence or even witnessed pogroms. When the US nearly dropped out of contention as a destination, they increasingly turned to Argentina, Brazil, or Canada. But those countries were also closing their borders as the world economic crisis took hold. Clearly, the international process of redirecting migrants from one country to another, which had functioned in a rudimentary way thanks to the Nansen passports, was no longer in force.

2.2 The "clean sweep": Mass flight and population removal in the 1940s

In the 1930s this breakdown was painfully experienced above all by people fleeing National Socialism. Immediately after Hitler's seizure of power, nearly 60,000 German citizens went into exile. Initially, the principal country admitting them was neighboring France, where 25,000 refugees chose to stay. Even at this early juncture, then, the exodus from Germany exceeded in quantitative terms the sum total of refugee movements out of Italy and all the other fascist or authoritarian regimes in Central and Eastern Europe. After Mussolini's seizure of power, not even 10,000 Italians fled Italy, and only smaller groups and opposition politicians went into exile from Poland, Hungary, Romania, Yugoslavia, and Bulgaria, evidence that Italian fascists and the authoritarian regimes in Eastern Europe were much less radical than the National Socialists.

Among the refugees from Germany, it was opposition politicians, journalists, and trade unionists who at first predominated. They were certainly fleeing for political reasons. But before long, German Jews had become the predominant group among the exiles. Superficially they were not any different from their fellow citizens, but they were persecuted, primarily because of National Socialism's racial ideology. Some historians, including Norman Naimark, categorize this early phase of persecution as "ethnic cleansing," which is why it is already being treated in this chapter.[33] France, in spite of serious economic crisis, held its doors open to refugees for five years. Arrivals from abroad, however, did not receive work permits. Infringements of the law and illegal employment were severely punished, sometimes even by deportation into the refugee's country of origin. Much like the situation facing Russians in Berlin during the 1920s, then, there were very few opportunities in France to earn a living outside of the self-organized refugee economy. The lack of work opportunities—a refusal to facilitate occupational integration that was a deliberate political act—condemned refugees to a *Luftexistenz* (airy existence), as Manès Sperber described it in a play on the Yiddish word *luftmensch* (an impractical visionary literally subsisting on air). Laconically, he expounded on the situation in Paris in the mid-1930s: "They were given to understand everywhere that the world did not need any emigrants and could barely suppress the suspicion that the defeat of those refugees had been their own fault and that they must have deserved it, too."[34] German Jews in growing numbers therefore moved on to Palestine, which became the most important country of exile for them until 1938. There, until survivors of the Holocaust started arriving from eastern Europe, the "Jeckes" (modern Hebrew slang for German Jews) constituted a major force in cultural life, especially in the "white city" of Tel Aviv.

The situation worsened after the Nuremberg Racial Laws were issued in September 1935. As a result of state-mandated discrimination and persecution, 70,000 Jews fled Germany. Following the "Kristallnacht" pogrom of November 1938, in which 400 people were killed and thousands of houses, shops, and synagogues ravaged, another 120,000 Jews emigrated.[35] Over the 1930s the social profile of the refugees changed as acts of repression became increasingly brutal. Beginning in 1935, more women and children, who were especially vulnerable, fled Germany. Yet the classic countries of immigration overseas treated refugees' visa inquiries and entry requests just as they did similar applications from other migrant groups, primarily with attention to utilitarian considerations. Families that were poor or had many children, single women, and old people had virtually no chance of being taken in.

After 1938, the expansion of the German Reich aggravated the international refugee emergency. Following the annexation of Austria and the destruction of Czechoslovakia, another 175,000 Jews headed into exile. Fresh waves of refugees had the side-effect, sought by the National Socialists, of helping to destabilize the remaining host countries and democracies. In France conflicts over refugee policy (which were linked, in turn, to the Spanish Civil War, about which more will be said in Chapter 3.2), contributed to the collapse of the leftist Popular Front government under Léon Blum.

Faced with flight on such a massive scale, the international community had to react. As early as 1933, the League of Nations, following the model of the commissioners for Russian, Greek, and Armenian refugees, appointed a High Commissioner for Refugees from Germany. This position was entrusted to James McDonald, a political scientist and diplomat from the United States whose appointment raised hopes that the US would overcome its isolationism and make a greater commitment on behalf of refugees. And yet the League of Nations gave McDonald little more than an office in Lausanne (not at the League's home in Geneva) and no dedicated budget.[36] The new commissioner was left with little choice but to beg charitable organizations for money; Jewish organizations in particular made donations to his office.

Ultimately, all efforts at coordinating the international distribution of the victims of National Socialism from one country to another failed—much as, eighty years later, the quota for refugees from Syria sought by the EU also collapsed. Only scholars, scientists, and some famous artists had a decent chance, but their admission depended on utilitarian calculations. The 212 German professors who found refuge in England, and the 143 who got to the United States promised to enhance the research climate of whatever country took them in. When McDonald called on countries to undertake a stronger effort against the causes of mass flight and adopt a more offensive stance against the Nazi regime, he got no support. In 1935 he resigned in protest, which was a logical and honorable thing to do but did little to help the refugees.[37]

At any rate, in 1938 at American initiative an international conference was called in the resort town of Évian-les-Bains to support Jewish refugees from Germany and recently annexed Austria. The thirty-two participating states could not, however, agree on an admissions quota. Moreover, Great Britain, which administered Palestine under a mandate from the League of Nations, limited annual immigration there to 12,000.[38] The background to this restriction had to do with the violence and occasionally pogrom-like riots between Arabs and Jews in 1936 and with the failure of the Peel Commission to mediate the conflict in 1937 by partitioning Palestine and arranging population shifts modeled on Lausanne.[39] But since this envisioned a resettlement of about 200,000 Arabs and only 1,250 Jews, the former resisted this vehemently and, at first, successfully.

In Europe and in North and South America, this sealing off of national borders had to do with the world economic crisis and, especially, the catastrophic status of the labor market. To this day, economic factors play an important role in the willingness to accept migrants of all kinds; in the 2015 "refugee crisis," poorer EU states and countries with high unemployment proved less receptive to helping than Germany, Austria, and Sweden. To be sure, Switzerland and Denmark, countries that are not exactly poor, also refused to take in a substantial number of refugees. Evidently, a country's policy toward refugees is not solely determined by its prosperity. Questions of national identity, cultural values, and the stance taken by mainstream parties toward right-wing nationalism can prove equally decisive.

In Europe in the 1930s, attitudes toward Jews were especially crucial. Through 1938, France and Czechoslovakia distanced themselves from the brutal antisemitism of the National Socialists and acted generously. Then, however, the Western powers left the last functioning democracy in Central Europe in the lurch, even though it was clear that this would again aggravate the international refugee emergency. After the Munich Agreement, around 190,000 people fled the Sudetenland, initially to the interior of Czechoslovakia and from there, to the extent this was possible, on to Western Europe. France was unable to withstand the additional onrush and decreed a halt to immigration in May 1938. This decision was also influenced by the burden of taking in refugees from the Spanish Civil War, who were crossing the border in ever larger numbers. Belgium and the Netherlands, in reaction to the panicky flight from Germany following the November pogroms, also closed their borders. In addition, more and more states deported people who were without a valid residency permit. As would happen again in the autumn of 2015, when many European countries and Germany's leading conservative media outlets changed the vocabulary of public discussion, refugees became "illegal immigrants."[40]

The traditional countries of immigration were also introducing ever stricter restrictions. In the United States, very low immigration quotas had been in force since the Immigration Act of 1924. And, although Canada did not actually fix an upper limit, after the outbreak of the world economic crisis it did deport more than 28,000 unemployed people between 1930 and 1935.[41] Brazil, Uruguay, Argentina, and Chile also closed their borders. Only Mexico, governed by leftist republicans, opened its doors to refugees in 1938–39.

Apart from this exception, the international community either ignored the persecution and suffering of refugees or at least did nothing to stop it. To the extent that countries of immigration were willing to take in refugees, economic criteria had priority. This utilitarianism contributed to a situation in which Jews were not accepted. A symbol of the international community's and especially the United States' failure was the odyssey of the *St. Louis*. In the spring of 1939 this passenger ship with 937 people on board spent more than a week circling the coasts of Cuba and Florida. Since no state was willing to accept the refugees (only 29 were allowed to disembark in Havana, thanks to the intervention of the captain), they had to return to Europe, where they were distributed among different countries. One fourth of them ultimately perished in the Holocaust.[42]

The *St. Louis* was sent back to Europe because the annual immigration quota for Germany and Austria had already been exhausted for refugees from

The 254 passengers of the *St. Louis* who were later murdered included the members of the **Dublon family** from Erfurt. Brothers Erich and Wilhelm Dublon, owners of a retail shoe company and two shoe stores, managed to get hold of a ticket for themselves and their families on the *St. Louis*. Up until the very end they were hoping to reach the US, which friends of theirs actually managed to do, but they, like almost all the ship's passengers, were sent back to Europe. At first the Dublons found accommodations in Belgium, where they were able to settle in rather quickly. Wilhelm Dublon's two daughters, Lore and Eva, were already back in school by the spring of 1940 and, after some initial difficulties owing to the foreign language of instruction, made it through the school year. On weekends the family enjoyed taking off on nature outings and walks in the woods, just as they had done back home. In one of his last letters to friends living in New York, Wilhelm Dublon described the situation in Brussels in April 1940 as "quiet" and "peaceful."[43]

A good month later, the Wehrmacht attacked neutral Belgium, and from then on the family had to hide. In the summer of 1942, the first member of the family was caught, the older brother Erich (age 50). He was deported to the Mechelen transit camp and from there to Auschwitz, where he died in the gas chambers. Wilhelm, his wife, and the two sixteen- and ten-year-old daughters were arrested in December 1943 and January 1944 and also taken to Auschwitz. The father, mother, and younger daughter were immediately sent to the gas chamber, while the elder daughter survived a few months longer as a forced laborer in the satellite camp of Golleschau. An entire family was extinguished. There was thus no one who could give witness to the fate of the Dublons. The family's history was finally treated in the framework of a multi-year documentation and research project about the passengers of the *St. Louis* put together by the United States Holocaust Memorial Museum, the findings of which were published in 2006 in the moving book *Refuge Denied*.[44] The book documents the life journeys of the survivors and of the other passengers on the *St. Louis* who came so close to being rescued but ultimately fell into the clutches of the National Socialists. The chances of survival were tiny for refugees in the Netherlands, somewhat higher in Belgium and France, while those accepted into England were the lucky ones.

(cont.)

(cont.)

In 2017 critics of President Trump, reacting to his provisional ban on taking in refugees, published the "St. Louis Manifesto" with the following hashtag: "We remember the victims of Nazism turned away at the doorstep of America in 1939. #RefugeesWelcome."[45]

these countries. The existence of that quota was, however, itself a sign that the US was at last taking some account of humanitarian concerns. In 1938 President Franklin Roosevelt ordered that the annual immigration quotas for refugees from both countries now constituting "Greater Germany" be merged so that the total now amounted to 27,370 people. This tripled the number of Jewish immigrants (which is what they still were in the eyes of officials) over the numbers allowed in four years earlier. In addition, the government removed time limits on tourist visas and eased other restrictions.

Just as important was the opening of Great Britain, which granted entry to 56,000 Jewish refugees from Germany, Austria, and Czechoslovakia on the eve of the war. This stance, in turn, motivated private aid organizations to finance the transport and placement of 10,000 Jewish children in England.[46] Latin American states now also behaved in a less restrictive manner, yet further evidence that international refugee policy can be shaped by models, good or bad.

Overall, about 270,000 German, 130,000 Austrian, and 33,000 Czechoslovakian Jews were able to reach safety before the outbreak of the Second World War.[47] Poorer families in Central Europe were unable to leave because high travel costs made flight unaffordable, while Polish Jews were in an even more desperate situation. About 100,000 of them fled to territories occupied by the Red Army after the invasion of the Wehrmacht. But the Stalinist Soviet Union—as Spanish Civil War fighters and Communists from Germany, Poland, and other countries had already learned—was a murderous country of asylum. Arriving Polish Jews were mostly deported to Central Asia and Siberia, where many died from adverse living conditions either en route or after their arrival. These deported Jews at least escaped the National Socialist extermination machine. After 1945 most of the survivors, along with the other *sybiracy* (these were mainly members of the Polish elites, civil servants, owners of homes or estates, as well as intellectuals who stood in the way of eastern Poland's Sovietization) returned to Poland, where the overwhelming majority were sent to the former German territories that were placed under Polish administration in the summer of 1945. In Silesia, Pomerania, and the other "recovered territories," Polish Jews were supposed to contribute to these regions' resettlement and Polonization. In line with the doctrine that these were originally Polish lands, this policy was called "re-Polonization," a further example of how different governments use the prefix *re-* for propaganda purposes. The largest communities now lived in Wrocław (Breslau) and in Lower Silesian Rychbach (subsequently renamed Dzierżoniów), where Jewish repatriates even formed the majority for a few years.

The attempt to integrate resettlers from central Poland, exiles from eastern Poland, remigrants from Western Europe, and the Jews into a new society failed. After the Kielce pogrom in the summer of 1946, where the death toll was 42, a massive wave of emigration took place that was nothing other than an additional stage in the flight from antisemitism in Europe. Most Jews wanted to go to the United States or Palestine but often had to stay put for the time being in the DP camps of occupied Germany and Austria, which will be discussed below.

By the mid-1930s, the protections for minorities embedded in the Paris Peace Treaties of 1919–20 were widely regarded as having failed. Poland, the largest state in East Central Europe, revoked minority protections in 1934—with the compelling argument that these protections would have to be valid for all European states if they were to have any validity at all. In the Paris Peace Treaties, France, Belgium, Italy, and even Germany, as a losing signatory from the First World War, had not committed themselves to any comparable concessions because, against all evidence, they insisted that they were already homogenous nation-states. The League of Nations could therefore do little to oppose National Socialist Germany taking ever harsher measures against its minorities during the 1930s.

The Munich Agreement of 1938, which stands for the failed policy of appeasement toward Hitler, finally removed minority protection in Europe for good. England, France, Italy, and the German Reich agreed to a reorganization of Europe on a foundation of ethnic boundaries. The border regions of Czechoslovakia, preponderantly settled by the German minority, fell to the German Reich, while the four signatory powers simultaneously concluded that a new border should also be drawn in southern Slovakia—in this case, to the benefit of Hungary. This was implemented at the end of 1939 in the First Vienna Arbitration. Each minority confronted the alternative of resettlement or assimilation. Following the Munich Agreement, around 190,000 Czechs fled the Sudetenland, while 120,000 people had to leave the territories lost to Hungary. After Slovakia became independent in the spring of 1939, another 50,000 Czechs were pushed out. There were no international aid programs of any kind for the roughly 300,000 Czech refugees, who could only hope for solidarity from their own nation-state, now seriously reduced and soon completely occupied, and from their families.

Following the example of the First Vienna Arbitration, two additional agreements were concluded in 1940, first between Hungary and Romania (in the Second Vienna Arbitration or, depending on one's interpretation, the "Vienna Diktat"), soon followed by another between Romania and Bulgaria (the

The desperate situation of Jewish refugees—and her personal fate—inspired **Hannah Arendt** in 1943 to write a now almost forgotten essay about refugees. The German-Jewish political scientist and philosopher was interned after the outbreak of the war with France in the Gurs camp as an "enemy alien." This kind of internment had an unholy lineage going back to the First World War, when hundreds of thousands of citizens of enemy countries landed in camps and died there by the tens of thousands from malnutrition, diseases, and epidemics. During the Second World War the danger this posed to interned German and Austrian Jews resided above all in the possibility that they might fall into the hands of the National Socialists after all. Arendt laments, in the lightly cynical and often desperate tone that pervades the essay, that "contemporary history has created a new kind of human being—the kind that are put in concentration camps by their foes and in internment camps by their friends."[48] From a purely legal point of view, Arendt was actually not an "enemy alien," since the National Socialists had taken away her German citizenship in 1937. Yet, as she noted disappointedly, the Jewish refugees from Germany, in spite of all their attempts at adapting to French society, were still regarded as "les boches."[49] After France's defeat by Germany, most of the Jews interned in Gurs and other French camps were deported to Auschwitz. Arendt escaped this fate by breaking out of the camp and, with the help of friends, finding her way via Marseille and Lisbon to New York.

There, in her essay "We Refugees," composed for the Jewish periodical *Menorah*, she worked up her experiences in France into a fundamental critique of the nation-state and international refugee policy. Arendt accurately observes that the Jews, in light of Europe's organization by nation-state, fell between the cracks of this order, and so she asks whether the obsession with defining a people as the residents of a state with fixed borders is still sustainable. She criticizes the limited willingness of states to take in refugees in spite of the acute threat and ends the essay by observing that the community of European nations was defeated by the National Socialists because it had allowed its weakest link, the Jews, to be excluded and persecuted. Arendt refers several times to the ghettos and concentration camps in Poland; apparently, as early as 1943 she was well-informed about the National Socialist machinery of extermination, whose origins she would analyze more thoroughly in her book *The Origins of Totalitarianism*.

In addition, Arendt's essay (one of her first English-language texts) pleads for more understanding for refugees. She writes: "We lost our home, which means the familiarity of daily life. We lost our occupation, which means the confidence that we are of some use in this world. We lost our language, which means the naturalness of reactions, the simplicity of gestures, the unaffected expression of feelings." In the collective we-form she laments the "rupture of our private lives" through the loss of and separation from friends and relatives. At the same time Arendt attacks the assimilation of refugees and especially of Jews: "We have become a little hysterical since newspapermen started detecting us and telling us publicly to stop being disagreeable. . . ."[50] She pleads for refugees to become "the vanguard of their peoples" and to advocate for their interests actively and publicly. While it is not entirely clear whether she refers here to Germans or to Jews as *her* people, it is also noteworthy that she speaks about refugees and not about exiles—apparently she did not regard herself as an exile.

In 2016, occasioned by the so-called refugee crisis of that year, the essay was republished in Germany and provided with a good afterword that placed the text in Hannah Arendt's broader oeuvre. In particular, her observations about fundamental human rights, the failed assimilation of the Jews, and the international order have a philosophical dimension. One may also interpret the essay, written primarily for a Jewish readership, in political terms. The joint proposal made in 2015–16 by the Christian Social Union (the Bavarian sister-party of Germany's Christian Democratic Union) and the Austrian People's Party (its counterpart there) to set up reception camps and hold refugees there without offering any prospect of asylum might signify a return to the practice of internment that Arendt criticizes in this essay.

Treaty of Craiova). These had to do with two long-disputed regions, Transylvania and Dobruja, and once again the "solution" was to draw an ethnic boundary and then to follow up with population shifts. Around half a million people had to leave their homeland. On paper they were "opting" for emigration, but in many places they were in reality fleeing from National Socialist riots and pogroms. The unholy tradition of the "right of option," established in Alsace in 1871, lived on after the First World War in the Paris Peace Treaties and in the Munich Agreement. In 1941 Bulgaria occupied large parts of Macedonia and Thrace. There the majority of the Serbian and Greek population was pushed out, while the Jews were handed over to the Germans and deported to Auschwitz. The "European peace order" propagated by Hitler on the basis of ethnically homogenous nation-states was, in the end, nothing more than an unstable war order generating even more violence.[51] Approximately six million people were resettled and expelled by the National

Socialists and their allies in Central and Southeastern Europe (not counting forced laborers and other displaced persons).

When the Nazi empire collapsed in 1944, there was no integration for the diverse population groups that had been pushed back and forth across Southeastern Europe in 1940–41. As far as is known, only a portion of those affected by these population movements returned to their old homeland after the war. Hesitation to return was linked to personal experiences with violence and the fact that many did not relish returning to an existence as an exposed minority. This frequently turned departure on account of ethnic cleansings into something permanent, whereas political refugees often tried actively and persistently to exert influence on their old homeland.

Flight and expulsion during the Second World War

The expansion of the war through Germany's attacks on Yugoslavia and the Soviet Union in the spring of 1941 (for only then and after Pearl Harbor did the assaults initiated by the Axis powers truly become a world war) had a mixed impact on the mass removal of populations. On the one hand, the Nazis and their allies halted the large-scale ethnic reshuffling of central and southeastern Europe set in motion by the Munich Agreement. All economic and military resources were now concentrated on the war at the eastern front. On the other hand, Germany's genocidal warfare uprooted more and more people. Frontlines were drawn and redrawn so rapidly and radically that it was hard to quantify precisely the scope of refugee movements caused by the war. Given the trajectory of the frontline, these movements at first affected Poland, and then in early 1940 the Western front, most of all. In France and Belgium alone, at least four million people were in flight.[52] This was, as mentioned, part of German military strategy, since streets clogged with refugees and a general climate of chaos prevented the French army from regrouping in the hinterland.

In Eastern Europe the Wehrmacht cracked down even harder on its enemies, in Poland during the autumn of 1939, in Yugoslavia during the spring of 1941, and in the vast expanses of the Soviet Union starting in the summer of that year. Because of the simultaneous recruitment of forced laborers and last minute evacuation of Soviet industries, it is almost impossible to calculate how many people fled from the approaching war fronts. According to official Soviet figures, it was fourteen million.[53] Gatrell assumes a figure of forty million civilians who became refugees in Europe as a result of the Second World War, four times the number for the First World War. Whoever could get to safety or be evacuated in time was fortunate, since the German occupation was synonymous with daily terror victimizing large numbers of civilians.

Conditions were especially bad in those parts of Eastern Europe where "wars within the war" erupted; here the Croatian-Serbian and Polish-

Ukrainian conflicts especially deserve mention. The Croatian fascists (Ustaša, which translates literally as "insurgence") took advantage of Yugoslavia's crushing defeat at the hands of the Reich to set up a nation-state of their own, which included Bosnia and Herzegovina. Much like what Hitler envisioned for Europe, this state was meant to be ethnically and racially homogenous. It was opposed by the large Serbian minority that actually constituted a majority in many places along the former Habsburg military border with the Ottoman Empire and in the north of Bosnia. The "solution" the Ustaša regime sought for the Serbian question was to assimilate one part of this minority (regarding them, in a way, as converted Croats), expel another portion to Serbia, and kill everyone who put up resistance. Hitler gave the Ustaša regime free rein to do this under the terms of the German-Croatian agreement of June 4, 1941, which granted Croatia permission to deport its Serbian minority to occupied Serbia and be compensated by taking in Slovenes expelled from the German Reich. But the Ustaše were in no position to organize such comprehensive population shifts, so local functionaries often resorted to brute force. Especially along the Drina, the river bordering occupied Serbia, horrific scenes played out. The Serbs were strafed and driven across the river. (Ivo Andrič described the harbingers of this tragedy in his novel *The Bridge on the Drina*, which he wrote during the war; in the 1990s there were massacres again, often at exactly the same sites as in 1941–42.) Within a mere matter of three months the German occupation administration counted 118,000 refugees from Croatia. The numbers were staggering and the refugees arrived penniless, robbed, and traumatized, so that the overwhelmed Wehrmacht soon re-sealed the border.

The closure of the border turned the ethnic cleansing into a genocide. In order to break the resistance of the partisans, the Ustaša kept on killing more Serbians and set up concentration camps like Jasenovac, where Croatian Jews and Roma were interned and killed alongside Serbians. Serious estimates put the number of Serbs killed in the course of the war in Croatia at 334,000 overall.[54] In return, Serbian Četniks (partisans loyal to the king) expelled and killed Croats and Bosnian Muslims because some of their leaders had formed an alliance with the Ustaša. The number of refugees in occupied Yugoslavia is hard to estimate because of the numerous local partisan actions, retaliatory measures, massacres, and expulsions. What we do know for certain is that several million people were uprooted or killed because, in each particular regional and local conflict, they belonged to the "wrong" nation or ethnicity.

The ideology of the Ukrainian OUN (the abbreviation stands for Organization of Ukrainian Nationalists) was similar to that of the Ustaša. The OUN wanted to reestablish the failed nation-state originally set up in 1918–19 under German dominance. Hitler, however, would not permit an independent Ukraine; as a result, leading nationalists like Stepan Bandera were even interned. Hence the OUN, unlike the Ustaša, did not have a state apparatus of its own to undertake mass expulsions or killings of minorities. Like the UPA (Ukrains'ka Povstans'ka Armija, the Ukrainian Insurgent Army), however, it did collaborate in the persecution of Jews and, after 1942–43, also went after the Polish minority. The number of Poles killed by Ukrainian partisans is estimated at around 30,000, while at least 300,000 fled in 1943–44 from Volhynia, Polesia, and Eastern Galicia, heading across what would later become the border river Bug into areas controlled by Polish partisans. There, in turn, the Ukrainian minority was persecuted, and several thousand people fled until, in a 1945 settlement analogous to the one moving Poles out of Ukraine, the "repatriation" of Ukrainians from Poland was regulated by treaty.[55] The common denominator of these incidents was the ethnic (and, in the case of the National Socialists, racist) categorization of the victims.

If things had gone the way the National Socialists wanted, these population shifts, which were intended to be permanent, would have been on an even greater scale. According to the "master plan for the East" (the Generalplan Ost), ten million Poles were to be evacuated from the annexed territories, a scheme analogous to that planned for Slovenians from so-called Lower Styria. These megalomaniacal plans were deferred in the summer of 1941 when the war against the Soviet Union took priority. Nevertheless, at least 365,000 Poles and about 30,000 Slovenes were forcibly expelled from their homes, and even more were taken away to do forced labor.[56]

The expulsion from the Warthegau (the German-occupied part of Poland annexed by the Reich) into the mercilessly exploited Generalgouvernement (German-occupied central Poland) was among the worst experiences of flight in the history of the Second World War, for there was no longer any kind of functioning state. Refugees were simply driven across the border or thrown out of the train at arbitrarily determined sites. The general level of distress in the Generalgouvernement was so great that local municipalities were unable to provide these refugees with food and living space. Somehow they struggled along, hunger was part of their everyday life, and often they had to move into the homes and apartments of deported Jews.[57] Even worse was the situation of the 110,000 people who in the winter of 1942–43 were driven out of the southeastern Polish city Zamość, which, like the Ukrainian town of Zhytomyr, became a laboratory for the Germanization of Eastern Europe. Overnight the entire Polish population was removed and replaced with German re-settlers, including the family of Germany's federal president Horst Köhler (in office 2004–10), who was born in 1942 not far from Zamość. In the summer and fall of 1944, close to a million people were deported as a punishment for the Warsaw Uprising. Overall in Poland, the Germans uprooted at least two million people, and deported three million Poles as forced laborers. Millions of Russians, Ukrainians, and Serbs, the latter especially despised by Hitler, suffered a similar fate.

The National Socialist expulsions and deportations prejudiced the fate of German minorities in Eastern Europe. The public in Great Britain and the United States was outraged at the violent Germanization of Poland. In 1941 the influential journal *Foreign Affairs* called for all the population shifts initiated by Hitler to be rescinded. German minorities were regarded as a fifth column of National Socialism and a threat to any future peace. In 1942 the Czechoslovakian president Edvard Beneš, in exile in London, was able to influence the revocation of the Munich Agreement. By way of compromise, Beneš offered to cede some small territories, and to assimilate one million Germans who would remain in Czechoslovakia.

In 1944–45 the Allies agreed that ethnic boundaries should be drawn in all of East Central Europe and national minorities dissolved. Winston Churchill got to the heart of the matter in a 1944 speech to the House of Commons when he proclaimed: "There will be no mixture of populations to cause endless trouble. . . . A clean sweep will be made."[58] This maxim applied not only to Germans, but also to Poles, Ukrainians, Hungarians, and Italians—in principle, to all national minorities. Here Churchill and Stalin made arguments that, on the one hand, were technocratic (modern means of transportation made it easy to resettle millions of people) and, on the other hand, simply alluded to the incipient fait accompli of mass flight already under way.

The Red Army's advance did indeed trigger a mass exodus. More than one million Finns, Estonians, Latvians, Lithuanians, Poles, Hungarians, and Romanians, some of whom had already lived through the terror of the Soviet occupation in 1939–41, set out toward the West. In some cases there was an overlap between spontaneous flight and organized evacuation, as in the case of the Karelian Finns. In East Prussia and other regions, by contrast, the National Socialists acted with complete impunity; up to the last minute they exhorted fellow Germans to hold out, and they shot alleged traitors, all of which worsened the conditions of flight. As a result, up to half a million Germans froze along the treks westward during the winter of 1944–45, drowned in attempts to cross the frozen Baltic Sea, or died from epidemics and malnourishment. Nevertheless, the conservative postwar government in West Germany laid all the blame for the so-called expulsion victims on the Red Army, Poland, and Czechoslovakia.[59]

Flight and population removal after the end of the Second World War
At the Yalta and Potsdam conferences, the chaotic conditions facing refugees in Germany were amplified by the Allies. In line with Stalin's demands, the victorious powers shifted Germany's eastern border substantially farther to the west than had originally been planned. By drawing the border at the Lausitzer Neisse river (instead of the Glatzer Neisse farther to the east) and west of the Stettin Lagoon, the territories of Upper Silesia, Lower Silesia (only

Görlitz remained in Germany), East Brandenburg, and most of Pomerania fell to Poland. It was clear that a Poland shifted westward by two to three hundred kilometers would not be able to exist with the German population present there. This minority would have constituted more than a quarter of the total population, and Poland already had had a bad experience with German revisionism in the interwar period. Czechoslovakia, similarly, was given free rein in dealing with its German minority.

In the spring of 1945, Poland and Czechoslovakia were already attempting to put in place a fait accompli. The Polish army chased more than a million people out of the regions that were close to the German border at the Oder and Neisse rivers. Czechoslovakia acted in a similar manner in the former Sudetenland; about 800,000 people were driven out in order to establish "facts on the ground" for a future peace conference and postwar order. In addition to wartime refugees, all these people were also traveling the roads of occupied Germany in the summer of 1945. By virtue of their geographical location, the regions most affected were the Soviet Occupation Zone (which later became the GDR), Schleswig-Holstein and Bavaria (both in Western-occupied Germany), and Austria. Several million people had to be provided with makeshift accommodations and food. Together with those bombed out, evacuees, and displaced persons, they formed an army of the homeless and the hungry (see Map 3 for the mass flight from Eastern Europe).

As in 2015, Austria, though primarily a transit country, also became a final destination for refugees. In 1945–46 about one million "German-speaking refugees" (as they were called in order to distinguish them from DPs and other groups) came to Austria from postwar Romania, Hungary, and Czechoslovakia.[60] The government under Chancellor Karl Renner, who had been born in Moravia himself and had supported the "Anschluss" annexing Austria to Germany, now accused the Sudeten Germans of having been a fifth column. Renner resorted to a classic "solution" for refugee policy: Austria simply sent the arrivals on with the argument that they were really Germans. The government also claimed that Austria was overwhelmed and, indeed, a victim of both the war and the National Socialists. After July 1945, the Potsdam Agreement furnished a legal pretext for getting rid of the refugees. Austria was not among the countries covered by the provisions for the removal of all Germans from Poland, Czechoslovakia, and Hungary, but it argued that it was acting in the spirit of the agreement by sending the refugees on to occupied Germany. The de-Germanization of Austria also encompassed other Germans who had settled there during the Nazi period.

Throughout the postwar period, German refugee organizations accused Czechoslovakia of brutality against the Sudeten Germans, especially because of the June 1945 death march from Brno, where up to 2,000 people died en route to the Austrian border, most from exhaustion. No one, however, counted the casualties after the refugee treks had arrived in Austria, where they were housed in camps and improvised accommodations before being driven on to American-occupied Bavaria. Eventually the "de-Germanization" of Austria was halted on American orders. It came to an end in September 1946, when the American army closed the Bavarian border to refugees arriving from Austria.[61]

The Austrian attitude adopted toward displaced persons was equally dismissive. The government in Vienna and the local authorities readily took the position that the DPs were a problem for the Allies, absolving Austrian officials of all responsibility. Through the repatriation of Soviet citizens and former forced laborers, Austria got rid of a majority of the DPs stranded there. At the beginning of 1947, there were nevertheless still almost 150,000 "foreign-language refugees" housed in camps. ("Foreign-language refugees" is how they were described in the official statistics, a legacy of the old ethnic-racial distinction between these refugees and "Volksdeutschen" that would later play an important role in questions of naturalization and legal integration.) The DPs were given only sporadic and scanty provisions, in order to forestall any requests they might make to stay. Moreover, they had no regular work permits, were viewed with suspicion by local neighbors, and were not infrequently subjected to verbal abuse. Ultimately the problem of the DPs was solved at an international level. In 1948 the US passed the Displaced Persons Act, as a result of which 329,000 DPs were allowed to immigrate. At the same time, the establishment of Israel ended the British quotas previously in place, along with the UK's de facto blockade of mass emigration to Palestine. (More details on the DPs and the roots of a more humanitarian refugee policy in the postwar period will follow in Chapter 3.3.) The history of the DPs in Austria and in occupied Germany does show, however, what happens to refugees when they arrive in countries where there is no solidarity based on common nationality or religious denomination.

In the spring and summer of 1945 the situation in Germany had gotten so out of control that the Allies attempted to defuse the chaos surrounding refugees at the international level. In July and August the "Big Three" met in Potsdam, where they agreed on the territorial division of the occupation zones and the main features of their administration. In Paragraph XIII of the accord agreed upon in Potsdam, the Allies stipulated the "transfer" of Germans out of Poland, Czechoslovakia, and Hungary and added that it should be carried out in an "orderly and humane manner." In the German literature on expellees, this accord is portrayed as a major violation of human rights. It was, of course, but in the years immediately following the war Germans could not count on much compassion. Stalin saw the expulsion as a just punishment for their having started the war, and both he and Churchill agreed that the high number of war casualties would have left plenty of room for Germans arriving from the East.

Among the several thousand Jewish displaced persons and refugees in occupied postwar Germany was a fourteen year-old girl named **Ruth Klüger**.[62] Along with her mother, she had survived concentration camps in Theresienstadt, Auschwitz, and Gross-Rosen before, finding a favorable moment to escape during one of the death marches in Lower Silesia, she ran away from her German guards. In the general chaos, Klüger, her mother, and another Jewish child mingled incognito with the German refugees; one might also summarize her experience as an instance of the suffering of one group enabling the survival of another. Klüger experienced this flight as liberation: "On those roads of eastern Germany we three were full of good humor: we were elated and in love with existence. It was a subjective state of mind and doesn't decrease the staggering number of victims by a single digit. Yes, we laughed a lot, for humor thrives on danger, for whatever reason. . . . One reason for our well-being was, without a doubt, that soon we were no longer starving."[63] On the long road from Silesia to Bavaria there were a few critical moments when the three women were almost recognized as Jews and might have been arrested again. But on one of the many stations of their flight, Klüger's mother succeeded in getting forged identity papers for herself and the two girls. As German refugees, the three were cared for by the National Socialist People's Welfare organization and evacuated to Straubing in Lower Bavaria, where Ruth Klüger experienced again a "dizzy sense of happiness, the very opposite of what the genuine German refugees experienced. For they had lost everything, that is, all their property, while we hoped to have gained everything, that is, the rest of our lives."[64] As it turned out, however, her father and her brother had lost their lives in a concentration camp.

After being liberated by the Americans in Straubing, the Klügers (who were natives of Vienna) were additionally fortunate in that the city commander from the American Army was of Jewish descent and found work for the mother. As a result, they did not have to live in a DP camp and could move about freely. Klüger used the opportunity to obtain a *Notabitur* (an "emergency" secondary school-leaving and university entrance certificate instituted in wartime) at a gymnasium in Straubing, then matriculated to the Philosophical-Theological College in Regensburg and was able, after a waiting period of two and a half years and a "jumble of requirements and quotas," to obtain an entry visa to the United States. There she studied at New York's Hunter College (where she was given credit for her courses at Regensburg, something that reminds us more generally how important it is for job certifications and educational degrees to be recognized) and in Berkeley. After initially working as a librarian, Klüger rose to become a well-known German studies professor. The concentration camp survivor, who characterized her profession as "lacking character . . . for someone like me," published numerous textbooks and essays, chiefly in English. Yet she remained enthralled by her native language: Both *Weiter leben: eine Jugend* (1993—the English edition entitled *Still Alive: A Holocaust Childhood Remembered* was published in 2001), her award-winning chronicle of surviving National Socialism, and her memoir *Unterwegs verloren: Erinnerungen* (2008) were written in German.

The Potsdam agreement, however, was simultaneously an attempt to channel the waves of refugees and to pause for at least a short breather on the matter of absorption; hence the talk of an "orderly" transfer. But this attempt did not succeed, since violence in the Kaliningrad region, Poland, Czechoslovakia, and Yugoslavia took on a dynamic all its own, slipping out of the hands of the central governments. In the spring and summer of 1945, local military garrisons, national committees, and security organs often went "wild," expelling the remaining Germans by brutal means. Sometimes material interests were at stake, in particular the question as to who could appropriate the nicest German house or the farm with the best land.

Early in 1946, the United States and Great Britain, acting as occupation powers, arranged with Poland and Czechoslovakia to take over scheduling the refugee trains traveling to the two Western allies' occupation zones. There, in the meantime, the authorities had constructed a system of reception camps providing preliminary medical care; arrivals were then moved on to makeshift quarters and, so far as possible, into permanent accommodations. Thanks to these efforts, approximately five million Germans "transferred" through 1948 arrived under what were, as a rule, more favorable circumstances. The refugees profited from the organizational capacity of the German bureaucracy, which only recently had been just as efficient organizing the displacement of millions, enslaving them for forced labor, and deporting them to concentration camps.

The initial chaos surrounding refugees in Germany and Austria and, above all, strategic considerations prevented this scenario from being repeated in Hungary. In principle, the German Reich's last ally in 1945 had to expect a similar collective punishment for those now stranded as ethnic minorities outside its shrunken borders; thus, for example, the Beneš Decrees in Czechoslovakia were directed as much against its Hungarian as its German minority. In Romania prospects for the Hungarian minority were just as dismal; hence, in 1944 the greater part of that minority fled from the Red Army and from the Romanians, who had changed sides just in time in the last year of the war. About 70,000 Hungarians also fled Vojvodina (now a Serbian province in Yugoslavia), not least out of fear of reprisals for crimes committed during the occupation. Budapest was overrun with refugees, even more of them than after the First World War, and the same was true for cities near Hungary's borders in the east and south.

In the midst of this acute emergency in the Danube region, Stalin ordered Hungarian refugees from Transylvania, who numbered about 400,000, to return to Romania. The logic behind this directive was the view that Romania, like Yugoslavia, was a multi-ethnic state.[65] Accordingly, the kind of ethnic cleansing that took place in Poland and Czechoslovakia should not be needed there. During the first few years after the war, party comrades of Hungarian and Jewish descent played a major role in the Communist Party of Romania, which had always been weak owing to the country's numerous historical conflicts with Russia and the bloodletting of the Stalinist purges. Analogously, the Communist Party of Yugoslavia also opened up to the country's non-Slavic peoples. In principle, Communist propaganda about the unity and fraternity of the nations included the Albanians in Kosovo, the Hungarians in Vojvodina, and the Italians in the upper Adriatic, on condition (needless to add) that all these groups behaved with absolute loyalty toward the regime. In the spring of 1946, a few hundred Communist workers from the Italian industrial city of Monfalcone even emigrated to Rijeka, taking over the homes of Italians who had recently fled that Croatian city, in order to assist in building socialism there.

Czechoslovakia also had to moderate its resettlement plans and, after the bilateral agreements of 1946, evacuated only a number of Hungarians equal to the number of Slovaks repatriated from Hungary (where there were a number of Slovak villages and settlements that were almost all dissolved after the Second World War). As a result, a large Hungarian minority was preserved in southern Slovakia. By contrast, the future Slovak capital Bratislava was profoundly transformed: until 1945, the city also known as Pressburg or Pozsony had been overwhelmingly German and Hungarian. Hungary and Yugoslavia concluded a similar bilateral agreement, though all it really did was confirm what had transpired in the flight of 1944.

The reciprocity of resettlements formulated in the postwar accords was never fully implemented. As happened also following the 1919 Treaty of Neuilly, the victors of World War II and their allies had the greater share of power, so were able to expel more people than the losers, and they did so. Nevertheless, the bilateral agreements limited the size of the populations that could be shifted from one country to the other. This signified, in principle, a return to the practices implemented after the First World War in the Treaty of Neuilly. Starting around 1948, the resettlement of national minorities in East Central Europe and Southeastern Europe came to a standstill.

The exception was Poland because, in spite of all its efforts in the struggle against National Socialism, it was treated like a loser of the Second World War. During the conferences with the Allies at Teheran and Yalta, the Soviet Union steadfastly insisted on retaining the eastern Polish territories that Stalin had annexed following the Hitler-Stalin Pact. Since the Red Army had reconquered eastern Galicia, Volhynia, Polesia, and the Vilna province in 1944, the Western powers could do little to oppose this. Soviet expansion left the Polish population in the eastern territories in an untenable situation. Already during the first Soviet occupation of 1939–41, they had become acquainted with every variety of Stalinist terror, from arbitrary police actions and deportations to Central Asia, to mass shootings by the NKVD. Among the Poles in L'viv, Vilna, Grodno, and many other urban centers, therefore, the prevailing mood when the Red Army marched in once again was apocalyptic, especially as more and more people fleeing Ukrainian partisans streamed into the cities.

When the Lublin Committee, the Polish government appointed by Stalin in 1944, concluded so-called repatriation agreements with the three Soviet Republics bordering Poland, the fate of the Poles in the eastern territories was sealed. (That this downgraded Poland to the status of a Soviet republic must have set off alarm bells among the Western powers, but they did not react.) The agreements contained provisions stipulating that these eastern Poles were to be "repatriated" into postwar Poland, voluntarily in formal terms, but de facto under direct or indirect compulsion.[66] In 1944–46, according to official information, 1,517,000 Poles left the eastern territories annexed by the Soviet Union. Taking into account those who had already fled and the forced laborers who were unable to return to their old homelands after the end of the war, the actual figure came to more than two million.

As a reciprocal measure, 482,000 Ukrainians and 36,000 Belarusians were "repatriated" into the Soviet Union from Poland. As in the case of the aforementioned peace treaties between Hungary and its neighbors, this was a bilateral scheme that greatly reduced national minorities on both sides of the border. According to the agreements, those repatriated were allowed to bring household goods and furniture (and the peasants even a few cattle) on the transport trains. More important for the subsequent integration of the eastern Poles was the allocation to them of former German property, arbitrary though the process proved to be.

One should not be deceived by these treaties' seemingly legal and constitutionally correct-sounding provisions or by their euphemistic terminology. There can be no talk of any "repatriation" in either direction, since those affected were not returning to their homelands but rather being robbed of them. What is more, many of the "repatriates" already had several stages of flight behind them, especially if they were from regions that had been contested by more than one group of nationalist partisans. In the cities that fell to the Soviet Union, the Soviet authorities arbitrarily refused to allot food ration cards and confiscated homes as needed. On the streets, insecurity was the rule. Gang crime was rampant, and there was constant fear of arrests by the NKVD. Repatriation, like all instances of flight, entailed an almost total loss of property. At most, those affected were able to save the few personal belongings they could fit in a few suitcases. Gone were their homes, their land, and (critically) also their jobs, which would prove a major hurdle for later integration in Poland.

In Dalmatia, Istria, and the hinterland of Trieste, there was yet another massive refugee movement. Between 1945 and 1947, nearly 300,000 Italians fled Yugoslav retribution against fascists. The Italians were under a cloud of collective suspicion (and indeed the Upper Adriatic really had been a hotbed of fascism before the war). In the first postwar years, Yugoslavia persecuted former fascists, but also many other opponents and bystanders, employing such Stalinist practices as show trials and penal camps.[67]

In principle, the redrawing of boundaries in the upper Adriatic region—which forced Italy in 1947 to cede Istria, the hinterland of Trieste, and a portion of Friuli—corresponded to the old principle of *cuius regio, eius religio*. The rulers of each region determined both its ideological orientation and the social order, including their ethno-national dimensions. The mass migration that took place across the new borders in the upper Adriatic region was inherent to the logic of this partition, which once again had been proposed by Great Britain.[68] The West, in this case Italy under the leadership of its long-serving prime minister Alcide De Gasperi, took in these refugees with a grand gesture because they were persecuted compatriots (here, again, national solidarity came into effect) and because they already fit into emerging Cold War patterns. Voting with one's feet was a way of calling into question the moral and political authority of the Communists: on one side of the border was the good, democratic West, and on the other side the evil, dictatorial East. That helped, much as it did in the Federal Republic of Germany, with the absorption and integration of refugees, but it did nothing to prevent the association of Dalmatian and Friulian Italians (the Associazione Nazionale Venezia Giulia Dalmazia, abbreviated as ANVGD) from drifting ever further to the right over the postwar period.

In the slipstream of the refugees from the upper Adriatic, Italy also took in 300,000 to 400,000 compatriots who were returning from the country's lost colonies in North Africa.[69] For Libya, in particular, the fascists had cherished ambitious plans: to construct an Italian colony on the other side of the Mediterranean, similar to French Algeria. These dreams ended in 1943 with the defeat of the Axis powers in Libya and Tunisia. The subsequent flight of most of the North African Italians also marked the beginning of the postcolonial remigration to Europe that would eventually include several million people (a subject to be treated in greater deal in Chapter 3.4).[70]

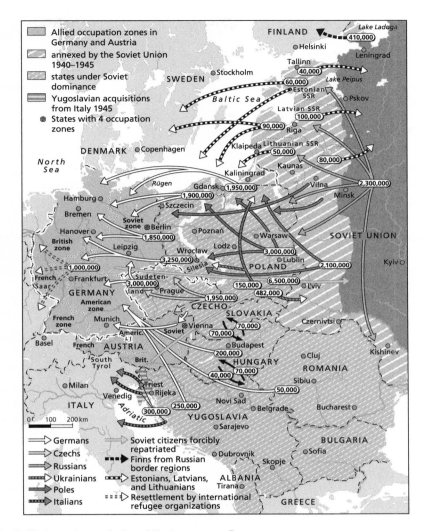

MAP 3. Flight and population shifts in postwar Europe

The absorption of twelve million refugees into occupied postwar Germany demonstrated just how far political solidarity could reach. In principle, this was a mandated absorption, since Germany's state and local authorities had no other choice than to follow the orders of the occupying powers and accommodate the refugees. In the fall of 1945, the governments of the German states of Saxony and Hamburg refused to take in any more refugees and began deporting them to neighboring states (mostly to Brandenburg from out of Saxony, and to Schleswig-Holstein from out of Hamburg). Some county administrations acted in a similar manner, pushing refugees out. The Soviet and British authorities eventually ordered the accommodation of refugees according to pre-set quotas.[71] What is striking is that there was hardly any open civilian resistance to this bureaucratic distribution of such masses of people. Needless to say, indigenous residents complained about the additional burden, but no riots or unrest ensued, as had happened in Greece in the mid-1920s or in postwar Poland. Was there a higher degree of co-national solidarity in Germany, and was this perhaps one of the many legacies of National Socialism? It is difficult to answer such questions, because no opinion surveys screening attitudes towards refugees were carried out in the tumultuous postwar years. (They were routine by 2015.) Nevertheless, we can gather some information based on people's actions, what they did or did not do. The main conclusion is that co-national or co-ethnic solidarity was not a given. It had to be created. Two factors hastened the integration of these particular refugees: there were no communication barriers as they spoke the language of their countries of arrival, and they already had citizenship, which facilitated legal claims and the starting of a new life.

Integration in early postwar Europe

There has always been a danger that talking about "the refugees" as a collective group neglects their internal differences. As the German case shows, postwar lives differed vastly, depending on the refugees' region of origin and the timing of their flight and arrival in their host country. Those who fled on their own initiative as the Red Army approached were relatively better off. (Marion Dönhoff, the longtime editor of the liberal German weekly *Die Zeit,* might be Germany's best known example; she rode on her own horse more than one thousand kilometers from East Prussia to the West. However, only the thin upper crust of society, to which Countess Dönhoff belonged, owned saddle horses who could carry them on the long journey westward.) Others were crushed by the unleashed dogs of war or, to put it more precisely, under the treads of Soviet tanks. Those who were not expelled until 1946 had the advantage that transports to Germany were now better organized than before, though on the other hand they would now arrive in a country already filled with refugees. The seasons also had a major influence. In summer the sun made people, often transported in open railway cars, uncomfortable; in the harsh winter of 1947, even more people froze in the trains, not only Germans from Poland, but also Poles who were repatriated from Western Europe.

It is just as hard to find a common denominator for all the many attempts at integration, for each such effort was different, depending again on the refugees' region of origin and where they were absorbed. In Poland, a host territory was available for expellees from the eastern parts of Poland annexed by the Soviet Union, but in the eastern territories that were formerly German expellees had to compete with re-settlers from central Poland who had frequently arrived immediately after the end of the war on their own initiative (with energy to match) and, above all, earlier. The "wild West," as Silesia, eastern Brandenburg, and Pomerania were sometimes called in 1945/46, was shaped by harsh struggles over houses, farms, and daily meals. Some re-settlers came chiefly to plunder, which was called by the originally Yiddish term *szaber*. Polish Communists believed that nationalism would serve as social putty, and they did succeed in drawing some former National Democrats to their side (*Endecja* was the Polish term for them—there are a number of continuities between the thinking of these National Democrats and that of today's right-wing nationalist PiS, the Law and Justice party, under the leadership of Jarosław Kaczyński.) They were unable, however, to prevent the new society from fracturing into the three aforementioned groups: re-settlers from central Poland, repatriates from eastern Poland, and so-called autochthones who, as former citizens of the German Reich, clung to the lowest rung of the pecking order.

The German refugees who in the young Federal Republic quickly renamed themselves "expellees" so as to underscore their permanent presence and status as victims (notwithstanding the Nazi past of many of the functionaries among them), as well as to reinforce their compensation claims, lived in a relatively well-ordered country. The Sudeten Germans were the best organized politically, a legacy of their prehistory as a national minority in Czechoslovakia. They had, moreover, left a prosperous industrial country and were therefore above average in education and professional training. By contrast, many rural workers from Pomerania or East Prussia, who had not seen much of the greater world outside their local farms, often felt completely lost in industrialized West Germany. They did not quite grasp where it was that they had washed up; which was indeed often a matter of pure accident. In 1952 legislation on compensation for their losses was passed in the form of an Equalization of Burdens Law, the *Lastenausgleichsgesetz*—whose very name conveys a recognition of the fact that the expellees (and those with bombed-out homes and properties) had endured more suffering than most in consequence of Germany's lost war. And perhaps it was this psychological dimension that was for them most helpful. The law foresaw the provision of substantial social welfare services (which most victims of National Socialism could only dream of): startup loans, study grants for children, and compensation for lost property, pecuniary losses, and losses of political capital that would ease the transition to a new life, at least for the younger generation. In the GDR, which competed with the Federal Republic over the excellence of their respective social welfare policies, re-settlers—they could not call themselves "expellees" on ideological grounds, and "refugees" was also unacceptable because that would have sounded too derogatory and might suggest to the SED (East Germany's rul-ing party) that theirs was a temporary residence—also benefited from a vari-ety of special services.[72]

The research literature is split over whether integration proceeded rapidly or whether the expellees remained disadvantaged into the next generation, as the sociologist Paul Lüttinger asserted in a 1986 essay about the "myth of rapid integration."[73] At the beginning of the twenty-first century, when the victim discourse surrounding expulsion reached a new peak (not least because many 68ers in Germany were dealing self-critically with their earlier aversion to this subject), there was an emphasis on the disdain, social exclusion, and discrimination experienced by expellees. Books like Andreas Kossert's *Kalte Heimat* (Cold Homeland) were representative of this genre.[74] In the immedi-ate postwar period, however, the main concern was reconstruction, not only of the entire country, but also of each person's own livelihood, and in this re-gard the expellees did not come off at all badly. Most of them achieved social advancement during the era known as West Germany's Economic Miracle, at least as measured against the poverty of the 1930s. Only the older genera-tion, especially the farmers, did badly.

The data on professional integration tend toward this conclusion. In 1959, when the sociologist Eugen Lemberg and the economist Friedrich Edding presented their multi-volume documentation about the "incorporation" of the expellees into the Federal Republic,[75] the number of unemployed among them had been reduced to one fourth of what it had been in 1950 (though it was down only by half during the winter, an indication of how dependent this group was on the construction trades and on low-skill jobs). The em-ployment rate among the expellees now began to approach that of the native population—at 63 percent for men, a value that today's Syrian refugees are likely to achieve in two decades at the earliest. (Coincidentally, however, it is exactly the same as today's employment figure for men with a Turkish mi-grant background.[76]) Many expellees went into public service, especially as teachers. The state also played an important role in professional integration, not only by awarding jobs but also, and even more fundamentally, by recog-nizing the expellees' educational and occupational credentials.

Yet the expellees themselves also could take a large share of credit for their rapid "incorporation." (The German word for this—*Eingliederung*—might be worth a semantic study all its own; this term for integration, the root of which means "limb" or "body part," like the Latin "corpus" in the English-language equivalent, only makes sense if one views society as a huge organism; any number of studies from the postwar period were shaped by this kind of col-lectivist and ethno-national thinking.) When necessary, they took on jobs for which they were overqualified, and they were extremely mobile geographi-cally. Here previous experience turned to their advantage. About half of the

1950s expellees had already been through dislocation, having left the original site where they had been absorbed in West Germany (owing to bomb damage in the major cities, these were predominantly villages, small and medium-sized towns) before now being relocated again within the Federal Republic. In the GDR and in Poland rates of geographical mobility were even higher, due in part to the failure of their land reforms, to collectivization (which started earlier in Poland than in the GDR but was then interrupted in 1956), and to Stalinist industrial policy. The dynamism of these societies cannot be replicated today—nor is it something that should be idealized, since there were many dark sides to postwar reconstruction. Its privations exacted a great toll from the expellees.

While relocation to big cities more or less fit in with that era's melting pot paradigm, so-called refugee industries present an independent development. At first they arose rather accidentally; owing to the housing shortage, refugees in 1945–46 were frequently accommodated in military barracks or in former camps and shanty towns near factories that had been relocated to the countryside because of the bombing. After the forced laborers exploited by the Nazis were repatriated, these industrial facilities often stood empty. Both the authorities and arriving refugees recognized their potential, and a deliberate effort was made to install factories, businesses, and specific occupational groups at these sites. Well-known examples are the municipality of Neugablonz near Kaufbeuren in southwestern Bavaria, where the jewelry industry of the northern Bohemian town of Gablonz was revived, Stephanskirchen near Rosenheim in Upper Bavaria with its textile industry, and the towns of Geretsried, Traunreut, and Waldkraiburg. The establishment of these "expellee cities" gave a boost to Bavaria's industrialization, and similar efforts were made in Lower Saxony and other primarily rural German *Länder*; one may, to an extent, compare this combination of refugee and development policy with the settlement of the Huguenots and their manufactories in Prussia. Sometimes there is even a geographical link, as in the case of the Franconian town of Bubenreuth, five kilometers from Erlangen-Neustadt, which had been built for the Huguenots. There, in 1949, violin-makers from Schönbach in the Bohemian region of the Egerland settled, increasing the population of Bubenreuth by 1,600. The town from which they came, by contrast, was never able to recover from its population losses; by 1950 only 2,200 people, half the number of its inhabitants before the war, lived in the municipality now known by its Czech name Luby.

At first the administrations of the *Länder* in the Soviet Occupation Zone also encouraged refugees to set up new industrial sites. Glass blowers from the aforementioned Gablonz settled in Lusatia, and cutlers in Brandenburg. But these firms had great difficulty obtaining essential raw materials, and from the outset the ruling Socialist Unity Party (SED) took an ambivalent attitude toward private enterprise. Moreover, for fear of revanchist tendencies, the SED wanted to avoid concentrating refugee groups from specific regions. As a result, nothing came of these attempts, and the enterprises folded soon after the establishment of the GDR. Attempts to establish refugee industry settlements in Austria didn't work either. There the government recognized the economic potential of the Gablonz glass industry and in January 1946 contemplated a settlement in Upper Austria, but in the end moving the refugees on to Bavaria took priority.[77] In West Germany the era of new and expanding industrial firms founded by expellees came to an end in the 1960s. Owing to structural changes in the economy and competition from East Asia, many of their companies, which were usually labor- and not capital-intensive (the refugees' capital having largely been lost in fleeing Eastern Europe), had to cease production. Nevertheless, businesses founded by expellees had employed 235,000 people by the end of the 1950s, and firms relocated from the GDR to the Federal Republic had created a similar number of jobs.[78] This was an important contribution to the early phase of integration, and a heartening one that raised the spirits of the refugees.

A peculiarity of integration among the German expellees of the postwar period—especially when compared with the Huguenots—was their marriage behavior. Although in the 1950s refugees were not exactly the best marriage prospects from a financial perspective, the number of their "mixed marriages" with natives significantly exceeded the figure for their endogenous marriages, and by the mid-1950s, 63 percent of the marriages made by expellees were exogenous. To put it another way, around 24 percent of all West German marriages in 1955 were mixed,[79] and this was also true of Catholics and Lutherans, whose marriage patterns had been markedly rigid, with few members out-marrying. This can only be explained by how thoroughly "on the move" German society was at the time. Individual inclinations apparently counted more than time-honored social barriers and conventions. That the war had created many widows looking for new partners also played a part. One might object, especially with a view toward the much lower level of family integration in the case of "guest workers" and later refugee groups arriving in Germany, that this peculiarity of the 1950s depended on the couples' sense of belonging now to a common nation. But this feeling of membership in a community should not simply be assumed, for it is equally apparent that many native West Germans were eager to leave their former denominational and social milieus behind.

In any event, the children of these marriages (between 1950 and 1957 alone there were more than 750,000 "mixed marriages") were no longer members of one group or the other, and their grandchildren certainly were not. This unusually rapid and extensive family integration explains why there are so many Germans today who have an "expellee granny." In terms of figures, this applies to at least 40 percent of the second generation born after 1945.

Although West German expellee associations always attracted just a small fraction of refugees as members, they successfully claimed to represent the entire community's interests. **Erika Steinbach**, a member of parliament for Germany's Christian Democratic Party (CDU), chaired the Federation of Expellees (the Bund der Vertriebenen, BdV) from 1998 to 2014. A closer look at her biography calls to mind Donald Trump's neologism of the "fake refugee," although we may assume the American president would find her politics attractive. Steinbach was born in 1943 in the small Polish town of Rumia, which fell to Poland under the Versailles Treaty and was occupied by the Wehrmacht in 1939. Among the occupying soldiers was Steinbach's father, a sergeant who actually came from Hanau in Hesse. Her mother was from Bremen and also had first settled in the Reichsgau of Danzig-West Prussia in the course of the occupation. In spite of this clearly West German origin, Steinbach was able to claim that she was an expellee under the 1953 Federal Expellees Act. That law gives virtually everyone born as a German in one the eastern territories lost by the German Reich (or in one of the areas where there was a German minority) expellee status.

Steinbach at first became a member of the expellee association for West Prussia (one of twenty regionally based associations of refugees [*Landsmannschaften*]), where she took on the role of a nationalist hardliner. She then used her position as head of the BdV to continue building up her profile on the right wing of the CDU. In 1991, right after she joined the Bundestag, she led a group of thirteen CDU/CSU deputies who voted against a definitive recognition of united Germany's border with Poland along the Oder-Neisse River. In taking this stand, she argued that "one cannot vote for a treaty that cuts off a part of our homeland." However, Rumia (Rahmel in German) had already been "cut off" in 1919 and not for the first time in 1945.[80] Steinbach's statement picked up on the fateful rhetoric of interwar revisionism that had contributed so much to the rise of Adolf Hitler. Helmut Kohl chose to ignore the nationalist right wing of his party, since his priority was obtaining approval from the Second World War's four victorious powers for unification with East Germany. The USSR, France, Great Britain, and especially the United States made it clear in the Two-Plus-Four talks that Germany's pending unification was conditional upon a definitive recognition of Poland's western border. In 1998, not least owing to her tough stance against Poland, Steinbach was elected chair of the BdV. Soon thereafter she established the foundation "Center against Expulsions," which since 2000 has been pushing to set up a memorial of the same name. It was

(cont.)

(cont.)

initially meant to be a memorial for German "victims of expulsion" only. Later the foundation tried to include other expulsions among the exhibits it organized in Berlin. This was a pretext for drawing an equivalency between the German expellees and the victims of the Armenian genocide and even the Holocaust.

The activities of the foundation and the reparations demands of the Preussische Treuhand (Prussian Claims Society, formally a firm but mainly run by functionaries of the BdV and individual Landsmannschaften), sparked a major crisis in German-Polish relations after the EU enlargement of 2004. In Germany, too, the tone and content of Steinbach's demands met with disapproval. In 2005 the German Bishops' Conference criticized the recent "demon of settling accounts," whereupon Steinbach accused this Catholic organization's chair, Cardinal Lehmann, of "outrageous remarks and lies." (She had already left the Lutheran Church because of ideological differences.) Steinbach then managed to convince the first Grand Coalition government led by Chancellor Angela Merkel (2005–2009) to decide in favor of establishing a "Memorial and Documentation Center for Flight and Expulsion" under the aegis of the BdV in Berlin.[81] There were repeated squabbles surrounding this center, which was to be housed in the very center of Berlin, until the 2016 appointment of a new director, not tied to the BdV, who steered the project onto calmer waters.

Merkel's concessions to Steinbach did not pay off politically. At the beginning of 2017 the rebellious member of parliament left the CDU and its parliamentary caucus in protest against the chancellor's refugee policy. In her resignation note withdrawing from the party, Steinbach linked the Middle East refugees, whom she designated as migrants, with terrorism and claimed that their mass admission amounted to opening the floodgates to asylum fraud.[82] This lack of empathy may perhaps be explained by her own biography, since Steinbach was a professional expellee, and hardly an actual one.

Conflicts like those surrounding Erika Steinbach, the longtime president of the Federation of Expellees (BdV) in Germany, highlight how troublesome the political integration of the expellees' lobbying organizations has been. In the early postwar years their involvement in government work was advantageous to the consolidation of West German democracy. On this basis the expellees' lobby succeeded in getting the Equalization of Burdens law passed, which had a favorable impact, in turn, on the professional integration of expellees and, by way of scholarships, on their educational opportunities. But gaining political recognition did not lead the lobby to adopt a constructive attitude toward Ostpolitik (West Germany's policy of détente with the Eastern Bloc) in the 1970s or toward the process of European unification after

1989.[83] Why this was so is explained by the profound traumatization numerous expellees experienced and by the self-radicalization that took place in the organizations representing them.

2.3 The case of Palestine

The refugee state Israel

While the Iron Curtain sealed the borders between East and West, the Pax Sovietica had the same effect on Eastern Europe. In 1948 a decade of mass flight and population removal came to an end. Yet if we look at Europe within a wider framework, that end was really a beginning. On the other side of the Mediterranean, a tragic history of displacements was just getting under way. In the British Mandate of Palestine, which required a significant troop commitment but generated little revenue (in India it was just the other way around), the Arab-Jewish conflict had been smoldering since the riots and pogroms of 1936. Although the Peel Commission's partition plan had been shelved in 1937, it remained an option.[84] Moreover, deadly terrorist attacks by the Jewish underground were demoralizing both the government in London and the army units stationed in Palestine. Britain therefore decided, as it had done before in India, to withdraw its army and leave management of the conflict to the newly created UN.

That this conflict was from the beginning configured bilaterally can also be attributed to colonial rule. "The Arabs," as the British classed them, were in fact a very diverse population, consisting of Muslims, Christians, smaller groups like the Druze, an educated urban middle class, peasants, and Bedouins. In the Jewish population there were Sephardic and some Oriental Jews, who soon came to be dominated by the Ashkenazim, recent immigrants from Central and Eastern Europe. In spite of these differences, the British government chose to define the population of Palestine according to linguistic criteria. There would be Jews and Arabs. This bilateral setup followed the imperial strategy of *divide et impera* (which also guided British policy in India, where colonial rulers grouped the population according to religion and pitted Hindus against Muslims). That the British colonial power dealt so differently with these two regions had less to do with previously existing ethnic differences than with European notions of society and nationhood. In 1947 a bare majority in the United Nations proposed partitioning Palestine into three regions: 1) an almost purely Arab region that would include the West Bank, a few adjoining municipalities in what would later be taken by Israel, parts of the Galilee, and Gaza; 2) a Jewish state on the coastal strip along the Mediterranean and in the Negev; and 3) a Jerusalem under international supervision. The different territories were connected only at a few junctures, so that military control over these links by Jewish or Palestinian

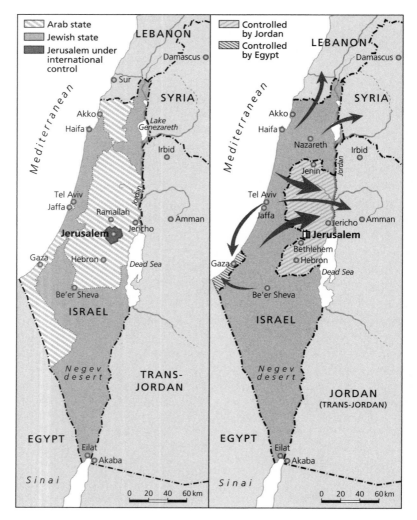

MAP 4. UN partition plan for Palestine (1947) and refugee movements related to the Israeli War of Independence (1948/49)

armed forces would determine the distribution of power in Palestine and over each partial state.

Upon the announcement of the partition plan, a wave of violence broke out, much like the one that erupted in India in 1947, and this ultimately segued into a civil war between Arabs and Jews. In the first phase of the war about 100,000 Arabs who had the necessary financial resources and lived in heavily contested places fled. By the summer of 1948 the number of refugees had risen to about 360,000 (see Map 4).[85] In the autumn and winter, their numbers doubled yet again. Initially this was related to the guerilla tactics of the Arab

Liberation Army (ALA), which gave the Israeli army a rationale for expelling the civilian population as well; this was later superseded by the deliberate seizure of land. David Ben-Gurion, the Polish-born founder of Israel, had already declared, before the outbreak of the war, that only a state with a clear Jewish majority was viable. (The current prime minister, Benjamin Netanyahu, seems to have a different opinion. In April 2019 he promised the annexation of the West Bank. If that were to happen under current conditions, it would turn the Israeli democracy into an ethnocracy.[86]) Ties to Europe also influenced the course of the war. At a critical moment the Jewish underground army received modern weapons from Czechoslovakia. There was an ideological background to this support in that the Eastern Bloc initially regarded the establishment of the Jewish state as an anti-colonial project, which it was in light of the conflict with Great Britain. But soon thereafter Stalin turned against Zionism and began to persecute Jews at home in the Soviet Union.

Idealizing a homogenous nation-state; employing a technical vocabulary that included terms like "partition," "transfer," and "population exchange"; harboring a collective suspicion of minorities; and a good portion of contempt for other people—these attitudes were consonant with those then current in Europe. From an Arab perspective, the mass immigration of European Jews amounted to a seizure of land by a colonizing power; indeed Jewish settlement in Palestine does share characteristics with other European settler colonies, such as Algeria. The chief difference was that the Jewish settlers had not arrived because of economic motives and as members of an expanding colonialist nation-state, but mainly as victims of persecution and as refugees. After the Holocaust, the foundation of a Jewish national state gained additional legitimacy and urgency.

The conflict over Palestine is therefore not conceivable solely as an Arab-Jewish or Near Eastern problem. European ideas and actors impacted the conflict in a variety of ways: because of the European legacy of colonial rule, the idea of a homogenous nation-state, movements of refugees, and especially because of the British army, which (as before in India) did little to counter the escalation of violence in Palestine. As the colonial masters withdrew, however, they did provide logistical support for the "transfer" (this term already appeared in the Peel Commission's 1937 recommendations) of Arabs and Jews with ships and trucks.[87] This brand of humanitarianism did perhaps save some lives, even as it simultaneously accelerated the expulsion of the Arabs.

The neighboring Arab states' assault on the tiny new state of Israel in May 1948 seemed to confirm Ben-Gurion's fears about the Palestinians as a fifth column of the enemy. Special units of the Israeli army expanded their ethnic cleansing efforts from the coastal region to Galilee, and began implementing them systematically, from village to village and neighborhood to neighborhood. The military's orders were clear: "In case of resistance, the armed forces must be wiped out and the population expelled outside the borders of the state."[88] Responsibility for the policy was assumed by a "Transfer Committee" in the Israeli government, which stipulated that none of the refugees were to return. There were, however, local exceptions, especially for Christian Palestinians, the Druze, and certain clans that had taken Israel's side. When the war ended in 1948 with a wholesale victory for the Israeli army, about 700,000 to 800,000 Palestinians were in flight. Compared to population shifts in India or Eastern Europe this was not a large number. But one has to consider this figure relative to the total population, for at the time only about 650,000 Jews were living in Israel. Moreover, this inflow of Arab refugees was a burden that was hard to manage for Israel's agrarian neighboring states. In Jordan after 1948, roughly every second inhabitant was a refugee, and in the Gaza Strip, which was annexed to Egypt after the ceasefire of 1949, 75,000 natives faced 200,000 refugees.

The Arab states retaliated in their own way. After 1948 and then in several waves following the Suez crisis of 1956 and the Six-Day War of 1967, around 800,000 Oriental Jews were expelled from the countries of the Near East and North Africa.[89] These refugees were fortunate, however, to have Israel as an exit option: a state resolutely defining itself as the homeland for all Jews everywhere, and therefore willing to accept and integrate them. In contrast to Jewish DPs, who often had to hold out in camps for years, the classic factors of "push" and "pull" used in migration research here interlocked. It was also helpful that not all Oriental Jews were expelled at one fell swoop, as happened with the Palestinians in 1948–49, but were instead driven out over a period of more than twenty years. To this extent the catchword "refugee state" has a double meaning in the case of Israel: on the one hand, it was a place where refugees from Europe, the Mediterranean, and the Near East were settled; on the other hand, it was a state that caused mass flight.

The Oriental Jews settled in places where refugees looking for shelter are often stranded, in the abandoned houses of other refugees. As Yfaat Weiss shows in a sensitive portrayal of the traditionally Arab neighborhood of Wadi Salib in Haifa, similar stories could be written about Jaffa (today a suburb of Tel Aviv), Tiberias, and other cities.[90] The former Arab neighborhoods with their winding alleys and mostly small houses were not prime real estate in newly founded Israel, certainly not compared with the bright Bauhaus-influenced districts newly built in the 1920s and 1930s.

Researchers studying the integration of refugees in Germany mostly focused on questions of social and cultural cohesion.[91] In Israel this was not the main issue. At the top of the social pyramid were the Zionists whose origins lay in Europe and who had already immigrated before the Second World War and formed the elite in government and the economy. Ranked just behind them were the Ashkenazim who arrived later, many having survived the Holocaust and endured internment in DP camps. Next were the Sephardim from Southeastern Europe and Asia Minor, followed in last place by the Oriental

Jews. In an unpleasant way, the latter reminded all the others, who still re-garded themselves as European, where it was in the world that Eretz Israel was located.[92] Centuries of living side by side with Arabs in the Ottoman Em-pire and its successor states, in Morocco and in Iran, had shaped the customs of the Oriental Jews, who struck the Ashkenazim as alien and, judged by the paradigm of civilization they had brought with them from Europe, back-ward.[93] These sharp contrasts have continued to shape Israel to this day, so-cially and politically.

The Israeli state, however, has made every effort to minimize the differences between its citizens. At the ideological level this happened through Zionism, which the Eastern Bloc countries demonized as right-wing nationalism after the state of Israel was established (an entire book could be written about the left-wing antisemitism underlying this stance), even though Israeli's found-ing nationalism was actually rather more socialist in character, as the kibbutz movement made apparent. In accordance with Israel's self-image as the home-land for all Jews, new arrivals were immediately granted citizenship, even though that was not necessarily in line with Jewish law in its orthodox inter-pretation. Traditionally, Judaism is defined matrilineally, and yet arrivals with a Jewish father and a non-Jewish mother became citizens on an equal foot-ing.[94] (This pairing of a non-Jewish wife with a Jewish husband was common among post-Soviet Jews, and it was also far from rare in the immediate post-war period, because more men than women had survived the Holocaust.)

Integration was advanced through the allocation of real estate and land that became available owing to the flight and expulsion of the Palestinians. This had obvious benefits for labor market integration, for it provided a source of livelihood. There was in fact a kind of work requirement for arrivals. Unem-ployment in the two decades after Israel's founding was not an issue, just as it was not in Europe. Furthermore, the state provided good instruction in modern Hebrew as a way of bridging cultural divides, and all arrivals had to pass a civics education course.

Israel, then, was the epitome of a refugee state; this is true even if one views the dedicated Zionists of the interwar period as voluntary migrants (and there are, as already mentioned, weighty arguments against this view). By 1951 ref-ugees and expellees from Europe, the Near East, and the Maghreb formed a majority of the population. In spite of the diverse backgrounds and traditions of the arrivals, a society emerged that had a pronounced national conscious-ness and a common will to defend the state and its territory to the utmost. The threat from abroad certainly contributed to this determination, since Is-rael had to wage three wars in 1948, 1967, and 1973, and in each of them it was not mere victory or defeat but the state's very existence that was at stake. A greater problem of integration than the aforementioned class differences or the marginalization of the Oriental Jews lay in the different ways Judaism as a religion had been interpreted. To this day the ultra-Orthodox enjoy a special status. They are not required to serve in the army, and are largely free to opt out of the labor market. How great a challenge this will pose over the long run, and at what cost, remains to be seen.

The success or failure of integration remains an open question as well for the Arab minority that was allowed to remain in 1948, and whose share of the population has since doubled to about a fifth of the Israeli total. The 1.6 million Arab Israelis of today can elect political representatives to a democratically constituted parliament and they do enjoy, in spite of their social and economic marginalization, a much higher standard of living than the population of all the neighboring states. That does not automatically turn them into loyal citizens of the state, however, even though there are no demonstrations of joy among Israeli Arabs, as there are in the Gaza Strip, when a terrorist manages every now and then to murder a Jew.

The refusal to integrate the Palestinians

In 1948–49 more than 80 percent of the Arabs in Israel had either been expelled or had fled on their own initiative.[95] Before 1948, presumably, few Arab inhabitants of Palestine would have been able to draw the Mandate territory on a map, and he or she would not necessarily have identified with a nation going by this name. Far away from the homeland, however, a Palestinian national consciousness spread and solidified. This was made possible by the very experience of flight and expulsion, and by the politics of the states that took in the Palestinian refugees.

Owing to its geographic location, Jordan was the country most affected; almost 80 percent of the refugees ended up there. They made up about half the nation's population, and significantly more in the relatively fertile West Bank. After the war of 1948 this region fell to Jordan, for whom the establishment of the Jewish state came in handy inasmuch as Jordan also profited from the partition of Palestine. Using both Arab and Jewish sources, the Israeli historian Avi Shlaim has meticulously assessed this community of interest between the Hashemite dynasty and the Israeli government.[96]

Owing to the massive number of refugees, integration was an imperative in Jordan. King Abdullah therefore conferred Jordanian citizenship collectively on Palestinian refugees in 1949, something that no other host country has done. This legal integration included work permits, passports, access to schools, and equality in other areas. Professional and social integration progressed less rapidly, since the Palestinians were mostly housed in camps, some of which still exist today. The basic problem was Jordan's low level of economic development. Settling refugees in rural areas was not possible on a large scale as land suitable for farming and grazing was in short supply. Over time, therefore, many camps turned into permanent settlements if the refugees did not immediately move to the outskirts of the major cities where they could find employment.

The legal inclusion of the Palestinians went hand in hand with a strict suppression of their Palestinian identity. In 1950 King Abdullah even decreed a ban on using the word "Palestinian" in official documents; this recalls the censorship of the terms "refugee" and "expellees" in the GDR, and is analogous to restrictions on usage in other Eastern Bloc states.[97] The Jordanian monarchy was not, however, an all-encompassing dictatorship, and aspirations for political emancipation could only be held in check for a limited time. The 1960s were the great era of anticolonial, Marxist-oriented liberation movements. Keeping in step with the times, the Palestine Liberation Organization (PLO) was founded in Cairo in 1964. The organization had an especially large number of adherents in Jordan and acted increasingly like a state within a state. It called for armed struggle against Israel and the annihilation of the Zionist state.

A more constructive approach to refugees was pursued by the Arab League in 1965 with the Casablanca Protocol, which urged its member states to grant the Palestinians free access to their labor markets and freedom of settlement. This happened fully sixteen years after the war of 1948, and without the establishment of the PLO and the self-organization of the refugees it would probably have taken even longer. Unfortunately, only in Syria did the agreement bring any concrete improvement; Lebanon and Egypt did not adhere to their own resolutions, whose implementation had been left open by the Protocol. Two years later Israel's neighboring states opted for military force again. Egypt placed several army divisions at the border on the Sinai peninsula and blocked access to the Red Sea, Syria marched onto the Golan Heights and shelled nearby kibbutzim from the hills, while Jordan hesitated to participate in these military operations. Israel, however, had anticipated the looming invasion by undertaking a preventive strike. Within six days (hence the war's name), in June 1967, the Egyptian, Syrian, and Jordanian armies were soundly defeated. This ended the dream of return for Palestinian refugees. And beyond that disappointment it added an additional 300,000 people expelled as a result of the war.

His defeat in the Six-Day War in large part relieved Abdullah's successor Hussein of his refugee problem, since Israel now occupied the West Bank. The military defeat, however, weakened the legitimacy of the monarchy and shifted the attention of the Palestinians to their situation in Jordan. In September 1970, the PLO attempted a coup, brought refugee camps and several cities under its control, and even undertook an assassination attempt on the king. The effort to transform Jordan into a Palestinian-dominated state failed, however. Hussein proclaimed martial law, suppressed the rebellion, and the PLO leadership was expelled along with around five thousand fighters.

After the revolt, King Hussein became even more determined to establish a social balance, though unavoidably limited by his country's poverty. One long-term consequence was that Jordan abandoned attempts to win back the West Bank. Hussein renounced this claim in 1988 when, in the aftermath of the first intifada, he abandoned Jordanian territorial demands in favor of a future Palestinian state. This was simultaneously linked to stronger protection of the border in the Jordan Valley. In the Washington Declaration of 1994, finally, the king recognized the existence of Israel. This recognition and the renunciation of the West Bank rested on Hussein's astute insight that Jordan, as the region's poorest state, had enough problems with the refugees already living there. His son and successor Abdullah II continued this policy and married a woman of Palestinian origin—an important symbolic act of integration. For Hamas and other radical groups, the monarchy's policy of peacefully settling differences at home and abroad constituted a betrayal, but so far Jordan has proved stable in spite (or perhaps because) of the wars in neighboring Syria and Iraq.

Jordanian policy toward the Palestinians may be contrasted with the refusal to integrate that characterized Lebanon, the second most important host country. The roughly 100,000 refugees who arrived in 1948 (in the meantime, vigorous population growth has raised their numbers to over 400,000) were not given citizenship in the decades to follow, nor were they granted any freedom of settlement, general work permits, or access to public schools.[98] For many years they could leave Lebanon only at the risk of being prevented from returning. In principle Lebanese refugee camps functioned like reservations, where Palestinians were held until they could return to their old homeland, no matter how long that might take. At the same time, like Syria and Egypt, Lebanon's government pointed the finger of guilt at its archenemy Israel, which it would have preferred to wipe off the map.

What explains this refusal to integrate? Here the history of Lebanon is of fundamental interest, because it makes plain the fact that integration can only function if there is a political and social aim behind it. The relevant question "Whither integration?" is also of central importance for today's Western societies. In purely economic terms, preconditions for integrating the Palestinians were favorable in 1948, since Lebanon was relatively prosperous; until the outbreak of the civil war in 1974, it was regarded as the "Switzerland of the Near East."[99] Moreover, the regions from which the refugees came (most were from the Galilee and Haifa) were geographically so close to Lebanon that there were very few differences between the Arab dialects and culture on the two sides of the border.

As a state, however, Lebanon did not function like Switzerland. Its political structure was (and still is) based on a complicated system of proportional representation and consociational power-sharing between different religious and ethnic groups.[100] According to the "National Pact" of 1943, Christian Maronites picked the president, Sunnis the premier, Shiites the parliamentary president, and the smaller group of Druze a few cabinet ministers. Parliamentary seats were also distributed according to proportional allotment based on religious and denominational criteria. (Here there are parallels to the late

Since refugee status among Palestinians is inheritable, Jordanian **Queen Rania** also counts as a refugee. The queen, frequently celebrated in the tabloid press of the West, was born in 1970 in Kuwait as Rania Faisal Yasin; her parents came from the West Bank, which they had to leave after the Six-Day War.[101] The father settled in Kuwait as a physician. His income allowed him to send his daughter to the New English School there, and then to the American University in Cairo. She could not study at a state university, because Egypt at the time excluded Palestinians from subjects like medicine, economics, political science, and journalism and, on top of that, demanded large tuition fees.[102] After the First Gulf War the Yasin family and 150,000 other Palestinians were expelled from Kuwait and went to the Jordanian capital Amman. There Rania, who obtained a business administration degree in 1991, worked in finance and marketing. Soon thereafter she became acquainted with Prince Abdullah, and in 1993 the couple married. In 1999 Abdullah ascended to the Jordanian throne upon the death of King Hussein.

At home and abroad, Queen Rania made a name for herself through her engagement on behalf of schools and hospitals, and, since the start of the civil war in Syria, through her advocacy for refugees. In the United States she became known above all through her children's book *The Sandwich Swap*, which she published in 2010 with two women as co-author and illustrator. The book deals with the conflict between two girls from different backgrounds, one of whom likes peanut butter and jelly sandwiches, while the other (whose parents come from the Near East) prefers hummus and pita. The food fight and the whole multicultural story have a happy ending, but that was not true of the attempt to translate the book into Hebrew. According to the Israeli newspaper *Haaretz*, Queen Rania rejected all offers from Israel to publish *The Sandwich Swap* there.[103]

In 2016 she visited a refugee camp on the Greek island of Lesbos and subsequently declared: "Refugees are not numbers. They are human beings like you and I, except they have seen unspeakable horror and have experienced unthinkable tragedy and hardship. They risked everything, their families, their possessions just to make it to safety. We need to bring humanity and compassion back into the narrative, because this crisis is about people not borders and barriers. It's about human dignity not deals."[104] She was apparently referring to the agreement between the EU and Turkey to repatriate and take in refugees (more on this in Chapter 4.2).

Habsburg Empire, which used similar methods in an effort to accommodate conflicting national claims; for example, by using regional compromises known as *Ausgleich*.) In the first three postwar decades this guaranteed a Christian majority in Parliament, although other kinds of coalitions were often formed.

This consociational system of power-sharing, which also applied to the executive branch, served in addition as the vehicle for distributing government expenditures; hence the resulting allocation of funds maintained a clientelistic power structure. There was in Lebanon, therefore, no nation-state of citizens *into which* the Palestinians could have been integrated. Apart from the preferential treatment accorded to Christians, which went back to French colonial rule (France had unwillingly conceded independence to Lebanon in 1943), the fundamental problem of proportional representation and the consociational system was that it rested on the assumption that the population distribution and percentages would remain stable. As soon as the balance changed—through higher birthrates (highest for Lebanese Muslims), different migration patterns (Christians went abroad more frequently), or exogenous shocks (such as the flight of Palestinians into Lebanon)—the system got out of joint. By 1975 conflict surrounding the consociational system of power-sharing led to the Lebanese civil war, which only ended in 1989 with a compromise based on denominational parity.

The Palestinians who had fled to Lebanon suffered in particular from the civil war, and in a certain way they had also triggered it. This, in turn, was related to the denial of integration, although one group of refugees was exempted from this refusal: The Christian-dominated Lebanese government, in accordance with the logic of the consociational system, had seen to it that refugees were accommodated separately in different camps based on their religion. But in the 1950s up to 30,000 Christian Palestinians, who made up a good 20 percent of the refugees, were awarded citizenship. This increased the number of Lebanese Christians and, in line with the demographic formula for forming governments in Beirut, their power. The Sunnis, by contrast, showed greater indifference toward their co-religionists from Palestine.[105]

Pan-Arabism did not function as a vehicle of integration, either, although this ideology was deliberately promoted by Egypt and Syria. In 1958 both countries even joined together in an explicitly Pan-Arab confederation (the United Arab Republic, which held together until 1961). This placed the Palestinians in the worst situation imaginable: because of their nationality they had been forced to flee their homeland, and yet—with the exception of Jordan—they never really arrived in another society. (To make the point in terms that are even more general, there was no national inclusion following upon their national exclusion. Their neighbors, the Jews, could have told them something about this based on their own history, but until the 1990s the relationship between these two military adversaries consisted of total speechlessness.)

Life without any prospects, poverty in the refugee camps, and the wealth gap between the refugees and natives were so unbearable that the Palestinians in Lebanon became even more radicalized than they had been in Jordan. The PLO again formed a state within a state and used the Lebanese refugee camps as a launching pad for guerilla actions and international terror attacks. Israel retaliated with massive bombings and a nearly two-decades-long occupation of southern Lebanese territory. In the end, it was possible to settle this bilateral conflict, although once again the resolution came at the expense of the Palestinians, who still had not become Lebanese citizens and were now forced to accept a variety of legal restrictions. To this day the Palestinians show up in the national and international statistics on Lebanon as a refugee population, even though they have been residing there for two or three generations, longer than the Syrians who began arriving in 2011.[106]

Egypt, one of the chief actors in the lost wars of 1948 and 1967, behaved similarly and, to this day, refuses to naturalize Palestinian refugees or grant them equal rights. At the same time, President Sadat disposed of a large part of his integration problem with the Camp David Accords in 1979, by leaving the formerly Egyptian Gaza Strip and its Palestinian population to Israel.[107] A good ten years after the peace settlement, the situation of the Palestinians remaining in Egypt worsened again, during the Gulf War of 1990–91, because they sided with Iraqi dictator Saddam Hussein, who promised to overturn the entire Near Eastern order and attack Israel. The United States, along with Saudi Arabia, intervened in favor of Kuwait, and Saddam lost the war. The Palestinians paid a hefty prize for the foreign policy of PLO head Yasser Arafat—who could have remained neutral. Kuwait expelled around 150,000 Palestinians workers, while another 250,000 who had fled from the Iraqi army were not allowed to return when the war ended.

The renewed and, this time, intra-Arab wave of expulsions following the Gulf War, together with the failure of the first intifada, contributed to Arafat's move away from violence. He engaged in the Oslo peace negotiations, which were also intended to find a definitive solution for the refugees. It was on this very point, however, that peace ultimately failed. Arafat insisted stubbornly on a "right of return" (to Israel, of course, not Kuwait), a notion that the Palestinians, owing to the daily misery and discrimination they experienced in their host countries, had been carrying around like a fetish.[108] Perhaps he needed to insist on the right of return in order to avoid violent conflicts between the increasingly fractious Palestinian militias.

At the beginning of the new century, Israel took a step in the direction of a two-state solution provided for in the Oslo Agreement. In 2005 the army withdrew unilaterally from the Gaza Strip, and Jewish settlers were forced to repatriate. This move was probably unavoidable as protection for the settlers' lives, since the Islamist Hamas, which had been gaining in influence since the 1990s, would not have tolerated a Jewish minority. The rest of this story reaches into the present; instead of using this opportunity for peaceful nation-building, Hamas repeatedly fired rockets into Israel from the Gaza Strip. Several times, in acts of retaliation and deterrence, Israel attacked the Gaza Strip and occupied parts of it. In this territory no bigger than 360 square kilometers (139 square miles) there now lived around 1.75 million people, instead of its original 75,000 inhabitants plus the 200,000 refugees who had arrived in 1948, almost all of them dependent on international assistance and food deliveries.

This leads us to the last important actor shaping refugee policy in the Near East, the UN or the international community. Because the partition plan for Palestine was drafted in the autumn of 1947 within a United Nations framework, the UN has felt responsible for the Palestinian refugees. In the tradition of the interwar period, at the end of 1949 a special agency was created for them, the United Nations Relief and Works Agency for Palestine Refugees in the Near East (UNRWA). As the long name indicates, this agency was meant to provide the Palestinians with the bare necessities and help them gain employment.

Originally there were large-scale plans to integrate the refugees through development projects, but later the agency's tasks were reduced to health and education assistance. Nonetheless, to this day UNRWA is the most personnel-intensive subdivision of the UN. It employs more than 28,000 people, many of them teachers. A major part of the Palestinian school system is maintained this way, and not without some small measure of success, since Palestinians are regarded in the Arab world as above-average in education attainment. Yet all these activities come at a price: the Palestinians are dependent on international donors. Since 1949 the US has been the largest sponsor, recently contributing about a fourth of UNRWA's budget. Without this support, the situation of the Palestinians would be even worse than it is, yet this external support also facilitated the refugees' host countries shirking their duties and the associated costs (which President Trump now uses as a pretext to reduce US funding for UNRWA).

Moreover, the social services provided by UNRWA affirm the Palestinians' refugee status, which is based on the notion that refugee status is inheritable. The world is now watching the fourth generation since the Nakba (the Arabic term for the catastrophe of 1948) grow up, but the UN still defines the recipients of its funds and services as refugees. One special passage in UNRWA documents even applies this status to Palestinians who have already received citizenship from host countries. The UN agency thus contributes to perpetuating a condition that, according to the Geneva Refugee Convention of 1951, should be temporary.

UNRWA, however, was not integrated into the UNHCR, established two years later. Initially, this was advantageous to the Palestinians, since they had their own refugee organization (UNRWA) responsible for them and better equipped financially than the UNHCR. Later this turned into a disadvantage, for it meant that the UNHCR was unable to exert any pressure on states hosting Palestinians to respect at least elementary refugee and human rights. Moreover, the regionalization of refugee welfare for the Palestinians ruled out any solution that might have enabled Palestinian refugees to move on to other countries, the kind of forwarding that has done much toward defusing and solving the problems of displaced persons in a variety of other postwar situations. For as many as 700,000 Palestinians, an international resettlement action could certainly have been managed. But it was blocked because, on the one hand, the Arab League states behaved with little solidarity for such a long time. And, on the other hand, because the expellees themselves wanted to remain close to their old homeland and insisted strictly on their right of return (a demand that rests on very shaky grounds in international law).[109] Invariably, a one-sided sense of victimhood is politically unproductive for refugees, and in the case of the Palestinians it was also abused to justify violence. In the end, the bare figures speak clearest when it comes to the failure of international and Arab refugee policy: today, owing to population growth, UNRWA is no longer responsible for 652,000 refugees, the number when the agency was founded, but for more than five million.

This exponential increase in the size of the problem shows that internationalism cannot substitute for nation-states as actors in refugee policy. The tragic history of the Palestinians also proves that a challenge as formidable as the legal, occupational, and everyday integration of a large refugee population can succeed only if host states make this a priority of the first order.

The turn to human rights

All the same, the hardship refugees faced in Europe and its adjoining regions toward the end of the 1940s did, to some degree, change the thinking about how to deal with flight on a massive scale. This rethinking began as early as 1946, in part because the problem was overtaxing the occupying powers. The Allies began to doubt whether forcible population shifts were really achieving their desired aim of stabilizing nation-states and protecting international peace. If the refugees were not to starve, the occupying powers would have to organize at least some basic care—a daily ration of food, clothing, accommodation and heating in the winter. All this was costly. In addition, it now dawned on the United States and Great Britain that political risks were involved. What would happen if the impoverished masses of refugees were to create unrest and back the Communists? As the scenario of the Greek civil war showed, this concern was not unfounded.

The governments in the Eastern Bloc, on the other hand, had a simple remedy available to them: the Communists confiscated the land belonging to big landowners and awarded their houses, apartments, businesses, and farms to those in need. In the West, where there was a commitment to fundamental democratic rights and the rule of law, which included protections for private property, confiscation in this manner was not possible. Other measures had to be taken to accommodate refugees and enable them to start a new life.

Moreover, there started to emerge, albeit hesitatingly, a moral disassociation from radical nationalism and the ethnic cleansing it unleashed. The West rediscovered human rights, the same rights that had been largely ignored in the reorganization of Europe at Yalta and Potsdam. This shift in opinion was initiated toward the end of 1945 by British and American journalists and intellectuals reporting from occupied postwar Germany. They denounced the mass misery and inhumane treatment of refugees in Poland and Czechoslovakia.[110] In the summer of 1946, the American secretary of state James F. Byrnes added his voice to theirs. With an eye toward the still pending peace treaty, he even called into question the postwar borders recently negotiated. The latter challenge was intended mostly as a warning to Poland and Czechoslovakia, but it was clear that American and British occupation authorities no longer wanted to remain silent while refugees were arriving from the East ragged, starving, and sick. This had less to do with compassion for the Germans, however, than with the difficulties of coping with this mass misery. In cooperation with German state and local authorities, the occupiers had to organize emergency medical care, laboriously nurse the refugees back to health, clothe them again, and put a roof over their heads.

In the gathering "Cold War," a term that Winston Churchill and the American columnist Walter Lippman brought into general use in 1946, human rights became an essential point of reference because they exposed a flagrant weakness in both the Soviet Union and its client states, the so-called people's democracies. More important, however, than any moral reservations about mass expulsions were the pragmatic considerations already mentioned, practical reasons that convinced even Stalin to spare Hungary (as he had not done for Germany) and stem the waves of refugees inundating the Danube region. De facto, the minor peace treaties concluded between Hungary and its neighbors in 1946–47 (see the discussion about them in the earlier section 2.2) also curtailed this population removal.

This move away from large-scale ethnic cleansing was also a salient feature of the conflict over Palestine. This may be discerned above all from what was *not* said in public. While Stalin, Polish Workers Party General Secretary Gomułka, and even democratic politicians like Czechoslovakian president Edvard Beneš were explicit in 1945 that they favored expelling national minorities, and that the personal suffering of those affected counted for nothing with them, the relevant discussions and resolutions of the Israeli government took place behind closed doors. Apparently, in 1948, the young state's leading elite did not want to say openly how they were thinking of proceeding against minorities. In South Asia, too, the page was turning. As of 1948, the founders of India and Pakistan started to dam the tide of refugees, moving away from the idea of homogenous nation-states and acting energetically against violent nationalists.

The Universal Declaration of Human Rights that was added to the UN Charter in December 1948 confirmed this humanitarian turn, though of course the document was no longer of any help to refugees of years gone by. The Genocide Convention, adopted almost simultaneously by the UN General Assembly, pointed in a similar direction and was meant to prevent a repetition of the Nazi persecution and the extermination of Europe's Jews.[111] It was, admittedly, not until the 1990s and the war in the former Yugoslavia that the Genocide Convention was used to protect refugees. But, in principle, the UN had already formulated the concept of genocide so broadly in 1948 that the international community could well have acted earlier against those responsible for causing mass flight. In the course of the postwar period, after all, the Holocaust became a benchmark for measuring all other crimes against humanity, and an admonition that it should never happen again. This required distancing oneself, at least verbally, from National Socialist persecution. The mass removal of populations and mass flight were, thus, not acceptable any more.

The passage of the UN Refugee Convention, along with the almost simultaneous establishment of the UNHCR, were drawn-out affairs compared with negotiations over accords. The delay had to do with the lines of conflict created by the Cold War and the skeptical attitude of the Eastern Bloc countries. Stalin and his allies refused to concede any kind of privileged status and special rights abroad to its citizens fleeing Communism, since they viewed these refugees as traitors and in fact persecuted them. In 1951, just after the start of the Korean War, a compromise was reached, although with the restrictions previously mentioned. The UN Refugee Convention was to remain valid for a limited period only and would apply only to Europe. It would exceed the scope of this book to cover the subsequent development of international refugee law, but the supplementary Protocol of 1967 deserves another mention. In principle, it expanded the UNHCR's radius of action to the entire world. This cannot be counted as a universal success for the UN or UNHCR, however, since to this day numerous states (especially in the Arab world) have not ratified the convention. Moreover, the UNHCR can only provide emergency assistance; there are no funds for more far-reaching measures supporting integration.

As the case of Syria since 2011 shows, even less has been done in the way of flight prevention. Russia in particular has boycotted almost all the measures proposed in the UN Security Council, with the result that only those ceasefires were permitted that served the Syrian regime under Bashar al-Assad. At the same time, the bombing war has been so brutal that the civilian population in the battle zones has hardly any choice but to run away. In spite of its role as a warring party, however, Russia is not taking in any refugees, but is leaving this to Syria's neighboring states and the EU, where Putin is simultaneously supporting right-wing populist parties that agitate against the absorption of refugees. If this irresponsibility catches on, we can expect terrible times to dawn again for refugees.[112] For there will always be more refugees (perhaps soon from Ukraine) and ever fewer states ready to take them in.

As the more detailed analysis of politically motivated flight in Chapter Three will show, the turn toward human rights in the late 1940s depended on very specific circumstances. Perhaps the so-called refugee crisis and the worldwide advance of right-wing nationalism is now bringing this era to an end.

2.4 Postcolonial flight and remigration

As the situation in Europe gradually calmed after 1948, the decolonization of Africa and Asia produced new waves of refugees. This was particularly true in the Mediterranean region, especially for Algeria and Palestine. Only a few months after the French defeat in the Indochina war, a war of independence broke out in Algeria. Inspired by Ho Chi Minh's success in Vietnam, the Front de Libération Nationale (FLN) waged war using guerilla tactics and deliberate terrorist attacks. The French army reacted by sending more than half a million soldiers to Algeria, shelling villages and urban neighborhoods in which rebels were suspected to be lurking, and with daily acts of repression. About 200,000 Algerians fled to the neighboring countries of Morocco and Tunisia, and another two million people fled to safer ground inside Algeria. While at first the war had tended to affect Muslim Algerians and out-of-the-way regions, over time the battles shifted more and more toward the coasts and the cities where Europeans, or people who defined themselves as such, lived. After eight years of war involving heavy losses and a coup attempt by right-wing officers, France inevitably realized that even this colony, which had a special status because it had been settled by the French and incorporated into the motherland, could no longer be held. In 1962 Paris accepted Algeria's independence, and more than 800,000 people were subsequently transported across the Mediterranean to France.[113]

To characterize this action the French government used the term "repatriation" (*rapatriement*). This allowed France to gloss over its military and political defeat, and it was also intended to facilitate the refugees' fresh start in their putative fatherland. It is no coincidence that there are similarities with the terminology here and that used in postwar Poland, where the euphemistic term *repatriacja* also served to make the loss of contested regions in the East palatable to the people. Algeria was not a colony like France's other overseas and sub-Saharan African territories. Administratively, the three Algerian *départements* were just as much a part of France as Alsace, Roussillon, and other borderlands. So, strictly speaking, the term "repatriation" was men-

UNHCR
The UN Refugee Agency

In view of all the terrible news for refugees over the past several years, the choice of Antonio Guterres as the new UN General Secretary was at least something of a positive sign. With this election in 2017, a former director of the **UNHCR**, the agency this Portuguese diplomat had run between 2005 and 2015, rose to become head of the United Nations. One may assume that this former Socialist prime minister of Portugal would advocate strongly for the interests of refugees. In the following profile we depart from the other analytical portraits in these insets, all of which highlight individual actors, because nothing embodies international refugee policy so much as this organization, the UNHCR. Its establishment in December 1950, just five months after the start of the Korean War, was close to a political miracle. It only happened because the tasks assigned to the UNHCR were at the time restricted to relieving suffering that resulted from mass flight during the Second World War, which preceded the organization's establishment, and caring for the remaining displaced persons. That is why the Soviet Union, after a long period of resistance, agreed to the founding of the UNHCR, even though it was clear that the grounds for persecution enumerated in the Refugee Convention could be utilized for making charges aimed against the Eastern Bloc. When it came to discrimination and persecution on racist grounds, however, neither the US nor the European colonial powers of that time could boast of clean hands, so the Convention provided for a kind of equilibrium between East and West at the level of human rights.

The UNHCR was confronted with its first major task just a few years later, in 1956, when it oversaw provisions for refugees from Hungary and arranged for their international resettlement. It also acted successfully as a mediator between West and East by, for example, managing the repatriation of minors who had spontaneously fled Hungary during the failed uprising.[114] The activities of the UNHCR were initially limited to Europe, thus adding a spatial limitation to the temporal restriction on its activities. Both the Palestinians and the refugees from the Korean War were supervised by independent UN sub-organizations, the UNRWA in the Middle East and the UNKRA in Korea. This was within the tradition of the interwar era, when the League of Nations appointed a special high commissioner dedicated to each of the major refugee groups.

In 1957 the UNHCR, which was headquartered in Geneva, expanded its radius of action across the Mediterranean when the Tunisian government asked for help in caring for refugees from the Algerian War. According to the supplementary protocol of 1967, the UNHCR's reach included refugees worldwide. But, owing to scarce resources, only emergency care could be financed. There

(cont.)

(cont.)

was no funding for measures aimed at permanent integration measures as originally envisioned. In any event, the Western countries who were the UNHCR's major donors were pursuing different aims; starting in the mid-1970s, they became increasingly concerned with stopping transcontinental movements of refugees.[115]

Since the end of the East-West conflict, the UNHCR has been increasingly concerned with war victims, as between 1992 and 1995 in Bosnia and Herzegovina. On a global scale, it has emphasized repatriation much more than it did during the Cold War. That is a legitimate and important goal, since refugees usually do wish to return to their old homelands; at least, that is what most of them want during their first years living abroad. But international policy makers should be aware that the very idea of repatriation depends on the notion that there is a "patria," which might not be the case after ethnic cleansing and the ravages of war. Sending refugees back to their former homelands also necessitates higher investment in former conflict zones.

In the last several decades, the UNHCR has increasingly taken care of "internally displaced persons" (IDPs for short), even though there are still no regulations for their protection beyond a general compliance with human rights. This, however, is the fault of the UN's member states, which have failed to grant the UNHCR more power to intervene within states. The UNHCR has, at the same time, neglected traditional areas of responsibility, such as investing in the permanent integration of refugees in the countries where they are exiled.[116] It should not be forgotten that the Geneva Refugee Convention contains a farsighted solution for reducing the global number of refugees: As soon as they are granted citizenship in the countries admitting them, they cease to be counted as refugees. This changes the status of refugee from permanent to ephemeral.

dacious, because the *patria* of the pieds-noirs lay on the other side of the Mediterranean.

Nonetheless, the state used this term to express its special sense of responsibility for the refugees arriving in l'Hexagone (metropolitan France). This had a positive influence on the course of the refugees' flight. The transports by ship across the Mediterranean were well organized, as were subsequent phases like the refugees' arrival in Marseille, their transfer to other locations, and their integration into France. Yet, as in other cases where a majority of the population senses that the terminology employed by the state is not entirely correct, a counter-discourse arose. This manifested itself not least in the unflattering label "pieds-noirs," which alludes to the arrivals' African home continent, their physique, and their feet.[117] In political terms, above all, the pieds-noirs had anything but an easy time. They were collectively under suspicion of having a right-wing radical and colonialist disposition, owing, among other reasons, to the coup attempt by the OAS, the Organisation de l'Armée Secrète. Similarly, Polish repatriates in the People's Republic of Poland were stuck with a reputation as reactionary die-hards still lamenting the loss of interwar Poland and the feudal order in the Kresy (the eastern territories in Lithuania, Belarus, and Ukraine that were once part of the early modern Polish commonwealth), as well as of cultural centers like Lwów (Lemberg in German, Ukrainian L'viv).

There is hardly any controversy today about how to evaluate the Algerian War in political terms; it was about colonial rule and an ensuing war of liberation. Yet the exodus of the Algerian French (all in all, more than a million people left the country) exhibited features of ethno-nationalist cleansing. While the FLN was officially secular, it also invoked Islam. Christians and Jews, including even Sephardim who had once fled Spain, were regarded as French and therefore as enemies. This exclusion and the attendant inclusion of different ethnic groups matched the pattern of nation-state formation in Europe, where in specific countries denominational criteria were also important for determining who could be a member of the nation and who not.

In general, European empires and colonial powers produced ethnically oriented national movements. This happened for a simple reason rooted in anti-imperialist and anti-colonial national movements. The oppressed nations were anxious not only to distinguish themselves from the ruling dynasty (and its elite) to which they were opposed, but also from "foreign domination" understood more broadly. In each case, accordingly, the issue was liberation from "the" Russians, "the" Turks, "the" Germans, and in Algeria from "the" French. Nevertheless, "colonial" and "imperial" are terms that cannot be used interchangeably as some continental European empires, the Habsburg monarchy for example, were imperial formations, but not colonialist ones. Colonialism rested on a differentiation among population groups that the authorities defined by racist criteria; this did not exist either in the Habsburg Empire, the Russian Empire, or vis-à-vis the Poles in the German Kaiserreich. This does not mean that the nationalism of non-colonial imperial nations was free of racism: the Germans did look down on the Poles as much as the Russians did on the inhabitants of Central Asia. But there was never, for example, any ban on mixed marriages as there was in colonial Africa or Asia.

The ethno-nationalist cleansing of Algeria did not conform entirely to the continental European pattern, since the FLN cracked down especially hard on the so-called Harkis, the roughly 180,000-strong Algerian auxiliary troops of the French army. This dimension of the conflict more closely resembled a civil war than an anticolonial liberation struggle. Persecution of the Harkis and, accordingly, their motive for flight was based on political retaliation, not on nationalism. Once the war had ended, the Muslim soldiers serving the French fell between the cracks no matter where they were. In

Algeria they were exposed to revenge by the FLN, and in France no one wanted them because there they were regarded as Algerians. Ultimately, about 90,000 Harkis (as many as 150,000 when family members were included) managed to get to France, often helped by former army comrades. The Harkis quite clearly presented a case of flight on account of immediate danger to life and limb, and they were accordingly regarded as "refugees" by the French authorities (in some respects comparable to the Afghani translators and other staff who assisted the NATO mission in Afghanistan, and were left with nothing in 2014 after most of the Western troops were withdrawn).[118] The motives and experiences of the Algerian French were different from those of the Harkis and depended on the time and place of their departure. A small share of them had been directly exposed to the war and already had several stages of flight behind them, while the larger share left Algeria after independence because there were hardly any prospects for their future in an independent Algeria. This push factor also was at work in cases of decolonization where no brutal war was involved as in Algeria.

France launched comprehensive aid programs for the refugees from Algeria. On their arrival they received immediate assistance for travel costs and relocation inside France, special support in searching for employment, and help with retraining and in their first year on the job; in addition, there were housing construction programs with special quotas for the "repatriés."[119] All this does not of course mean that the local population welcomed the pieds-noirs. Often they felt abandoned and rejected, much like the German refugees who arrived from Eastern Europe in the early postwar years.[120] An additional measure, which could be compared to West Germany's equalization of burdens for expellees, was the set of restitution payments for land left behind, funds the Algerian French could use to replace their lost agricultural property. Overall, between 1962 and 1970, the French state spent more than 16 billion francs for these integration programs, a gigantic sum at the time (in today's purchasing power it corresponds to around 17 billion euros, a sum one must also measure against the scope of public spending at the time.)[121] The pieds-noirs were thus, like the postwar German expellees (or the Salzburg Protestants and Huguenots a good two centuries earlier), "privileged refugees." These large government expenditures paid off. From an economic perspective, the French from Algeria integrated rapidly. As early as their first generation, there was no longer any appreciable lag behind the native population, although neither the children of the refugees nor the "Metropolitan" French should be seen, of course, as a single homogeneous entity.

Equally beneficial was the economic upswing of the first three postwar decades. Although a total of two million people came to France from its lost colonies,[122] they were absorbed by the labor market in much the same way as guest workers from Spain and Portugal. Immigrants from the Maghreb and sub-Saharan Africa, however, usually had to make do with simple jobs, in trade, on factory assembly lines, or as workers in construction, with women frequently working as cleaning ladies.

These jobs, with the exception of the industrial ones, were badly paid and highly susceptible to fluctuations in the business cycle. This meant that the inexorable rise of unemployment, in the aftermath of the first oil crisis and during the 1980s, hit postcolonial immigrants especially hard, for they, in contrast to the pieds-noirs, did not receive any special support from the state. The same was true for the guest workers in Germany who, in contrast to the expellees, did not receive integration assistance. Instead, they were offered financial assistance in 1983's remigration program to help them leave the country. To this day, many of the problems in the French banlieues and in some troubled neighborhoods in Berlin, Hamburg, Duisburg, and other major German cities go back to the formation of a new kind of class society based heavily on one's country of origin. Owing to high unemployment and a lack of prospects for the second and third generations, this can correctly be characterized as social disintegration.

In an article for the journal *Annales* a good ten years ago—that is, well before the great financial crisis of 2008–9—the sociologist Dominique Schnapper postulated a phenomenon she called "downward assimilation" to describe the trajectory of French immigrants from the Maghreb and sub-Saharan Africa.[123] Concretely, this means a marginal existence in society without opportunities for regular employment. Incomes, accordingly, are low, which also means that it is hard to find a wife and start a family. Injured male pride and a lack of economic prospects become breeding grounds for radical Islamists. It is from this milieu (and not from the circles of actual refugees fleeing Syria and Iraq) that the terrorists came who perpetrated the murderous attacks of 2015 and 2016 in France.

When it comes to the pieds-noirs, there are fewer social problems than political ones. To this day, the municipalities and regions in which the refugees from Algeria settled are among the strongholds of the Front National, for in spite of elaborate integration programs, many pieds-noirs remain embittered over the loss of their homeland.[124] From the outset, they held it against President de Gaulle and his party, the Gaullists, that France had been defeated in the Algerian war of independence, and so with the establishment of the Front National in 1972, conservative Gaullists found themselves facing political competition from the radical right. Although the party's founder, Jean-Marie Le Pen, is not a French Algerian, he served in the Algerian War of Independence and thus exuded personal credibility to the pieds-noirs. Today these two milieus—the radical nationalist and petty bourgeois Front National voters, on the one hand, and the postcolonial-influenced banlieues, on the other— are proving either impossible or extremely difficult to integrate into mainstream French society.

Great Britain, the Netherlands, Belgium, and later Portugal also experienced mass flight and remigration from their colonies.[125] Demographers estimate the number of "white" returnees from the former British colonies at 380,000 to 500,000 people, with an additional 1.3 to 1.7 million non-white immigrants also emigrating to the United Kingdom. The Netherlands had to absorb 312,500 returning immigrants from Indonesia, 106,000 of them as "evacuees" in 1946–49, the other two thirds following independence. Among the returning immigrants there were also 12,500 Moluccans who had served in the Dutch army.[126] Great Britain and the Netherlands had the advantage that postcolonial remigration extended over a long period of time, easing the absorption of the arrivals. Belgium, by contrast, had to rush to evacuate its citizens because of the sudden reversal in the Congolese war of independence. Within two and a half weeks, the Belgian government flew 25,000 people out of the Congo in an airlift; overall, 38,000 Belgians abandoned the country that would later become Zaire.[127]

While the Belgians, like the Algerian French before them, were clearly fleeing a war, the inhabitants of other European colonies in Africa, Asia, and the Caribbean tended to emigrate in response to a lack of future prospects. Characterizing all these migratory flows as "remigration" (an overgeneralization much like the concept of repatriation) is inaccurate as it conceals the fact that many citizens of the colonial powers had lived overseas for quite a few decades, or even over several generations, and often felt more at home in the colonies than in their putative motherland. In spite of all the things that distinguished the colonizers from the colonized, a common everyday life and a unique culture had developed overseas. This culture had an impact on literature in particular, as in the gloomy colonial novels of Joseph Conrad (originally Józef Korzeniowski), who had such a sharp eye for cultural and social conflicts in part because he came from a small town in eastern Poland shaped by its multicultural mix. In the Netherlands there emerged an entire literary genre, *Indische letteren*, that garnered new and well-deserved attention (at the latest) with the turn of the millennium in the wake of Postcolonial Studies' emergence.

Even more powerfully affected by its overseas territories was tiny Portugal, to which more than 600,000 people immigrated after its belated farewell to colonialism between 1974 and 1976. Considering that the country had a total population of nine million, this remigration, mainly of refugees fleeing the wars in Angola and Mozambique, came as a far greater challenge to Portugal than the comparable flights to France or the Netherlands.[128] In addition, the so-called *retornados* arrived just at the moment when the postwar boom in Europe was coming to an end, which cast an additional cloud over their prospects for professional integration. One country frequently overlooked in the context of decolonization after 1945 is Italy, probably because it had already lost its colonies during the Second World War. Barely 400,000 people arrived in Italy from today's Ethiopia, Eritrea, Somalia, and especially from Libya, a country that, like Algeria, was intended as a Mediterranean settler colony.

In concluding this excursus on postcolonial migration, it needs to be stressed once again that in many cases this particular variety of migration involved fleeing wars of liberation and civil wars.[129] In addition to Algeria, we could consider other former African and Asian colonies in greater depth, recognizing that one needs to differentiate among different phases and stages of escalation in each given conflict. (This is obviously a subject that could fill an entire book on its own.) Since decolonization and postcolonial nation-building frequently went hand in hand with ethno-national exclusion, it was often race or nationality that decided who *had* to flee and who could stay. These criteria simultaneously determined who *could* flee based on whether the "motherland" was ready to take them in. Recognition (or continuity) of citizenship, with all the social rights this entailed, was mostly denied to members of colonized nations. In this matter of inclusion and exclusion based on ethnic and racist criteria, European colonialism experienced a final climax whose consequences have left their mark to this day.

At the same time, the absorption of postcolonial refugees in Europe illustrates what national solidarity (always, of course, a politically willed, "constructed" solidarity) is capable of achieving: Each government treated its "repatriates," "returned migrants," and "homecomers" from overseas as compatriots. Here, the biologically tinted concept of mother- or fatherland proved quite helpful. Even if attitudes inside the host society were not so unambiguous, integration usually proceeded quite smoothly. This was attributable to the fact that the refugees and immigrants from the colonies, with the exception of Italy and Portugal, arrived during the *trente glorieuses*, the three decades of the great postwar boom. Europe's willingness to integrate is also worth mentioning here because of the number of arrivals; at four to five million they vastly exceeded all subsequent refugee waves, including those of 2015.[130]

However, adding to the non-white refugees, there soon followed a great many migrant workers, for European colonialism continued to cast a long shadow. These groups found it much harder to find a place in their host societies. This was true also for those groups who had to flee because they were colonized people who had served their colonizers, like the Harkis, Moluccans (who, analogously to the Harkis in French Algeria, had served in the Dutch colonial army in Indonesia), and the Sikhs (many of whom had been in service to the British in India). They shared the experiences of being excluded along with other African, Asian, and Caribbean migrants who made it to Europe in the wake of decolonization.

The late case of Cyprus

The Cyprus conflict, which triggered the next massive flight to Europe following the Algerian War, also had its roots in colonialism. In 1960, when Great

Britain granted independence to the island, which the UK had until then governed as a colony, Greek Cypriots thought it almost self-evident that they would continue to play political and economic roles in the future. Then, in 1963, President Makarios dismissed the representatives of the Turkish minority from his government and terminated the previous power-sharing arrangement. A serious outbreak of unrest resulted, which could only be contained through international mediation. The UN formed its own blue helmet troop, the United Nations Peacekeeping Force in Cyprus (UNFICYP), to uphold the fragile peace between the two nationalities.

This peace was over and done with, however, as early as 1974, when a group of Greek Cypriots came to power in a coup and sought annexation to Greece, then also ruled by a military junta.[131] In Turkey, which at this time had a democratic government, the coup reignited the old enmity with Greece, a hostility that had not really ended with the Treaty of Lausanne. The Turkish army invaded the Mediterranean island to protect the Turkish Cypriots and occupied a large area, today's Northern Cyprus. This escalation of the conflict set off two refugee waves: about 165,000 Greek Cypriots fled to the southern part of the island; in a countermove, 45,000 Turkish Cypriots went north. At this point the UN intervened again, stationing blue helmets along the military frontlines to keep the parties separate. In 1975 the Security Council negotiated an accord that called for a population exchange whereby the minorities remaining on both sides could take their belongings and resettle on the side of the island where each was in the majority.[132]

In Cyprus, then, the model of ethno-nationalist partition developed by Great Britain was being applied once again. Unlike earlier agreements (Neuilly and Lausanne after the First World War, and the peace treaties of 1946–47 following the Second World War), the accord on the Cypriot population transfer merely validated the movement of refugees that was already under way and did not generate any new population shifts. Nevertheless, the case of Cyprus confirms every kind of basic reservation that has been advanced against these kinds of "solutions." In spite of various mediation efforts, the island remains divided to this day. Since the Cypriot Greeks and Turks have now been living for two generations in nationally and religiously homogenized parts of the island's territory, it is questionable whether they could accustom themselves to a culturally, denominationally, and politically re-pluralized society should Cyprus ever be reunified.

Moreover, it is unclear how the return of refugees could be achieved. Owing to the inheritability of refugee status (there are parallels between this situation and that of UNRWA and the Palestinians discussed earlier) and to population growth, the refugee population on Cyprus has since grown to more than 260,000. Inheritability not only entrenches the ethno-nationalist way of thinking that is among the major causes of mass flight in modern European history. It also perpetuates a one-sided victimhood status for refugees, which would be a powerful obstacle to any attempt at reunifying the island.

After 1974 Europe and its neighboring regions enjoyed a lengthy pause where the flight from nationalism was concerned. This coincided with a long period of peace (apart from the civil war in Lebanon, which barely affected Europe, since at that time the vast majority of refugees from that conflict either stayed in that country or fled to Syria), with the EC's coming to terms with almost all its minority problems (with the exception of the situations in Basque country and Northern Ireland), and with the belief (then widespread in both East and West, and actually quite sympathetic, though unfortunately false) that nationalism was a thing of the past.

2.5 Ethnic cleansing in the former Yugoslavia

The wars of Yugoslav succession

As the Iron Curtain and Berlin Wall came down in the autumn of 1989, no one could imagine that two years later the continent would again become the scene of nationalistically inspired wars and waves of refugees. To be sure, there was an early intimation of this in the summer of 1989 in a remote and therefore little noticed part of the continent: in June the Bulgarian government suddenly opened its border with Turkey, and within three months more than 300,000 members of the Turkish minority fled; these were ethnic Turks whom state and party leader Todor Živkov had been harassing since the mid-1980s with a campaign of Bulgarianization, forced name changes, and a ban on circumcision.[133] Anti-Turkish nationalism and the opening of the border served as a safety valve to distract from the misery wrought by the dysfunctional planned economy and state socialism. This massive flight was certainly the consequence of flagrant human rights violations; yet the West, following the principles of the Cold War, had no wish to intervene in the domestic affairs of individual Eastern Bloc countries, so that Živkov's nationalistic Communist regime remained undisturbed.

This nonintervention did not escape the notice of Slobodan Milošević, then the head of the Serbian Communist Party. In June 1989, at almost the same time as the exodus of the Bulgarian Turks, he stoked the flames of pan-Serbian nationalism with his infamous speech delivered in the Field of Blackbirds (the Kosovo Polje, site of a fourteenth-century battle between Serbian and Ottoman armies). In front of a huge grandstand laid out like an altar, Milošević celebrated the national unity and heroism of the Serbs. Because of a recent coup-like takeover of regional party leaderships in Kosovo, Vojvodina, and Montenegro, the speech intensified Slovenian and Croatian fears of a new Serbian claim to leadership and recentralization. (Tito had given Yugoslavia a very decentralized structure in his 1974 constitutional reform.) It was this power conflict, economic decline, and controversial economic reforms that led to the collapse of Communist Yugoslavia.

That it collapsed violently was due to discord over the territorial order and to traumatic memories of the Second World War, which Milošević revived for his own purposes.[134] Slovenia, Croatia, and (after some delay) Bosnia and Herzegovina sought independence on the basis of the republic's existing borders. In opposition to this, Milošević and the representatives of Serbian minorities in Croatia and Bosnia that allied with him demanded ethnically defined borders amounting to a Greater Serbia. In the spring of 1991, in anticipation of the referendum on independence in Croatia, there were already several local outbreaks of violence that resulted in dozens of deaths. After Slovenia declared itself independent, the Yugoslav People's Army (JNA), which was quickly transformed into a primarily Serbian army, intervened there militarily. The JNA soon retreated after encountering surprisingly strong resistance.

In Croatia, by contrast, Milošević and his allies put their bets on violence and outright war. Paramilitary units composed of dedicated nationalists and common criminals played a key role in the warfare, above all the "Tigers," under the leadership of the warlord "Arkan" (Željko Ražnatović). The JNA and the paramilitary units devised an effective division of military labor: first the official army bombarded the disputed territories with artillery, then the Arkan Tigers and similar units moved in. Frequently, and in full public view, they killed the local Croat leaders, as well as advocates for a multicultural Yugoslavia. Among the victims were also very many Serbs; which means that one cannot reduce this war (any more than the later war for Bosnia) to an ethnonational conflict.

This display of violence served to intimidate the non-Serbian population to such an extent that many would take to their heels on their own. Within three months, Serbian militias following this strategy had occupied a third of Croatia, and about 200,000 people fled the contested territories. Battles were especially fierce for Vukovar, which Serbian artillery largely razed to the ground. There the "Tigers" (the official name of the irregular soldiers was the Serb Volunteer Guard) even marched through hospitals executing supposed enemies.[135] In view of this escalation of violence, the UN Security Council, following several unsuccessful tries, negotiated an armistice at the beginning of 1992. Thereafter the situation calmed a bit because the lines of demarcation inside Croatia were secured by the United Nations Protection Force (UN-PROFOR). The stationing of almost 15,000 blue helmets, however, came at the price of ratifying the Serbian conquests de facto and of giving refugees no hope for returning home. (It has been much the same since 2014 in Eastern Ukraine, though the units stationed there are from the OSCE.)

The ease with which Croatian territory was occupied encouraged Serbian minority leaders to proceed in similar fashion in Bosnia and Herzegovina. In

March 1992, even before the referendum on independence there, the JNA and paramilitary groups struck in the east and north of the republic, and within a few months they had conquered almost all the territories where Serbs constituted a substantial minority. The Bosnian Serb nationalists around Radovan Karadžić justified this deliberate escalation of violence by arguing that they wanted to protect the Serbs from a genocide like that of the Second World War. Since some witnesses to the earlier genocide were still alive, this propaganda fell on fertile ground.

In the first few months of the war, the Bosnian Serb army (Vojske Republike Srpske, VRS), which had hived itself off from the JNA in May 1992, already had conquered such strategically important territories as the corridor surrounding the northern Bosnian city of Brčko and the area around Prijedor, where the majority of residents were Croats and Bosniaks. As in Croatia, the military action was accompanied by massive ethnic cleansing, an expression that entered the vocabulary of the international community and media at this time. In the course of the war's first few years, almost two million people fled the wide network of frontlines in Bosnia and Herzegovina. This flight was not the worst fate that could have befallen them, given shootings, local massacres, and the concentration camps the Serbian forces had started operating.

The spring of 1993 brought a "war within the war" that saw the official Army of the Republic of Bosnia and Herzegovina (ArBiH) and the Bosnian-Croatian army (the "Croatian Defense Council in Bosnia and Herzegovina" or HVO) contesting control over territories in central Bosnia and the area around Mostar. Apart from these conflicts over power and territory, strains occasioned by mass flight contributed to the escalation. The Bosnians driven out of eastern and northern Bosnia had to be housed somewhere, and in many places this shattered the local balance between the nationalities and led to new outbreaks of violence. Indirectly, the Croatian-Bosnian conflict strengthened the Serbian side. In the spring of 1993 two thirds of Bosnia and Herzegovina were controlled by the army of the self-proclaimed Republika Srpska, and around 2.2 million people, half the prewar population, was in flight.[136]

As with almost all instances of flight attributable to civil wars, the majority of war victims fled at first to other locations inside their own country. Bosnian refugees clustered above all in urban centers like the besieged city of Sarajevo, around the industrial city of Tuzla in central Bosnia, and in enclaves like Bihać in the northwest and Srebrenica in the northeast, where the Bosnian army put up resistance to the VRS for a long time and even mustered an effective counteroffensive in the autumn and winter of 1992–93. In the spring of 1993 the UN declared a total of six cities and their environs "United Nations Safe Areas" in order to provide better protection for their inhabitants and the refugees who were stranded there. Fleeing to the EU therefore subsided, which was the intent of the UN's move. Yet Bosnians continued to be expelled from the Republika Srpska, or else made their own escape attempts, fleeing the daily discrimination and abuse they were facing there.[137] Here the distinction between preventive and retroactive flight was fluid.

Limited humanitarianism: The refugee intake in the EU

Even as early as the first few months of the war in Croatia, refugees were already arriving in the EU and heading toward Austria. At first most of them found shelter with relatives and friends, but they still had to register with the authorities. By the end of 1991, Austria already had a tally of more than 11,000 Croatian refugees; the following year, it was the Federal Republic of Germany that became the most popular destination. There, over the course of the war, 350,000 refugees were taken in from the former Yugoslavia. In relation to the overall number of refugees from Croatia, Bosnia, and Herzegovina, Germany's share was approximately one seventh, far fewer than people often imagine today. Yet at the time this influx was perceived by the German public as a burden. In relation to their overall populations, Austria and Sweden were taking in more war victims, at 90,000 and 120,000 each, and this was also true of Denmark, the Netherlands, and Switzerland.[138]

The choice of these destinations can only partly be explained by their geographic location. Croatians and Bosnians were for the most part trying to reach those countries where relatives and friends were already living because they had arrived earlier as guest workers. Their flight, in other words, was shaped by older networks of migrants. As will be shown in greater detail in Chapter Three on political flight, this is a common pattern: labor migration and flight migration readily spill over into each other—in both directions. To this extent, the moral distinction between "good" refugees and profit-oriented "economic refugees" that was used at the beginning of the 1990s to legitimate restrictions on the right to asylum is dubious from a historical perspective. But at the same time, discourses like this can serve as a gauge indicating whether good times or bad times prevail for refugees in different host countries.

The flight from Yugoslavia marked a decisive turning point for international refugee policy. In the first four decades since the passing of the Geneva Refugee Convention, wars and civil wars were not recognized as grounds for fear of persecution and subsequent flight. Refugee and asylum policy in the West is still very much shaped by the Cold War (this context will be treated in greater detail in Chapter Three on politically motivated flight). That means that refugees tended to have the best chance for gaining asylum and permanent absorption if they could demonstrate danger to life and limb on political grounds. Radical ethno-nationalism, as discussed at the beginning of this chapter, ranks among the most formative *political* ideologies of European modernity, but despite that status, it took more than a year after the outbreak of the war in Croatia before the international community and the EU summoned up the will to condemn Great Serbian nationalism. This hesitation had a historical background (the right lessons are not always drawn from history), since Serbia had been on the side of France and Great Britain in two world wars. The complete destruction of the city of Vukovar in eastern Croatia, the artillery bombardment of Dubrovnik, and the siege of Sarajevo with its high toll of victims combined to sway public and political opinion over the course of 1992; the West could no longer dismiss the conflict as a mere civil war. In the meantime, the Serbian military had largely decided the war in its favor. Milošević and his allies lost the media war over the former Yugoslavia, however, due in part to the pictures coming out of the concentration camps in Omarska, Keraterm, and Trnopolje of emaciated inmates who recalled those liberated in 1945 from German concentration camps, and to the pitiful condition of the refugees. The media also reported in meticulous detail on the atrocities committed by the VRS and paramilitary units.[139]

While it was overwhelmingly men who were interned in the concentration camps, the story of what happened to a number of women slowly came to light during the summer. Especially in northern and eastern Bosnia, paramilitary units and the VRS operated more than a dozen bordellos in which Bosnian women were often detained and raped. In October 1992, the UN began systematically documenting the mass rapes, and after the end of the war some of the perpetrators received sentences from the International Criminal Tribunal for the former Yugoslavia (ICTY).[140] Still unpunished are the far more numerous individual cases in which soldiers molested women, often within sight and hearing of their relatives, in order to humiliate the women's families and the nation the soldiers were fighting.

It is encouraging that the revelation of mass rape and forced prostitution in Bosnia and Herzegovina led to the punishment of at least some perpetrators, another positive outcome. Ever since this subject came under increased scrutiny, there has been renewed discussion of earlier cases coincident with flight and expulsion. In the Federal Republic of Germany this attention centers on the women who had found themselves in areas conquered by the Red Army in 1945.[141] For a long time, discussing their rapes had been taboo, even though postwar West German research on expellees always emphasized the victim status of the refugees and noted that there was a higher proportion of women among them. The American historian Norman Naimark, above all, deserves credit for adopting a gender perspective and drawing attention to the persecution and abuse of female refugees.[142]

The brutality of Serbian warfare did have the effect that those expelled from Bosnia and Herzegovina met with solidarity abroad, even though the general political and economic context for such solidarity was unfavorable. At the end of 1992 the Federal Republic of Germany slid into a recession after its brief unification boom, and unemployment was also on the rise in Austria, Sweden, the Netherlands, and other European countries. Nevertheless, most EU states and Switzerland granted asylum collectively, dispensing with the usual case-by-case assessment, to those arriving from Bosnia and Herzegovina and seeking protection.

This gesture of generosity, however, was linked to a time limit on admissions. After the reason for flight expired—meaning once the war had ended—the refugees were supposed to return home. Social welfare benefits were also cut back significantly in 1993 and turned into in-kind benefits so as to remove any material incentive to flee to Germany. Yet the "social welfare tourism" (*Sozialtourismus*) that has recently been the subject of much polemical discussion (in 2013 the term received the "Non-Word of the Year" award annually bestowed by a panel of German linguists) played no role at all. A look at the escape routes out of war regions shows that refugees primarily go to countries they are capable of reaching and where they have personal contacts.

The Federal Republic was especially resolute in implementing its announced policy of repatriating refugees once the war in the Balkans had ended. After the Dayton Accords, the vast majority of the 350,000 war refugees had to leave Germany. In Austria, by contrast, more than 80 percent of the arrivals from Bosnia and Herzegovina received a permanent residence permit, and in Sweden the number was even higher.[143] There is a clear correlation between these figures and the situation in the relevant labor markets. Through 2012 Austria enjoyed the lowest unemployment rate of any EU country, so that most refugees there had already found a job and were still needed at work. In Sweden, too, though the country experienced a deep crisis at the beginning of the 1990s, unemployment never reached German levels.

The Bosnians paid a price for their entry into the labor market in that they had to accept jobs well below the level of their occupational skills. Doctors were turned into nurses, engineers into auto mechanics, and skilled working women into cleaning ladies. Here again, it is worth taking a closer look at Austria, where there were far more refugees in relation to the overall population than in Germany, and where the proportion of those arrivals allowed to stay was also comparatively high. There is a problem in the official statistics here, as in most other Western countries, in that the data are differentiated according to country of origin, but there is no distinction between the refugees of the 1990s and the guest workers who came earlier.[144]

From the Austrian statistics it emerges that the refugees, much like the guest workers, were compelled to accept menial jobs as laborers and in the service sector. This can be gathered indirectly from the findings of a study conducted soon after the intake of the refugees, which showed that 55 percent of the Bosnians living in Austria were employed below their skill level, a significantly higher share than for any other group of migrants.[145] The only explanation for the gap between them and the Turks, Serbs, Croatians, and migrants from other states has to be that the refugees from Bosnia and Herzegovina had been "de-skilled." It also gives food for thought to consider that, as of 2013, half of all immigrants still were not working at jobs in line with their educational attainment.[146] The lower one's entry level into the labor market, the harder it is to climb to a higher rung.

This is a double loss: for the host countries, who are dependent on well-trained immigrants, and for the refugees, who often have to work low-paying jobs that are too physically exerting for them. There is also a gender component here in that women are more frequently affected by de-skilling than are men. And this downward mobility obviously entails disadvantages for the next generation as well. The Austrian statistics show that the parents of refugees were more likely to have completed secondary or university education than did their children who had grown up in Austria. This certainly is not the fault of the parents, since refugees almost always aspire to see their children enjoying a better life than theirs.[147] And this again raises the question of what direction integration is taking, whether toward the middle of society or toward the margins or even the lower end of the social hierarchy. In spite of these deficits, the labor market integration of Bosnian refugees has been a major success in all countries of admission, except Germany, which chose to repatriate the vast majority of the Bosnians after the war had ended.[148]

The idea of repatriation, which conditioned the way refugees from Bosnia-Herzegovina were taken in more than it did any previous group, is older than the Geneva Refugee Convention. In principle, repatriation accords with the interests of most refugees, at least at the beginning of their stay abroad, since most want to return home. This wish, however, rests on a recollection of what the old homeland was like before war broke out, when it had not yet been overrun by violence and destruction. As many returnees to Bosnia could not help but notice, that was a homeland that no longer existed. Ethnic cleansings had profoundly changed or destroyed local communities, and frequently the houses and apartments left behind were either no longer inhabitable or were occupied by different families. For the most part, therefore, former owners sold the properties restituted by the terms of the Dayton Accords and moved to regions where their own nationality was dominant.[149] In spite of the costly programs of return and restitution financed by the UN and EU, therefore, only about 500,000 international and domestic refugees returned to their hometowns.

To this extent, the "repatriation" of refugees (taking the term literally) proved to be a fiction. Refugees may have been returned to their country of origin, but it was rather rare for them to settle in their own home places. The fiction that they did so was constructed above all with a view toward the public in Germany and other host countries. The Federal Republic could present itself as generous and humanitarian when it came to supporting refugees at the start of the war and then, by repatriating basically unwelcome guests, preserve the illusion that it was still *not* a country of immigration. The heaviest price for this was paid by refugee children, who were uprooted from their schools and local surroundings in Germany and then had to integrate for a second time back in their old homeland.[150]

Humanitarianism also needs to be evaluated critically with a view toward its impact on the war itself. The West and the UN supplied "safe havens" in the Balkans with food, medicine, and clothing, and thus saved many human lives. The airlift to relieve the besieged city of Sarajevo was the most costly international relief program in Europe since the United Nations Relief and Rehabilitation Administration's activities following the Second World War. And yet this intervention left a bitter aftertaste, since pleas issued by the government in Sarajevo that the weapons embargo be lifted were not heard. Had they been heeded, this might have prevented the genocide committed against the defenseless and unarmed civilian population of Srebrenica. Another consequence of the embargo was that the Bosnian Serb army was able to bombard Sarajevo and the other besieged cities for more than three years with impunity. The victimization of the Bosnians and, linked to that, their self-victimization in politics and the media, ultimately made for a convenient excuse. They allowed the West to conceal how, in spite of all the lip service it paid to a multinational and democratic Bosnia, it had supported the government in Sarajevo only half-heartedly. The government, in turn, used the victimhood narrative, which it has been deliberately disseminating to this day, in order to advance Bosnian nation-building.

The Dayton Accords did not bring either the wars of the Yugoslavian successor states or the mass refugee waves to an end (see Map 5).[151] Peace came about not least because the fortunes of war shifted in the summer of 1995—to the detriment of the Serbs, above all in Croatia. In August 1995 the Croatian army marched into Krajina and liberated the Serbian-occupied territories with lightning speed in "Operation Storm." This could happen because the Croatian Serbs, like the VRS, had to defend overextended frontlines and because their army, as measured by the size of the occupied territory, lacked sufficient manpower. Many potential recruits had fled to Serbia or abroad. The appeal of Serbian nationalism turned out not to be as great as many in the West maintained. The Croatian-Serbian army's military collapse, fear of retaliation, and the initially brutal action of the Croatian army, which fired on civilians and set numerous houses on fire, triggered the greatest mass flight in the former Yugoslavia since the summer of 1993. Some 180,000 Serbs fled hastily out of Croatian Krajina and into other occupied territories. The exodus continued after the battles were over, though now mostly in the form of auto convoys and with buses. Apparently, the remaining Serbs could not imagine existing as a minority in Croatia.

This scenario was repeated in Bosnia when the suburbs of Sarajevo and a number of other local districts were placed under the control of the central government in accordance with the Dayton Accords. About 50,000 Bosnian Serbs thereupon packed their belongings and emigrated to the Serbian-ruled

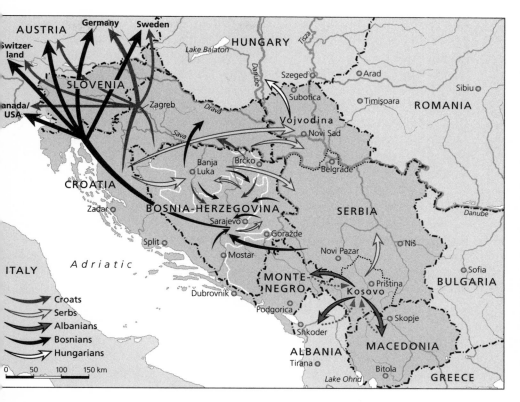

MAP 5. Movements of refugees as a result of the collapse of Yugoslavia

part of the country. This exodus may be characterized as ethnic "self-cleansing." The nationalist leadership of the Republika Srpska deliberately promoted the exodus in 1996 by urging Serbs (via print media, leaflets, and radio) to leave and by making arrangements for them to do so. From the perspective of migration history, the relationship of "push" to "pull" factors reversed in the case of these movements of refugees; the nationalist summons to return home (pull) played a more important role than the pressure of persecution (push). At any rate, the close entanglement between flight and absorption made it possible for Serbian refugees to take a large proportion of their household goods along with them. Unlike almost all other twentieth-century refugees, they did not arrive at their destinations completely impoverished and traumatized. All the same, leaving their homeland entailed a loss of jobs and social status.

The West appeared to be unmoved by the mass flight of the Serbs. There were only a few protests against the persecution and murder of Serbian civilians in Croatian Krajina (even at the International Court of Justice in The Hague, these war crimes and crimes against humanity remained unpunished), and there was no attempt to stop the exodus from Sarajevo. This had to do with diminished empathy for the nation that, in the view of many, had started the war to begin with. It also reflected the fact that the refugee waves of 1995 did not reach the EU. The Serbian refugees, numbering around 250,000, were absorbed by Yugoslavia and, to a lesser extent, by the Republika Srpska in Bosnia. Milošević steered some of the inbound refugees toward Kosovo, so as to increase the Serbian share of the population there, but most moved to Belgrade or to Vojvodina, the more prosperous parts of Serbia.

The role that mental and geographic distances can play is also illustrated by the second great center of conflict in the 1990s, the Caucasus. There, between 1988 and 1993, a total of about 1.5 million people were expelled from their homes, including 340,000 Armenians who had fled from pogroms in Baku and other Azerbaijani cities in the late Soviet Union. Between 800,000 and a million people fled the autonomous Republic of Nagorno-Karabakh, which had seceded from Azerbaijan (and from adjoining territories), while 230,000 Georgians had to leave the renegade province of Abkhazia.[152] This mass flight left the West and Europe largely untouched, since these refugees, like the Serbs of 1995, did not get as far as the EU. Much like Eastern Ukraine today, Nagorno-Karabakh is regarded as a conflict in suspension, though one that could become acute at any moment, as demonstrated by the fights that suddenly flared up in 2016. Today, owing to heightened mobility, refugees from the Caucasus would certainly head in the direction of the EU, and among the Chechens this has already been happening since the late 1990s. Yet, ultimately, the conflict surrounding Nagorno-Karabakh has eluded control by the West. The region's chief supplier of weapons and supreme regional power is, as in eastern Ukraine, the Russian Federation.

2.6 The (ir)responsibility to protect

The Kosovo crisis

The Dayton Accords of 1995 regulated the postwar order in Bosnia and Herzegovina, but not in Kosovo, where the collapse of Yugoslavia had, in many respects, begun. This was due to Milošević being allotted a place at the negotiating table; although he did have to bury his vision of a Greater Serbia, he still was needed as a partner to the accord. Milošević misunderstood this to mean that he would again have a free hand to mistreat minorities in the dominion he ruled. The state he was governing continued to go by the old name "Yugoslavia"; but it was mere presumption to call it by that name.

The prospect of permanent and even more intense discrimination changed the nature of resistance for the Albanians in Kosovo. Led by the writer Ibrahim Rugova, they had pursued a strategy of nonviolent resistance through 1996, demanding only that their regional autonomy, abolished in 1989, be reinstated. This restraint reflected their fear of the kind of escalation that happened in nearby Bosnia. Yet soon after Dayton, the UÇK (Kosovo Liberation Army) carried out attacks on police stations and other government offices. The Serbian security forces reacted with ever stronger repression, which only provoked more counter-violence.[153] In 1998, when a deployment of paramilitary units (including, once again, the "Arkan Tigers") was added to this volatile mix, the situation escalated further. In this first phase of the Kosovo conflict, approximately 300,000 people fled, 30,000 of them abroad.

The West, however, did not want a repetition of the Bosnian scenario. US Secretary of State Madeleine Albright, who had herself grown up as a Czechoslovakian refugee, warned against "appeasement." Initially the West imposed economic sanctions on Milošević's Yugoslavia, followed in 1999 by an ultimatum for negotiations on the status of Kosovo. When the negotiations collapsed early in 1999, NATO started an air war, bombing Belgrade and other Serbian cities as well as critical infrastructure. In Kosovo itself, the situation again worsened as about 600,000 people—one third of the Albanian population—now found themselves in flight. Thanks to aerial support and weapons deliveries from abroad, the UÇK gained the military upper hand and, faced with impending defeat and bombardment, Milošević gave in and accepted de facto secession.

The Kosovo conflict, especially the action taken by NATO, has divided world opinion to this day. At the time, advocates of intervention made their case by invoking the massive human rights violations committed by the Milošević regime, the violent action taken against the Albanians who accounted for the vast majority of the population in Kosovo, and the mass flight this brutality set in motion. Influential Western politicians, among them Madeleine Albright, brought forward historical arguments, including analogies to National Socialism that culminated in comparisons between Milošević and Hitler.[154] Specific events also played a role, like the Račak massacre, although it could not be clearly proven who should answer for the roughly forty Albanians killed there or where exactly it was that they lost their lives. There was also a lot of media commotion over the never-verified "Horseshoe Plan" whereby Serbia sought to drive the Albanian minority out of Kosovo in a pincer movement.

Regardless of how one evaluates this reporting and these specific events, they distract us from the central question: Should foreign states intervene militarily in order to prevent mass flight from nationalist persecution? Those in favor of intervention formulated some wording to express what they deemed a "Responsibility to Protect" (R2P), according to which the international community has a responsibility and even a duty to protect civilians from the worst kinds of human rights violations and ethnic cleansing.[155] After what happened in the former Yugoslavia, this sounded like a fine idea in the late 1990s: flight would be prevented by nipping it in the bud and not just curbed only once entire peoples had already hit the road.

Opponents of such interventionism countered by pointing out that national sovereignty is the foundation of the international order and world peace. According to this perspective, the attack on Yugoslavia set a dangerous precedent contrary to international law, since the UN Security Council had not given its approval. Furthermore, the critics explained, the UÇK was responsible for the escalation, because its terror attacks had provoked the Serbian security forces and ultimately NATO's intervention. And, indeed, since the nineteenth century the repertoire of radical-nationalist tactics in Southeastern Europe included the deliberate use of attacks in order to escalate violence and provoke intervention by the great powers.

From a historical perspective, the Kosovo conflict may be situated schematically along two time axes, one retrospective and the other prospective, or to put this in simpler terms: either as the endpoint of a past development or the point of departure for something yet to come. Taking the second perspective unavoidably draws one's attention forward to the Iraq War of 2003, since this intervention was also defended with arguments about human rights and did not have UN Security Council approval. From this point of view, the Kosovo conflict was not a further stage in the historical development of Western human rights and refugee policy, but rather the point of departure for a misguided interventionism. In view of the chaos that erupted in Iraq after the invasion of the coalition led by the US and of the mass flight that Mesopotamia has experienced since then, the verdict of contemporary history seems clear.

This also applies to Kosovo, since the interventionists' intended policy of flight prevention, while ultimately effective on behalf of the 600,000 Albanians who fled and were soon able to return to their homes, did not work for the roughly 250,000 Serbs, Roma, and members of other minorities who had to abandon their homeland after NATO's intervention. Here there was a mixture—similar to what we saw in 1995 in Croatia and Sarajevo—of ethnic cleansing and Serbian "self-cleansing." After the multinational Kosovo Force (KFOR), led by NATO and supported by neutral states, was sent in, things calmed down. Yet even KFOR could not prevent country-wide riots and pogroms in 2004, when Albanian nationalists killed nineteen people, drove out over 4,000 Serbs who had remained behind, and set thirty monasteries and churches on fire.[156] The ongoing violence against minorities, the problems encountered in building a Kosovar state, and the experience of rampant corruption and criminality perhaps make an even stronger case against intervention (ex post) than did the reservations already articulated at the time (ex ante) in terms of international law.

This finding is disheartening, especially as regards the history of flight from nationalism, a lengthy history replete with victims. For in Syria since 2011 we have seen what can happen when the West does not intervene. The civil war in Syria (see Chapter 4.2) has led to ethno-national segregation and the flight of more than ten million people. Also, in the former Yugoslavia, after 1993, the perpetrators of ethnic cleansing were brought before the International Criminal Court in The Hague, on the strength of resolutions passed by the UN Security Council. In Syria (and in Iraq), the perpetrators have so far been able to act largely unchecked, with corresponding consequences for the civilian population. To this extent, unfortunately, it is to be expected that the history of flight from nationalism will also need to be updated in the future.

Summary

Throughout the nineteenth century in Europe, nationalist mechanisms of exclusion and inclusion were superimposed on older, religious lines of demarcation. Then, in the twentieth century, modern nationalism led to an unprecedented rise in the numbers of refugees. Nationalistically motivated expulsions first devastated southeastern and then, after the Munich Agreement, Central and Eastern Europe. In Europe and its near neighborhood, about thirty million people were forced to leave their homelands permanently because of their nationality ethnicity. This variant of persecution and flight was thus by far the most common. It is linked to wars, for only in the context of war could major population groups be put to rout. Yet the flight from nationalism usually reached its apex after the end of each war. Hence we have to pose the question yet again as to what aims the states and politicians participating in each of the relevant peace accords and postwar orders were seeking to achieve.

In the age of nation-states, international politics followed a logic we would today regard as repulsive: until the middle of the twentieth century, mass population shifts were viewed as a legitimate means of stabilizing nation-states and promoting international peace. The permissive and sometimes supportive stance of the international community, in combination with the radicalization of nationalism, triggered a spatial and social escalation of population removal. The first schemes for an "exchange of minorities" affected only disputed regions, were meant to be voluntary (at least on paper), and covered only about a third of each respective minority. But after the Treaty of Lausanne, which also led to a more stringent implementation under the Treaty of Neuilly, entire states became ethnically homogenized. There were no longer any exceptions, and minorities were removed as completely as possible. In spite of the refugees' suffering, "Lausanne" became a model for the "solution" of minority problems. By the end of the 1930s, Great Britain referred to "Lausanne" on several occasions, as did Hitler in his vision of a "new Europe" based on ethnic borders and ethnically homogenized nation-states. The main difference between the Western and the German interpretation of Lausanne was the murderous racism of the Nazis, which inspired fascist Croatia and Romania to stage their own partial genocides.

When the fortunes of war changed, the fate of the German minorities in Eastern Europe was sealed. As early as 1941, Western public opinion and governments agreed that the Nazi resettlement of ethnic Germans in occupied Poland had to be undone. Moreover, by 1942 there was already an Allied consensus that Czechoslovakia could not and would not want to live with a sizable German minority. Hence, the "clean sweep" proclaimed by Winston Churchill at the end of 1944 made common sense by contemporary standards. Apart from the Germans, the peoples affected were—in descending order—Poles, Jews, Ukrainians, Italians, Finns, Hungarian, Bulgarians, Romanians, Slovaks, Estonians, Latvians, Czechs, Belarusians, and Lithuanians, as well as a variety of smaller ethnic and national groups. In the decade between 1938 and 1948, half a continent was on foot. Since many men were drafted into the armed service, women and children were obviously predominant among these roughly twenty million people who lost their homelands forever in postwar Europe.

Because of the difficulties involved in managing such masses of refugees and the well-founded fear that they were creating a breeding ground for Communism, the Western powers began to distance themselves from large-scale ethnic cleansing after 1946. They also grew more sensitive to political refugees from Eastern Europe (for this, see Chapter 3.3). Stalin, who certainly had no moral scruples, reversed course for pragmatic reasons as well. He intervened to prevent the larger Danube region from falling into the same kind of chaos as had prevailed in occupied Germany. Nevertheless, this curtailment of ethnic cleansing was motivated mostly by pragmatic, not humanitarian, considerations. Although the Universal Declaration of Human Rights passed in 1948 was in tacit contradiction to all the postwar treaties stipulating the removal of national minorities, postwar refugees could not base any legal claims on a UN declaration. The only immediate impact of the growing awareness of human rights was that the governments of newly independent Israel, India, and Pakistan did not openly advertise mass scale population removal as a "solution" to their domestic problems and as a way to create a lasting peace. Nevertheless, mass flight was still a predictable result of war, communal violence, and nationalist expansion.

Because of the suffering it inflicts on its victims, "ethnic cleansing" has been viewed as a serious human rights violation since the beginning of the 1990s—therein lies a deeper reading of this irritating term. "Ethnic cleansing" was prosecuted as such before the International Criminal Tribunal for the former Yugoslavia in The Hague (ICTY). In handing out sentences for genocide, however, the judges held back from equating the two crimes. Ultimately, the deliberate killing of around eight thousand Bosnian men fit for military service in Srebrenica was the only act punished as genocide, not so for "ethnic cleansing" and many other crimes against humanity. This restrictive jurisdiction on genocide is controversial, but it does distinguish the crime of ethnic cleansing from genocide defined as the deliberate and mass killing of persecuted minorities.

Ethnic cleansing, in contrast to genocide, rests on the idea that the minority in question has a home (though somewhere else) and that there is a country that can be regarded as the destination to which they can be transferred. The formula *"Heim ins Reich"* ("back home to the Empire") invented by Hitler got to the heart of this as early as 1938, and Czech officials shouted the slogan mockingly at the Sudeten Germans as they chased them across the border to "their" nation-state in 1945. The existence of an unwanted people's external nation-state at least meant that there was an entity that should feel responsible for these people. It was the reverse of the situation faced by refugees from the Russian Revolution, by the huge number of Jews who were fleeing an increasingly violent antisemitism, and by the Syrians of today who have managed to make it as far as Europe. For all their suffering and misery, most victims of ethnic cleansing had an apparatus of government administration to which they could turn in the countries of arrival. They were uprooted and impoverished, but not entirely defenseless at the moment of their absorption. This was reflected in contemporary writings and recollections; in spite of miserable living conditions in occupied Germany's reception camps, for example, the Sudeten Germans taunted with "Heim ins Reich" were initially delighted to have left what they perceived as hell and to now be in Saxony or Bavaria.

Whatever the theoretical value of this distinction, in practical, everyday reality national solidarity often did not extend very far. Arrivals were assaulted with insults, frequently housed for years on end in camps and barracks, chased from the fields, and made to stand at the very end of the job queue. Yet most had command of the host country's language, received (or retained) that country's citizenship (which is why, according to the Geneva Refugee Convention and its forerunners, they were not usually registered as refugees), and also benefited from social welfare services, to the extent these were available.

There is no reason whatsoever to idealize the national solidarity practiced by the host states, since it was expressed in a wide range to their refugee policies. They extended, if one looks (for example) at the period after the Second World War, from legal equality and welfare state privileges being granted quickly, as in the case of the German expellees, all the way to deliberate ostracizing, which is how Palestinians were treated in most of the states neighboring Israel (with the exception of Jordan). The point here is that refugees' room for maneuver is fundamentally restricted. What matters most in every one of these cases is the attitude of the host society and its political elite. The quantity and quality of the solidarity that ensues from shared nationality is not predetermined; it is instead a construct to which different sides contribute:

the "expelling states," the refugees, and the host countries and societies. Which side contributed more or less depended on a hierarchy of power that was different and remained variable in each given case.

Although it was modern nation-states that first produced national minorities, and thus the "minority problems" that accompanied them, there was a plus side in that national solidarity helped defuse a number of "refugee crises." The integration of refugees proceeded most rapidly when different groups arrived over a short timespan. One example of this is what happened in the early Federal Republic, when millions of expellees, GDR refugees, and ethnic emigrants from Eastern Europe arrived in the first decade after World War II. The binding element here was postwar reconstruction (which also helped paper over social and political conflicts within the Eastern Bloc), something that consisted not only in the rebuilding of the country as a whole, but also the reconstruction of families and individual livelihoods, both private and professional. Israel, another "refugee state," also formed a melting pot made up of very different groups, though one should not downplay the social and cultural differences that distinguished European Ashkenazim, Sephardim, and the long-marginalized Oriental Jews from one another. In both these cases, moreover, refugees were lucky that a long-lasting economic boom began soon after their arrival, an upswing abetted by the influx of a new reservoir of labor.

The situation was much worse for refugees who were persecuted because of their nationality or race but did not have a state of their own. For centuries this applied to the Jews, and to this day it has resulted in disadvantages for the Roma in a number of European countries, as well as for the members of other stateless nations like the Palestinians and the Kurds. Because the international order is based on nation-states, these nations have fallen between the cracks; they are ostracized and expelled from their countries of origin but do not have a destination in any country that can advocate for them and serve as their refuge.

Since the late nineteenth century, Jewish minorities compensated for lacking a state of their own by founding civic organizations that were active across borders. Jewish NGOs were among the first and most important actors providing refugee welfare services, and they were also decisive in getting the Paris Peace Treaties to implement rudimentary minority protection. But these efforts helped Jewish minorities and refugees in the interwar era only to a limited extent; they continued to suffer discrimination and persecution. In the period following the Second World War the problem for Jewish DPs was resolved only when the State of Israel was founded in 1948 and they could emigrate there. The price for this solution, however, was the Israeli War of Independence and the mass expulsion of the Palestinians. The refusal of most of the states adjoining Israel to integrate the Palestinians and the inheritability of their refugee status according to the statutes of UNRWA have exacerbated this refugee problem.

There are also unsolved problems left over from mass flight in Europe. Within the EU, Cyprus ranks first in this regard. In spite of several attempts to mediate between representatives of the Greek and Turkish Cypriots, a rapprochement, or even a revocation of the island's division accompanied by a return of refugees, still seems a long way off. At least no armed encounter menaces Cyprus today; the conflict really is *frozen* (in contrast to most conflicts designated as such). In Bosnia and Herzegovina one cannot be so sure of this. There the leadership of the Republika Srpska, one of the two entities in the federal state of Bosnia and Herzegovina, has crippled joint government since 1995 by issuing a variety of vetoes in the state executive and by boycotting administrative work and the parliament. This political blockade weakens the rule of law and economic policy in the federation, and it has undermined its every effort at gaining EU membership.

There is a perilous trouble spot lurking inside the way the history of the Bosnian war has been processed. The governing SDA party (the abbreviation stands for Stranka demokratske akcij [Party of Democratic Action]) is formally secular but de facto Muslim-dominated. It persistently underscores the victim status of the Bosnians and, only recently, brought Serbia once again before the International Criminal Court in The Hague on charges of genocide (appealing a negative ICC verdict from 2007), which the Bosnian Serbs persistently reject. This stubborn stalemate between the two nationalities may strengthen identification with one's own nation and each group's regional government (Bosnia and Herzegovina is a federated entity), yet it prevents the divided country from growing together as one.

What is more, the integration of returned refugees will only be able to make progress when an economic upswing finally sets in. And given how dysfunctional the state is, an economic upturn is not readily foreseeable. Since 1995 Bosnia-Herzegovina has been steadily falling behind economically, until it is today the poorest of the six former Yugoslavian republics. With an unemployment rate of nearly 28 percent, it has a GDP of 5,500 dollars per capita (only Kosovo was even poorer). Even more worrisome is the fact that imports are almost double the volume of exports; this makes Bosnia (like the Palestinian Authority) extremely dependent on outside donors and on remittances from co-nationals living abroad. This oppressive poverty of a major part of the population leads to new flight, though now mostly for economic reasons.

As European unification moved forward after the turn of the millennium, it was hoped that Europe would no longer experience war and the mass flight that ensues from war. When Russia annexed Crimea and intervened in Eastern Ukraine, these hopes were dashed. Anyone in the Donbas who openly proclaims allegiance to Ukraine or speaks Ukrainian on the street puts himself at risk. For that reason, and because of the misery that accompanies every war, at least 1.5 million Ukrainians have fled since 2014, about two thirds of them to other parts of Ukraine and another third to Russia.[157] The conflict surrounding Eastern Ukraine is still confined to this region, and most refugees from the Donbas and Crimea have found accommodations in Kyiv and other Ukrainian cities. Should the Russian president decide on a renewed round of escalation, however, and expand the war to other parts of Ukraine, the EU will have to adapt to waves of refugees, just as it did in the 1990s.

It is also in this context that one must warn against the current political renaissance of nationalism. At the beginning of the twentieth century, no one could have imagined the abyss into which radical nationalists would plunge Europe or the problems that movements of refugees would bring in tow. These lessons of history should not be forgotten, and this has been one of my reasons for writing this book.

3

POLITICAL REFUGEES AND THE EMERGENCE OF AN INTERNATIONAL REFUGEE POLICY

3.1 The making of the modern refugee in the "long" nineteenth century

The series of revolutions that took place beginning in 1776 reminds us that it makes no sense to treat Europe as a closed territorial unit. To understand European history properly requires a wider framework that takes in the trans-Atlantic world. Indeed, the history of political flight began on the American side of the Atlantic, with the American Revolution. In terms of sheer numbers, political ideologies are less relevant as a cause of mass flight than ethnic cleansing. But it is political refugees who have shaped overall perceptions of refugees in the Western world and in international law. Hence they require special attention.

Historiography has always been dominated by the winners of wars, revolutions, and other major conflicts. Less is known about the losers, who tend to be forgotten by history. This is also true of the British Loyalists who succumbed in the War of Independence. Somewhere between 300,000 and 400,000 people in North America took the side of the British, who had also brought in tens of thousands of mercenaries, mostly from German states like Hesse, to fight the insurgents. Most of the Loyalists wanted to stay and were allowed to do so.

Yet, as Maya Jasanoff has shown in her remarkable book on the Loyalists, around 60,000 were either forced to leave their homes in the original thirteen states or chose to do so. These refugees had a variety of motivations for fleeing, including political convictions, fear of retribution, and a desire to escape the violence that accompanied the American Revolution. In many places it was fought like a civil war, which had the impact of an additional push factor. African Americans had their own motives. Having gained their freedom in return for service in the British army, they feared being re-enslaved by the war's victors.[1]

Most refugees at first emigrated to nearby states and territories like Canada and Florida. Many went back to the British Isles, while some migrated to the Caribbean islands. Around 2,000 African Americans even migrated, by way of Nova Scotia, as far away as West Africa, where they founded a new colony, symbolically named Freetown.

The British Empire was successful in settling the refugees from its former colonies because it perceived them as its citizens. It also offered quite generous compensation for lost property and land. This meant that the empire reproduced old class structures and did not treat all refugees as equals. Nevertheless, these measures taken by the government in London greatly reduced its colonial refugees' grievances, at least on a material level. As one may gather from Jasanoff's biographical sketches, the integration of the American refugees worked out quite well. The British Empire, she claims, also profited by developing a new, more liberal spirit as it absorbed the Loyalists.

The French Revolution produced about twice as many refugees as the American Revolution. The main reason was the Jacobins' Reign of Terror. The execution of King Louis XVI and Queen Marie Antoinette in 1793, and the subsequent suppression of the opposition in Paris and the Vendée raised awareness of what could happen if one did *not* flee the country. Between 100,000 and 150,000 French people therefore went into exile. Some members of the high aristocracy and representatives of the ancien régime who were in exposed positions had already left the country in the years preceding the Terror. In order to leave, they needed above all to overcome two obstacles: One was the ring of passport inspection posts surrounding Paris that the Jacobins had put in place. (There was some unintended continuity here with a practice dating back to Louis XIV and the era of Huguenot mass flight.) A second set of hurdles was posed by France's external borders. The revolutionary government wanted to know who was fleeing abroad because they suspected, not incorrectly, that the opponents of the revolution would be gathering abroad to form a counterrevolutionary alliance. A third problem was a lack of receptivity in the neighboring countries, where the French were often suspected of being supporters of the revolution.[2]

As a rule, the only refugees accepted in the states of the Holy Roman Empire adjoining France were those who could prove that they could pay for their own livelihood. For about half of them this was not a great problem, since as members of the nobility, the upper-middle class, and the clergy, they had sufficient funds at their disposal. The nobility made up 16.8 percent of the refugees, far larger a share of the exile population than of the population back in France; 11.1 percent were upper-middle class; and the clergy comprised 25 percent, most of whom where priests and monks, so that men predominated overall. The equally numerous peasants, artisans, and workers, classes of refugees who more frequently came from regions near the border, scratched out a living at a subsistence level and lived in constant danger of being sent home impoverished.

The reason for this was a lack of political solidarity. The European elites were horrified at the execution of the royal couple and at the Jacobins' Reign of Terror, but this did not result in any broad, socially embedded counter-movement. A bit of political history may explain why: counterrevolutionary conservatism only developed as an ideology and party movement in the course of the nineteenth century, and even then solidarity and internationalism were hallmarks of liberals and the left, not of the right. An additional reason was apprehension lest there be spies and revolutionaries among the refugees. Fear of infiltration by enemy forces became a recurrent feature of attitudes toward political refugees during later waves of exile, as demonstrated by reactions to refugees from the Russian Revolution, or by the hunt for Communists (real or imagined) masterminded by Senator Joseph McCarthy during the 1950s in the US, which was temporarily closed to outsiders. Today's deliberate fusion of debates on refugees with fear of Islamist terrorism is in line with this baleful tradition. Yet we know of several recent cases from Germany (and elsewhere) in which refugees reported terrorists to the police and thereby prevented violent assaults. (In October 2016 an Islamist bomb-maker living in the eastern German city of Chemnitz, where he was registered as a refugee, was able to evade the police until two fellow Syrians in Leipzig turned him over to the authorities.[3]) Back in the late eighteenth century, in the societies of Europe's early modern anciens régimes, it was the aristocratic elites who tended to be more open to receiving their persecuted peers. Moreover, at all the European royal courts and governments there was a demand for experienced civil servants, scientists, and military officials, so that quite a few refugees were able to find good positions. Some families enjoyed rapidly rising careers, among them the Ficquelmonts and Mensdorff-Pouillys, who were elevated to earldom by the Habsburgs. As the example of the latter family shows, however, this ascent was predicated on a major effort at assimilation. The Pouilly family adopted the German-sounding name Mensdorf (at the time still written with only one f) and, when their two sons were recruited into the Austrian army, called attention to the family's origins in Lorraine (parts of which came under French rule only in 1766) while concealing their French connections.[4] Whether this was absolutely necessary is another question. After all, in the Age of Enlightenment all things French continued to enjoy a dominant cultural status in Europe (see Chapter 1.2 for more on this). Hence there was great demand for French language teachers, translators, tailors, and jewelers, as well as for fencing and dance instructors.

The largest diaspora, around 25,000 French refugees, formed in London, which could be reached more quickly by ship from most of France than Germany, a destination requiring a long overland journey. Active counterrevolutionaries assembled at the Rhine in Koblenz, where they plotted a military intervention. But they had to flee again after French forces conquered the city in 1794. For many refugees, France's expansion into neighboring countries resulted in an exile in several stages; some fugitives were even driven as far as Galicia in the very east of the Habsburg Empire or to the Russian Empire. At first the refugees expected that their flight would be temporary and behaved accordingly. The former elites of the Absolutist state especially pinned their hopes on an invasion by the European great powers, but their armies of mercenaries were crumbling before the French Revolutionary forces already as early as the War of the First Coalition (1793–97). Thereafter many of the less affluent exiles returned, as inconspicuously as possible, to their old homes, taking advantage of the 1795 demise of the Jacobin Terror. An additional incentive to return was provided in 1802 when Napoleon proclaimed an amnesty for refugees of the revolution. On the whole, then, the first mass flight in European history that was politically or ideologically motivated remained a mere episode.

This outcome is notable inasmuch as it is distinctly different from the fate of the Huguenots. Only rarely did religious refugees return to France, even though there might have been several opportunities to do so, as in 1787 when Louis XVI revised the discriminatory Edict of Fontainebleau. To be sure, the change in generations needs to be kept in mind: by this time, the third or fourth generation of Huguenots had already grown up outside France. Moreover, religious refugees and victims of ethnic cleansing typically perceived their flight and expulsion as definitive, even though there might have been opportunities to resettle in their old homeland. What weighed against their return were apparently such factors as their experiences in the "old country" as members of a persecuted minority, the traumas induced by flight, and the awareness that they would once again be regarded as outsiders should they choose to return. Conversely, one can view the decision to opt for a permanent new home abroad as an indicator of how well these refugees integrated into the societies that took them in. Successful integration and a close mental and emotional attachment to one's country of origin need not, however, be mutually exclusive. Political exiles in particular often performed a balancing act between their two homes, trying to provoke changes in the old homeland even as they integrated into their new environment.

A second grave trouble spot in late eighteenth-century Europe was Poland. In 1791 the Polish parliament (the Sejm) adopted Europe's first constitution—*ex oriente lux*! In contrast to what happened in France, this constitution was not the product of a revolution, but rested instead on a gradual accretion of civil liberties guaranteed by the Sejm and the estates. In principle, this progression from group to universal rights is comparable to the trajectory of early modern England. The May Constitution, along with Poland's attempt to modernize through Enlightenment reforms, induced Czarina Catherine

II to intervene militarily. Unlike revolutionary France, Poland was quickly vanquished, not least because it was surrounded by three conservative great powers. In the ensuing Second Partition of 1793, Poland lost extensive territories in the country's east and north, and the constitution was rescinded. Tadeusz Kościuszko, a commander in the previous Polish-Russian war, rose up against this. The uprising he led—the Revolution in Europe's east, as it were—failed. As a result, Poland was, in 1795, partitioned once and for all among its neighbors Russia, Prussia, and Austria. With this violation of international law—until then no large European state had been dissolved in this manner—the long history of Polish exile began.

While Poland was under Napoleonic rule, the country briefly hoped that it might be reestablished as a state, and roughly 100,000 Polish soldiers served in Napoleon's Grande Armée. But after Napoleon's catastrophic defeat in the Russian campaign, the Russian army marched back into Poland and, in 1815, the Congress of Vienna decided to partition Poland once more. The largest part of the country fell to the czar, who became the king of Poland as well. The great powers assured that the so-called Congress Poland would have autonomy within the Russian Empire (in principle this is comparable to the outcome of the Yalta Conference 130 years later, although socialist Poland did become a formally sovereign state). This autonomy did not last long, for in November 1830 an uprising erupted that occasioned the largest political movement of refugees to date in the nineteenth century.

The Grande Émigration of 1831

The uprising was poorly prepared. The social foundations were lacking for a revolution like the ones that took place in France or Belgium. Polish national consciousness and political awareness had not penetrated far into the peasantry, which made up the mass of the population. This meant that the insurgent army's mobilization was faltering and ultimately had to admit defeat before the superior power of Russia. Much like what happened between 1789 and 1794, this failed Polish uprising had ideological links to revolutionary movements in other parts of Europe. In July 1830, an alliance of the upper middle class, artisans, and workers overthrew the reactionary Bourbons who had returned to the French throne after the Congress of Vienna. This was followed in August and September by a revolution and independence in Belgium. There was also unrest in a number of mid-sized German states, among them Saxony, Bavaria, Baden, and Württemberg. There the monarchs reacted to protests by conceding more rights to the citizenry. In France the newly installed "Citizen King" Louis-Philippe, who was elected by the parliament, even swore allegiance to the constitution. The liberal revolutions and upheavals of 1830–31 thus planted a number of constitutional monarchies. In the end, this was a smart compromise, even if it left many social problems unsolved.

The life of **Tadeusz Kościuszko** (1746–1817) stands both for the global dimension of the revolutionary era at the end of the eighteenth century and as the archetype of the activist political exile. Kościuszko came from a landowning family in Polesia (today a part of Belarus); in the stratum of minor nobleman to which he belonged, the *szlachta*, Polish national consciousness was especially pronounced.[5] In 1769, thanks to a fellowship from an aristocratic Polish family, he was able to start studying at the French military academy in Paris. There he also got to know the dark side of the ancien régime. Kościuszko was unable to find a position in Poland's downsized army after the First Partition of 1772, so three years later he left for America, where he engineered the building of fortresses during the War of Independence, successfully secured the border with Canada, and won several battles. For his services he was promoted to brigadier general in 1783 and awarded a 500-acre estate. Kościuszko could have settled into a quiet life in the United States, but instead he returned to Poland. There he caused a stir when, in the spirit of American abolitionism, he cut the corvée obligations of his serfs in half. In 1789 Kościuszko was made general in the Polish army and again won several battles in the Polish-Russian War of 1792. These victories, however, did not prevent Poland's defeat.

The revolutionary National Assembly in Paris awarded him French citizenship for his services on behalf of liberty. Subsequently, in Paris, Rome, and Dresden, Kościuszko planned yet another uprising—this time against Russian domination. In 1794, the intended revolution foundered again at the hands of on the Russian army and an alliance of the three conservative partitioning powers. Following this defeat, the Polish revolutionary survived two years of hard prison time in St. Petersburg, before Czar Paul pardoned him following the death of Catherine the Great. Kościuszko then went back to the United States, made over his landed estate to Thomas Jefferson—in a will that also stipulated freeing all of Jefferson's slaves—and returned with his American fortune to Europe. In 1798 in Paris he took part in the formation of a Polish legion, but then after a personal meeting with Bonaparte he distanced himself from Napoleon, whom he accurately described as the "gravedigger of the revolution." Consequently, Kościuszko spurned the offer to assume an elevated position in the Grand Duchy of Warsaw, the Polish state created in 1807 by the grace of Napoleon, and went into exile in Switzerland. In 1815 he took part in the negotiations at the Congress of Vienna, where Czar Alexander sought his approval for the establishment of a semi-autonomous Poland under Russian rule. Kościuszko rejected this plan, returned to exile, and died two years later.

In Poland things moved in the opposite direction. Russia and its allies Prussia and Austria teamed up to intensify political repression. Czar Nicholas I, who governed with an iron hand after the Decembrist revolt of 1825 (an unsuccessful uprising of liberal nobles), took drastic and ruthless measures. He had 54,000 Polish rebels deported to Siberia, often along with their families, and confiscated countless landed estates. In addition, the czar canceled the autonomy of Congress Poland and installed the supreme commander of the Russia army, General Ivan Paskevich, as Polish viceroy. He presided as military dictator over a brutal regime that promoted Russification. The occupiers closed the University of Warsaw, Russian became the official language and the language of instruction at all secondary schools, and leading administrative positions were filled with Russians. Prussia reacted to the uprising in much the same way; in the Grand Duchy of Posen and West Prussia, a systematic Germanization got under way.

Poland's military defeat and the excessively harsh actions taken by the partition powers triggered a mass flight. In contrast to what had happened in the late eighteenth century, when Polish republicans got lost in the turmoil of the Coalition Wars, the Grande Émigration became a permanent point of reference for the European public. This was attributable to the international dimension of the upheavals of 1830–31. The uprising in Poland was, as already mentioned, the only revolution of that period that was violently suppressed and failed completely. International solidarity, correspondingly, was considerable.

The first station in the flight of about 6,000 Polish refugees (they were predominantly soldiers from the rebel army) was, in most cases, Saxony. In 1831 that kingdom's liberal bourgeoisie was able to push through its demands, so that on September 4, the king issued a constitution and transformed Saxony into a constitutional monarchy. Only a few days later a rebellious Warsaw surrendered to the Russian army. The Grande Émigration this set off thus happened at a propitious moment for the Polish refugees. The bourgeoisie in Central and Western Europe was highly politicized; and Saxony, moreover, had close ties to Poland because of their shared history in the Polish-Saxon Union of 1697–1763. The refugees were therefore received with great sympathy, especially in Dresden and Leipzig, even though it was no easy matter to accommodate several thousand war veterans. Aid committees and charitable collections pitched in to find lodging and provide food for the defeated rebels.

Only a few Poles were able to remain in Saxony, however, because Prussia would not have tolerated the formation there of a politically active diaspora. Much the same was true for the other states in the German Confederation, where the Austrian chancellor Prince Metternich had created a centralized system of police and spies via the repressive Carlsbad Decrees of 1818 (a response to two political murders). Yet, precisely because of the suppression and persecution of the German opposition, the Polish freedom fighters were everywhere welcomed cordially, sometimes even enthusiastically. New words were coined to express this enthusiasm. There were *Polenvereine* (associations supporting Poles), *Polenlieder* (songs for Poland), and there was *Polenschwärmerei* (a form of infatuation that might be translated as "Polish fever"). [6]

France and Belgium reacted to the punitive suppression of the uprising by granting generous terms of asylum to the refugees.[7] These included open-ended residency permits and protection against deportation (a precursor to the Geneva Refugee Convention's principle of non-refoulement) and even financial assistance to secure a living. The "brothers from the north" received an annual subsidy to their income in amounts that depended on their profession or previous social position—it ranged from 270 francs (for simple soldiers and artisans) to 3,000 francs (for former ministers and generals with families).[8] This generosity rested on two foundations: on the fact that the number of refugees was manageable and could easily be accommodated in Paris, which had three quarters of a million inhabitants at the time, and on political solidarity. Some among the new French elites had firsthand experience of political persecution themselves, gained under the Bourbon restoration. Furthermore, among the liberal bourgeoisie in the period between the Congress of Vienna and the revolutions of 1848, there had developed an internationalism similar to the kind later encouraged by Marxists in the Socialist International.

This internationalism also shaped the 1832 Hambach Festival organized by the German opposition in southwestern Germany. The festival was the first mass meeting of the German national movement, yet on display at that event's procession, alongside numerous flags showing the German national colors black, red, and gold, were Polish, French, Greek, and Serbian flags.[9] The Grande Émigration from Poland continued to have an impact. And at that time the Serbian Revolution also aroused much public interest in German-speaking countries, most notably for the founder of modern historical scholarship, Leopold von Ranke.[10] The dominant conservative powers Austria and Prussia found in the Hambach Festival, and especially in an 1833 assault by revolutionary students on the Frankfurter Wache (the police guard station in Frankfurt that was also the site of the German Confederation's treasury), a pretext for launching a broad-based campaign of suppression. Student fraternities (hotbeds of nationalist and liberal ideas in Germany at the time) were banned, censorship was reinforced, and warrants were issued for the arrests of numerous people.

A "Black Book" listed the names of more than 1,800 opposition figures who were "wanted," including 259 people who had fled abroad. This book is a valuable source for the history of political flight, because it gives precise details about the occupation, age, and gender of the refugees. Two thirds were academics, half of these students and therefore young, while women constituted (as is usually the case among politically motivated refugees) only a small minority.[11] On the whole, therefore, this was a social elite, well equipped to start life over in whichever country took them in.

The political refugees from the era prior to the revolutions of 1848 were not, however, thinking about permanent exile. Instead, they lived in hope of influencing political developments back home. Initially, therefore, they continued pursuing their political activities in Switzerland and France, the two countries that were their most common destinations. Prussia and Austria put pressure on tiny Switzerland, above all, to prohibit any opposition activity. This pressure was passed on to the refugees by the Swiss authorities, who even threatened the exiles with expulsion if they continued to be politically active. France acted in a less restrictive manner, although after 1837 it did cut support payments. This had an impact, above all, on the Spaniards who had fled the earliest of the Carlist Wars, a dynastic and political conflict between adherents of absolutism and a constitutional monarchy.

In addition, more and more members of the opposition were arriving from Piedmont, where King Carlo Alberto, installed in 1831, reigned in a close alliance with Austria and persecuted the opposition just as severely as Metternich did in the German Confederation. Since at this time the Veneto, Lombardy, Parma, and Tuscany were under Habsburg rule, the long arm of reaction extended far. Parisian officials counted 624 Italian exiles along with 5,150 Polish and 580 Spanish refugees.[12] In Marseille, close to what was then the border with Piedmont, even more Italians had found sojourn.

The watchful Austrian and Prussian authorities astutely noted that, although the flight of opposition figures abroad weakened political resistance at home, its center of gravity was merely shifting. Prussia therefore turned to persecuting the Polish opposition in a new and perfidious way: by banishing them into overseas exile. In November 1833 the government put 650 Poles in Stettin onto a ship that was supposed to sail to the United States. The banished even received a lump payment of forty dollars—no trivial amount at the time—so that they could permanently settle overseas.[13] The exiles, however, mutinied during the crossing, because they wanted to stay in Europe and continue there the struggle to liberate their fatherland. They disembarked in England and France and organized a small army with the aim of rushing to the assistance of democrats who had risked an uprising in Frankfurt am Main earlier that year. When the Polish freedom fighters learned that the assault on the Frankfurter Wache had failed, they went to Switzerland in order to take part in an attempted invasion of Piedmont (see the account of this incident in the portrait of Mazzini). This led to massive diplomatic complications and protests by the neighboring states. Like Mazzini, the rebellious Poles were deported to England. The English right of asylum was the most liberal in

Among the 1,500 Italians who fled to France in 1831, **Giuseppe Mazzini** (1805–1872) stood out both politically and intellectually. As a law student in Genoa, Mazzini organized conspiratorial meetings in a secret lodge, while at the same time publicly demanding a democratic Italian nation-state. Denounced by an informer, he sat out three months of imprisonment in the winter of 1830–31; then, following his release, fled to Marseille. There he founded his first exile organization, "La Giovine Italia," which became the model for numerous similar associations, including "Young Germany, "Young France," and "Young Switzerland." The "Young Czechs" (a left-liberal and decidedly national party that played an important role in Bohemia starting in the 1870s) and the "Young Turks" (a revolutionary movement of the late Ottoman Empire, see Chapter 1.5) also harked back to this model. The common aim of these organizations was to found national movements and nation-states. In Swiss exile in 1834, Mazzini expanded his ideas to a pan-European level. Italians, Germans, and Poles banded together fraternally in "Young Europe," an association committed to a federation of European nations and republics. Mazzini thus became a visionary thinker on behalf of a united Europe.[14]

The charismatic intellectual's attempts to launch a revolution in his homeland were less successful. The volunteer forces that marched into Piedmont from France and Switzerland failed miserably, and some close friends of Mazzini were sentenced to death and executed.[15] The ill-considered action taken by Mazzini's insurrectionist allies meant that his position in Switzerland was no longer tenable. The king of Piedmont demanded the extradition of Mazzini, who had been sentenced to death in absentia. But the Piedmont monarch was opposed by the citizens of the Grenchen, a municipality in the canton of Solothurn where Mazzini had found refuge. They organized a signature campaign and tried to hide Mazzini. Tracked down by the police, the democratic revolutionary was forced to leave Switzerland within twenty-four hours and fled to London.

In order to fend off impoverishment in England, Mazzini composed numerous additional writings and matured as a political thinker and philosopher. In 1848 he took advantage of the revolution in Lombardy to return to Italy, initially to Milan and then, after the invasion of the Austrian army, to Rome, where he lead the revolutionary triumvirate early in 1849. Any further development of the Republic of Rome was inhibited, however, by the French army, which intervened in favor of the Papal States. Mazzini had to flee to London again, but ten years later he inspired Garibaldi and his "Expedition of the Thousand," which finally brought about Italy's long-awaited unification. In London Mazzini continued trying to build an effective democratic exile organization, and in 1864 helped found the first International Workingmen's Association.

Alongside his activities as a dedicated republican, Mazzini's scholarly treatises on literature and music are notable. In these works he calls for the creation of a "European music" fusing together diverse national styles.[16] His way of classifying European culture was admittedly based on national stereotypes, but Mazzini was also a great European in his capacity as a philologist, historian, and political philosopher.

Europe, although the state did not provide any kind of material support. This meant that poverty and hunger were problems, but there was no ban on political activity in Switzerland or (later) in France.

The "Forty-Eighters"

Metternich's harsh actions and police state he staffed with informers charged with spying on the liberal opposition in the end only provoked more resistance. When a series of bad harvests in the mid-1840s coincided with the overthrow of France's "citizen king" in 1848, the proverbial "revolutionary spark" rapidly spread from Paris to central and southern Europe. Only the Russian and Ottoman empires remained calm, for the most part, which had to do with their remoteness, but also with the lack of organized opposition there. The revolutions of 1848–49 had a different quality from those of 1830–31, because they did not stop at a bourgeois uprising; workers, at the latest in a second phase, also got involved. This wider cast of actors, however, had the negative effect of splitting the opposition into liberals and democrats. The Prussian, Austrian, and other governments exploited this division, playing on the bourgeoisie's fear of a proletarian revolution. France even experienced a kind of counterrevolution: Napoleon III, a nephew of the emperor, saw his chance when a power vacuum ensued, and in 1848 enthroned himself as president and then, four years later, as emperor, following in the footsteps of his far more famous and successful uncle.

In Prussia and the Habsburg Empire, which at the time included the Italian territories mentioned above, the rulers banked on ruthless force to break the revolution. In 1848 the Austrian government sent its armies to Milan and to Prague, and finally ordered them to invade Austria's own capital, where numerous revolutionaries were executed, including Robert Blum, a delegate to the National Assembly in Frankfurt who, as such, really should have enjoyed immunity. The trail of blood ran onward to Lemberg, where the army and the Polish National Guard bombarded the city with artillery fire. In 1849 the Habsburgs allied with Russia in order to suffocate the last fires of revolution in Hungary.

The excessive use of the military and police created a spiral of violence that constitutes the second major difference between 1848 and the uprisings of 1830–31, when Poland had been the only country where there was a protracted deployment of armed force. Now the revolutionaries were defending themselves by force of arms and raising their own armies and national guards. Government repression provided another motive for flight; numerous 1848–49 revolutionary activists were now threatened with summary court-martial and the death penalty. Conversely, this meant that the host countries were confronted with refugees who in some circumstances had committed crimes, ranging from plunder to politically motivated assaults.

The third qualitative difference between the revolutions, which for reasons of space can only be briefly addressed here, was their increasingly national orientation. Italians, Hungarians, Poles, Romanians, and others went to the barricades not only in the name of liberty, but also on behalf of their respective nations. This is why the revolutions of 1848–49 are occasionally referred to as the "Springtime of the Peoples," a factor that the multinational empires correctly viewed as an existential threat.[17] The suppression of the opposition therefore had an anti-nationalist thrust, so that here nationalist and more universal motives for flight were fused.

It never came to a countrywide revolution in Poland, because the opposition in the largest, Russian-ruled part of the partitioned nation was still exhausted from the uprising of 1830–31, and the Czarist police had the situation under control. In Austrian-governed Galicia, however, the Polish National Guard occupied the provincial capital in Lemberg, while in Prussian-administered Posen there was an uprising under the leadership of the Parisian émigré Ludwik Mierosławski. In 1847 he had been sentenced to death in Berlin as ringleader of an attempted uprising, but in the midst of the turmoil surrounding the revolution in Prussia, he was able to escape from prison (see the concluding chapter of this book on these kinds of existential experiences). The failure of Polish independence efforts was politically predetermined, because the Frankfurt National Assembly backed Prussia's territorial claims and supported its rule over the Grand Duchy of Posen and West Prussia. In doing so the National Assembly was adhering to the misconception that it could bring about the unification of Germany on the basis of Poland's continual partition. This turning away from the ideals of pre-1848 liberalism, like the liberals' alliance with the German crown, was one of the ways in which the German revolution of that year went astray. The Prussian military quickly moved to suppress the uprising in Posen, and Mierosławski fled to Italy, where he fought in the front rows of the Sicilian revolution. After that failed, he rose to become the supreme commander of the revolutionary army in Baden, which was also defeated in 1849. Mierosławski fled with his remaining soldiers to

Switzerland; and once again, this professional revolutionary managed to save his skin at the last moment.

In the end, none of the revolutions of 1848–49 was successful—at least not if one uses advances in the cause of human rights and democratic participation as the measure of success. All of the constitutions that had been negotiated were eventually quashed (with the exception of the Kingdom of Piedmont's), while Prussia and Austria in particular imposed and implemented hundreds of death sentences. Abroad in the West, however, these repressive measures aroused just as much sympathy, outrage, and ultimately solidarity as Russia's actions against Poland had evoked in 1831.

This wave of persecution was the actual hour of birth for the "Forty-Eighters," whose very name betokens their elevated political status. Not until 1968 has a single generational cohort succeeded in establishing itself so prominently in the discourse of the European public (and also, from that time forward, in the trans-Atlantic public). The political presence of the Forty-Eighters exceeded by far the actual number of refugees from these revolutions. When the last embers of the revolution were finally suffocated with the surrender of the Hungarian army in August 1849, another five thousand freedom fighters fled. At first they moved into the neighboring Ottoman Empire, whereupon Vienna and St. Petersburg exerted strong pressure on that regime to extradite them. The reform-oriented Sultan Abdülmecid I, however, did not give in to these demands, invoking Western European asylum laws.

The new refugees brought new energy to an already existing Polish diaspora that, as of 1842 under the leadership of Count Adam Czartoryjski, had founded the town of Polonezköy (the name translates to "Polish Village") on the Asian side of the Bosporus. Several refugees, including General Józef Bem—the winner of more than a few military laurels (in 1831 for the November Uprising in Poland, in 1848 for the defense of Lemberg and Vienna, and then in 1849 in the Hungarian army)—thanked the Ottomans for asylum by converting to Islam. Bem became Murad Pasha and was able to launch a career in the Ottoman army, though he died only a year later during a military campaign in Syria.

Most Hungarian and Polish revolutionaries, however, eventually emigrated to France and Great Britain. Today the Orbán government in Budapest views refugees coming from third countries as "illegal immigrants"; following this legal interpretation, most of the revolutionary refugees from 1848–49 and Hungarian national heroes like Lajos Kossuth would also have qualified as illegals. Overall, the number of permanent exiles in Western Europe was limited to between 12,000 and 15,000 people.[18]

The most important country of exile was initially, as it was also in the case of the German Forty-Eighters, France. There the government again paid refugees an allowance toward living expenses. Political complications prevented a German Grande Émigration, however. Refugees from Germany (who had already fled in 1848) and French republicans took part in the May 1849 revolution in Baden and smaller upheavals in the Palatinate. This interference from across the Rhine provoked strong protests; the government of Baden imprisoned several French revolutionaries; it apparently had some leverage against the French government. France then got its citizens released by undertaking to change its refugee policy.[19] The German revolutionaries (at this time there were barely a thousand of them) were interned in two large camps far from the border. (What Hannah Arendt later experienced, as depicted in Chapter 2.2, was really not so new.) When Baden issued a partial amnesty in favor of the insurrectionists, France advised them to return to their old homeland. In order to encourage remigration, the government cut the support payments on which the interned refugees, for lack of work opportunities, were dependent.

This growing rejection of political refugees was related to the authoritarian course adopted under the rule of Napoleon III. More and more, refugees were attacked as troublemakers. Foreign Minister Alexis de Tocqueville accused the refugees of simply looking for an opportunity to "strike the final blow against the European order and in particular against the current social order in France."[20] In the United States Tocqueville is known above all for his admiration of the American Revolution and of the Americans' public spirit. For these he is readily quoted to this day, while his remarks about democratic refugees seem to have been forgotten. After Napoleon's coup d'état of 1851, attitudes hardened, and the situation of the Forty-Eighters became completely untenable. A number of the 1831 emigrants even felt compelled to move on. Joining these refugees were more than 1,500 French opposition figures, who first fled to Belgium and then on, for the most part, to England.[21]

It is hard to say what kind of impact this turn against exiles, a reversal in domestic politics that ran contrary to France's almost sixty-year tradition as a country of exile (in the 1820s even the reactionary Bourbons had admitted a few hundred political refugees), had on the integration of those Poles who remained in French exile. As late as the third and fourth generations, according to researcher Jerzy Borejsza, they kept their Polish identity and language and aspired to return to Poland.[22] This may have applied to a few tradition-minded families, but it was usually only the hard core of this (or any other) diaspora that remained devoted to its homeland's nationalism. Keeping the second or third generation emigrants committed was much harder, and usually only a fantasy cherished by radical nationalists. Owing to industrialization, France at this time was an immigration country that absorbed most refugees as it did the much larger number of economic migrants.

Since France was closing its doors, there was a greater surge of refugees heading to Switzerland. After the defeat of the revolution in Baden in the summer of 1849, an entire army of more than ten thousand soldiers sought refuge in Switzerland. Initially there was great sympathy for the revolutionaries; much as they had done for the Huguenot refugees, Swiss citizens founded aid committees and collected donations. Only half a year later the attitude toward the refugees turned hostile: they had to be fed and housed and were increasingly competing for jobs with the native Swiss.[23] Individual cantons were no match for the onslaught and shuffled the refugees to and fro until the government in Bern, in accord with the new constitution of 1848, finally assumed responsibility. The Swiss federal government appointed a refugee commissioner with far-reaching powers and distributed the refugees according to a fixed formula. (The European Union obviously lacked this kind of central government in 2015; whether such a policy should be implemented is another question.) Even as this internal Swiss distribution was getting under way, the powerful neighbor to its north was already pressuring Switzerland to stop accommodating refugees near the border. The minimal distance according to a government decree had to be eight hours on foot, which corresponded to a good thirty-eight kilometers; political activity was deemed undesirable and could result in immediate deportation.

The main goal of the Swiss federal government and the refugee commissioner it had appointed was to reduce the number of refugees, whether by way of remigration or by moving them on to third countries. To this end Switzerland, like France, even funded refugees' trips to England or overseas.[24] Through this combination of financial incentives and political pressure, the number of refugees by the end of 1850 sank to about 2,000 and a year later to only 500 people. Before leaving, to be sure, the refugees had to sign a statement that they were leaving Switzerland voluntarily. Nevertheless, the political leaders of the revolution, threatened by immediate danger to life and limb, were treated more generously. Richard Wagner, for example, for whom there was an arrest warrant because of his participation in the Dresden May Uprising of 1849, was able to remain longer in Switzerland. In cases like his, private connections mattered; Wagner was supported by the wealthy Wesendonck family. He had in fact developed a romantic relationship with his hostess, which apparently inspired him to compose *Tristan und Isolde*. It could be said, therefore, that the flight to Switzerland proved productive even for the arts.

In view of the redirection of refugees from France and Switzerland, England and the US moved to center stage as countries of exile, becoming even more important than before as places of refuge. Both countries, as a matter of principle, refused to deport refugees who had committed political offences and crimes. Refugees were not required to report to the authorities and were free to practice their professions. This liberal refugee policy was coupled, however, with a social welfare policy that was just as laissez-faire. In contrast to France or Switzerland in 1831 and 1849–49, refugees in the Anglo-American countries received no social welfare benefits. For the new arrivals in the expensive world metropolis that was London, this often spelled rapid destitution. Karl Marx is a prominent example since, unlike Mazzini, he was not especially successful as a journalist. The manufacturer's son Friedrich Engels, however, supported him financially, which enabled Marx to continue writing.

The refugees were grateful for their reception but at the same time complained of the indifference of the Londoners.[25] Even prominent Forty-Eighters like Gustav Struve and Karl Heinzen left England for the US because they saw no way to earn a living in London. Finally, by the end of the 1850s, the British government was actively supporting emigration to the US in order to defuse social tensions in London and rid the country of refugees regarded as political troublemakers. In 1858, however, when the French government sent a list containing names of its own citizens along with opposition figures from Italy who struck the authorities in Paris as too subversive to be harbored in nearby England, London coolly explained that nobody could be forced to emigrate to the US against their will.

In spite of widespread distrust of radical revolutionaries and their agitation, the British government was permissive when it came to refugees' efforts to assemble. Thus, in addition to a variety of refugees' organizations that formed in London, there was also the Comité central démocratique européen, whose first manifesto the tireless Giuseppe Mazzini composed. Its list of members reads like a "who's who" of the refugee scene at that time. In addition to Mazzini, it included Arnold Ruge; Alexandre Ledru-Rollin, an opponent of Napoleon III; Lajos Kossuth, the Hungarian defense minister in 1849; Ion Brătianu, a leading Romanian politician; and the journalist Wojciech Darasz, who had to leave France like other exiled Polish activists.[26] All of the refugee organizations, however, suffered from internal conflicts that went back to their political fragmentation into groups of liberals, democrats, and radicals. The greatest challenge in exile, though, was daily survival. Poverty, misery, and illnesses like tuberculosis were rampant among the refugees; Wojciech Darasz died of TB soon after the founding of the committee.

Until then, political refugees from Europe had tended to view exile in North America rather skeptically because they feared that it would take them too far from the action where they could no longer influence the course of events in their old homeland. (This attitude was rarer among exiles who had fled religious or nationalist persecution—see Chapters 1 and 2 of this book—who tended not to succumb to such illusory hopes.) This was also the thinking of the reactionary governments in Berlin and Vienna; Prussia and Austria tried to scotch Polish opposition by banning it to North America. They did not always succeed; two hundred Poles who had been forcibly shipped to Trieste in 1849 mutinied on the way there (cf. a similar case of Prussian Poles from 1833, discussed in Chapter 3.1) and finally landed in French Algeria.[27] France's transformation from a republic to a monarchy entailed a similar change of climate vis-à-vis refugees. Napoleon III did not want to have a democratic international in his country, and at the beginning of the 1850s the increasingly authoritarian emperor began sending ships full of opposition activists overseas.

With the advent of steamship travel, however, the US moved closer to Europe, economically and politically. (The first steamships crossed the Atlantic in 1838.) This lent new relevance to the founding myth of the US as a sanctuary of freedom, and the same was true for its attitude toward political refugees, which Thomas Paine had captured in his polemical treatise from 1776, *Common Sense*:

> Every spot of the Old World is overrun with oppression. Freedom hath been hunted round the globe. Asia, and Africa, have long expelled her, Europe regards her like a stranger, and England hath given her warning to depart. O! receive the fugitive, and prepare in time an asylum for mankind.[28]

In line with this maxim, which by 1848 had lost none of its topicality, the US remained fundamentally a country that welcomed refugees from Europe.

This opening, however, rested (political convictions aside) on America's self-image as an immigration country. Because the Forty-Eighters were highly educated, they were particularly sought after as immigrants. In the 1850s, moreover, there was still a lot of good agricultural land available for settlers, and on the east coast and along the Great Lakes, industrialization was taking off and along with this came a huge demand for both skilled and unskilled labor. These opportunities drew about 80,000 to 100,000 Germans, who emigrated in the wake of the political refugees. They frequently shared the political convictions of the Forty-Eighters; hence they were often perceived as such by the American public.[29]

The number of genuine revolutionary refugees was much smaller. Probably there were at most a few thousand people who moved to the United States for reasons that were primarily political, and almost all of them were Germans.[30] The Italian, Hungarian, and Polish Forty-Eighters preferred European countries of exile, including the Ottoman Empire. Trans-Atlantic labor migration from these countries was in its early stages as refugees from East-Central and Southern Europe had not yet developed adequate networks in the US that they could rely on, and they saw the New World as much too distant from their old homeland.

In the US the German Forty-Eighters earned such a lasting reputation not least because some of them, in the course of their lives as Americans, rose as high as the Polish military hero Kościuszko had nearly a century earlier during the War of Independence. The American Civil War helped numerous refugees to a military career, sometimes taking them from simple soldier to high officer. Friedrich Hecker, the radical democrat from Baden after whom the "Hecker Uprising" of 1848 was named, made it as far as colonel, and the former war minister of Baden's revolutionary government, Franz Sigel, advanced as far as brigadier general. The latter played a key role in the Civil War by recruiting emigrants, and some regiments from the armies of northern states were predominantly German. Civilian career advancement was no less impressive: Lorenz Brentano, who in May 1849 headed the revolutionary government in Baden, became a congressman and later American consul in Dresden. Carl Schurz, another revolutionary, rose to become secretary of the interior responsible for all federal public lands. The list could be extended to include business leaders, but focusing on only the most famous figures would be misleading. It is more important that the vast majority of refugees integrated; and most succeeded in doing so by the first or second generation.

The absorption and social rise of political refugees from Europe fortified the founding image of the US as a sanctuary of freedom and opened the way for those migrants who came to America out of more material motives. At the same time, it relativized the strict distinction between political refugees and labor migrants, which is implicitly inscribed in the Geneva Refugee Convention and shapes public debates about flight and asylum to this day. As in later periods, the reasons for flight and the motives for migration coalesced. What was decisive was the attitude of the host societies. The fundamentally positive attitude toward refugees in the US helped labor migrants from Central and Eastern Europe obtain a social bonus.

This, in turn, affected later refugees, such as the Russian and Polish Jews who arrived at the end of the nineteenth century. Owing to the hegemony of white Anglo-Saxon Protestants and traditional Christian antisemitism, American society was admittedly less open to them. Yet it was certainly recognized that emigration was just about the only way to escape the pogroms. By contrast, Chinese labor migrants were strictly banned from entering the US by the 1882 Chinese Exclusion Act. Apart from the moral support that refugee groups were sometimes accorded, depending on their ethnic or national background and political orientation, refugees received no government services of any kind. Special integration programs were initiated 120 years later, at the end of the 1970s (more on this later in Chapter 3.5). Whether government services would have accelerated integration in the nineteenth century is another question. Refugees integrate most easily when they do not confront a fully entrenched social order and a majority population but can instead start their new life in a mobile and fluid immigration society.

In one respect, however, the highly politicized refugees from Europe were in for a disappointment: the US, in spite of its democratic self-image, rejected intervening in the domestic affairs of other countries on behalf of the persecuted and oppressed. The first cracks in this splendid isolation only appeared on the eve of the First World War. Numerous civic aid organizations then took the lead, and American NGOs became increasingly active in Europe, advocating for refugees. At first this usually happened in the context of solidarity with ethno-nationalists; for example when Jewish organizations supported persecuted Jews back in the old country. There were also some NGOs that based their missions on universalistic convictions about human rights, such as the Carnegie Foundation during the Balkan Wars of 1912–13, when it documented numerous war crimes and the suffering of refugees, thus drawing the attention of the world public to their fate. In addition, the Quakers supported and operated numerous refugee camps in the period following both world wars.

The protections for minorities written into the Paris Peace Treaties[31] acted indirectly to prevent additional instances of massive flight from East-Central and Southeast Europe. US, Jewish, and humanitarian NGOs also made major contributions to improving the status of minority populations in the Paris accords. As shown in Chapter Two, movements of refugees among national minorities had largely come to a standstill by the mid-1920s. This was largely a consequence of the political and economic stabilization of Europe, that is, to weaker push factors, but also to diminished receptivity among the countries that were traditional destinations for refugees.

The growing distrust of refugees was symptomatic of the political polarization of Europe. Among those who had been politically persecuted in 1830–31 and 1848–49, the dominant groups were bourgeois or, to some extent (as in Poland and Hungary), aristocratic liberals. But in the late nineteenth century, the profile of international exile—whether in Switzerland, Paris, London, or New York—began increasingly to include socialists, anarchists, syndicalists, and other radicals. Some of them did not shy away from violence and would commit spectacular assassinations, such as the one that took the life of the Austrian empress Elisabeth in Geneva in 1898. Attitudes toward political refugees and exiles, accordingly, became much less welcoming, as anxiety mounted that migration might bring with it political dangers.

These fears recurred in later periods, for example after the First World War, when refugees from the Russian Revolution began arriving and, more recently, over refugees from the Middle East. Although many Syrian and Iraqi refugees were in fact fleeing the terror of the so-called Islamist State, they have been associated with that terror ever since the assaults in Paris, Brussels, Nice, London, Manchester, Stockholm, and Berlin.

In the United States, it is the president himself who pushes this line. Immediately after assuming office, Donald Trump declared a 120-day moratorium on taking in refugees. Although he partially rescinded this measure half a year later in response to a court order, the freeze remains in force for refugees from Syria and other zones of conflict in the Middle East.[32] Sanctions of this kind, targeting certain countries, were not even imposed during the waves of assassinations around the turn of the nineteenth century and during the 1930s, when exiles from Southeastern Europe committed a number of spectacular and suicidal terror attacks.

A policy of excluding refugees and other migrants ultimately rests on the construct of an ethnically defined nation. In Europe nation-building built on exclusion and ethnic homogenization has a long and disastrous history. In the US it contravenes the country's more than two-century-old self-image as a bastion of freedom and a sanctuary for refugees. For this reason, too, it is worthwhile lingering on the history of the Forty-Eighters, even if they have attained a rather mythical status. The unusual aspect of this myth is that it has repeatedly wandered back and forth from one shore of the Atlantic to the other and thus has never been entirely forgotten on either side of the ocean. The Forty-Eighters are a matter of trans-Atlantic interest, much like the revolutions of the late eighteenth century.

Political refugees of the long nineteenth century stand out in the history of that era also because of their extra-political accomplishments. Frederic Chopin, Adam Mickiewicz (the Polish national poet), and Richard Wagner achieved world renown as artists in exile, and they were followed in the twentieth century by Marc Chagall, Igor Stravinsky, Pablo Picasso, Czesław Miłosz, and many other painters, musicians, and writers. Culture and their host countries would be poorer without them. This applies to political history as well, a field in which refugees often exerted great influence, as they did on the trade union movement and radicalism in the US.

3.2 The Russian Civil War and the nascent international refugee regime

The Russian Revolution gave rise to the first politically motivated mass flight that affected the entire world. At first the waves of refugees affected the vast Russian Empire itself. Already during the First World War, as we have seen, an estimated six million people were fleeing, although this flight was not politically motivated only, but also a response to other varieties of forced migration, such as evacuations and deportations ordered by the Czarist military. The defeats of 1916 and 1917, when Russia lost Poland, the Baltics, and parts of Ukraine, intensified these movements of war refugees. After the Bolsheviks seized power, the world war segued almost seamlessly into the Russian Civil War, which again forced millions of people into flight. Exactly how many refugees there were, however, is hard to estimate in light of rapidly shifting frontlines and the general chaos of the times. According to recent estimates, the civil war cost about three to four million civilians their lives, and there were probably three to four times as many refugees.[33] The great majority of them at first moved within the vast expanses of the Russian Empire; today they would be designated internally displaced persons. Boris Pasternak recorded the massive uprooting and associated misery in his *Doctor Zhivago*, which can also be read as a novel about universal human displacement and hopelessness.

Soon enough, this mass flight from the Russian Civil War became an international problem. It was as if big stones had been thrown into a puddle; wave followed upon wave as Russian refugees were driven first into the immediate surroundings of the disintegrating empire and then, over the course of time, out into the wide world.[34] Contemporary observers put the number of international refugees at about two million. Although this figure may be somewhat of an exaggeration, it holds up if one includes the "repatriations" to Poland and other states that some refugees seized on as an opportunity to escape the hell of the civil war and the early Bolshevik terror. "The Russians" in fact covered a variety of groups. Immediately after the murder of the czar's family and the initial looting of the aristocracy's landed estates and bourgeois residences in the cities, it was above all the social and political elites who got themselves out of harm's way. The escalating civil war then ultimately affected all strata of society, but only those who had money for train tickets, passage by ship, and, when necessary, to pay human smugglers could flee. In a recent biography of his family, the historian Mark Mazower has recorded in graphic detail how his grandfather, with the assistance of a smuggler, managed to get to Lithuania, Poland, and finally England; unfortunately, we have few such individual case studies.[35] Owing to the collapse of state power, pogroms spread like wildfire, which led at least three hundred thousand Jews to flee. Finally, toward the end of the civil war, tens of thousands of White army soldiers needed to be evacuated. Hence, as is usually the case in instances of politically motivated flight, there was a surplus of men among the fugitives.

Initially, most refugees fled to countries immediately adjoining the former Russian Empire, which was now of course the Soviet Union. Tens of thousands came to ground in Warsaw, Bucharest, Istanbul, and the Manchurian city of Harbin. The populations in the Russian quarters of these cities were, however, always in flux, as permanent prospects for making a living were scarce. Other conflicts, both historical and contemporary, contributed to the hardships. Until the "great retreat" of 1915, large parts of Poland had been ruled and oppressed by Russia for more than a hundred years. In 1920 the Soviet-Polish War broke out, so that even for years to come Russians were viewed with suspicion, if not as outright enemies. It was of little help to the Russian refugees, therefore, that they shared with Poles a common opposition to the Bolsheviks. Only in exceptional cases did Russian refugees receive permanent residency permits, and no social services at all were available to them.

In Romania there was also a long prehistory of Russian domination, in this case within the framework of the czarist empire's protectorate over the two Danubian principalities (1828–54). When there were conflicts in the Balkans, moreover, Russia repeatedly supported Slavophile Bulgaria against Romania. As in Poland, therefore, Russian refugees received no government support, this in spite of Romanians' political sympathies for the "White Russians." Bucharest tolerated the Russian refugees only if they promised to move on quickly.[36] A separate problem in Poland and Romania was anti-semitism, which was directed against the Jews among the refugees, but also struck non-Jewish refugees who were lumped with the Jews and mistreated just as badly.

When existing escape routes narrowed, the refugees adjusted their strategies. For example, a number of Russians and Ukrainians used Poland's opening to Polish repatriates as a way of getting to the West. After the Polish-Soviet Treaty of Riga was concluded in 1921, between 1.1 and 1.3 million people left for Poland. Recent studies have concluded that at most half of them were actually from Polish families.[37] The Baltic states recorded having even more repatriates in proportion to the size of their populations, 215,000 for Lithuania and 130,000 for Latvia, according to Gatrell's estimates.[38] Since the repatriates often arrived traumatized by the turmoil of war and without even the most meager of possessions, it seems appropriate to call them refugees even if they were actually not, according to the League of Nations' definition at that time. They did have, as a rule, the advantage of being able to obtain citizenship quickly in the country where they were taken in. For stateless refugees—statelessness was one of the criteria in the League of Nations definition—acquiring citizenship was much more difficult.

An exodus from the Ukraine followed the suppression of the Ukrainian People's Republic. Some 35,000 Ukrainians fled immediately to the West, and later even more came.[39] They were not really welcome in Poland, because the reestablished Polish state wanted to keep its Ukrainian minority as small as possible. Lacking further prospects, most Ukrainians moved on to Canada and the US, where there were already numerous Ukrainians who had come prior to 1914 as labor migrants.[40] In Prague, too, a large Ukrainian diaspora formed parallel to the Russian one. All of this demonstrates once more that political flight is linked to other forms of migration and that often the paths to exile were paved in advance by earlier labor migration.

Oppressive poverty and the lack of future prospects in Poland and Southeast Europe heightened migration pressures on Germany and especially on its capital city. Since the nineteenth century, Berlin had been a magnet for Jewish and East European migrants. Added to its attractions was its location on the way to North Sea ports and thus to the most important emigration routes to North America. When the refugees from revolution and civil war in Russia started arriving in the hundreds of thousands, however, they quickly perceived that they were not welcome in Berlin either.[41] It was very hard to obtain a permanent work and residency permit there, which forced them into the shadow economy and into accepting jobs for the proverbial "starvation wage," which then intensified competition with the native lower classes.

In November 1923, growing social tensions in Berlin's Scheunenviertel, the central gathering point for refugees from Eastern Europe, led to a pogrom. The police managed to get the violence under control; and unlike the pogroms in numerous Russian, Ukrainian, Polish, and Romanian cities, there were no deaths in Berlin. Yet the looting and violence on the streets acted as a push factor on the refugees. According to official French counts, 72,000 Russians (among them also many Russian Jews) came to France, above all to Paris.

The United States was also a desirable destination for Russian refugees. Here, however, there was a new set of hurdles. In 1921 the US enacted a quota system for immigrants that favored "white" Central and Northern Europeans over refugees from Southern and Eastern Europe. The Immigration Act of 1924 sealed off the US even more, and with a racist bias. Other overseas countries like Canada, Australia, Brazil, and Argentina remained more accessible until the outbreak of the Great Depression. But their immigration policies also had a utilitarian orientation. What chiefly mattered was the economic value of migrants, not humanitarian assistance for refugees. Not least for that reason, about 100,000 Russians remained in Germany until most of them had to pack their bags again when the Nazis came to power.

The international emergency posed by the plight of the Russian refugees was resolved when they took their fate into their own hands. Through letters and other channels of communication, they kept in touch with compatriots abroad and learned from them where conditions were best for finding temporary accommodations and work, and where prospects for the future were brightest. Their social status gave them access to this information as most of the refugees belonged to the upper classes, bourgeoisie, or intelligentsia, and quite a few of them spoke French, German, or English, which helped greatly in gathering essential information about their host countries. When it came to overcoming immediate hardships, what proved especially helpful were emergency associations, private initiatives, and clubs created on short notice, but most important of all were the refugees' extended families. Using these networks, refugees found their way to many different countries on all of the world's continents, as far away as Australia and South Africa.

The League of Nations developed into the most important international refugee organization of its time. When it came to money and material support, the High Commissioner for Russian Refugees had nothing to offer, but Fridtjof Nansen succeeded in implementing certain norms on how refugees were to be treated. With the invention of the Nansen passports named after him, the Norwegian philanthropist was able to put in place three essential innovations: first, an international system for forwarding and taking in refugees under the umbrella of the League of Nations; second, the cooperation of most of the nation-states organized within the League (it was the member states that were responsible for issuing the Nansen passports); and, third, the principle that refugees should not be sent back to their countries of origin, the places from which they had fled.

Progress was erratic, as the fate of the East European Jews stranded in Danzig (see Chapters 2.1 and 2.2 on this) and the forced repatriation of Galician refugees out of Vienna show; nevertheless, Nansen's measures marked the beginning of an autonomous international refugee policy. The title given to him in the documents of the League of Nations makes this clear, for as of 1922–23 the national attribute was dropped. Nansen was no longer High Commissioner for *Russian* Refugees; he was High Commissioner *period*, responsible for all refugees. In the 1930s, this changed again, and each commissioner was assigned to one specific group of refugees. But when the United Nations created the UNHCR, the concentration of all competences into one institution remained the rule.

Europe's economic recovery played a strong role in improving the legal position and treatment of refugees as well. France in particular readily accepted refugees and other migrants in the 1920s in order to close the demographic gap that the First World War had rent in the national fabric. Then, when underlying economic conditions worsened with the Great Depression every European country found itself faced with an army of unemployed. This brought social welfare systems to the brink of collapse, and the mood turned against all kinds of migrants, including refugees. The growing nationalism and xenophobia even extended to people who had already been integrated into the labor market for several years. Thirty thousand Ukrainian and other East European workers were deported from Canada at the beginning of the 1930s, a number of former Russian refugees lost their work permits in France, and refugee existence became more precarious all over the world.

Jewish refugees suffered doubly under these worsening economic conditions, for antisemitism was also on the rise and borders were closing. The next major group affected by the decay of the nascent international refugee regime was the Spanish fleeing their country's civil war after 1936.

3.3 Flight from fascism

Most refugees from National Socialism arriving in France after 1933 had at least one advantage: they were members of an educated elite. Many already spoke a foreign language or knew how to learn one, and as a rule they were well connected. The lucky ones had some savings they could bring along. (On the refugees from Nazi Germany, see Chapter 2.1.) By contrast, most of the Spanish refugees arrived in France with few social and cultural resources at their disposal. To be sure, they were not citizens of a former and future enemy country, but they came as France's poor southern neighbors. Already in the 1920s, numerous Spaniards had immigrated to France as agricultural workers. Because of their poverty they occupied a low rung of society, living mostly on the edges of cities and villages, and were in many respects comparable to the agricultural laborers from the Maghreb in today's Spain.

The first great wave of refugees arrived following the collapse of the northern front in the summer and autumn of 1937, when the Spanish republican government lost all of the regions along the Atlantic coast to the rebels under General Franco. About 120,000 Spaniards fled to France, mostly under chaotic circumstances and only with the clothes on their backs.[42] The leftist Popular Front government under Léon Blum initially sympathized with the republican refugees and distributed more than 25,000 of them to municipalities willing to take them in. Their best chances to be admitted were in places where Socialists or Communists governed, and there was also some support from the churches. But as the number of refugees grew, their chances for acceptance diminished. With increasing frequency, the Spaniards were seen as a burden and a danger to domestic peace, as an "invasion," or even as a "plague."[43] The denigration came primarily from the right, but sometimes also from the left, as in the case of fishermen along the Atlantic coast who protested against Spanish competitors.[44]

The government soon reacted with stronger border controls, a promise to repatriate the Spaniards as soon as possible, and by the end of November 1937 with a directive according to which only those refugees could stay who had sufficient means to support themselves.[45] This harder line was not enough to slow the rise of right-wing parties, which spread hate propaganda and promised to halt the admission of refugees altogether. Much like countries ruled by centrist or leftist parties today, the Blum government's reputation suffered. Leftist stalwarts now accused the Popular Front of betraying both its own ideals and the Spanish republicans. It was owing in part to this persistent controversy over how to deal with the civil war and the Spanish refugees that Léon Blum had to resign as premier in 1938.

French society and the rest of the international community showed more empathy to only one group, namely children. When Bilbao fell in the summer of 1937, 4,000 children were transported by ship to Great Britain, followed later by evacuations to Belgium, which accommodated 5,000 children, and to the Soviet Union; neighboring France, took in 20,000 children, the largest contingent by far.[46] This distribution was largely the product of an international conference that convened in Paris on November 20 and 21 in 1937 and was dedicated to providing for and forwarding refugee children. As a result, even faraway Mexico took in 436 Spanish minors. In all 33,000 children were brought to safety. This relief campaign and overseas transports were successful acts of international humanitarianism.

The aftereffects extended well beyond Spain; in 1938–39, within the framework of the so-called Kindertransport program, 10,000 Jewish children were brought from Germany and Austria to Great Britain and thus saved from death in Nazi concentration camps. These successes in rescuing refugee minors stand in sharp contrast to the Évian Conference, which looms so large in the historiography of the late 1930s. Much depended, on the one hand, on the timing—in 1937, when the Paris conference took place, attitudes toward refugees were not quite as negative as they would become a year later—and, on the other hand, on the activities of NGOs. It was civil society, not a government, that organized and paid for the Kindertransport on the eve of the Second World War.

When Valencia, Barcelona, and a besieged Madrid fell in 1939, this aggravated the situation once again, both inside France and internationally. The French government under its conservative premier Édouard Daladier, one of the signatories to the disgraceful Munich Agreement, tried to close the Spanish border. When the border posts were overrun, the government hastily erected concentration camps—which were actually called by that name.[47] Interning the refugees, however, solved nothing. Owing to overcrowding in the camps, food rations had to be cut, and outbreaks of epidemics intensified French fear of foreigners. The refugees were desperate, and the only conceivable way out was through some kind of private connection or service in the Foreign Legion.[48]

France proposed that the Spanish government set up internment camps along the Spanish border—which the Francoists of course rejected—and started negotiations with Franco about a massive repatriation. Even the evacuated war children entered into the discussion, since the Spanish government accused host countries of "stealing" the children. There were indeed lots of problems in orphanages that housed the children and among the families who were searching for them, for they had been traumatized by war and flight, usually spoke no French, and suffered from homesickness. Many of the institutions were therefore rather relieved when they were able to send their charges back to Spain after 1939.[49]

Attitudes toward refugee minors—here, once again, a detour into the present seems appropriate—have changed since 2015. Skepticism is growing all over Europe, due in the first place to the large number of "unaccompanied minors" (in Sweden they make up a third of all refugees), and second because of overburdened social workers, who have great difficulties in dealing with these frequently traumatized youths. In Germany in 2017 a criminal case in Freiburg attracted much attention when an Afghani minor (who turned out to be several years older than originally reported) raped and murdered a university student. The age and asylum status of refugee minors now receive a good deal more scrutiny, especially as the age of young people can be determined more reliably today with the aid of biometric examinations, a tool not yet available in the case of the Spanish Civil War children. At that time, though, there was also no legal possibility of arranging for refugee children who had already fled to rejoin their families. Today the humane principle of family reunification can conceivably create a false incentive for the migration of unaccompanied minors that would not exist if war orphans were to be brought directly from Syria or its neighboring states to Western countries of asylum. How one might configure Western humanitarianism so that it actually helps the neediest—refugee minors undoubtedly fit into this category—will be discussed in greater detail at the end of this book in Chapter 4.3.

For the Spanish Republicans stranded in France, there was still one last resort, which was moving on to a third country. It was a stroke of luck that at the time Mexico happened to be ruled by a republican party. Twenty thousand Spaniards found refuge there; some were even picked up by ships specially prepared for them and, upon their arrival, they received government support to aid them in starting a new life. This example shows again what political solidarity can accomplish. (It was a solidarity, however, that was not extended to Jewish refugees. In 1937 the Mexican government issued a decree against the admission of Jews.) Other traditional countries of immigration like Argentina, which was then governed by conservatives, were afraid that they might be importing Communists and anarchists along with the refugees. Hence only a few thousand Franco opponents found accommodations there, usually on the strength of private connections.

The Soviet Union, which was the only state to support the Spanish Republicans openly and with weapons deliveries (in 1937 France had imposed a weapons embargo, which was intended to prevent an escalation in the civil war but indirectly strengthened the Francoists), was far away and could only be reached by ship. There up to 10,000 Spanish Communists were taken in. They had a rough time, however, for many were again persecuted for deviations from the party line and, due to fears of Western infiltration, imprisoned or killed in Stalinist gulags.

The US, by contrast, dropped out as a country of refuge for Spanish Republicans owing to its quota system, which had little room for Southern Europeans. And soon there would be even less room for refugees from Spain. In 1938–39, President Roosevelt made a major share of the entire immigration quota available to persecuted Jews. The quota system was in general an obstacle to flexible refugee policy. Its breakdown of immigration by country of origin—ostensibly utilitarian, but subliminally racist—made it hard to react to acute crises in a humanitarian spirit. President Roosevelt recognized this when he opened the quotas for imperiled Jews from Central Europe. But in 1938–39, his power apparently did not reach far enough that he could persuade Congress to adopt a fundamentally different refugee policy. The consequences of this rigidity are also demonstrated, tragically, by the case of the *St. Louis*, which was not allowed to moor in Florida because the 1939 immigration quotas had been exhausted. Ultimately the refugee ship was sent back to Europe, where about a fourth of its passengers were killed in the Holocaust. This horrible ending could not have been foreseen in 1939; nevertheless, the contradiction between utilitarianism and a humanitarian refugee and immigration policy was apparent to all.

In the end, therefore, a majority of the Spanish Civil War refugees remained captive in their own country or were sent back there. What happened with the deportees has barely been researched, since failed flight is just as much a poor stepchild of refugee research today as remigration was in migration studies until about thirty years ago. Politically less prominent refugees probably had a better chance of flying below the radar once they got back home. Their opportunities were also favored by the circumstance that millions of people were wandering about in Spain and ultimately making their way back to their homes. All those who were politically suspect in the eyes of the Francoists, however, could look forward to trials, internment in camps, and possible execution. Only in the late 1990s was there any nationwide investigation of the fascist era's numerous mass graves, since a cloak of silence was spread over the crimes of the Franco dictatorship following Spain's democratization in the late 1970s.

In spite of the forced repatriations, however, one should not condemn France and its refugee policy out of hand. After all, around 150,000 Civil War refugees did find refuge there in an extremely tense economic and political situation.[50] On the other hand, more than 250,000 people were "repatriated" to Spain, if one may use this euphemistic expression. The failure of French and international refugee policy post-1938—after its positive start in the 1920s—can be attributed above all to the lack of political solidarity that had already prevented a spirited intervention in favor of the legitimate Spanish government. The longer the Civil War lasted, the greater the fears about whom one might be bringing into the country: undoubtedly paupers and freeloaders, according to contemporary perceptions, and in the worst case troublemakers and revolutionaries. The sheer number of refugees was also a factor. France and the international community were simply overburdened. The treatment of Spanish Civil War refugees was, therefore, yet another testament to the Western democracies' failure to meet the challenge of fascism in its many interwar varieties.

That fascism should be considered in the plural is demonstrated in a surprising way by the third largest wave of mid-1930s refugees, which saw National Socialist Germany, of all places, becoming a country of exile. In June 1933, the Austrian government banned the Nazi party in order to contain the spread of National Socialism. The leaders of the party, however, remained active in the underground and, one year later, organized a coup against the clerical-fascist Dollfuß regime. The chancellor was murdered according to plan, but overall the coup failed and ended with thirteen death sentences after a series of trials. In 1933 and 1934, therefore, over 15,000 Austrian National Socialists fled to the German Reich.[51] This number may seem relatively tiny, but in places like the Wolfsberg in Carinthia or Leibnitz in Styria up to 11 percent of men between the ages of 20 and 24 fled to neighboring Germany. To this day both localities are bastions of the right-wing nationalist Freedom Party of Austria, the FPÖ, which advocates an extremely restrictive refugee policy.

There were, in principle, three ways that Spanish Civil War refugees might find refuge in French exile: If they were rich enough, they might be able to support themselves in spite of the ban on employment. Artists like Pablo Picasso and musicians like the cellist Pau Casals also had relatively good chances to be permanently accommodated. A third possibility was volunteering for service in the Foreign Legion, which could mean being sent to the French colonies. For all other refugees the prospects were usually dim, which is why most returned to Spain.

Among these unsuccessful refugees, probably numbering more than 200,000, was **Manuel Alarcón Navarro**, forty years old at the time of his flight. He is one of a million refugees whose name has played no role in previous histories of this period because they left scarcely any historical records behind. The biographical sketch presented here relies on a private family archive consisting of a small box of photos and some fragments of letters. One could probably find ten thousand such archives in Europe if one were only to make the effort to gather them from family members willing to share them.[52] On the basis of these scanty sources it may be deduced that this worker from the Andalusian province of Almería took the side of the Republican government in the Civil War.[53] In the spring of 1938 he volunteered for the army, which retreated to the north after several severe defeats. A year later Alarcón was in flight again, presumably as part of the *Retirada*, the retreat of the defeated Republican army, heading toward France, where he was interned in the refugee camp at Vernet d'Ariège.

In the autumn of 1939, he returned to Spain because the French repatriation effort left him no alternative. In addition, he was worried about his wife and five children, aged one to thirteen, who had stayed behind in Almería. Alarcón was apparently convinced that the punishment for veterans of the Republican army would not be so severe, since the Civil War had been over since April. He paid with his life for this miscalculation. According to the last signs of life transmitted to his family, Alarcón was interned in the concentration camp at Miranda del Ebro, where he died.[54] For a long time the relatives of men persecuted by the Franco regime were kept in the dark about the fate of their sons and fathers; officially, they were simply regarded as having "disappeared." Following the end of the Franco dictatorship, Alarcón's wife had him declared dead after undertaking a fruitless search with advertisements in three national newspapers, so that she could at least receive a widow's pension.

(cont.)

> *(cont.)*
>
> One could fill many books and graveyards with unsuccessful refugees like Alarcón. One of his victims, indirectly, was his eldest daughter, who died of tuberculosis at sixteen. His single widow with her many children could not afford any effective treatment for her, which would have required a dietary routine of healthy nutrition and regular visits to a sanatorium.

The failed coup in Austria and flight into the German Reich had serious international repercussions. Mussolini ordered the Italian army to the Austrian border at the Brenner Pass in order to demonstrate his support for his allies, the clerical fascists. Hitler, on the other hand, was forced to distance himself from the coup attempt, so that the Austrian refugees and fellow Nazi party members were taken in rather reluctantly and quietly rather than with open arms and noisy propaganda. In order to prevent further diplomatic tensions, the Nazi regime moved the Austrian Legion formed by these refugees to northern Germany, where it was finally dissolved a few years later. The move and shutdown had little to do with foreign policy considerations, however, but instead with a conflict inside the Nazi regime. The Legion was close to the SA, which had lost a power struggle with the SS.

In September 1938 there ensued the next massive flight in the direction of Nazi Germany. After a failed attempt at an uprising and the proclamation of martial law in the border regions of Czechoslovakia by President Edvard Beneš, more than 30,000 members of the Sudeten German Party (SdP) settled in the German Reich. Hitler presented the refugees as victims of nationalist tyranny and thus gained one more argument he could use in his effort to persuade France and Great Britain that the so-called Sudetenland should be ceded to Germany. These refugees, of course, were no victims of political persecution. During the negotiations on the Munich Agreement they had carried out 230 raids on Czechoslovakian border posts, police stations, and administrative buildings. This deliberate escalation brought about the desired result for Hitler, and the Western powers surrendered Czechoslovakia to Germany's superior strength. Just two weeks following their flight, the functionaries of the SdP marched triumphantly back into their homeland.[55] This return of refugees, certainly the fastest in twentieth-century European history, may at first glance look like an isolated episode. But on second glance it shows that not all political refugees are innocent victims of persecution. The victims of the new European order reached with the Munich Agreement were the approximately 200,000 Czechs, Jews, and German opposition figures, above all Social Democrats, who had to flee into the Czechoslovakian interior after the border territories seceded.[56]

For many this proved a dead end, since after the Évian Conference there were hardly any states taking in political refugees. Ultimately their fate was little different from that of the Spanish Republicans, since the spread of fascism meant the same thing for both groups: namely, that there were hardly any countries left as destinations. France, Belgium, the Netherlands, and Great Britain held that they were already overwhelmed by refugees from Germany and Austria.

By the end of the 1930s the at first tentative acceptance of political refugees, followed by the ultimate refusal to accept them at all, deepened the loss of prestige suffered by the remaining Western democracies. In France the debate over refugee policy, one of the largest areas of conflict in domestic politics in 1938–39, contributed to the collapse of several government cabinets. Moreover, the potential of the refugees for the impending war effort was insufficiently recognized. Refugees, to be sure, had the possibility of volunteering for the Foreign Legion and the French army, but their forced repatriation to Spain nonetheless robbed France of huge military potential, since many Spanish Republicans had military training and combat experience. Instead, French society became demobilized from within and without. This paralysis contributed to its rapid and devastating defeat by Nazi Germany in 1940.

Another factor contributing to the French defeat was the National Socialists' wanton reliance on mass flight as a strategic instrument. The occupation of Belgium in May had already caused a mass flight even larger than that of World War I, with up to two million Belgians fleeing from the German army to France. The rapid advance of the Wehrmacht through northern France and the faltering defense of Paris at the beginning of June triggered another wave of refugees. More than one million Parisians tried to get out of the capital; all in all, between eight and nine million people were on the run.[57] The Belgians and French fleeing the Blitzkrieg so severely clogged French roads that they prevented France's own army from a timely mobilization with adequate reinforcements. This refugee chaos, which is vividly described in the novel *Suite Française* by Irène Némirovsky,[58] had been factored into the Wehrmacht's strategy. Marshal Pétain then used it in order to gain popularity for himself and his defeatist stance. In several speeches in which he pointed to the suffering of millions of refugees inside France, he promised the nation peace and the refugees a speedy homecoming.[59] To put the point somewhat more dramatically: the refusal to take in refugees in 1939 was like a curse that backfired on France.

3.4 The early Cold War and displaced persons

International scholarship is not entirely agreed on when exactly to date the beginning of the Cold War. Winston Churchill's speech about the "Iron Curtain" in Fulton, Missouri, during the summer of 1946 is often suggested, while other historians opt for the Berlin Blockade of 1948.[60] In the Baltic region this lingering and long-lived enmity showed itself even earlier in the form of yet another mass flight. In the summer of 1944, when the Red Army occupied Estonia, Latvia, and Lithuania for a second time, a new mass exodus began from these countries. Their inhabitants had experienced Stalinist terror and deportations during the first Soviet occupation in 1940–41, and they knew what awaited them. In addition, some Estonians, Latvians, and Lithuanians had collaborated with the Nazis because of their anti-Communist convictions, and for other reasons. Hence, by the end of 1944 about 50,000 people were attempting a last-minute escape across the Baltic Sea.

Stalin viewed the Baltic refugees as traitors and a danger to the Soviet Union and demanded that the governments of Sweden and Finland hand them over. Finland found itself in a weaker position than Sweden because it was preoccupied with the evacuation and reception of about 300,000 refugees from eastern Karelia, which it had had to cede to the Soviet Union. Moreover, it did not have full sovereignty in foreign policy after its defeat by the Red Army. The government in Helsinki, therefore, feared that it might have to hand the Baltic refugees over to Stalin. Some 7,200 Estonian refugees got the hint that they should make their way through to Sweden via the west coast of Finland. Eventually, more than 50,000 people were repatriated from Finland to the Soviet Union, often against their will. The Swedish government, by contrast, decided for the time being not to cave in to pressure from Moscow, and so it took in the refugees from the Baltic permanently.

For Sweden this added considerably to a burden the country was already shouldering, since toward the end of the war about 150,000 war refugees from Norway and Finland were still sheltering there, as well as several thousand exiles from Germany and Austria (among them future chancellors Willy Brandt and Bruno Kreisky). Up through the end of 1944 these were joined by 32,000 refugees from Estonia, and the capital city of Stockholm became a "Baltic metropolis."[61] This openness toward refugees from the eastern shores of the Baltic rested on historic and even some national ties, for until 1940 a small Swedish minority had resided on the Estonian Baltic islands, and these Swedes had fled after Estonia was annexed by the Soviet Union. Moreover, Sweden had a tradition as a country of asylum, so the media treated the refugees sympathetically. At the end of 1944 and in 1945, Swedish newspapers were full of stories about adventurous escapes in small fishing boats that foregrounded in touching terms the human side of the operation.[62] Thus was born the heroic figure of the Cold War refugee, which returned later in different forms in the US and Germany, especially after the building of the Berlin Wall.

Sympathy for the politically persecuted was on the rise again early in 1945 when Sweden participated in emergency assistance to concentration camp survivors from Poland. Sixteen thousand people arrived and were cared for by NGOs and aid workers from the civilian population. This humanitarian action was initiated by the Swedish Red Cross functionary and philanthropist Count Bernadotte. Two years later, the UN appointed him negotiator in the Jewish-Arab conflict in Palestine, where he was assassinated by a Zionist paramilitary unit in the fall of 1948. While the Estonians, Latvians, and Lithuanians were taken in as political refugees, the Swedish government officially classified the Poles as "repatriates." In fact, one third of them returned to their homeland in 1945–46. Although Poland was still governed by a coalition with the participation of the Peasant Party, the Communists were already taking over power. At the beginning of 1946, Sweden also made a small concession to Stalin: 146 Estonians and Latvians who had demonstrably fought on the side of the Germans were extradited to the Soviet Union.[63] In addition, there was a ban on political activity by exiles.

While the Swedish Social Democrats distanced themselves from the anti-Communist refugees under prime minister Tage Erlander, the level of civil-society engagement increased. The churches collected donations, as did the Red Cross, and native fishermen participated in rescue operations on the Baltic. Moreover, the government saw to it that the refugees were spread out across Sweden: moved out of the overcrowded capital of Stockholm to Göteborg, Malmö, and the country's interior. This forwarding of refugees was intended, however, not only as a way of easing their integration, but also as a deterrent to organized political activity and collective movements of the sort that might trigger conflicts with the Soviet Union. All in all, the Swedish government acted rather defensively, out of foreign policy considerations, in contrast to civil society's less guarded behavior.

Outside support played an important role in coping with the flight from the Baltics. Via the War Refugee Board, the US participated financially and organizationally in aiding the refugees from Estonia and promised to take some of them off Sweden's hands. Some years later, in fact, the center of emigration really did shift—as in the case of Latvians, Lithuanians, and Ukrainians—to North America. The refugees from the Baltics enjoyed a special status in the US, not least because the United States had not recognized the annexation of the Baltic states by the Soviet Union in 1940 (in contrast to the Swedish government, whose behavior was more compliant). Accordingly, the renewed occupation of 1944 was also deemed a violation of international law, and the refugees to be in need of protection, as far as the US was concerned. Overall the "refugee crisis" in the Baltic region was resolved thanks to three factors: the vigorous solidarity of Sweden, the first host country; the manageable number of refugees; and the internationalization of the problem by redirecting the refugees to North America.

At that time there was a southeast European equivalent to the situation in the Baltic region. Following the war's end a civil war erupted in Greece, a conflict in which the Communists initially brought parts of the north under their control.[64] The popularity of the Left dated back to the incomplete integration of refugees from Asia Minor and the presence of the *slawophono*, the unrecognized Bulgarian and Macedonian minority. Yet the fate of the Communist partisans was sealed by the partition of Europe in the run-up to the Conference of Yalta. Greece fell into the Western zone of influence, and the Soviet Union adhered to the agreements. After his break with Stalin, Tito did not wish any conflict with the Western powers, and without support from abroad the forces of the partisans were not sufficient to offer permanent resistance.

In 1949 the last Communist units fled to Albania and Bulgaria. In total, the wave of refugees, including family members, numbered around 100,000 people. The Eastern Bloc made use of this situation in a large-scale propaganda campaign. In 1948 they had already started an international solidarity action for the Greek refugees in which the Soviet Union, Albania (at the time still loyal to Moscow), Bulgaria, Romania, Czechoslovakia, the GDR, and Poland participated. These states presented the Greeks as victims of Western imperialism and fascism, founded aid committees, provided housing, clothing, and jobs, and distributed the refugees among themselves.[65]

Special empathy was enjoyed by 28,000 Greek children and youngsters. They did not fit into the heroic imaging of antifascist resistance fighters, but they provide further evidence of the growing sensitivity toward children that had already saved the lives of 10,000 Jewish minors from Central Europe on the eve of the Second World War. This increasing focus on children changed the attitude toward refugees in both the East and West; it "humanized" the arrivals, who had previously been viewed all too often as a gray mass and as freeloaders.[66] In contrast to human rights and the rights of refugees that derived from that human rights, notions that the Communists rejected as hypocrisy, caring for children was popular on both sides of the Iron Curtain.

That this was not entirely a consequence of humanitarian ideals becomes obvious in the context of Stalinism. The USSR aimed to raise each child to become a "new man," an ardent supporter of the party, and viewed grown-up refugees as a reserve army against the possibility that the constellations of the Cold War, with its entrenched frontlines, should change again. The hope for a revolution back in the old homeland helped the exiled Greeks stick together in faraway Tashkent, where the largest contingent of more than 13,000 people was accommodated and the refugees founded a "Greek people's democracy."[67] Yet their harsh everyday life as industrial workers (the Greeks there were replacing repatriated Japanese prisoners of war), the rough climate in Central Asia, oppressive surveillance by the NKVD, and unbridgeable differences between them and the native Uzbeks prevented the Greeks from putting down permanent roots.

In the GDR there was a similar outcome to the Greek story: the grown-ups were kept under surveillance by the Stasi and did not integrate to any significant extent into East German society. Young people in the children's camps (the largest of which was in the Dresden suburb of Radebeul), resisted the traditional German educational drill to which the Communists subjected them, especially as many of them had suffered before under the Nazi occupation of

Greece. After the fall of the Greek military dictatorship in 1974, most GDR Greeks returned to their homeland, which many of them had never seen before.[68]

In Poland there was a connection between taking in the Greeks and the flight and expulsion of the Germans. The largest contingent of the 13,000 civil war refugees, about 4,000 people, were settled in Zgorzelec, the part of Görlitz east of the Neiße river that had fallen to Poland. There, at the end of the 1940s, room was still in plentiful supply as the resettlers from Central Poland and the refugees from Eastern Poland were not numerous enough to replace the Germans who had been expelled.[69] Most of the Greeks moved away again from this gray border town, however, with many of them heading to Wrocław and then, in the second half of the 1970s, back to Greece. As in the GDR, integration was a failure here in spite of much political propaganda and expressions of solidarity toward the Greek refugees.

What the Baltic and Greek Communist emigrations, for all their differences, had in common was the way they functioned to confirm the ideological positions of the two rival Cold War blocs, allowing both East and West, as well as formally neutral countries like Sweden, to celebrate their alleged moral superiority over the competing system. The media boosted circulation with adventurous stories of flight, and people in the host societies had an opportunity to demonstrate their helpfulness. Sweden distinguished itself in particular here, and its welcoming tradition lived on in later years. The country's openness to asylum seekers from all over the world became part of Sweden's national identity, at least for the liberal mainstream of society. Sweden's much-discussed problems with the Middle East refugees since 2015, and also with earlier arrivals, may reside in the discrepancy between its intention to do good for refugees (as well as for others in need) and the limited integrative power of Swedish society, a capacity that is, after all, not unlimited.

In the 1970s neutral Sweden, Austria, and the West in general were clear winners in the competition over the refugee policies. Whereas in the course of time almost all of the Greeks returned to their old homeland, most Baltic emigrants remained in the US, Canada, and Sweden. Although there were a few prominent exceptions—including three exiles who later became heads of state (Valdas Adamkus in Lithuania, Vaira Vike-Freiberga in Latvia, and Toomas Hendrik Ilves in Estonia)—on the whole the number of returnees remained negligible. In the end, though, Greece and the Baltics were only sideshows in the nascent Cold War.

The displaced persons

The greatest refugee drama was played out in the center of Europe, and it refutes all the myths about the good, humanitarian West always striving to uphold human rights. Among the legacies of the Second World War were about seven to eight million displaced persons in the parts of Germany and

Austria occupied by the Western Allies. Almost as many DPs remained behind in the Soviet sphere of influence. These were prisoners of war, including former soldiers of the Red Army, forced laborers displaced and enslaved by the Nazis, Holocaust survivors, and other civilians.

For the victorious Allied powers, the sheer number of DPs—the term then covered all those people in Europe located outside the borders of their homeland—was the greatest challenge. It was a challenge aggravated by the circumstance that several million German refugees and evacuees were already entering occupied Germany and Austria in 1945. In retrospect, it almost borders on a miracle that this chaos could be managed in the face of severely destroyed cities, train stations, and railway networks. Immediately after the end of the war, the Allies returned a majority of the prisoners of war and forced laborers to their countries of origin. In May and June 1945 alone, more than five million people were repatriated, more than 80,000 daily on average.[70] Moreover, the occupying powers succeeded in preventing massive outbreaks of epidemics. This was also true in Hungary, Greece, and Italy, which housed at least 700,000 refugees in each country, and in Poland even more. There were, to be sure, local outbreaks of typhus, cholera, and the ever-present tuberculosis, but no widespread deaths as was the case after the end of the First World War and following the Treaty of Lausanne.

In making this logistical accomplishment possible, an important role was played by the United Nations Relief and Rehabilitation Administration (UNRRA). It was founded in 1943, two years before the UN, on the initiative of the United States, which provided nearly two thirds of the new organization's budget. UNRRA secured nourishment for millions of DPs, supplied food for the return transports, and was a cornerstone of care in Poland after repatriation. UNRRA was explicitly not responsible for German refugees from Eastern Europe. For obvious reasons, there was no international empathy for them immediately following the war, so German officials were supposed to take care of their own uprooted countrymen.

At first, rapid repatriation accorded with the wishes of most East European prisoners of war and forced laborers. After years of deprivation they wanted only one thing: to return home, back to the old country. The problem was that this homeland often did not exist anymore because it had been destroyed in the war, as was the case, for example, with the Polish capital Warsaw. Since the Soviet Union had annexed almost half of the Poland's prewar territory, at least 300,000 Polish forced laborers could no longer return home from Germany. Moreover, freshly liberated Poland quickly turned into a dictatorship. In the summer of 1945 the first show trials began against the non-Communist resistance fighters of the Armia Krajowa (the Polish Home Army had been the strongest resistance group by far), and in many rural regions groups of partisans took to the forests and continued to fight, now against the Communists. This civil war–like situation, the arbitrariness of the security forces, and the frequent arrests and disappearances of people created a climate that the Polish historian Marcin Zaremba has accurately captured as "the great fear" in his book by that name.[71] After a fraudulent referendum that the Communists had organized in the summer of 1946 as a substitute for free elections, the police, state security apparatus, and the Soviet NKVD persecuted the opposition even more severely. Representatives of the old political and social elites, resistance fighters, and well-known intellectuals now fled in ever greater numbers to the West. At this time the number of Polish DPs in the Western occupation zones of Germany and in Western Europe was estimated at about 400,000.[72]

Many people also became de facto refugees by resisting the repatriation to Poland. The Communist takeover motivated a growing share of former soldiers who had fought on the Western side against Nazi Germany to stay in the West. Several thousand Poles had distinguished themselves in this capacity in France and in the air war surrounding England, and about 80,000 soldiers of the Anders Army (named after its commander General Władysław Anders) later found their way via the Soviet Union and Iran to the Allies and contributed significantly to their victories in North Africa and Monte Cassino. These soldiers, refugees many times over, could not go back to Poland. What awaited them there were show trials, camp imprisonment, and in the worst case death.

In addition, the pogrom in Kielce in June 1946 (discussed in Chapter 2.4) set off an exodus of Polish Jews. They may have had the US or Palestine in mind as destinations, but their escape route frequently led them across occupied Germany. After the February 1948 coup in Prague, more and more Czechs and Slovaks went into exile, as did Hungarians, Romanians, Bulgarians, Croatians, and Slovenians, in addition to the Ukrainians and Balts already mentioned. The latter could argue that they were not even Soviet citizens and thus not subject to repatriation. From the perspective of the Western powers this meant that all their post-1946 efforts at international resettlement had scarcely reduced the number of DPs. It looked like an insoluble problem.

Stalin hermetically sealed off the Soviet Union from the outside, thus erecting a second Iron Curtain within the Eastern Bloc, but news nonetheless filtered through about what was happening to the forced laborers and prisoners of war who had returned home. They fell under suspicion of collaboration—in the end, they *had* been working for the enemy—and of treason. The punishment for these offenses was internment in the gulag or punitive deportation to inhospitable regions. The terror of Stalin, the NKVD, and the Red Army had already driven millions of Russians, Ukrainians, and other Soviet citizens into the arms of the Wehrmacht and farther westward during the war. Among the anti-Communist refugees there were such allies of the National Socialists as the soldiers of the "Russian Liberation Army" (better known as the Vlasov Army—its commander, Soviet Lieutenant General Andrey Vlasov, had

Also among the refugees of the Cold War was a then eleven-year-old Prague-born girl named Marie Korbelová. Like many an East-Central European exile, she already had, in spite of her young age, several stages of flight behind her. In the spring of 1939 her father, the diplomat Josef Korbel, had fled Czechoslovakia for London after the invasion of the Wehrmacht. This flight from the National Socialists was politically motivated, but it saved the young Marie from likely death in a concentration camp because, as it would later emerge (although her converted parents had kept this secret from her) the family was of Jewish descent. In 1945 the Korbels returned to Prague, where Marie's father entered diplomatic service again under President Edvard Beneš and was sent to Belgrade as ambassador. After the Communist putsch in Czechoslovakia in February 1948, Korbel defected from Yugoslavia via England to the US, was given political asylum there, and became an American citizen in 1957. The diplomat was also able to gain a foothold professionally; thanks to the sponsorship of the Rockefeller Foundation he got a teaching position as a political scientist and founded a graduate school in international studies at the University of Denver.

His talented daughter Marie married into a wealthy American newspaper dynasty and, now under the name of **Madeleine Albright**, studied at Wellesley College, Johns Hopkins University, and Columbia University in New York. Her language skills, which she had acquired at home, proved advantageous, giving her access to other Slavic languages in addition to her native Czech. Albright wrote her master's thesis on the Soviet diplomatic service and her doctoral thesis on the role of the press in the Prague Spring. Subsequently, however, the mother of three children moved into politics and became a legislative assistant to Senator Edmund Muskie. Zbigniew Brzezinski, a child of Polish exiles who rose to become national security adviser to President Jimmy Carter, recruited her in 1978 for a position on the National Security Council. She was able to avoid the usual career slump after the Republicans took over under Ronald Reagan by returning to an academic life. She held teaching appointments at various universities and worked on the side as a foreign policy adviser to prominent Democrats like Walter Mondale.

After his first electoral victory in 1992, Bill Clinton appointed her UN ambassador, and in his second term she rose to become the first woman secretary of state in the United States. In this capacity Albright advocated a resolute stance against Serbian President Slobodan Milošević and convinced Clinton during the Kosovo conflict to bomb the Serbian remnant of Yugoslavia. Her

human-rights credentials, coupled with the formula of a "responsibility to protect" (see Chapter 2.6.), added weight to her position, one shaped not least
by Albright's own childhood in the period following the Munich Agreement
and the failed appeasement policy toward Hitler. This was also true of her
tough attitude in the Cold War, which was fortified by detailed knowledge
about changes going on behind the Iron Curtain. Like her mentor Zbigniew
Brzezinski, this background knowledge facilitated judicious accommodation
toward the Eastern Bloc when that approach was appropriate. Albright's
flexibility contributed significantly to détente and the peaceful end of the
Cold War.

At the same time, the careers of these two academic policy-makers (Albright
and Brzezinski) shows the major influence East-Central European emigrants
had on American foreign policy. And in Hungarian-born George Soros, this network had an ally who used his enormous fortune toward the end of the 1980s
to exercise direct influence on his old homeland and vigorously support opposition activities and institutions throughout the Eastern Bloc. Madeleine Albright's biography thus stands for more than an exemplary career following
on a privileged flight and reception in her new country. Her life story shows
also that countries that take in refugees can profit from them politically.

switched sides in German captivity), the Cossacks under the command of
seventy-year-old civil war veteran General Pyotr Krasnov, collaborators of the
SS division in Galicia, the Latvian Legion, and similar units, but also several
hundred thousand innocent people who had suffered under Stalinist terror
in the 1930s or during the first Soviet occupation of Eastern Poland and the
Baltics from 1939 to 1941. In total, the refugees from the Soviet Union, at up
to two million, probably exceeded the numbers resulting from the Russian
Civil War in the early 1920s.

It was their misfortune not to be perceived as refugees. This was in part
because they rarely got as far as France, England, or the US, and therefore were
unable to influence public opinion there. At the Yalta Conference, Stalin energetically demanded the "repatriation" of all Soviet citizens stranded in Germany, Austria, and other European countries. He made this demand partly
owing to his notorious lust for vengeance and partly because he feared a
strengthening of the anti-Soviet diaspora. The Western powers, still closely
allied with him, readily acceded to this wish because they found Stalin's reck-
oning with former enemies and collaborators to be legitimate and also
because this at the same time relieved them of their own huge refugee
problem.[73]

In February 1945, accordingly, the Soviet Union and the US secured an
accord on repatriation to the USSR. The agreement was not made public,

probably because it made no distinction between collaborators, prisoners of war, and civilians, which put it in contradiction to both the American legal tradition and the Geneva Convention's stipulations about the treatment of prisoners of war from 1929. For Stalin, keeping this secret fulfilled another purpose: When officers of the Red Army inspected the DP camps in the Western occupation zones, their inmates were in the dark about collective repatriation and about the rules that applied. As soon as the DPs declared that they were Soviet citizens or were identified as such by representatives of the Soviet Union—the power of definition lay with officers of the Red Army and numerous NKVD functionaries—they were subject to repatriation. There was ample opportunity, in theory, for camp denizens to cite the Geneva Convention on prisoners of war, but hardly any DPs knew about this, and it would in any case only have helped men fit for military service.[74]

On the basis of these agreements and the force exercised by the Soviet Union, 2.7 million people were handed over to the Soviet Union through September 1945 alone. In some cases the repatriations were linked to spectacular secret service operations and abductions, above all in the divided cities of Berlin and Vienna. In 1945 Soviet security forces in Austria arrested more than a hundred Russians who had just attended a church service.[75] Among the people delivered to Stalin were refugees from the 1920s who had Nansen passports and were not even citizens of the Soviet Union. This collective repatriation of prisoners of war was also dubious under the terms of international law, especially as it included thousands of forcibly recruited soldiers from regions that the Soviet Union had occupied and annexed after the Hitler-Stalin Pact. The refugees, both the innocent and those who really had collaborated with the National Socialists, reacted with acts of desperation. Some DPs attempted at the last moment to break out of the camps, while others committed collective suicide. On the bridge over the river Mur in Judenburg in the Austrian province of Styria, where the British army handed over 4,000 Cossacks to the Soviets, numerous people leapt to their death.[76]

The US was hardly shaken by these postwar tragedies because they took place far away in Europe, and America had other priorities. Solidarity demonstrations in New York, Washington, and other major cities had more of an impact. These rallies were called by refugees from the interwar period, now diaspora members in a position to come to the defense of their threatened and persecuted compatriots. Advocates and lobbies for the refugees also acted behind the scenes to influence the government. Their voices and votes counted, especially around election time. Moreover, anti-Communist governments-in-exile functioned as instruments of power in the impending Cold War, subverting the Soviet Union's claim to power over Eastern Europe and the territories annexed by the USSR. As of December 1945, the US responded by beginning to limit repatriations to the Soviet Union, and Great Britain gradually conformed to this new line. In 1947 there was an official rupture of the repatriation agreements, and in 1948 the US prohibited Soviet officers from continuing to visit DP camps in the American occupation zone.

With the Berlin Blockade, there was a further hardening of the Western stance. From now on, refugees from the Eastern Bloc were presented as virtual heroes, pioneering freedom fighters, and crown witnesses against the "totalitarian" Stalin regime. The concept of totalitarianism and the equivalence it suggested between National Socialism and Communism dates back to this period. Heroic refugees were also fodder for the film industry. In 1949 in Vienna, which had proved its worth as a shooting location for the film noir spy drama *The Third Man*, Metro-Goldwyn-Mayer produced the *The Red Danube*. This movie mixed a political plot about the forced repatriation of Soviet citizens with a private drama, and drew suspense from the search operations of the Soviet secret service, which was also hunting for Russian opposition figures and refugees in the British and American zones. The love relationships all end tragically: a Russian ballerina jumps from the window before the NKVD can capture her, and before that a Russian scholar shoots himself for the same reason. But these victims do not die in vain, as the film's male protagonist, a British officer, addresses the Western powers at a UN conference in Rome and moves them to stop the forced repatriation of Soviet citizens.[77]

The cinematic happy ending for the Soviet refugees not yet handed over had a real-world background in actual power politics: At roughly the same time that repatriation was stopped, George Kennan, the great Russia expert and architect of American foreign policy during the early Cold War, was shaping a more active refugee policy. Kennan's Policy Planning Staff (PPS) at the State Department recognized the political potential that lay in defectors from the Soviet Union and Eastern Bloc. His aim was to endow the image of the defector with the greatest possible public appeal in order to demonstrate the West's superiority over the Soviet Union. The high number of refugees from the Eastern Bloc living in Western Europe—650,000 DPs according to PPS estimates (including more than 200,000 Poles; 170,000 Jews; about 150,000 Estonians, Latvians, and Lithuanians; and at least 110,000 Ukrainians)[78]— were now no longer to be seen as a burden but as an opportunity. Kennan advocated bringing scholars, scientists, and journalists, above all, to the US and deploying them there in the struggle against the Soviet Union. In 1948 the Displaced Persons Act was enacted, a law that allowed 329,000 DPs to immigrate to the US.

The case of the Eastern European displaced persons thus exemplifies the kind of reassessment that refugees may experience. While the Western powers were still viewing and treating the Soviet DPs collectively as collaborators in 1945 (correctly in the case of the Krasnov and Vlasov armies), a few years later they were stylized as victims of Soviet tyranny and the NKVD, which was also justified in many cases. We see here again that the possibility of flight and the emergence of escape routes are less in the hands of the refugees themselves and more dependent on potential host countries. In this case, two factors in particular were at work: the Cold War confrontation between the US and the Soviet Union and the activities of diaspora organizations that put pressure on the government in the United States. The latter factor, together with the UK's financial exhaustion, also explains the contrast between the policy of the US and that of Great Britain, which was more hesitant about reassessing its policy regarding the DPs.

After the Korean War erupted, a military component was added. In 1950 Congress enacted a law allowing the US army to conscript up to 12,500 "unmarried aliens." This was followed in 1952 by another law actively promoting defection, the United States Escapee Program, which was allocated 4.3 million dollars.[79] As the name of this program demonstrates, it was not congruent with the Geneva Refugee Convention concluded at the same time, for the latter spoke of "refugees" rather than "escapees," a conceptual confusion which proves that the United States still lacked a rigorously thought-out refugee policy. At this time, strategic considerations clearly outweighed humanitarian concerns.

Owing to a fear of agents and spies, as well as to Senator Joseph McCarthy's witch hunt against alleged Communists, chances for being admitted to the US worsened in the early 1950s. This made fleeing the Eastern Bloc riskier, and there were a number of cases in which Western border officials in Germany and Austria judged fleeing across the Iron Curtain to be an illegal border crossing and turned back refugees, as a rule with fatal consequences for those involved. The *New York Times* criticized these actions and lamented in 1951 that an "escapee" had a "better than two-to-one chance of being jailed promptly like a common criminal."[80] The window for DPs to immigrate closed once again; about 175,000 of them remained stuck in refugee camps in West Germany and Austria at the beginning of the 1950s.

Lengthy stays in camps—the very antithesis of integration—led to massive social problems. The American sociologist Edward Shils, who researched numerous DP camps in 1946, described the refugees as apathetic, bad-tempered, and irrational in their political views; the children he described as living "in hordes . . . and by marauding, . . . undisciplined, untrained, ready for any political disorder and without any sense of communal responsibility."[81] Such assessments were widespread, and they created a vicious circle. The worse the image of the DPs, the less willing potential host countries were to take them in. This, in turn, extended the length of stays in the camps, often well into the 1950s, and created a variety of social and psychological hardships. One of the greatest problems was that the DPs had—apart from jobs in the administration of the camps—scant opportunity to pursue employment. In order to increase their food rations and save money for emigration, they were frequently dependent on semi-legal or illegal jobs, including bartering and black market ventures.

Tensions did lessen over the course of the early 1950s as the old camp population slowly melted away and hardly any new refugees arrived to take their place. For in spite of all its sharp lines of demarcation, the dynamics of East-West conflict in some ways functioned like a system of intercommunicating pipelines. The friendlier the reception given by the Western powers to the "defectors," "escapees," and "refugees" from the East, the more rigorously Eastern Bloc countries sealed off their borders. One telling example of this zeal is a bizarre episode related by the Polish historian Dariusz Stola: In June 1953 two young Poles paddled a float into the Baltic in an effort to reach the Danish island of Bornholm. They were discovered, however, by the Polish coastguard, which thereupon summoned 116 soldiers, eight airplanes (five of them Soviet), a tugboat, sixteen fishing trawlers, four military vehicles, and two dogs to assist in the capture of the two refugees.[82]

Even more dangerous was overland flight, since the Polish borders with the GDR and Czechoslovakia were closed and these two states were increasingly vigilant about guarding the Iron Curtain. The inner-German border in the 1950s still presented the smallest hindrance; shooting at the external borders of Czechoslovakia on the other hand was severe, and from 1952 to 1965 alone twenty-nine Poles met their death there.[83] By comparison, diplomats and economic functionaries with travel permits had it relatively easy. From 1948 to 1950, 205 Polish diplomats defected, and in Paris in 1951 it was the turn of Czesław Miłosz, the future winner of the Nobel Prize in literature. In 1934 he had studied for a year at the Sorbonne, so Paris was an obvious choice.

The slowing of flight from east to west indirectly facilitated the further development of international refugee policy. Stalin had long regarded international refugee politics and institutions as instruments of American imperialism. Hence, the Soviet Union viewed the International Refugee Organization (IRO), which was founded in 1946 under the auspices of the United Nations to supplement the work of UNRRA, with extreme skepticism and refused, a few years later, to extend its mandate. In 1950, however, the Soviet Union gave up its blockade and consented to the establishment of the UNHCR.

The American government at first behaved just as ambivalently toward the UNHCR as it had toward refugees from Eastern Europe. For years the US strongly resisted the establishment of the refugee aid agency; once it was in existence, Congress cut its already meager support of 50,000 dollars because the first High Commissioner, Gerrit Jan van Heuven Goedhart, a Social Democrat from the Netherlands, was not to the US's liking politically.[84] On top of that, the United States did not sign the Geneva Refugee Convention but only much later the supplementary 1967 Protocol. In Eastern Europe the

After the Second World War, Paris emerged once again as the intellectual epicenter for exiled Poles, while the government-in-exile, reduced to insignificance, remained in London. This stature was attributable above all to the Instytut Literacki (Literary Institute) in Paris and its publication *Kultura*. That journal's central personality was the former government official, journalist, and world war veteran **Jerzy Giedroyc**. Yet *Kultura* functioned above all as a collaborative publishing venture and authors' collective. The Parisian journal published different genres of literature: poetry (including numerous poems by Władysława Szymborska, who later joined Czesław Miłosz as a recipient of the Noble Prize for literature), political essays that ranked among the masterpieces of this genre, memoirs, short stories, and excerpts from novels. This meant that every issue of this literary and cultural review was varied in design. There was no comparable German-language publication in the postwar period; the closest equivalent in the United States was the *New York Review of Books* (which was established in 1963 and at times also provided a forum for and about refugee and dissident intellectuals from Central and Eastern Europe). *Kultura* printed, in addition to the works of exiles, numerous Polish authors who had remained in their homeland and were banned or heavily censored there, including the beatnik Marek Hłasko, who wrote the most exciting books of the 1950s and 1960s, as well as the dramatists Zbigniew Herbert and Sławomir Mrożek. Also appearing in the magazine were translations of the Russian authors Boris Pasternak, Anna Akhmatova, and Alexander Solzhenitsyn. In this way *Kultura* shaped intellectual and cultural life both in exile and in Poland.

The political significance of *Kultura* was much greater than one might anticipate for a cultural journal. It softened the sometimes stubborn anti-Communism that shaped all of the East European diasporas (which led to conflicts in the case of Miłosz and contributed to his 1953 departure for the US), functioned as a channel of communication for international and national opposition to the Communist government in Poland, and promoted reconciliation with the Ukraine, Belarus, and Lithuania. Jerzy Giedroyc and his allies were of the opinion that Poland needed to take leave for good of its lost eastern territories and abandon any claims to cultural hegemony in order to put relations with its eastern neighbors on a new footing. This insight is all the more remarkable in that it was held by exiles who, like Miłosz and Jerzy Stempowski, came from these very regions. They were thus giving up on their old homelands, a painful step that only a few German expellees took so decisively and so early. *Kul-*

tura supported the Ukrainian, Lithuanian, and Belarusian independence movements, regularly printed texts by authors from these Soviet republics, and thus anticipated Polish and European foreign policy as it took shape in the 1990s. Alongside *Kultura*, the Literary Institute also put out *Zeszyty Historyczne*, an influential historical journal that treated Poland's conflicts with its neighbors and Polish-Jewish relations.

Another reason why Poland's exile community in Paris bloomed so vigorously was that it had an actual brick-and-mortar home, a place that functioned a bit like a beehive. In 1954, thanks to a fundraising drive among *Kultura*'s readers and large individual donations secured by some of the journal's contributing authors, Giedroyc bought a spacious house in the Parisian suburb Maisons-Laffitte.[85] There was enough room now for all the editors' offices, a large salon, and a guest room in which authors and newly arrived refugees could be accommodated. The social contact this enabled played an even more important role than the material help offered, inasmuch as the Polish exiles, like all of their companions in misfortune, often suffered from loneliness, homesickness, and a feeling of alienation. In 2000 *Kultura* was closed at the request of Giedroyc, who saw the journal's historic mission as fulfilled. Maisons-Laffitte, however, lives on as a museum commemorating the Polish exile and the Literary Institute.

Voice of America and Radio Free Europe nevertheless disseminated the image of a free West that welcomed the persecuted and those in flight. De facto, owing to the hunt on Communists under Senator McCarthy, this was not the case. The Refugee Relief Act of 1953 tied the award of an immigration visa to at least two years of good conduct, proof that one was not a Communist, and extensive medical tests, requirements that were not easy to meet, with the result that between 1953 and 1955 only 563 immigration visas were awarded instead of the 58,000 envisioned in the Refugee Relief Act. Moreover, in this same period refugees from China and Vietnam could not find any way at all into "white" America, Canada, or Australia. With the DPs in mind, *Harper's Magazine* wrote of a "national disgrace" and condemned the way the US was again sealing itself off.[86]

The Eisenhower administration circumvented the problem by providing generous subsidies to the refugee camps in Europe and helping refugees transit on to other countries. Washington paid for ship transports to Canada, which took in 123,000 DPs between 1948 and 1951, and to Australia, where 182,000 DPs were accommodated.[87] It was the countries of immigration that selected the refugees, however, and they did this according to their traditional utilitarian criteria: The immigrants had to be healthy and practicing professions that were in demand. A missing phalanx on a finger, frostbitten toes, or traces of an earlier bout with tuberculosis on an X-ray sometimes sufficed to disqualify applicants and prolong their waiting period in the camps. Refugee policy continued to rest on utilitarianism, not humanitarianism.

The problems facing Jewish DPs could largely be solved in the 1950s because there was now a State of Israel. If one sets aside the founding idea of Zionism and the national ideology associated with it, then Israel was above all a state of refugees who, persecuted on nationalist, racist, and occasionally also political grounds, came to her shores from every European country. From 1945 to 1948, because of British restrictions on Jewish immigration to Palestine barely 50,000 European Jews were able to immigrate, more than half of them illegally. At least 12,000 Jews were therefore stuck in Italy, where they wanted to ship out for Palestine, and 25,000 were interned on the British-governed island of Cyprus.[88]

Much like the passenger steamship *St. Louis* on the eve of the Second World War, there also was a ship that symbolized the stray paths now taken by Jewish refugees and immigrants en route to Israel, in this case a decommissioned and rebuilt American postal ship that the Zionists aptly renamed the *Exodus*. In the summer of 1947 in the French port of Sète, 4,500 Jews boarded the *Exodus*, hoping to get to Palestine. There, however, the ship was turned away by the British authorities. After a lengthy odyssey, a PR disaster for British foreign policy, the *Exodus* finally ended its journey in Hamburg. In the country of the murderers, as the Jewish DPs saw it, they were forcibly brought on land. After the establishment of Israel, restrictions on Jewish settlement came to an end, and within the next year and a half, 340,000 Jews immigrated in spite of the ongoing war of independence. Just about as many followed in 1950 and 1951.

The situation eased in those DP camps that still remained, not least because of the economic upswing in Europe, which was in turn related to the Marshall Plan. The idea of integrating displaced people through economic development also played an important role outside Europe, above all in India,[89] and it was propagated by the UNHCR.

Another accomplishment of the early postwar period was the shaping of an international refugee regime. Because of the DPs, forwarding refugees to third states became just as much an established practice as the coordination of activities by the UNHCR would become later. This proved extremely helpful, since in 1956 Europe was again, and unexpectedly, confronted with several hundred thousand refugees. Even more fundamental, however, was the *politicization* of flight: whoever emigrated across the Iron Curtain had very good chances of being recognized and permanently taken in. That is also the reason why almost all cases of flight between 1946 and 1989 are treated here in the chapter on political flight.

3.5 Open doors to the West: 1956, 1968, and the "boat people"

The Hungarian crisis

The year 1956 shook the entire Eastern Bloc to its core. The key event was the Twentieth Party Congress of the Soviet Communist Party, at which the party leadership conceded the crimes of Stalin. This confession weakened party elites in the Eastern Bloc states, which had stood loyally by Stalin and promoted other similar personality cults. Party leaders in Poland and Hungary fell from power. There was already discontent among the population because postwar reconstruction and Stalinist industrialization had been rushed forward in both countries at the expense of consumers. There were frequent shortages of foodstuffs, soap, and the simplest consumer items, while at the same time work requirements were constantly being pushed higher.

In East Germany and Czechoslovakia in June 1953, workers rose up in protest against their Communist rulers, and three years later there was a similar sequence of events in Poland. In Hungary a popular uprising broke out following conflicts within the Communist party and the forcible suppression of a student demonstration on October 23, 1956. The government was toppled, and Imre Nagy (who was later executed) became premier. The rebels succumbed to the illusion that the West would support them and that Hungary would be able to achieve neutrality on the Austrian model. At first the Red Army retreated from Budapest, but on November 4 it reentered the Hungarian capital with massive reinforcements. Soviet tanks steamrollered the uprising until mid-November.

As early as the last week of October, when the outcome of the uprising was still uncertain, several thousand people sought refuge in Austria. Among the refugees there were several party functionaries and even around 120 staff members of the Communist secret service (the Áltamvédelmi Hatóság, abbreviated ÁVH).[90] It may seem paradoxical at first glance that Communists were running away from their own party comrades, but the persecution of one party faction by another already had a long history going back to the Stalinist purges of the 1930s. In spite of the first refugees' dubious political background, the Austrian interior minister granted asylum on October 26 to all arriving Hungarians. After the violent suppression of the revolution on November 4, the flight from Hungary increased dramatically. On that day alone 6,000 people, including 1,000 soldiers, crossed the border into Austria.

At this time flight abroad was still easily achieved because the Politburo of the Hungarian Socialist Workers' Party, within the framework of de-Stalinization, had decided in May 1956 to dismantle the barriers along the border and defuse 700,000 mines. Moreover, numerous border officials sympathized with the rebels and waved them through.[91] This window of opportunity for a nearly effortless border crossing did not remain open for long, for on November 6 soldiers of the Red Army and Hungarian units loyal to the regime were posted at Hungarian-Austrian border crossings. As of November 9 they had begun shooting at refugees with live ammunition, and in some cases even pursued them into Austrian territory. There were, however, a few escape hatches that remained relatively safe, including the bridge at the village of Andau in Burgenland and the reed belt of Lake Neusiedel. (Burgenland is the easternmost province of Austria, and the southern end of the lake—Neusiedlersee in German, Fertöd in Hungarian—is shared by both countries.) Over the course of November more than 110,000 refugees reached Austria along these routes, on some days as many as 8,500 people. These waves of refugees prefigured those who would cross the same border six decades later in the autumn of 2015. Overall, according to official figures, almost 180,000 Hungarians fled to Austria through February 1957. They were joined by 20,000 refugees who had originally sought refuge in Yugoslavia—a secure "third country" in today's terminology. The sum of 200,000 refugees was tiny compared with the numbers of 1945 or 1946, but they arrived within a short period of just a few months and weeks.

For those fleeing Hungary, it proved advantageous that Austria had coped with a much larger wave of refugees only a decade earlier. Although there were still almost 40,000 DPs living in Austria in 1956, this was 100,000 fewer than at the end of 1947.[92] As a result there was still room to absorb newcomers, partly in existing refugee camps where 47,000 "new refugees" (as they were called in contrast to "old refugees") were accommodated. New camps were set up as well, including the one in Traiskirchen, which later achieved prominence beyond Austria because, in addition to various Cold War refugees, it housed very many Soviet Jews. As a result of détente, about 250,000 of these Jewish refugees were allowed to leave the Soviet Union via Austria and then resettle in Israel, the US, and other Western countries.[93]

In 2015, Traiskirchen made headlines again. The camp was so severely overcrowded with refugees from the Middle East that many of them had to sleep out in the open air. Critics condemned these conditions and blamed them on Austria's conservative interior minister, alleging that they were deliberately engineered to force a reversal in the refugee policy of the country's ruling Grand Coalition of Social Democrats and Christian Democrats from the People's Party. By November and December 1956, however, the existing accommodations could no longer suffice to take in all the Hungarians, so the authorities requisitioned gyms, parish halls, boardinghouses, and private accommodations. No one had to sleep out in the open or suffer from hunger, which was no mean accomplishment under the circumstances.

In Austria the hospitality extended to the Hungarian refugees has hardened into a myth. De facto, the mood toward the refugees had already veered in a negative direction as early as November 1956. The authorities, municipalities, parishes, and aid organizations were simply overtaxed. Moreover attitudes toward the arrivals changed the moment they no longer behaved like supplicants but began instead to articulate demands and look for work. In the autumn of 1956, a psychological study devoted to the refugees (which also wisely looked at native Austrians) observed that an unconscious attitude prevailed among the native population to the effect that "this group of people should display the attitude of poor, hopeless children. . . . If refugees socialize in the same *Espresso* [an Austrian term for a kind of small coffee house—PT], act spontaneously in some other way, occasionally buy something nicer in the same store, then a kind of aggression sets in almost following a set pattern."[94] Also stoking resentment were free tickets refugees were given for Viennese streetcars and other social services. Sixty years later a debate over whether Syrian refugees should be allowed to use local public transportation for free would again trouble Vienna, and the Austrian government would attempt once more to divert attention from its own problems by calling ever more loudly for international support. At the beginning of the Hungarian crisis, any number of states had announced that they would take in refugees, among them France, Great Britain, and Canada (the latter country even without an upper limit).[95]

When it actually came to redirecting refugees toward other countries, however, there were some hitches. At first these concerned practical difficulties—it is not easy to organize transportation for tens of thousands of people—but they also derived from the traditional immigration countries' insistence that their usual safeguards be observed, including protracted health tests for the refugees. There were even demands that these be conducted *before* the refugees' departure, meaning while they were still in Austria. Moreover, in keeping with the wonted logic of selection, highly skilled men and young families, who predominated among the Hungarian refugees, were readily taken, while women, especially single mothers, children, old people, and the infirm remained behind. The Austrian Foreign Ministry complained vehemently about this. As a concession, American Vice President Richard Nixon paid a state visit shortly before Christmas and traveled with a large delegation to the transit camps in Eisenstadt and Traiskirchen. The trip was at least a token expression of solidarity, and it produced a lot of press photos that served to prepare the American public for taking in the Hungarian refugees.

The plan to redirect these refugees to other countries did get off the ground after all with some delay, and the situation began to ease in mid-January. This had to do, on the one hand, with an accelerated reception process in a total of thirty-seven states on five continents and, on the other, with the closing of Hungary's western border together with the last of the remaining escape hatches. The number of refugees in Austria therefore declined in the summer of 1957 to around 20,000, of whom the majority ultimately stayed put in the country.[96] Austria owed the easing of its burden mostly to the US and Canada, which took in 38,000 and 35,000 Hungarians, respectively. The US thereby surpassed its original commitment twofold, followed by Great Britain which took in 20,690, the Federal Republic of Germany with 15,380, Switzerland with 12,810 (making it the country that accepted the most refugees in proportion to its population), and France with 12,405. Even former party members were allowed to enter and stay if they signed a declaration stating that they had not joined voluntarily. The motive for this generosity was not political alone, as the crisis coincided with an economic boom in all Western countries that raised demand for labor.

This willingness to take in refugees was based on the premise that there would be no further inquiry into their exact motives and background. Otherwise it might not have escaped notice that many Hungarians were coming not only from heavily contested Budapest, but also from the country's western regions.[97] This was an exodus that cannot be explained solely by the suppression of the uprising and the persecution of its sympathizers; rather, it is much more credibly accounted for in many cases as a simple consequence of the opportunity offered to flee. Proximity to the border—and an awareness that living conditions were better in Austria—surely played a role, for more than 4 percent of the population fled from the northwestern Hungarian *komitat* (county), while the comparable number leaving from the eastern half of the country was only 0.4 percent, ten times less. Finally, it needs to be added that drawing attention to these patterns is not intended to discredit political refugees in retrospect, but merely to point out that a mix of motives influenced flight. For these many-faceted choices the French historian Stéphane Dufoix has coined the apt term "micro-decisions." And they are certainly detectable in almost every instance of flight.[98]

Since the international task of forwarding the Hungarian refugees was largely finished after a good half year, they did not in the end spend too much time living in camps. That was perhaps the greatest mark of the operation's overall success. This haste was not unwarranted, as by the end of 1956 the authorities were already diagnosing a widespread "camp psychosis." According to observers, this state was characterized by a "lack of individual initiative, misjudgment of reality, corresponding overreaction, and a general inability to control socially undesirable impulses."[99] In short, the refugees were in a foul mood. There was little for them to do in the camps other than wait and see, and many were also plagued by constant worry about their relatives. Only about 3,000 refugees received a work permit in Austria, and these as a rule only allowed simple work by the hour, like shoveling snow. The situation of the Austrian labor market at the time dictated these restrictions, for although the unemployment rate had sunk to 5 percent in 1956, Austria's delayed economic recovery (compared with Germany's) meant that there were still five applicants for every open position.

The lack of good prospects in Austria, combined with anxiety about starting all over again in far-distant lands, separation from family, and homesickness, impelled 13,000 refugees to return to Hungary over the next several years.[100] The remigration of refugees is, as we have seen before, a topic that has not been well researched. In this case, there were many young people among the returnees, who had spontaneously set off from home without thinking too carefully about what their prospects might be. Return was, moreover, encouraged by an amnesty for all refugees proclaimed on November 29, 1956.[101] Canceling criminal sanctions was a wise move on the part of the new party leadership under János Kádár and an early signal of the new party line that came to be known as "Goulash Communism." As long as people were silent about politics, a condition the returnees understood, the party would guarantee them a decent living standard.

The UNHCR did a good job both in repatriating the Hungarian refugees and forwarding them to third states, and by this means enhanced its acceptance in Hungary, the Soviet Union, and the Eastern Bloc as a whole, where it originally had been rejected as a Western invention. Its success in the West was even greater: the governments of the host countries could now stage themselves as benefactors. The communist countries countered that the West was taking in refugees in order to exploit them as cheap labor. The charge was not entirely bogus, as Stephen Porter has shown with the example of DPs brought to Louisiana to work for minimal wages in sugar plantations.[102] However, this abuse was soon ended following protests by priests and NGOs, and the propaganda war around refugees ended in the 1950s with the clear victory of the West.

This had positive reverberations for the refugees. The Hungarians were widely seen as noble refugees fleeing acute persecution and Soviet tanks. This image was reflected in the pictorial language of press photographers, who frequently took pictures of refugees in three-quarters profile and other flattering poses that made their faces look somewhat weary but determined and sharply chiseled. In brief, these refugees were no pitiful, starving victims of political disaster. In the iconography of the time, they were heroes of freedom.

The Hungarian crisis set the scene for what would become a tradition of generous asylum legislation in most Western countries. Especially in Sweden, which took in many emigrants from Poland as well as from Hungary in 1956, and in Austria, a critical part of each country's identity would be its openness as a sanctuary for the politically persecuted. One should not overstress Austrian hospitality and humanitarianism, however. That country's postwar myth notwithstanding, the priority there was always on redirecting refugees to other countries. Yet the effectiveness of myths, as is well known, does not rest on their truth so much as on their power to persuade and on the perpetual retelling of the narratives. The fact that Austria and Sweden accepted an especially large number of refugees in proportion to the size of each country's population in 2015 (measured against the size of its population, the number was much higher in Sweden than in Germany), together with the high level of civil society support for refugees in all three countries, can be traced back, however, to these identity-forming moments during the Cold War. Despite their geographic distance from Hungary, the US and Canada were also affected by the events of 1956. From then on until the mid-1980s, both countries were open to the Cold War refugees who would soon arrive, not only from Europe but also from nearby Cuba. Initially there was a clear preference for white refugees of European descent, but this racial preference diminished as the numbers of refugees from Cuba grew, and later even more with the influx of the refugees from Indochina.

A turn toward humanitarianism in fact affected the entire international community. In 1958 the UN proclaimed a "World Refugee Year." The underlying idea was to use the momentum in international refugee policy following the Hungarian crisis to find permanent accommodations for all the other displaced people still housed in camps. There was a special focus on the hardcore of DPs and a renewed effort at international resettlement. In Geneva, London, Manchester, and other English cities (the idea for the "World Refugee Year" came from Great Britain) activists set up model tents resembling the shelters in refugee camps and distributed leaflets and other materials with information drawing the attention of passersby to the fate of refugees.[103]

The notion that it might be possible to solve all refugee problems in one fell swoop will strike us as naïve today. It was also Eurocentric, since at the same time violent conflicts were brewing on other continents that would keep the world in turmoil for decades to come. In immediate proximity to Europe the Algerian war was heating up, the Palestinians driven out of Israel continued to subsist in makeshift camps, and the massive expulsion of Jews from Arab states had also begun (in 1956). In addition, millions of people were losing their homes as a result of conflicts over decolonization and the global Cold War. Yet it was hoped that at least Europe would be free of refugees; and that was the unarguably noble proposition that the organizers of World Refugee Year had in mind.

Moreover, resettling the last remaining European DPs fit in with the logic of the Geneva Refugee Convention and its impetus to integration. As soon as refugees became citizens of a new state, their status as refugees ended. Lacking a homeland was thus not a permanent fate but a condition looking to be terminated. In the so-called Third World, the UNHCR attempted to tie the absorption of refugees to development projects. But all such projects fizzled early for lack of financial resources; to this extent, the limits of international refugee politics and of humanitarianism were already visible by the end of the 1950s.

Flight from East Germany

In Cold War Germany, refugee politics had higher relevance than in any other country (with the possible exception of Israel: see Chapter 2.3). Germany had been divided between West and East since 1949, so that people living in the Federal Republic and the German Democratic Republic could constantly compare their rival systems one with the other.[104] The comparison ran against the GDR. Because the Soviet Union had dismantled East German industrial plants and the Communist regime in East Berlin had nationalized industry and trade, the GDR had, from the outset, a lower standard of living. On top of that there was political repression, which became increasingly harsh. These two factors motivated ever more people to flee to the Federal Republic. Even before the uprising of June 17, 1953, a million East Germans had crossed to West Germany.

Whether this could properly be classified as flight, and whether these migrants should be viewed as refugees worthy of protection, was at first open to dispute. In 1949 West Germany's first cabinet under Chancellor Konrad Adenauer shared the view that "the greater part of the migrants" consisted "of criminals and political agents." Only a small portion, about 7 percent, could genuinely be regarded as politically persecuted.[105] This skepticism toward the arrivals mirrored American attitudes during the McCarthy era. Accordingly, discussions in the young Federal Republic initially turned on how to dam the flow of migrants. Even tighter control over the line of demarcation with the GDR and repatriation of the migrants—in other words, an Iron Curtain hoisted by the West—were contemplated at this time.

In spite of pressure from some West German *Länder*—interestingly, from those federal states that were farther away from the GDR and therefore had taken in relatively fewer refugees than the border provinces—these demands were not politically feasible. Closing the border and sending back the refugees would have meant giving up the dogma of an indivisible Germany, the Federal Republic's claim to be the sole legitimate German state, and the policy of national citizenship associated with this claim. Furthermore, what was happening right at the border demonstrated that the East Germans were not deterred by the increasingly severe border controls of the Red Army and NVA (the National People's Army of the GDR). The refugees had their own agenda. Higher hurdles on the Western side of the Iron Curtain would hardly have diminished the influx.

Given this situation, the West German federal government attempted to regulate the admission of refugees and the procedures for recognizing them, so as to achieve greater control over the flow. The Federal Emergency Admission Act (*Bundesnotaufnahmegesetz*) passed in the summer of 1950 set the terms under which one would be recognized as a refugee. There had to be "imminent danger to life and limb, to personal liberty, or other compelling grounds" for leaving the Soviet Occupation Zone.[106] Only a minority of the refugees could prove this level of endangerment, so in 1950 and 1951 more than 60 percent of the applicants in the aforementioned emergency admissions procedure were rejected. The remaining 173,000 applicants were designated as "illegals" and therefore ineligible to claim social welfare assistance or other government services. Because of damage from wartime bombing, the main problem was a lack of housing. West Germany's two reception camps, at Uelzen in Lower Saxony and Gießen in Hesse, were permanently overcrowded.

Yet—and the situation is much the same with today's rejected asylum seekers—it remained unclear how to proceed further with the petitioners who were not accepted as refugees. To deport them to the GDR was hardly possible for political reasons, and certainly far from feasible on purely practical grounds. So the problem with the many "illegals" was solved by tolerating them and then, after 1952, granting them a more generous degree of recognition. This is demonstrated by the share of positive responses to the emergency admission procedure, which rose to over 80 percent in 1953 and reached nearly a 100 percent toward the end of the decade. The more open attitude toward the "Soviet Zone refugees" (the official German term was *Sowjetzonenflüchtlinge*, *Sowjetzone* being the scornful West German name for the GDR) was inherent in this very designation, which became more widely accepted at the beginning of the 1950s. The term was also meant to distinguish these newcomers from postwar expellees, whose lobbies kept an eagle eye on their social welfare privileges.

Pursuant to the Emergency Admission Act (which as of the summer of 1951 also applied to West Berlin), Germany's *Länder* and the federal government decided on admission quotas. According to this arrangement, North Rhine-Westphalia (West Germany's most populous and industrialized state) was to take in 65 percent of the refugees in the first few years, in return for which the state would receive added housing construction funds.[107] This heavy burden on one single state made sense inasmuch as the refugees would be able to find work relatively easily in the Ruhr region owing to the boom in heavy industry. In the following years the distribution of refugees among the regions changed several times, with the consent of the relevant *Länder*, according to the "Königstein formula," which calculated apportionment based two thirds on the level of tax receipts and one third on population size. This laid the foundation for the refugee policy that has lasted to this day, and which also served as the basis for distributing the 2015 Middle East refugees.

At the same time, a difference can be detected in the enforcement of international refugee policy: while the admission quotas for Germany's federal *Länder* were binding, forwarding refugees at an international level after the Hungarian crisis was based on voluntary commitments that some states broke (France, for example, which was preoccupied with its own postcolonial flight, took fewer Hungarians than announced), while others kept their promises (West Germany), and yet others exceeded them (Switzerland, the US, and Canada). The situation is much the same in the EU today, except that most member states are even less faithful to their commitments than was the international community in 1956. The West (including formally neutral Austria and Sweden) held together better than the European Union does today.

The generous interpretation of the Emergency Admission Act and the grounds for flight enumerated therein had the vacuum cleaner effect that some federal and state ministries in Germany had feared: more and more East Germans fled to the West, above all via the eye of the needle that West Berlin had become after the inner-German border was closed early in 1952. In the first half of 1952 alone, 200,000 GDR citizens arrived (among whom men were clearly predominant through 1957). For their benefit a new airlift was organized—one that has undeservedly fallen into oblivion, overshadowed by the famous airlift of 1948. Beginning in February 1953, airplanes made daily flights ferrying up to 1,400 people from West Berlin to West Germany. A total of about 108,000 people were flown out in the first four months of 1953. In the two big reception centers in Uelzen and Gießen (later joined by other camps), they were then registered, interrogated, investigated, fed, and moved on. Logistically this was an immense achievement, and equally purposeful assistance in integration followed.

The US participated in this largest of all Cold War refugee movements both organizationally and financially. It provided planes for the airlift and gave the Federal Republic fifteen million dollars to build housing, a generous cash injection that signaled an about-face away from America's indifferent attitude toward German refugees and expellees after 1945.[108] In the postwar period the latter were consistently excluded from all services provided by UNRRA and the American government because the Western powers regarded them as a purely German problem and showed little empathy toward the perpetrators of the Second World War.

American support draws attention once more to the Cold War context. Without the East-West conflict, West Germany, which had to absorb refugees numbering in the tens of thousands every month, might presumably have behaved differently. As the aforementioned debates of 1949 and the recurring demands to impose an upper limit on migration from the GDR show, neither national nor political solidarity was a given.[109] If after 1953 the East German refugees were also taken in so willingly, it was in considerable part because the government under Chancellor Adenauer knew how much the exodus was damaging the GDR both economically and politically.

As if there were not enough intra-German refugees, between 1949 and 1961 they were joined by around 475,000 ethnic German emigrants from Eastern Europe (called *Aussiedler* or *Spätaussiedler* in German), who were fleeing both Communism and daily discrimination based on their nationality.[110]

The postwar apex of this exodus was reached in 1957 and 1958. Its main country of origin was the People's Republic of Poland (it would retain that status until 1989), and most of these emigrants came from the regions of Silesia and Masuria. Though ten years had passed between the end of the war and the temporary opening of the East European borders for Germans willing to emigrate, one can view this migration movement as a kind of *delayed flight*. When it came to individual families, ethnic discrimination played a greater role than political oppression in general, even if Stalinism started earlier, was harsher, and ended later in the areas where German minorities were settled in postwar Poland.[111]

More than a hundred thousand of these ethnic German emigrants had been kept as skilled labor after the war, for example in Lower Silesian Waldenburg and in the Northern Bohemian glass industry. In addition, in 1946–47 about a million former citizens of the Reich chose the option to stay that was offered to "autochthons" in Poland. The legal foundation for this was a kind of *Volksliste* in reverse (the *Volksliste* being the Nazi-era list used to distinguish ethnic Germans from other groups in occupied territories). To be eligible for inclusion, one had to show proof of Polish ancestors, relatives, language proficiency, or national spirit. Once included, the so-called autochthons would be able to evade forced resettlement in line with the Potsdam Agreement, although they then would suffer the repressive measures of a regime that was just as nationalist as it was Stalinist. Many soon regretted the decision to stay in Poland, especially as their siblings and cousins had often been resettled after the Potsdam Agreement and were already living in Germany. The members of this minority therefore had Western connections and they knew about the economic miracle in West Germany. In fact, even in the GDR, the standard of living during the mid-1950s was noticeably higher than in Poland.

In addition to the East-to-West migration after 1945 of ethnic German and Polish refugees leaving the lost eastern territories, there was a later westward migration in 1956 of Poles who had not been removed after the Second World War but were detained in the Soviet Union, mostly on collective farms or as experts in industry. Between 1956 and 1959, they were allowed to depart. The Polish "repatriates" from the Ukrainian, Belarusian, and Lithuanian Soviet Socialist Republics replaced the 248,000 ethnic German refugees who went to West Germany in 1956–59. Four thousand two hundred Silesians, most of them miners, gave preference to socialist East Germany.[112]

The ethnic Germans from Eastern Europe constituted, as discussed, only a small share of the immigration to West Germany, while the number of refugees from the GDR during the 1950s was six times higher. Overall, 3.1 million recognized refugees and ethnic emigrants came to the Federal Republic in this decade, in addition to about a million GDR citizens who were not taken into consideration under the emergency admission procedure but were nonetheless allowed to stay. In spite of this hard-to-manage mass flight, the newly founded Federal Republic committed itself from the outset to treating the ethnic emigrants as fellow Germans. They were immediately awarded citizenship, a privilege compared to the DPs and the later guest workers.

The Federal Expellee Act of 1953 regulated their "ethnic inclusion" (*Volkszugehörigkeit*) as Germans; the arrivals merely had to prove that they had declared their allegiance to "Germanness" (*Deutschtum*) back in their homeland. Through the early 1990s this opened the door to an additional four million people and ended the unclear legal status for refugees and ethnic emigrants from Yugoslavia and Romania, who in the early postwar period often had to struggle to receive German citizenship. The Federal Republic viewed the ethnic German emigrants to a certain extent as successors to the expellees. This status came with a variety of advantages, including the provision of services within the framework of the statute on equalization of burdens and the Federal Expellee Act. Also availing themselves of these higher levels of integration assistance were 682,000 refugees from the GDR who originally came from Silesia, East Prussia, and other lost territories and who were therefore recognized as expellees.[113]

This national solidarity with German refugees, expellees, and ethnic emigrants had two foundations: One was the assumption of common nationality— here the National Socialist idea of the *Volksgemeinschaft* (the ethnically and racially defined national community) continued to reverberate. Second, and much as in the case of the Hungarian refugees, there was the view that Communist countries were totalitarian regimes. The Germans who remained in the Eastern Bloc were indeed subject to discrimination through restrictive language laws, at work, and in everyday life. Poland and the Soviet Union, the two states that had suffered the most under the Wehrmacht and German occupation, treated the remnants of their German-speaking populations with especial harshness.[114]

After Stalinism came to an end, the oppression abated, especially in Hungary and Romania, where the German minorities were left comparatively undisturbed. Accordingly, the reasons for emigrating changed: whereas at first political motives were foremost, later emigration had more to do with improving one's standard of living. It was also valid to question whether refugees from the GDR left solely for political or also for material reasons.

These questions, which were still being asked in the first years after the Federal Republic was founded, faded with the advent of the economic miracle. The West Germans' initially mixed attitude toward refugees from the GDR was hardly surprising given that there were still 635,000 unemployed expellees from Eastern Europe in 1950. They thus constituted a third of all the unemployed, double the figure for their share of the population. This was especially the case for people over fifty, the less skilled, and former farmers, whose chances of employment were slim.[115]

In the following decade, both the young Federal Republic and the refugees from different regions were in luck—plain and simple. In the exact same years as most of the GDR citizens and ethnic emigrants were arriving in West Germany, the economic boom was beginning to gain traction to such an extent that the labor market could absorb them. That this was possible may be attributed not least to the refugees themselves, who took any job, frequently well below their skill levels and in different branches from the occupations in which they had been employed back home. While refugees from the GDR were overwhelmingly male, among the expellees there was a surplus of women. There were 1,136,000 million women for each one million men; among the native population, the surplus of women was similarly high.[116] The gender balance had changed, however, by the end of the 1950s as more women and children fled the GDR. Here we see a pattern frequently encountered in refugee waves: first the men flee and try to find work in their new home, and then they are joined by family members.

Given the overwhelming scope of flight from East to West, it went long unnoticed that in fact about half a million people were moving in the opposite direction, from the Federal Republic to the GDR.[117] Familial or occupational reasons often played a role here, so that one cannot speak of flight in the narrower sense. One example is the family of Chancellor Angela Merkel, whose father went to the GDR as a Lutheran pastor. But cases like that of the folksinger Wolf Biermann show that migration from West to East was not always entirely voluntary. Returning exiles and Jewish concentration camp survivors (Biermann's father was Jewish) did not have it easy in the early days of the Federal Republic. In everyday life and in dealings with public officials and the legal system they were constantly encountering former Nazis, some of them simple party members, some of them known criminals who had taken part in their persecution. Some Jews and Communists found this unbearable and thus crossed to the GDR for political reasons. After the ban on the KPD (the Communist party in the West until it was readmitted under the new initials DKP as détente got under way in 1968) in the summer of 1956, there began a wave of persecution against its members and sympathizers, with prosecutors initiating proceedings in 125,000 cases. In the end, only 6,688 of these resulted in sentences (there were 40,000 political sentences issued in the GDR that same year), but even those who were not sentenced often lost their job or suffered other disadvantages.[118] This threat of persecution gave some ten thousand people a manifest reason to flee West Germany. The leadership of the KPD, in anticipation of the party's ban, had absconded ahead of time to the GDR.

In spite of this counter-movement, it can be said without any exaggeration that the young Federal Republic was a land of refugees. Within just fifteen years, if one includes the period of Allied occupation, West Germany took in more than eight million expellees, four million GDR refugees, as well as nearly half a million ethnic German migrants, and assisted (on top of this effort) in

There is a temptation to pick out especially prominent people when writing the history of refugees. The noncommissioned officer **Conrad Schumann** belongs to that great (but by no mean gray) mass of refugees who left hardly any traces behind of their lives apart from a few Stasi (East German secret police) files and that world-renowned picture showing him taking a leap to freedom over barbed wire freshly rolled out along the Bernauer Straße (one of the streets at the border between East and West Berlin). As he leapt, Schumann threw his machine gun behind him, and at exactly that moment a young trainee waiting to take snapshots during the construction of the wall pressed the shutter release on his camera. The contrast between Schumann's martial uniform and the weapon he threw away, between the barbed wire tangle and his leap across it, guaranteed the picture its global career.

Schumann made the decision to flee rather spontaneously. The young man, a shepherd by trade from the Saxon village of Zschochau, had volunteered for the East German riot police reserve. For him, police service meant upward mobility, and yet according to his Stasi file he had volunteered for political reasons. In the file there is an obviously pre-formulated sentence: "Because of atomic armament in West Germany [in the early 1950s the USA had begun to station atomic weapons there—PT] I have come to the realization that I should help defend the achievements of the German Democratic Republic."[119] The then nineteen-year-old Schumann almost certainly had no inkling of where he would be deployed, and certainly not that a wall would soon be erected on the border between Berlin's Eastern and Western zones. The immediate occasion for his desertion from the border troops, according to his own testimony, was a tear-filled event at the border wall, when a small girl who had been visiting her grandmother in East Berlin was not permitted to return to her parents in the Western part of the city.

Schumann was not happy, however, with his decision to flee. According to statements from his wife, whom he met soon after his resettlement in Bavaria, he was plagued by pangs of conscience on account of the parents and two siblings he had left behind in the GDR, as well as by constant fear of persecution by the Stasi. Materially, Schumann lacked for nothing; after working for a time in a nursing home, he got a good-paying job as a machinist for Audi. Schumann was not eager to appear in public, but he was repeatedly invited to political

(cont.)

(cont.)

events like the 750th anniversary of Berlin in 1987, the event where Ronald Reagan uttered the famous words: "Mr. Gorbachev, tear down this wall!" The fall of the wall did not bring Schumann any new zest for life; he suffered from depression and committed suicide in 1998 at the age of 56.

the international endeavor to forward refugees from Hungary. Only Israel had a greater claim to being a "refugee state," and there absorption was also guided by the premise that the arrivals were preordained citizens of the same nation. As noted earlier, other forms of solidarity, of a religious or political-ideological sort, were also at work in the history of massive refugee movements, yet the construct of the "nation" has been perhaps the most important factor supporting the integration of refugees in modern Europe. Not to be neglected here, admittedly, is the context of the Cold War, which unexpectedly reached a new climax in 1960–61.

The building of the Berlin Wall put a sudden end to inner-German flight. Whereas 207,000 Germans fled from East to West in 1961 (according to the data recorded in the course of the emergency admission procedure), the number of refugees in the following years sank to a few thousand. The wall refugees, however, soon became icons of the Cold War.

The Berlin Wall, as is well known, was not entirely insurmountable. Tunnels were dug in various places to aid excapees. Most spectacular of all were: an escape using a self-made cableway from the House of the Ministries (the former Luftwaffe building used to house the East German Council of Ministers), the breakthrough of a locomotive heading to Spandau, escape attempts along the Spree river, and various hot-air-balloon transits. All these adventures reinforced the Western image of the heroic Eastern Bloc refugee. More numerous, though, were cases of GDR citizens whose freedom was ransomed by the West German government; between 1961 and 1989, that was the means by which almost 300,000 East Germans got out of their country. (Western-aided escape is a research topic in its own right and therefore omitted here.) Media images of people killed at the wall also confirmed conventional wisdom about the GDR as an inhumane and violent regime. Fleeing East Berlin in fact cast the entire Eastern Bloc in a bad light, which helps explain the escapees' ready acceptance in the West.

The suppression of the Prague Spring

The perception of the Eastern Bloc as a collection of totalitarian dictatorships was confirmed in a shocking manner when the Soviet Union and its allies marched into Czechoslovakia in August 1968. With the suppression of the Prague Spring, all hopes for a "socialism with a human face" died. There was no armed resistance and also no subsequent escalation of violence as happened in Hungary in 1956, and consequently no mass flight out of Czechoslovakia following the invasion. Measured against the size of the population, the numbers that left were not even half as large as in Hungary. In absolute numbers, however, both incidents of flight were equally significant.

Initially, as after the Hungarian crisis, the most important country of refuge was Austria. Ninety-six thousand Czechoslovakian refugees crossed into the country between August and the end of October 1968, when Austria's borders were again sealed. In addition, just as the Warsaw Pact states invaded Czechoslovakia, 66,000 Czechs and Slovaks on summer vacation in Yugoslavia found themselves cut off from their homeland. Most of them eventually returned, however, so that the total number of refugees in 1968 rose only to around 100,000.[120] Then, in the two decades that followed, an additional 140,000 Czechs and Slovaks left their homeland, largely driven out by intensified suppression of the opposition following the declaration of the "Charta 77."

Austria's response to the refugees was similar to the reaction a decade earlier to the Hungarians. In today's lingo one might summarize the attitude both of government and society as one of "Refugees Welcome." There were numerous demonstrations of solidarity. The "Children's Friends" (a Socialist welfare organization), the Catholic charitable relief group Caritas, and a variety of organizations representing Viennese Czechs organized donation campaigns, arranged emergency accommodations in schools, distributed free tickets for public transportation, and even gave out gasoline coupons. The Interior Ministry issued a blanket proclamation declaring that all refugees from the ČSSR were to be treated according to the Geneva Refugee Convention.[121] But in the end only about 10,000 Czechs and Slovaks applied for asylum in Austria in 1968 and 1969, because if they did so they were required to hand over their passports and therefore would not be able to travel on to third countries. As in 1956, Austrian hospitality depended on the premise that most refugees would be moving on. Those Czechs and Slovaks who remained in Austria had the advantage of fitting into the population in terms of outward appearance, for they came from a country that was by this time nearly as prosperous as Austria and culturally similar as well, despite the language difference. In general, Viennese Czechs and Slovaks integrated quickly, as demonstrated by the fact that only a small number returned to the old homeland after 1989. There were, however, a few prominent returnees, including the adviser to President Havel and later foreign minister Karel Schwarzenberg.

Owing to its geographic location, the Federal Republic was also an important country of refuge. Bavarian authorities made gymnasiums and other emergency accommodations available close to the Czechoslovakian border, and the refugees received additional care in a central reception camp in Zirndorf outside Nuremberg. In West Germany, a country more deeply affected by anti-Communism due to its frontline position in the East-West conflict, the reception was not quite as unconditional as in Austria. Critical voices, for example, warned that there were many Communists among the refugees. This was actually true, since most of the Prague Spring's protagonists were members of the Czechoslovakian Communist Party.[122] In the end, however, political solidarity with the refugees prevailed; as in Austria, they received asylum without too much fuss, and even those who were rejected had nothing to fear as there was a guideline, in effect since 1966, that prevented the deportation of Eastern Bloc refugees back to their countries of origin. Through 1989 a total of 22,654 Czechs and Slovaks entered the Federal Republic.[123]

As it had twelve years earlier in 1956–57, Switzerland too contributed to preventing a "refugee crisis" after the Prague Spring. About 13,000 Czechs and Slovaks were taken in and quickly integrated into the Swiss labor market under a special regulation. Somewhat simplified, this regulation said that the Czechoslovakians were not to be counted against the quota on foreigners that normally applied to labor migrants, which was intended to limit immigration deemed detrimental to the Swiss.[124] The rest of the Czechoslovakian emigration was dispersed among France, the Scandinavian countries, the US, Canada, Australia, and a number of other states. It was renewed vindication for the system of international resettlement that had functioned equally well when it enabled Soviet Jews to leave their country for the US or Israel via Austria.

The West's receptivity also had to do with the good press generated by a few spectacular flights that once again confirmed the Cold War's pattern of friend and foe. A few days after the invasion of the Red Army in Czechoslovakia, for example, a twenty-three-year-old man on the last leg of an escape route to the Bavarian border hid himself under the axle of a truck and then sprinted the last few meters into the West. One day later, a driving instructor from Prague succeeded in fleeing with his girlfriend by circumventing the closure of gas stations in Prague, overtaking the tanks rolling southward and westward on side roads, and then arriving in the Upper Austrian town of Freistadt just in the nick of time before the border closing. And, much like what happened in the case of Conrad Schumann at the Berlin Wall in 1961, there were also some uniformed soldiers who deserted by throwing down their weapons and running into the West.

Western newspapers were happy to document these cases thoroughly, with photos of the harried and relieved refugees adding emotional impact to their stories. In August 1968 in the Bavarian Forest town of Philippsreut, press reports attracted curious onlookers who, according to their own testimony, wanted to support arriving Czech refugees. They really did help them in some cases, but their actions were apparently too much for the German border police to handle. They closed off access to the border and called upon their own citizens to go home.[125]

In a very similar way to what happened after the Austrian-Hungarian border was sealed off and after the Berlin Wall was built, East and West functioned like a system of intercommunicating pipelines. The more the West celebrated shrewd, courageous, heroic refugees, the more rigorously the embarrassed Eastern Bloc states guarded their borders. One aspect of this rivalry was the order to shoot that cost more than 250 East-West refugees their lives on the inner-German border and along Czechoslovakia's external frontiers. The West's receptivity to refugees was never put to the test long term, however, due to the rapid abatement of the flight from Czechoslovakia. The ČSSR government's multiple offers of amnesty for returning refugees through the autumn of 1969 helped stem the flow. How many Czechs and Slovaks ultimately remigrated is not well researched, but it was certainly several tens of thousands, including the aforementioned Adriatic vacationers (a summer trip to Yugoslavia was at that time a privilege, so most of the people involved were likely doing quite well under socialism).[126]

As we have seen, the heroes and victims of the Iron Curtain confirmed stereotypes about the Eastern Bloc and the clichéd self-images of Westerners, including by those from neutral states who could congratulate themselves for their virtuous refugee policies. Thus, in a 1974 retrospective the long-serving Swiss Federal President Kurt Furgler described his country's acceptance of the Czechs and Slovaks as a "model of international solidarity" that underscored the neutral role of Switzerland and its engagement in the international community.[127] In patting his country on the back, the Christian Democratic head of state did not mention the Swiss economy; Czechs and Slovaks, it is worth noting, had arrived at a time when, as in West Germany and Austria, workers were being sought and deliberately recruited. Yet it was apparently advantageous to stress ethical values and portray one's country as a refuge of liberty. One should not view this self-congratulation too cynically, for statements like Furgler's do prove that humanitarianism was becoming increasingly a political asset.

For refugees these were good times; and, accordingly, they integrated quickly. Frequently the first generation of East European exiles was hardly recognizable as such; at most, a slight accent might give them away. The second generation, as a rule, was fully absorbed. Whether that was a good thing or not is another question, one that depends on each society's self-image. Even in income and social status, there were hardly any differences between East European refugees and the native population (the same was not true of wealth of course, for that is not built up so quickly). Another reason why the refugees of 1956 and 1968 succeeded in becoming upwardly mobile is that they came in large part from the educated classes and other social elites. The success of their integration is demonstrated by how few became remigrants to Hungary or Czechoslovakia after 1989. Those prominent exiles who did return to their old homelands were treated shabbily when it came to the restitution of their assets.

In the US and Canada, the Cold War refugees were more apt to seek a self-definition that included their country of origin and its culture. Hence there was a new cohort of "hyphenated Americans," some of whom were active in diaspora organizations. Politically active exiles remained a tiny minority, however, even more so by the second generation.

The "boat people" and global resettlement

If one extends one's view beyond Europe, the term "Cold War" seems inadequate, for in other parts of the world there were real proxy wars involving heavy casualties. Vietnam was contested almost uninterruptedly for thirty years. As a result of the First Indochina War, several hundred thousand Vietnamese had fled their country already by 1954. Among the Western countries only France was affected; it took in 25,000 to 30,000 refugees from its lost colony.

After Vietnam became independent and divided, 930,000 people fled from the Communist north into the south of the country, and 140,000 moved in the opposite direction, often under chaotic circumstances.[128] In the south refugees were resettled in huge development projects or along the borders with North Vietnam, Laos, and Cambodia. It was thought that this pattern would prevent the infiltration of Communist partisans, but it did not work out that way. On the contrary, it intensified political and social tensions.

In the 1960s the war with North Vietnam led to another surge in the refugee population. In 1968 Vietnamese authorities counted more than 1.3 million refugees, and in 1971 the number reached six million.[129] Vietnam's eastern neighbors were also massively affected by American aerial warfare and their own civil wars. In Laos around 700,000 people fled, first from American bombing, then from the partisan war. The situation was even worse in Cambodia, where up to three million people were on the run. Many of them eventually perished in the concentration camps run by the Khmer Rouge. When the Vietnamese army toppled Pol Pot's genocidal regime, it set off another mass flight. According to UNHCR statistics, 237,000 Cambodians arrived in camps run by the organization in Thailand; even more languished near the border, which the Thai government closed several times out of fear of Communist infiltration.[130]

In 1975, when the US submitted to defeat and withdrew from Vietnam, it evacuated around 130,000 people, most of them collaborators and allies in the South Vietnamese governing apparatus, soldiers, and police whom the Americans preferred not to see fall into the hands of the Communists. The legal basis for this evacuation was the "Indochina Migration and Refugee Act" passed in May 1975, the first law calculated to provide access to the United States for large numbers of Asian refugees. Under the same circumstances today, the US government would likely be warning that opening the flood-gates risked letting dangerous enemies into the country, but Republican President Gerald Ford had no qualms. Nor did he, like Donald Trump today, suggest that the intelligence services and police might not be acting in the best interests of their own country.

The Saigon evacuation operation was only the beginning of massive flight out of Vietnam. Owing to the nationalization of business, collectivization of agriculture, Communist reeducation in labor camps, and plain hardship, about a million Vietnamese left their homeland in the second half of the 1970s, some by land to Thailand and China, and more probably by sea. In the flight from Vietnam there was also another ethnic component, for the refugees included around 250,000 Chinese who, as in other Southeast Asian countries, were a major segment of the economic elite. This put the UNHCR to the test yet again; under the aegis of the refugee aid organization, most members of this minority were brought to the People's Republic of China, some of them also moved to Hong Kong. Other minorities allied with the US, such as the Hmong in Laos, who suffered from Communist retribution as well, and came under intense pressure to leave.

After 1978 more and more desperate Vietnamese attempted to cross the South China Sea to reach Malaysia, Singapore, Indonesia, or the Philippines. Pictures of these "boat people" moved the Western world and especially the US. Their ships were primitive, not equipped for long distances and storms on the high seas, and they often sank. The American public, feeling guilty over the conduct of the war, felt responsible.

Vietnam's closest neighbors along the South China Sea, the ASEAN countries, bridled at the arrival and reception of the refugees, and international law did not oblige them to help as they were not Geneva Refugee Convention signatories. In light of this emergency, the US again intervened. At the beginning of 1978, President Jimmy Carter ordered that 7,000 refugees be taken in, and three months later Congress resolved to let in 25,000; this in spite of negative public opinion polls and resistance among the Republicans. Opponents of this humanitarian action warned that it would only intensify the exodus from Vietnam. And that is just what happened; around 400,000 refugees immigrated to the USA through 1980. By taking in these so-called Indochina refugees, American society distanced itself by word and by deed from the war in Vietnam and from the country's history of racial discrimination on immigration.[131]

How radical this turnaround was can only be appreciated by taking a long look into the historical background. In 1882, with the Chinese Exclusion Act, the US had banned East Asian immigration. The Immigration Act of 1924 reaffirmed the exclusion of Asians and extended it to Southern and Eastern Europeans, who got only a very small immigration quota. Thus the numerous East European Jews were indirectly excluded as well. After the Holocaust, the US made an exception for 329,000 DPs. Here, again, a guilty conscience was at work, in this case on account of the rejection, toward the end of the 1930s, of so many Jews who had then perished in the Holocaust.

Taking in the Indochina refugees also represented a major departure from the standards applied by previous US immigration policy. As in Canada and Australia, utilitarian criteria had been primary. Only those who promised to be useful to their new country could immigrate. One may find this utilitarianism amoral: toward the end of the 1940s, for example, old and infirm DPs were frequently sorted out of the immigration mix. Yet there is an advantage to the utilitarian standard in that it can generate or strengthen consensus in favor of immigration. For this reason, the self-image of the US as an immigration country was never really lost, in spite of its being breached in 1924. (And perhaps one will soon have to add "and not breached again until 2016." For Donald Trump, influenced by his senior adviser Stephen Miller, is questioning this consensus as no other American president before him has done.) Taking in refugees from Southeast Asia, by contrast, was justified on moral grounds and lent to international refugee policy a normative orientation that remains dominant to this day.

Strong normative convictions were not only widespread among liberals and the left, but also among Republican "Cold Warriors." In 1979 California Republican senator S. I. Hayakawa stated that taking in refugees constituted a moral asset for the US in the global Cold War: "By welcoming Indochinese refugees to the United States we will once and for all show up the present government of Vietnam as the totalitarian, racist tyranny that it is. Morally, we shall have won the Vietnam war."[132]

It would be misleading, however, to focus too much on American political debates. The comprehensive resettlement of the refugees from Southeast Asia was possible, among other reasons, because the US was supported by a broad Western coalition. Canada and Australia (which had stood with the US politically and militarily in the Vietnam War) each agreed to take in more than 100,000 refugees, and eventually they took in almost twice as many. For both these countries, as for the US, this was a reversal of an earlier whites-only immigration policy. Taking this step had sociopolitical relevance that extended well beyond refugee policy.

France, which as the region's former colonial power had especially close ties with Southeast Asia, accepted more than a hundred thousand Vietnamese immigrants. The other member states of the European Community also participated, as did neutral states like Switzerland and the Scandinavian countries. At 16,000 people, Norway took in the largest number of boat people in relation to the size of its own population.[133] Even isolationist Japan, which never, before or after, granted refugees entry in any appreciable numbers, allowed 11,300 Vietnamese into the country. As in 1956 and 1968, then, many countries shared the burden of this international resettlement.

The commitment of the Western states to refugee relief was the basis for the "Orderly Departure Program" that the UNHCR arranged after lengthy negotiations with the ASEAN states. Malaysia, Singapore, Indonesia, and the Philippines agreed to temporarily take in boat people if third states would later permit them to immigrate. After this conditions improved in the improvised refugee camps, where crime and prostitution were rife due to daily hardships and the lack of job opportunities.[134]

In Southeast Asia and the West, a debate grew up around whether taking in and forwarding refugees from Vietnam might not motivate additional people to venture out onto the open seas, thereby risking their lives—much like what is happening today on the overseas escape routes of the eastern and central Mediterranean. In the end, this was not the decisive question. The flight across the ocean abated when the Vietnamese government, in a move analogous to what China started doing in 1979, took a first step toward liberalizing its economy and allowing peasants to sell a portion of their harvests on the open market. This incentivized agricultural production and increased the food supply. In addition, the Communists stopped enforcing their strict reeducation policy. Today, to be sure, it would be incomparably more difficult to achieve a similar improvement of living conditions in the Middle East. In Syria no end to the civil war is in sight, Libya is de facto a failed state, and the other North African countries have grave economic problems that even a major push toward reforms would not easily remedy.

Taking in the Vietnamese refugees was simultaneously a stellar moment for civil society initiatives. In 1978 André Glucksmann, who had himself grown up as a child of refugees, Jean-Paul Sartre, Raymond Aron, and other French intellectuals founded operation "Un bateau pour le Vietnam." In Germany the journalist Rupert Neudeck and Heinrich Böll, the Nobel Prize-winning novelist, adopted this idea and raised donations to build the Cap Anamur.[135] This rescue ship criss-crossed the South Chinese Sea, where it saved more than 11,000 human lives and brought them directly to Germany.

Under the banner of a universal humanitarianism, the old ideological fronts of the Cold War softened, both in France and West Germany. The boat people tended to be anti-Communist refugees, but the leftist intellectuals around Sartre and Böll did not fault them on that account. On the contrary, the acceptance of the refugees elevated the status of migrants in the eyes of Marxist-influenced intellectuals and social scientists. In a sense, they replaced the working class as both an object of study and of sympathy. In a reciprocal gesture, conservative politicians and media hardly objected to the leftist exiles who were among the roughly 2,000 Chileans entering West Germany at around the same time.[136]

In the case of Neudeck (the German journalist who spearheaded the Cap Anamur campaign), his own biography played a role in his efforts on behalf of refugees. In 1945, at the age of six, he had to flee with his mother from

Danzig; later, the years he spent as a Jesuit imparted the sense of mission that convinced him to dedicate the rest of his life to humanitarianism and to building up an aid organization. At the same time, the emergence of refugee NGOs gave an ever-stronger normative tilt to the activities of those committed to this cause. In a reversal of the earlier formula applied to refugee policy, the new precept was now humanitarianism instead of utilitarianism (see Chapter 4.3 for a discussion of these two principles). The extent of humanitarian consensus and solidarity with the Vietnamese was due, not least, to the amount of coverage Western media in the 1970s devoted to the boat people. Other refugees, for example the seven million people who fled to India between 1970 and 1972 as a result of the civil war in East Pakistan, today's Bangladesh, affected the European or American public only marginally; the same is true for Africa's many refugees.

In spite of all the sympathy for the Vietnamese refugees, there were problems encountered in forwarding them. It was in logistical terms no easy undertaking. The West German Foreign Office pointed out that under the 1910 law of the sea convention, the Federal Republic was merely responsible for refugees rescued from ships under the German flag.[137] Several times, however, the Cap Anamur took on refugees who had been saved by other ships. While these acts of assistance defused the situation on the high seas, they helped only a little to ease the situation in the refugee camps. Thus, for example, until the late 1980s there were 28,000 Vietnamese stuck in the infamous Indonesian camp Pulau Galang. Only after the end of the Cold War could they be repatriated. The goal of repatriation began to play a more important role in international refugee policy after 1989, whereas during the Cold War all sides had acted on the assumption that returning to a Communist country was not possible.

In 1982, in the face of rapidly growing unemployment, the Federal Republic imposed a freeze on taking in Vietnamese boat people. Following public protests, this measure was rescinded, but it shows that the consensus that had emerged since the Hungarian crisis for the unconditional reception of refugees was beginning to weaken.[138] This was related to the arrival of ever more refugees from Turkey following the military coup of 1980, from South Asia following the outbreak of civil war in Sri Lanka, and especially from Poland. The total number of asylum seekers, in the meantime, fell again after the brief outlier year of 1980, when it reached 108,000. The change of attitude in Germany and other Western countries, then, cannot be explained by any strong surge in refugees.

Instead, the turnabout in German "foreigner policy" was mostly a side effect of the worsening economic situation. (The term Ausländerpolitik had emerged in the course of Germany's guest worker recruitment effort of the 1960s, though semantically it included refugees.) After the first oil crisis in 1973–74, all West European countries imposed a freeze on recruiting guest workers and other labor migrants. At first the policy toward refugees remained untouched by this change, as the case of the Vietnamese boat people shows. But after the second oil crisis and the deep recession of the early 1980s, foreigners in general were increasingly viewed as a burden. This was also the period that witnessed the first terror attacks by right-wing extremists. In 1980, two Vietnamese boat people died after an arson attack in Hamburg. But, on the whole, neo-Nazi terror tended instead to push Germans toward showing solidarity with the Vietnamese, as would be demonstrated by the protest against the aforementioned admission freeze of 1982.

In the very same year, the new Christian Democratic-Liberal coalition in Bonn issued a comprehensive program for the return for guest workers. Between 1982 and 1984 it had the desired result: up to 416,000 more foreigners moved out of the Federal Republic than moved in. The program primarily targeted Turks, but they relatively seldom took advantage of it, because economic conditions had worsened back in the old country. At almost the same time the government under Chancellor Kohl passed the Asylum Procedure Act, which imposed a one-year work ban for asylum applicants in addition to cuts in social services. The argument for this measure was that it would prevent covert labor migration.[139] Refugee policy was thereby linked quite openly and officially to "foreigner policy" in general.

The Asylum Procedure Act seemingly fulfilled its desired goal. In 1983, the number of asylum applicants sank to 19,700, one fifth the number in 1980.[140] Whereas 80 percent of asylum applications had been decided positively through 1980, the acceptance rate through 1985 declined to less than a third. To be sure, the ban on deportations to Communist countries introduced in 1966 continued in force. Refugees from Poland, Czechoslovakia, and other Eastern Bloc states who had their applications for asylum rejected were nonetheless tolerated, as a rule, and received residency permits. Yet, while all arrivals from the Eastern Bloc were until the early 1980s regarded as victims of totalitarian regimes in need of protection, they now saw their motives questioned, both in individual cases when they applied for asylum and, above all, in public discourse.

While it was generally expected that East European refugees would integrate quickly, expectations for the boat people were much more pessimistic. The reason was that the Indochina refugees were outwardly recognizable as foreign, had a relatively low level of education (or were even illiterate), and had grown up in a very different culture. This was particularly true of the Hmong, an ethnic group that lived in Laos, the mountain regions of North Vietnam, the south of China, and remote parts of Thailand. Following the old colonial strategy of divide and rule, the French government had employed the Hmong as auxiliary forces. Communist retribution after the first Indochina War drove them to side with the United States and drew them into the Vietnam War. After the defeat of the US, the Hmong were collectively condemned as traitors (although some of them had fought on the side of the Communists) and came under intense pressure to emigrate.

Back in the old country the Hmong had lived predominantly from agriculture, hunting, and fishing. Theirs was also a strongly patriarchal society, where polygamy was common practice, as was levirate marriage (whereby a widow is obliged to marry a brother of her deceased husband). Moreover, when the Indochina refugees arrived on Western shores, the long postwar boom in Europe and the US had ended. The newcomers confronted a labor market much worse than what Hungarian, Czech, Slovak, and early Cuban refugees had faced. Initial conditions for integrating these Indochina refugees were thus markedly less favorable than for the earlier Cold War refugees.

The Hmong were settled predominantly in California and the Midwest. The distribution was based on a country-wide formula, but the refugees could also express their wishes. The ones who arrived later frequently oriented their choices toward already existing contacts. It was clear from the start of the resettlement program that these impoverished arrivals would need massive government assistance. The Carter administration thus developed welfare measures of a novelty and scope that matched the size and unusual nature of this large-scale project. These efforts can be seen as a late apogee of post-New Deal welfarism. The social policy put in place for the refugees was based on what would later be labeled "public-private partnership." The federal government paid for initial transportation and housing along with language training, and it reimbursed the individual states for their expenses. (In 1980 and 1981, the federal government spent 1.7 and 2 billion dollars, respectively, on support for Indochina refugees.) But once the refugees were housed in the receiving communities, most of their care was taken over by local church members and civil society organizations. This certainly promoted social integration, but this division of labor can also be viewed critically as an attempt of the government to avoid responsibility for refugees once they were settled.[141]

One should not draw too rosy a picture of how that care worked out in the case of the Hmong. The values and habits of the locals, mostly white and monolithically Christian in rural parts of Wisconsin and Minnesota, differed quite radically from those of the refugees. The Hmong had, for example, no clear concept of private property similar to the host society's, since many of them had lived from hunting and fishing in forests and waters that were perceived as a common resource.[142] So there was a rash of complaints about trespassing on private property and illegal hunting. That led to serious incidents, even years after the refugees were first admitted. In 2004 a Hmong hunter who felt threatened when confronted by a group of white hunters who taunted him with racist slurs shot six of them.[143] In fact, many Hmong complained of racist insults and discrimination on other occasions—on the street, in stores, and at school. But it is clear that this particular shooting and other cases of violence which received a lot of media attention were exceptions.

By all the usual measures of integration—occupational and social status, educational level, income, real estate holdings, and social mobility—the Hmong and their descendants integrated rather well into mainstream society. That is the conclusion of sociologist Jeremy Hein, who has drawn on carefully selected local case studies and data for publications on the Hmong that span his entire scholarly career. Hein characterizes their experience as "one of the most positive interracial exchanges in US history."[144] Studies on the second generation confirm his conclusions, especially as regards the Hmongs' educational aspirations and achievements.[145] This is all the more remarkable given that the Hmong remain poorer than the average white inhabitants of Wisconsin and Minnesota. In general, class-based comparisons between refugee groups and poorer US-born citizens tend to lend even more support to a positive assessment of recent US integration history.

Literature written from a more culturalist and subjective viewpoint arrives at more critical conclusions. Here the stress is on the experience of discrimination, the "kinship ties" among the Hmong (kinship is, of course, a classical topic for cultural anthropologists), and on their sense of separateness. Anthropologists have also raised doubts about the record of good school performance and pointed to the high rate of truancy, especially among girls. According to Hang, these problems are attributable to hierarchical gender structures in traditional Hmong society, which does not treat female education as a high priority, and which clash with the greater freedom of other American teenagers that Hmong youth observe and imitate.[146] Closer parental control is impossible in many families, since both parents need to work to boost their low incomes. These findings look surprisingly similar to what social scientists have observed among Turkish guest workers and their descendants in Germany.[147] Hence, gender disparities and role models are in these cases the biggest problem, and not the religious differences that are frequently cited as the source of problems with Muslims, as if all of them were ardent believers. And of course class matters, maybe more than race, which is so dominant in US academic discourse (for understandable reasons in view of the history of race discrimination, but I sometimes wonder why liberal academics especially have paid so little attention to issues of class in the past three decades). The cutbacks on expenditures for refugees under the Reagan administration certainly did not help to diffuse class differences between refugees and the receiving society.[148]

Historians are not trained to make policy recommendations, yet the conclusion for refugee policy seems clear: More attention should be paid to promoting female education in schools, professional training, and career advancement. Social scientists and historians must also address why there are disparities between the conclusions drawn by different researchers study-ing the Hmong. The main reason would seem to be an old hermeneutical trap: the research questions and approach predispose the results. A possible way out might be to analyze more thoroughly what people do (which would also be in line with Simmel's stress of agency), as opposed to what they say, for the latter depends a lot on the questionnaire. Do the Hmong have a ris-ing number of good jobs earning them a decent income? Are there regular everyday social encounters and contacts between various social groups (which should be defined not only by race but also by class)? And, last but not least, is the number of mixed marriages and blended families on the in-crease? The answer to all these questions is encouraging. In spite of the criti-cism raised above, developments in academia suggest as well that progress is under way. The very existence of a journal titled *Hmong Studies* is a sign that this diverse diaspora community has created an elite of its own that is taking an active interest, alongside other Americans, in the history of their group and their lives in the US. Tellingly, there is no such journal in Germany for much larger groups of immigrants like Turks, Poles, former Yugoslavians, and Italians.[149] Maybe traditional immigration societies like the US are bet-ter able to integrate refugees than the more sedate and homogenous societies of the old continent. But even in Europe the historical record is good, espe-cially for Southeast Asian refugees.

3.6 Flight from Poland and the first turn against refugees

At first glance, the imposition of martial law in Poland in December 1981 seems to mirror the pattern of Hungary in 1956 and Czechoslovakia in 1968. An attempt to liberalize the political and economic system was followed by a phase of violent suppression. Poland had already lived through two episodes in which the government blew hot and cold between reform and repression, one following the thaw of 1956 and the other after the student revolts of 1968. In the summer of 1980, there was yet a third wave of protests. Following price hikes for basic foodstuffs, Polish shipyard workers in Gdańsk, Gdynia, and Szczecin went on strike, and the protest soon grew to encompass the entire country. At first the Communists made concessions to the strikers and even registered the independent trade union Solidarność. This did nothing to im-prove the dire economic situation: foreign debt was devouring 82 percent of annual export revenues, and the shortage of consumer goods got worse, which resulted in more strikes and a radicalization of the opposition in 1981.

After barely one and a half years of political tug-of-war, General Wojciech Jaruzelski took drastic measures, and under martial law the People's Repub-lic of Poland was transformed into a socialist military dictatorship. The gov-ernment had about 3,000 Solidarność activists arrested, 10,000 people were interned, and more than 12,000 members of the opposition were sentenced for political transgressions.[150] Moreover, the government issued orders to shoot in case of resistance, and in the Wujek coal mine in Katowice the security forces killed nine miners. Jaruzelski later argued that his aim in imposing martial law was to prevent a Soviet intervention as in Hungary and Czechoslovakia. That was a self-serving argument, as the military forces of the Soviet Union were tied up in Afghanistan. (Nonetheless Erich Honecker, the general secretary of East Germany's ruling Socialist Unity Party, really did call for an invasion of Poland, and the hardliner regime in Czechoslovakia stood for a similar tough line.)

Because it was the country's own army that intervened, Poland's case differed in two essential respects from the refugee crises of 1956 and 1968: There were no pictures in the media of Soviet tanks or heroic resistance against "the Russians." Also, apart from its location on the Baltic Sea coast, Poland did not border any Western country. Hence there were no pictures of heroic refugees daringly charging the border at the last moment, and no major refugee wave toward the West materialized. The imposition of martial law and the acts of repression associated with it paradoxically led to a decline in departures from Poland, for the GDR, out of fear that there might be a spillover effect from Solidarność, had annulled visa-free travel between the two countries in the autumn of 1980. Moreover, martial law hindered the mobility of citizens; travel applications were processed sluggishly and the allotment of foreign exchange reduced. Any kind of mass flight to Austria or West Germany, and from there to Canada and the US, where there were large Polish diasporas, was therefore not possible for purely practical reasons. Nevertheless, in 1981 alone Polish border troops arrested 800 "refugees to Western countries," as official diction labeled them. An additional 84 Poles were taken into custody attempting illegal border crossings to the West from the GDR and Czechoslovakia.

Restricting the history of Polish society in the 1980s to its state and territory alone would abridge that history just as much as in earlier periods. The Warsaw historian Dariusz Stola estimates that, at the time of the 1981 coup, about 300,000 to 400,000 citizens of the People's Republic of Poland were residing abroad in the West, officially mostly as tourists, but in fact with the goal of earning money on the side there. After the imposition of martial law, at least 150,000 of them decided not to return home, and in the winter of 1981–82 about 50,000 applied for asylum in Austria, West Germany, the US, and Canada.[151] This was flight of a certain kind, even if it produced no television pictures of waves of refugees or dramatic scenes alongside the Iron Curtain.

Austria remained one of the few escape hatches opening into the West, just as in 1956 and 1968, since Poles had been able to travel there without visas since 1972. As a rule, Czechoslovakia waved travelers through if they were using the country as a way station en route to the West. In 1981, 29,000 Poles applied for asylum in Austria, and the Cold War international system for forwarding refugees geared up for another round: in the first half of 1982 more than 10,000 Poles were transported out of Austria to the US, Canada, Australia, Switzerland, and West Germany.[152] More than just humanitarian considerations underlay this procedure. Australia, for example, sorted the immigrants according to occupational criteria, and the US also paid close attention to whether it could or could not use a particular applicant. Canada, by contrast, invented a new category of "Eastern European self-exiled persons."[153]

In the meantime, the Polish government lowered the level of repression. In March 1982, Interior Minister General Kiszczak informed imprisoned members of the opposition via the press that they could apply for passports. The background for this move was overcrowding in the internment camps and prisons, and security authorities overburdened by the need to keep the opposition under surveillance. In passports, however, a clause was inserted stating that the bearers were only entitled to leave the country one time. De facto, then, these were emigration papers. In the course of 1982 more than 3,200 applicants received this emigration passport, but then only 1,070 left. This was due in part to rigorous inspections by Western authorities, who suspected that the Polish government might be trying to foist common criminals on them (as the Cuban government had done in the Mariel Boat Lift), and therefore demanded documentation on the political activities of potential emigrants. Also responsible were prominent opposition figures who protested against this deportation practice in disguise. In 1983 Adam Michnik, one of the imprisoned leaders of Solidarność, accused General Kiszczak in an open letter of breaching Polish and international law. In fact the refusal to permit reentry was just as much a violation of international law as the German Democratic Republic's practice of expatriation (as in the case of the East German dissident folksinger Wolf Biermann). A second charge made by the opposition was that the government was attempting the corruption of dissidents. Michnik declared pointedly that, in spite of the adverse conditions of imprisonment, he was not going to exchange his cell for "capitalist luxury."[154] A third argument equated flight with defeatism. This objection was in the tradition of the French Revolution, the history of which was well known to Michnik and other champions of Solidarność.

Outside the jails, Poland's standard of living was not much better than what Michnik and his imprisoned allies experienced. During martial law almost all basic foodstuffs were rationed; and meat, dairy products, butter, and even sugar were scarce. Daily life was a constant struggle for survival, especially for families with children—and Poland at the time had a high birth rate. Hence, the millions of food parcels sent from West Germany amounted to more than a symbolic gesture. One can also view this action as yet another example of how humanitarianism had become internationalized in the left-liberal spectrum of West German society. In August 1982, on the occasion of the two-year anniversary for the official recognition of Solidarność, there were mass protests, and in Gdańsk security forces shot and killed five demonstrators. In the face of this desperate political and economic situation, flight from Poland accelerated once again. Stola puts the number of people he classifies as part of the "martial law emigration" at 100,000.[155] Those he has in mind are citizens who had protested against the Communist dictatorship in different ways, could not put up with "actually existing socialism" any longer, and were led to emigrate by force of circumstance (cf. the concluding chapter on the existential experience of flight).

The most important escape route ran (as already mentioned) via Czechoslovakia to Austria and its capital city of Vienna. There, however, the mood toward the Poles shifted, a consequence of their large number, their obvious poverty (which distinguished them from the Czechs and Slovaks of 1968–69), and their trading activity at flea markets like the Mexikoplatz. In West Berlin, too, voices complaining about the "flood of Poles" and "illicit Polish moonlighters" grew louder.[156] In swear words like "Polacks" there was a lingering after-effect (similar to what was happening in the GDR) of Nazi-era anti-Polish prejudice, something that in the 1980s had not been confronted or reappraised nearly as much as antisemitism, which by now was largely scorned, at least in public.

There was also a political problem: The governments of chancellors Schmidt (in West Germany) and Kreisky (in Austria) still clung to their 1970s policies of détente. On several occasions, therefore, Schmidt distanced himself from Solidarność, which struck this Hanseatic Lutheran as too Catholic, nationalistic, and irrational. Although Schmidt and Kreisky condemned the imposition of martial law, they did not want to break off all contact with the government of the coup plotter Jaruzelski.

That empathy for refugees was no longer extended to the Poles, and that it abated even further by the mid-1980s also had to do with changes in Poland and the Eastern Bloc. In 1983 Jaruzelski revoked martial law and promulgated an amnesty that allowed more than half of those interned to go free. More prisoners were released a year later, and in 1986 the Polish version of perestroika commenced. This meant that the phase of harshest persecution was over, which in turn undermined the political credibility of asylum applicants who, because of the double border obstacle on the way to the West, did not come across in any event as archetypical Cold War refugees but instead, for the most part, as visitors with tourist visas. In spite of all the American lip service paid to the Polish opposition, the US embassy officials in Warsaw were stingy about granting visas; apparently, they too feared a mass immigration like the one following the Second World War.[157]

By the mid-1980s the number of Poles heading West already exceeded, many times over, the volume of the exodus after 1956 and of the later Czechoslovakia exodus of 1968. There were simple demographic reasons for this:

Poland had about one and a half times as many inhabitants as Hungary and Czechoslovakia had taken together. Seen this way, the 530,000 Poles who (according to official emigration statistics from 1983–88) were no longer returning to the People's Republic did not seem like such a great number.[158] Yet these arrivals were burdening national social welfare systems and aid organizations throughout Western Europe. In 1987 the Italian Catholic welfare organization Caritas complained of the large number of Poles availing themselves of social assistance. This clerical institution made a point of adding right away that inhabitants of Third World countries were in much greater need of support. The Austrian government complained about "false refugees."[159] The Federal Republic of Germany reacted (as already mentioned above) by tightening its asylum policy, and in West Germany the acceptance quotient for Polish applicants seeking asylum fell to 3 percent in 1988. Czechs, Slovaks, Hungarians, and citizens of other Eastern Bloc countries were now also granted full asylum status less frequently.

While the West German government was behaving ever more coolly toward asylum applicants from the East, one part of society in the Federal Republic was opening itself up to the world and its problems. This new attitude found expression in the new "third world shops," in fundraising for the Sandinistas in Nicaragua, and also in a growing sensitivity to global refugee waves. Finding in these causes a kind of substitute for the classical leftist class struggle agenda at home, the West German Left increasingly turned to humanitarianism and hopes for a post-national society envisioned as a community enriched by refugees and migrants from all over the world. In conservative circles, among the older generation, and in the countryside, by contrast, the old mistrust of foreigners lived on and soon was directed also against those who so vehemently advocated a multicultural society.

These tensions within German society persist to this day and have preshaped attitudes to the "refugee crisis" of 2015. Three large groups may be distinguished here: the first is afraid of foreigners at large and so rejects migrants of any kind; a second group either wavers or is largely indifferent to migrants, but is motivated by the ethical consideration that politically persecuted persons should be recognized as refugees, so long as not too many of them come; and finally there is a third, significantly smaller group, that enthusiastically favors an open and multicultural Federal Republic and therefore willingly takes in refugees.[160] In contrast to the US, however, there has never been in Germany a vigorous and intellectually demanding debate about what multiculturalism means both in theory and everyday life.

This basic constellation of views existed with some variations in all European societies west of the Iron Curtain; it was only the proportions of the groups that fluctuated depending on the social and political context in each country. In Sweden with its strong tradition of social action by Protestant congregations, an accepting orientation toward the "Third World" and openness toward refugees predominated. In more rural and Catholic France there was less of the same openness, although the governing Socialists kept in place their cosmopolitan asylum policy. However, the National Front party very early supported a xenophobic nationalism; in fact the party was founded in part to address a refugee problem that still has not been fully resolved. In 1992 in Austria, the FPÖ, which moved to the far right after Jörg Haider was elected party chairman in 1986, launched the Foreigner Referendum. ("Austria first" was the slogan of the referendum's founders; Donald Trump, it would seem, was not terribly original.) To be sure, the openly xenophobic politics of the FPÖ did set off a major counter-movement which, like the Germans who protested the arson attacks on Turks in Mölln and Solingen in 1992 and 1993, organized candle-lit demonstrations against the right-wing initiative. The referendum failed miserably, but the FPÖ succeeded in permanently changing Austria's political climate.

In the US, by contrast, the consensus in favor of taking in refugees held because it was fed by two sources: on the one hand, the humanitarianism of the civil rights movement and, on the other, the anti-Communism of the Republicans and a segment of the Democrats. This led to a privileging of refugees from Communist countries, initially from Europe, but in time from all over the world.

The ethnic German emigrants from Eastern Europe

The simplest and safest way to leave Poland and other East European countries was an option open to persons of *Aussiedler* status (ethnic German emigrants) as defined in West Germany's Federal Expellee Act.[161] As explained in the beginning of the previous chapter, within just three years of the end of Stalinism around a quarter of a million ethnic emigrants resettled in Germany. This window was shut again in 1960, and over the next fifteen years the numbers of returnees fluctuated between 15,000 and 30,000 annually. The Federal Republic, in light of its healthy economy, easily managed this influx.

The ethnic emigrants alleviated the labor shortage that had mainly been covered by guest workers since the building of the Berlin Wall. At first, beginning in 1956, it was Italians who came, followed by workers from countries that were to become members of the European Community in the 1980s, such as Spain and Greece, the NATO member Turkey, and, as the sole socialist country, Yugoslavia. In this way 2.5 million guest workers immigrated to the Federal Republic, a number that climbed as high as four million people if family members were counted.

While the recruitment of the guest workers ended in 1973 because of the recession that followed the first oil crisis, the influx of ethnic emigrants increased significantly in the framework of détente. In the second half of the 1970s, just as happened two decades earlier, more than a quarter of a million ethnic emigrants arrived in the Federal Republic. In 1981 more than 50,000 evacuees emigrated from Poland alone, most of them just shortly before the imposition of martial law. As the title of the much-discussed family memoir and autobiography *Wir Strebermigranten* (We Striver Migrants) by Emilia Smechowski indicates, their German background and the discrimination arising from it in the 1980s was at best a secondary motive for their emigration.[162] Most of the families from Poland had at most one German grandparent, and even that grandma or grandpa was often someone who may have been registered on the German "people's list" (*Volksliste*) during the Nazi occupation and not someone who necessarily identified as German. All the more reason for these emigrants, who were actually Polish, to conform to the majority culture once they got to Germany (an objective to which the hard-to-translate title of Smechowski's book alludes).

The government of Helmut Kohl that came to power in 1982 knew in principle that the motivations for this emigration were changing, and that most cases were not delayed escapes due to nationality issues, but instead emigration primarily out of economic motives—a flight from a socialist economy of scarcity, as it were. Nevertheless, the German government held fast to nationality as a legitimate foundation for accepting immigrants. It was urged to do so above all by the expellee associations, lobbies that were regaining influence under Chancellor Kohl and hoped to win new members from among the ethnic emigrants. The constant emphasis on their Germanness seemed anachronistic in the 1980s, but the two-sided autosuggestion on which it rested proved useful: based on this nationalist premise the emigrants received extensive assistance in integrating, and in return they quickly conformed to the national majority. At the same time, it enabled them to distinguish themselves from the guest workers, especially from the Turks, who had to take a backseat in the social hierarchy of the Federal Republic.

In 1988 the number of ethnic emigrants from Poland jumped to a new record level of 140,000 people.[163] In 1989 a quarter of a million Silesians, Masurians, and other Polish citizens immigrated on grounds that they had proof of German ancestry. (At the time there was a joke circulating that the only proof required was a German shepherd.) The cultural contrast between the immigrants of the first three postwar decades and these new evacuees was marked; 90 percent of them spoke Polish at home. It was different with the Germans from Romania, for they had done more to preserve their German culture and language and had settled abroad as self-contained communities. Their numbers also increased abruptly, while the number of emigrants from Transylvania and the Banat fluctuated between 12,000 and 15,000 from 1980 to 1988 (most were "ransomed" by the Federal Republic) and climbed to 111,000 people in 1990.

This scenario was repeated in the collapsing Soviet Union. As soon as it was possible to do so, the Volga Germans who had been carried off to Central Asia and Siberia and their descendants set out for the idealized homeland of their distant ancestors. When Mikhail Gorbachev proclaimed glasnost and perestroika in 1986, exactly 753 ethnic German Soviet citizens were allowed to emigrate to the Federal Republic. By 1990, 150,000 people were in the process of emigrating, and in 1994 the highest level of emigrants from what was now the post-Soviet region was reached.

Here two push factors converged: In the 1990s the successor states of the USSR were in an economic depression on the scale of the 1930s Great Depression. In Uzbekistan, Kirgizstan, and Georgia, there were even local outbreaks of famine. Daily misery intensified a nationalism that was already present and inflamed conflicts over the allocation of resources. Since most descendants of the Volga Germans had adopted Russian as their everyday language during their banishment, in Central Asia they were often looked upon as Russians and as representatives of foreign domination. If one wishes to summarize the motives for the departure of 1.5 million post-Soviet emigrants, discrimination (both old and new) against a national minority would head the list, coupled with the hardships of the post-Communist transformation.[164] The latter also afflicted ethnic Russians, eight million of whom moved out of Central Asia into the Russian Federation. An additional factor in the resettlement was a social dynamic that operated on both meso- and micro-levels: as soon as one part of a village or of another settlement community had emigrated to Germany, family members and friends followed suit. Entire small towns and villages were emptied out by this chain migration.

As the case of the ethnic German emigrants clearly illustrates, flight depends in many cases not only on the pressure of persecution (the factor foregrounded by the Geneva Refugee Convention), but also on opportunities— in this case the opening of borders after the end of the Cold War. In addition, there was the fact that wealthy West Germany acted like a magnet. The total number of arrivals from post-Communist Europe rose from 377,000 in 1989 to nearly 400,000 in 1990. The post-Soviet ethnic emigrants, however, only very rarely communicated with each other in German; at most, German had been the language of their grandparents. This was attributable not only to Communist language policy, but also to their social integration in the Soviet Union, which (in spite of the discrimination against them) had been quite successful in the workplace, in everyday life, and through mixed marriages. At the same time, more and more people were applying for asylum in the Federal Republic. The number was 121,000 in 1989, 193,000 in 1990, and 256,000 in 1991. By the time the figure rose to over 400,000 asylum applicants in 1992, the increase was already related to the war in the former Yugoslavia.

After the end of state socialism, then, a number of different waves of flight and migration reached a culmination point; in principle the situation was comparable to the 1950s, but with a different ethnic mix. First and foremost, just as at the start of the Cold War, there was intra-German flight. In 1989 880,000 East Germans left the GDR via Hungary, the ČSSR, and finally across the border dividing Berlin once the wall was opened. From 1990 to 1994 an additional 1.4 million East Germans migrated to the West, though (at the latest) after a decision was reached in the spring of 1990 to complete an economic and currency union between the two German states, one could no longer call this flight. While the intra-German migration was not called into question politically, the steep increase in the number of ethnic emigrants and asylum applicants elicited reactions that, on close examination, extended across the entire partisan spectrum. The right wing of the Christian Democratic Union and its Bavarian sister party the CSU joined the right-wing nationalist Republikaner (though they were soon at loggerheads with each other over this) in taking aim at asylum applicants in particular. The anti-nationalist left, by contrast, focused on scrutinizing the nationality of the ethnic German emigrants and criticizing the preference given to this one immigrant group.

In fact, the ethnic emigrants did acquire German citizenship, on the basis of the German Expellee Act of 1953, after only a brief test. In addition, they received assistance in the search for housing, subsidies for basic and advanced vocational training, and were eligible for pensions and unemployment insurance. These privileges were justified by the notion that the *Aussiedler* were a special case, as victims of the Second World War and as Germans who had been subjected to discrimination and persecution because of their nationality. Even if policy toward German minorities differed widely from one country or period to another—the worst case was their collective punishment and humiliation in the Stalinist Soviet Union, Poland, and Czechoslovakia—there was some justification for this national solidarity, however selective and however much it may have been rejected by many West German leftists.

The Cold War context also played an important role here, since the Federal Republic had acted for almost forty years as the savior of its fellow Germans from Communist dictatorship. In the 1970s and 1980s this role legitimated the morally ambiguous ransom of ethnic Germans from Romania and other Eastern Bloc countries, as well as of GDR citizens eager to leave East Germany. By way of summary, then, it is fair to say that the absorption of over four million ethnic German emigrants was based on a mixture of national and political solidarity.

With the collapse of the Soviet Union and the granting of generous minority rights in Poland and other post-Communist states, this legitimization for the Federal Republic's role was no longer valid. Accordingly, resistance built up against the immigration of these so-called *Aussiedler*, who in fact were no longer clearly identifiable as German owing to their generally poor command of the German language. In 1990 integration assistance for the ethnic emigrants was cut, replaced by a lump-sum "integration payment." The War Consequences Settlement Act of 1993 (*Kriegsfolgenbereinigungsgesetz*—its interminable name referred only to the Second World War, although the law also provided a settlement for consequences of the Cold War) discontinued resettlement on this model. Only those born through the end of 1992 could still submit an application, and ethnic German emigrants were also required from now on to provide evidence of the "acute pressure of persecution." This became practically impossible for residents of East Central and southeast European states that had, in the meantime, entered into association agreements with the EU. In 1996 there followed regulations requiring language tests, which could lead to the loss of residence rights even after admission to the Federal Republic. The federal government's "Commissioner for Matters Related to Ethnic German Resettlers" justified this restriction by saying that these emigrants' "declining language skills" would "result in a general loss of acceptance in the population."[165] At almost the exact same time, the federal government enacted cuts in the ethnic emigrants' pensions (their employment before arriving in Germany had once been factored in, but now it was only partly counted if at all) and added as well a fixed abode requirement (so as to distribute the arrivals equally across the entire federal territory).

These restrictions fulfilled their most important aim: they reduced the number of arrivals as of 2006 to well under 10,000 each year. The drawback was that the restrictions, which were intended to deter additional immigrants from Russia and Central Asia, had a negative impact on the integration of those ethnic emigrants who had already resettled in Germany. Conventional wisdom blames the significantly slower-paced and more confrontational pattern of integration that characterized the mid-1990s on the greater linguistic and cultural distance between the ethnic emigrants and their new home. Yet this culturalist argumentation is insufficient. A sharp rise in unemployment and drastic cuts in government assistance also intensified the problems of the German-Russians. Thus, for example, the eligibility period for the government's integration allowance (a kind of substitute for an unemployment benefit, and a grant that had already been cut) was reduced to six months in 1994. At the same time, the government canceled its assumption of living expenses for retraining and other job qualification measures, and even cut language courses to six months. It should have been obvious that the Russophone immigrants could hardly learn German in so short a time (and this should be just as apparent today when it comes to refugees from the Middle East). The upshot in this case was de-qualification, so that most of the ethnic emigrants had to accept jobs well under their level of education and training.[166]

Moreover, because of growing unemployment and poverty, they became increasingly reliant on helping themselves. In the second half of the 1990s, therefore, neighborhoods and streets grew up in cities both large and small that were colloquially referred to as "Little Kazakhstan" or the "Russian Quarter" (parts of Berlin-Lichtenberg, for example). Postwar Germans were not used to ethnic neighborhoods like these until Turkish guest workers formed them prior to the post-Communist *Aussiedler* wave, though they are very common in the US, Canada, and because of decolonization also in France, the UK, and the Netherlands. West German society has grown more accustomed to diversity over time, yet the public's expressed concern about "ghettos," "ghettoization," and the presumed failure of integration is little more than a variation on the theme of the outsider's distrust of concentrations of foreigners. Russian (and Turkish) quarters in fact offered their inhabitants security in surroundings that were increasingly hostile, especially in the 1990s when unemployment soared and social tensions were on the rise. It was also unfortunate that the majority society knew (and wanted to know) little or nothing about the history of their new fellow citizens.[167] The closing off these enclaves from the outside as well as the slow pace of professional and lifestyle integration, in turn, intensified the host society's skeptical attitude. An additional consequence was an increase in conflicts between the ethnic German emigrants and other immigrants, above all with the descendants of Turkish guest workers. The higher share of ethnic emigrants' votes that now go to right-wing nationalist parties can also be traced back to the 1990s and problems with integration.

The connection between cuts in welfare services and later social problems needs to be underlined, especially at the present juncture. At the moment right-wing nationalist and, in the meantime, even conservative parties and governments in Europe are advocating and implementing cuts in social services for the refugees of 2015. They argue that their aim is to deter the influx of new illegal migrants supposedly attracted by lavish welfare payments. It is unlikely that such measures would significantly reduce either the migration of refugees or other forms of immigration. Even if the new arrivals were excluded from welfare payments, they would all the same be attracted by Western European living standards, which remain much higher than in the Middle East. That pull factor would be only minimally reduced by cutting benefits. The relevant push factors—civil wars and failing states—are also not going away. Last but not least, it should be remembered that flight is a matter of survival for many refugees.

What is certain, however, is that cuts in social benefits, especially for language and professional training, delay integration and shift burdens into the future. There also is a connection between external closure and internal tensions. This was one of the reasons for the arson attacks and pogrom-like incidents in Germany in the early 1990s. This specter has not yet come to haunt the United States, but the physical wall that President Trump intends to build at the Mexican border would certainly have an impact on inter-ethnic and racial relations in the US.

Political closure and social emancipation

The 1980s, therefore, brought about a rupture in refugee policy. There was an abatement of the former political solidarity from which Hungarians profited in 1956, Czechs and Slovaks in 1968, and then the Vietnamese boat people at the end of the 1970s. The tendency to seal off Europe from immigration affected both refugees who were persecuted and threatened existentially, among them the leading activists of Solidarność and left-wing intellectuals following the military coup in Turkey, and the numerous "optional" refugees who might have remained in their old homeland but preferred, for a variety of micro-motives, to leave (more on these distinctions in Chapter 4.4. on experiences of flight).

Owing to the shift of mood against immigration, West Germany even issued repatriation programs for guest workers and their descendants. Legally, labor migration and migration by refugees remained separate issues, but they are connected in public opinion and as political issues. The ending of guest worker recruitment in 1973–74 left asylum law untouched at first. Then, ten years later, with flight to Germany increasing substantially, there was a tightening of asylum law and cuts in social services. The goal of the recruitment stop and the legal measures was the same; both were intended to achieve a reduction in immigration. A second connection was semantic. The invention of new terms like "economic refugees" and "pseudo-asylum seekers" cast doubt on the motives of refugees and their fundamental legitimacy.

Discourses against immigrants in general and against refugees in particular resulted, at the beginning of the 1990s, in Germany once again sealing itself off from the outside world. In 1992, as the number of asylum applications in Germany grew to more than 400,000 while at the same time there was an increased influx of ethnic German emigrants, the governing Christian Democratic Union, its coalition partners the Liberals, and the *Länder* governed by the Social Democrats agreed to the so-called asylum compromise.[168]

This curtailment of the right to asylum in the Federal Republic's postwar constitution had far-reaching consequences not only for Germany, but also for the entire EU. From now on refugees ran a high risk of having their asylum applications rejected if they were entering Germany from a state in which the Geneva Refugee Convention and the European Human Rights Convention were in force. That was undoubtedly the case for Germany's western and southern neighbors: the Benelux states, France, Denmark, Switzerland, and Austria, and as a result of the revolutions of 1989, post-Communist Poland and Czechoslovakia. So it was now legally possible to send back refugees who had entered Germany from any neighboring country.[169] In principle, a refugee could only arrive in the newly united Germany by air (hence the conspicuously large transit zones in international airports) or by sea. Entering by land was no longer possible for refugees, at least not if they wanted a chance at asylum and being taken in permanently.

This change in refugee and asylum policy, however, was different from one country to another. In France, governed at the time by the Socialists, the humanitarian consensus held longer, and the same is true for Sweden.

In some ways, the US acted in line with Germany. In 1996 the Congress passed new asylum laws containing a paragraph about "safe third countries." These measures were a part of the Illegal Immigration Reform and Immigrant Responsibility Act (IIRAIRA). Asylum seekers who entered the US via Mexico and Canada could be sent back to these countries.[170] It is significant that this legislation mixed asylum and immigration issues (curbing illegal immigration was its main aim). The conflagration of labor and flight migration sowed some of the seeds of the later widespread backlash against humanitarianism. However, there also was a humanitarian side to the asylum reforms, since wars, civil unrest, natural disasters, and gender-based discrimination became more widely accepted as legitimate grounds for granting victims refugee status.[171] And there was still a degree of rhetorical restraint: neither Ronald Reagan nor George W. Bush talked about "fake refugees."

Historians and migration specialists should reject political polemics. Nevertheless, the academic community should not idealize refugees and labor migrants either. It is a legitimate question to ask, to what extent has the status of "refugee" been (mis-)used by labor migrants?[172] At first glance this seems a valid concern, for ever since European Community members closed themselves off to labor migrants from outside Europe in 1973–74, the number of asylum applications and of refugees has noticeably increased. (This European closure was only directed toward the outside, not internally. Within the European Community labor migration was made easier, step by step, in line with the efforts at European integration that culminated in the Single European Act of 1987.[173]) The same is true for the US, where attempts to curb legal labor migration from Central America has had an effect on the number of asylum applications.

Yet, even if one were to throw all the varieties of migration into the same basket (which the IIRAIRA did), a strong correlation between mass flight and political crises and wars becomes evident. The military coup in Turkey and the proclamation of martial law in Poland in 1980–81 were massive push factors, as was the collapse of the Eastern Bloc and the Soviet Union in 1989–91, soon followed by the war in the former Yugoslavia. To impute to all the people who arrived from these countries that they had come to Western Europe or the US out of economic motives precisely at this time is nonsense. Even if migrants' micro-motives had shifted from political suppression (which was waning) to economic distress (which was on the increase), the immediate triggers for the major waves of flight usually remained the same: violence, either experienced firsthand or anticipated, and a fundamental lack of prospects at home.

While Western governments, beginning in the 1980s, were increasingly closing off their borders, or at least taking some measures to reduce forced migration and flight, there were countervailing tendencies at work in the societies they governed. These societies were emancipating themselves—as they were in other areas, ranging from environmental policy to military armament—from government policy and questioning the legitimacy of the government to regulating all kinds of affairs (I am avoiding here the term "big government," which is a myth, especially in the US). After the NGO Cap Anamur, other organizations emerged, such as Pro Asyl, founded in 1986 in reaction to that decade's restrictions on the right and recognition of asylum and dedicated to looking after recently arrived refugees in Germany. There were similar initiatives in France, the Netherlands, Italy, and other West European countries; and in the US the American Civil Liberties Union acts as a strong lobby for the rights of refugees.

The arguments advanced by the NGOs were above all humanitarian in nature: it is a duty to help people in distress. This humanitarianism, however, came at a price, since it meant that the debate was increasingly shifted onto a normative plane. Norms, however, change over time, while upholding them depends on the given political context. By contrast, utilitarian arguments, usually invoked to justify or discourage migration in general, have been used less since the 1980s watershed. It remains an open question what makes sense politically, since the right-wing nationalists now governing some countries reject both kinds of argument, humanitarian and utilitarian. Yet it remains a lesson of history that refugees almost always increase the welfare of the nations taking them in, and that they also enrich their host countries culturally. There have only been a few exceptions to this rule, in cases where the host countries have rejected equality and integration for refugees. For the countries of origin, by contrast, a massive flight of their citizens always means a loss.

Summary

Compared with incidents of flight that are motivated by religious or nationalist persecution, the numbers of refugees that one can specify as politically persecuted in a narrow sense is rather small. Yet it is precisely these political refugees who have had the major impact on their host countries and on international law, especially the Geneva Refugee Convention of 1951. The reason for this has something to do with the fact that political refugees have overwhelmingly been members of a social elite. They were able to express themselves in the countries that took them in, and frequently also lobbied for human rights and on behalf of other kinds of refugees. At the same time, they stayed connected to their countries of origin, and not infrequently viewed their exile as a passing affair. As early as the nineteenth century, these exile activists imprinted a positive image of refugees in Western societies.

The first refugees subject to political persecution from the period of the American Revolution would, however, probably arouse little sympathy today: they were not freedom fighters, but loyalists to the English crown and supporters of British colonial rule over America. The roughly 60,000 refugees who fled the American Revolution had the advantage that their "mother" land really behaved as such, like a parent, redirecting them to new places where they could begin life anew, and generously compensated them according to their social status (which also lead to the reproduction of class). Today's UN is unfortunately not as powerful and effective as the British Empire. Its work is in most cases restricted to supplying emergency relief to refugees. The EU also is neither an empire nor a state, though the opposite is sometimes asserted, but merely an institution whose undertakings depend for their success on the willingness or unwillingness of its member states.

Soon after the American Revolution, the European revolutions of the late eighteenth century created a second mass flight of conservatives, and these refugees, from the French Revolution, had it harder than the American Loyalists. The anciens régimes in Europe rejected the Republic and the Jacobins, and they intervened militarily against revolutionary France. Toward the refugees, however, who were French and thus regarded in principle as suspicious foreigners, they showed at best a limited solidarity. The host societies of the day were not politicized to any significant degree, so it was only the governing dynasties and nobility that evinced a certain empathy. But they were not interested in sharing their positions at court and in the feudal estates with the refugees.

The ideals of international solidarity and fraternité remained a domain of liberals and the left throughout the entire "long" nineteenth century. The slogan of the 1831 Polish freedom fighters from 1831, "For our freedom and yours" ("Za wolność naszą i waszą"), got to the heart of the matter. After the failure of the uprising, Polish emigrants (who knew that their exile would last a long time) were frequently greeted with enthusiasm, housed for free, and supplied with food. The Western liberal constitutional states (France under Louis-Philippe, the recently independent Belgium, Switzerland, the United Kingdom, and especially the US) held their doors open for refugees, at least in principle. In Switzerland especially, exiles had at times to accept restrictions such as a ban on political activity, but they were protected from deportation and thus from counterrevolutionary persecution in their countries of origin. These principles amounted to a *non-refoulement avant la lettre*.

The relatively welcoming reception given to political refugees was related also to the manageable size of these refugee streams. In the end, the Grande Émigration out of Poland included only 6,000 permanent exiles; from the countries in which reactionary forces had emerged victorious in 1848–49, a total of 12,000 to 15,000 freedom fighters went into exile.

Although in no case did exiles achieve major changes, let alone an overthrow of the conservative order back in their homeland, refugees like Giuseppe Mazzini, Lajos Kossuth, and Arnold Ruge played the publics of their host countries and the Old Continent like virtuosos. The US in particular defined itself as a sanctuary for political freedom fighters and nurturing this self-image produced circumstances favorable for refugees; in principle, the situation recalled the late-seventeenth-century age of religious refugees. The biggest problem here was the struggle for everyday survival, for the very countries that took in the refugees most readily, England and the US, offered no material support or permanent social services. France, by contrast, behaved quite generously, although Napoleon III broke with this tradition because he did not want to import agitators—which political exiles frequently were—into his country.

Because of political polarization in the second half of the nineteenth century and the assassination attempts made by the first international terrorists at the fin de siècle, suspicion of political refugees increased in all of the potential host countries. The myth of the Forty-Eighters continued to be operative, however. Alongside Switzerland and other small countries like Belgium, France was again ready, after Napoleon III was deposed, to take in political emigrants permanently.

The situation became far more difficult for people fleeing the Russian Revolution and civil war. This can be attributed to their unprecedented numbers, the long prehistory of Russian hegemony over the eastern part of Europe, and the devastation of the First World War. Russia's immediate neighbors were overwhelmed by masses of refugees, granted them only short-term accommodation, and later attempted to rid themselves entirely of Russian refugees. Germany, Berlin in particular, was a second stop for many refugees, but there hyperinflation and economic chaos reigned. Anti-Communism might have been a bridge between refugees and the various European societies that took them in, but anti-Communism at the time was not as ideologically well developed as it would become later during the Cold War. Moreover, anti-Communism had been coopted by radical nationalists and anti-Semites who rejected foreigners, and therefore refugees, on general principles.

Nationalism and antisemitism were also spreading in the US. The influence of these ideologies and a fear of competition on the labor market by new immigrants led to the Immigration Act of 1924, which established national quotas for migrants. There were no exceptions made for refugees, or in general on humanitarian grounds. In the other former European settler colonies, too, utilitarianism took precedence over humanitarianism. Immigrants were only welcome to the extent that they promised to bring advantages to the societies taking them in. Refugees, however, were predominantly destitute and needy; and hence, in principle, less welcome.

Nevertheless, the rudiments of an international refugee policy did emerge in the 1920s and would eventually serve as a template for refugee policy after the Second World War. Within the framework of the League of Nations, the newly introduced High Commissioners for Refugees took on as their first task the care of stateless Russians, Armenians, and other persecuted Christians from Asia Minor, and then, after 1933, of refugees from Germany. A high commissioner for Jewish refugees was never installed, however, although these were especially numerous and endangered. In the 1930s the international community famously failed to meet this challenge. Antisemitism was certainly a major motive for the refusal of so many countries to take in Jews.

Things were little better for the Spanish Civil War refugees, a failure that would have repercussions for the Western democracies. In 1940, one of the reasons France was in such a state of political and social exhaustion when the German army marched in was that it had been unable to reach a consensus on how to deal with its refugees. Consensus was also lacking in the US, where President Roosevelt succeeded only in opening up already existing immigration quotas for the Jews. Congress did not want to approve a larger aid operation or indeed make any fundamental changes in the country's immigration policy. Thus, the tragedy of the *St. Louis* symbolized a much larger problem.

The West did, however, learn its lessons from the mistakes of the 1930s and from the Holocaust. The Human Rights Charter of the UN and the Geneva Refugee Convention of 1951, based on the Charter, established a cluster of inviolable basic rights and protections for the individual (in contrast to the collective minority protections of the interwar period). To be sure, the implantation of conventions of this kind are dependent on the goodwill of all involved and subject to political cycles. Violations, moreover, are far from sanctionable.

A look at refugee policy in the late 1940s reveals profound contradictions between the values advocated by the West and actual policy. Almost at the same time that the international community, at the insistence of the US and its allies, was discussing the 1948 UN Human Rights Charter, there was still a consensus that ethnic cleansing was a legitimate way (albeit a last resort) to settle conflicts and create a new postwar order (see Chapter 2.3). Accordingly, some fifty million people were put to rout in Europe, Palestine, and India. Similarly questionable was the treatment of the displaced persons from the Stalinist Soviet Union, who for too long were repatriated notwithstanding their backgrounds and political views. Here, too, finding a pragmatic solution to a problem—woe to the groups that were viewed or defined as such!—trumped moral considerations. The treatment of Jewish DPs in the first three postwar years was especially disgraceful when one considers how many of them had just survived German concentration camps.

The admission of DPs into the United States in 1948, however, does mark a milestone in international refugee policy. Here, for the first time, humanitarian concerns counted for more than the merely practical objective of getting refugees off the nation's back. A decisive factor behind this humanitarianism was the martyrdom of Jews in the Holocaust; after 1945 Jewish refugees could no longer be treated as they had been before the Second World War. And, as the fate of East Europe's DPs makes plain, the Cold War catalyzed a different attitude toward refugees in general. As of the summer of 1946, Ukrainian and Baltic DPs got a more sympathetic hearing (from the Americans somewhat earlier than from the British) when they resisted forced repatriation to the Soviet Union. Anti-Communism, however, was a double-edged sword and could also be used as an instrument against Eastern Europeans. Starting in 1950, owing to deliberately incited panic about Communist spies, the US for a number of years admitted almost no new refugees into the country. After 2016 these deep-seated historical anxieties resurfaced. Since taking office, President Trump has fostered fear of "Islamic terrorists"; all one has to do is substitute "Islamic terrorists" for "Communist spies" and the echoes ring loud and amazingly true.

In 1950, the establishment of the UNHCR created the first international institution for refugees that could claim universality. While the Geneva Refugee Convention, because of resistance from the Communist countries, had initially been restricted to Europe and to persons displaced before the Convention was passed, over the next several decades that agreement achieved a global reach. The most important steps in that direction were the Hungarian crisis of 1956, when the UNHCR earned recognition in the Eastern Bloc; the Supplementary Protocol of 1967, in which the Convention was extended to the entire world; and the international resettlement of the so-called Indochina refugees at the end of the 1970s. In was during that decade in particular that humanitarian values and the international agreements based on them began to pick up serious momentum. This had much to do with the ideological competition of the Cold War; and also with the power of autosuggestion: by taking in refugees, the West was able to show its benevolent, humanitarian side.[174] This motivated an openness toward refugees from Communist countries, first from Eastern Europe, then from Latin America and East Asia.

On top of that, in 1956 and 1968, the Soviet Union did the West a favor, unintentionally. The Red Army was dispatched to seal off the borders of Hungary and Czechoslovakia again after a brief opening. Both of these refugee crises ended before the West's receptivity had been durably tested, setting off what might be termed a third "Golden Age of European refugees." That age (if one wishes to call it such) lasted a good quarter century, from the end of the 1940s until the closure toward Polish refugees in the mid-1980s (and the equivalent restrictive move in the US after the Mariel Boat Lift—for more on this, see Chapter 4.1).[175]

In this era, humanitarianism, as we have seen, displaced the utilitarianism that previously had been the prevailing philosophy (for a discussion of these two principles, see Chapter 4.3). Refugees were taken in above all because of their status as persecuted victims, not out of consideration for whatever usefulness they might bring to the countries taking them in. This moral dimension, which characterizes the civil rights movement in the US as much as it applies to the 68ers in Europe, has certain drawbacks, however. To begin with, it turns refugees into objects of pity, unable to affect their own fate as subjects of history. On second glance, moreover, the status of a persecuted person turns out not to be cut and dried. Refugees seldom abandon their homeland for one motive only. Many Eastern Bloc refugees also left because they knew that living standards in the West were higher.

The remarkable thing about this quarter century is that no one really scrutinized why people were fleeing. The West, when taking in refugees from the Eastern Bloc or Southeast Asia, proceeded from the very general assumption that these were victims of Communist dictatorships. At most it was ex post facto that refugees were asked about their political convictions and activities. Western host countries behaved very generously even in highly doubtful cases. Thus, for example, members of the Hungarian, Polish, and then in 1968 of the Czechoslovakian Communist parties who had fled their countries were admitted to the US.

When détente arrived on the scene and the Eastern Bloc countries were no longer to be viewed as totalitarian dictatorships but in a more complex way, the friend-versus-foe scheme of the early Cold War sounded less convincing. Moreover, the citizens of the Federal Republic of Germany and Sweden, two countries with an especially strong asylum tradition, experienced an influx of Poles coming as harvest workers and as tourists. The growing exchange between East and West made it clear to all sides that Poles, Hungarians, and citizens of other Eastern Bloc countries (to the extent they were allowed to travel) were not coming to the West for political reasons only.

Yet, all in all, the attitude toward refugees remained affirmative, because the moral convictions of the civil rights movement and (in Europe) of the student movement continued to penetrate Western societies more and more deeply. Conversely, it was also characteristic of détente that conservative politicians and parties began to accept moderate or radical leftists more readily, as for example from Chile after a right-wing dictator seized power there. Two decades earlier these same refugees would have been under suspicion of being agitators or spies; by the end of the 1970s, some of them were even allowed (after resistance from influential Republicans) to come to the United States.

This openness toward refugees and intensified humanitarianism also correlated with the economic boom of the first three postwar decades, and the corresponding high demand for labor. Hence, as in the 1920s, refugees were taken in rather willingly. This was especially true of West Germany, which after the arrival of eight million expellees took in an additional five million refugees from the GDR and ethnic German emigrants from Eastern Europe. It is therefore no exaggeration to call the Federal Republic a "refugee state."

Postwar German history leads to another conclusion about the coincidence of prosperity and receptivity to refugees. The same two decades that saw the

Federal Republic taking in around thirteen million refugees also witnessed the postwar economic miracle. Without the gigantic reservoir of labor provided by refugees, the miracle would have been somewhat less miraculous.[176] Taking in and integrating thirteen million people between 1945 and 1961 rested, however, on a double legitimation, political and national. In advancing the cause of expellees from East Central Europe, the government's first appeal was to national solidarity, but it simultaneously pilloried Poland and Czechoslovakia as brutal Communist dictatorships. It was made clear to West Germans that there could be no question of returning refugees to their old homelands, and that therefore they had to be integrated into their "new homeland."

In France national solidarity legitimized taking in and lavishing public expenditures on the pieds noirs, even though there was political dissent against them, specifically over colonialism and the French Algerians' contribution to it. Among the Vietnamese, by contrast, humanitarian motives predominated.

Not one of the host countries regretted its decision to take in refugees. Everywhere, the Cold War's political refugees integrated well and rapidly. This point requires special emphasis, because for some groups like the Indochina refugees, the Hmong in particular, the initial prognosis was negative. It was predicted that their lifestyle as peasants, fishers, and hunters, and their lower level of education would work against them. Nonetheless today the Hmong in the US are just as well integrated as the Vietnamese in France who have so enriched France's cities as "traiteurs" (caterers) with their delicatessens and snack bars.

Yet in the 1980s, when the postwar boom fizzled and unemployment was on the rise, a more defensive attitude could be detected everywhere in the West: at first toward labor migrants, and then also, with a decade's delay, toward refugees. In West Germany the recruitment of guest workers came to a halt in 1973, followed ten years later by the first cutbacks, initially in social services, for refugees. In addition, access to the labor market was restricted. This was justified by the argument that there should not be any incentive for immigrating in a quest for asylum. The upshot, however, was that refugees were now seen more than ever as a burden on the welfare state. As demonstrated by the case of the Polish refugees in the 1980s, Cold War political solidarity was on the wane. No longer was anyone who managed to get over the Iron Curtain automatically a good refugee worthy of protection.

Matters were much the same across the Atlantic. After taking in a small contingent of Poles immediately after the proclamation of martial law, the US refused to accept a larger number. In spite of American sanctions against the regime of General Jaruzelski, the Poles were not regarded so much as an oppressed people as a poor one whose immigration ought to be prevented. But the government of President Reagan did not revoke the Refugee Act of 1980.

Even under this Republican president (as later under both Bushes), the US accepted contingents of resettled refugees. To this extent the humanitarianism of the 1970s endured—until the year Donald Trump won the presidency.

In present day Europe there are similar trends. Those countries in which right-wing nationalists govern or share power favor cutting off refugees, now often criminalized as illegal migrants. As discussed earlier, however, such ideas and the dissension they evoke were already present in the 1980s. Between the 1980s and the present day lies a long period of time, which will be discussed in greater detail in Chapter Four. Here the focus will not be so much on flight itself as on the Western world's refugee policy, the relationship between normative and utilitarian standards, and reaction to the massive exodus out of the Middle East since 2011.

4

REFUGEE POLITICS AFTER THE COLD WAR

4.1 Humanitarianism after 1989 and "Fortress Europe"

Nineteen eighty-nine was widely celebrated as the year when Western values, human rights, and democracy triumphed in Europe and beyond. Euphoria over the fall of the state socialist dictatorships in Eastern Europe did not last long, however, especially inside those very societies. The collapse of the Soviet bloc's planned economies and of their Cold War–era economic union caused a deep recession in all the post-Communist countries. Unemployment, a phenomenon unknown on that side of the Iron Curtain prior to 1989, rose steeply, millions of people fell into poverty, and life expectancy in the former Soviet Union sank to the level of developing countries.

In most post-Communist countries, the pendulum in economic policy now swung in the direction of neoliberalism, which at the beginning of the 1990s had attained global hegemony.[1] The dissidents and revolutionary mass movements had fought dearly for human rights, but they did not bring human dignity or social protection to the masses of the population now suffering from steep economic decline. Democracy may have been a cherished ideal, but as a political system it encountered skepticism. Moreover, the cuts in social expenditure and radical reforms were presented everywhere on the grounds that "there is no alternative." This anti-political slogan (once invented by Margaret Thatcher) may have helped to push through reforms, but it cut short political debates and thus also weakened the young democracies. In combination with the widespread corruption that accompanied privatization, this resulted in low electoral participation and—if one may project today's political science vocabulary back onto the past—in a "crisis of democracy."

Economic decline, moreover, abetted the rebirth of nationalism that had already played a major role in mobilizing societies in the autumn of 1989. In 1991 Europe's last multinational states dissolved, first in Yugoslavia, where the Serbian head of state and party leader Slobodan Milošević banked on a strategy of violence and the establishment of a Greater Serbia. After a failed coup against Mikhail Gorbachev, the Soviet Union was dissolved at the end of 1991. Although there was no civil war, there was considerable violence in the Caucasus, the Central Asian Fergana Valley, and Transnistria. Czechoslovakia partitioned itself without any violence, undoubtedly taking heed of what its people and leaders had witnessed in nearby Yugoslavia. In the autumn of 1991, the first refugees from Croatia were already reaching the newly independent state of Slovenia, Hungary, Austria, and Germany. In 1992 the trail of refugees from Bosnia and Herzegovina extended as far as the Netherlands, France, and Sweden (see the details in Chapter 2.5). This was a refugee wave almost on the scale of what Europe would later witness in 2015.

Prevailing conditions for absorbing the 700,000 refugees from the former Yugoslavia into the EU—about two million people were fleeing within or between the successor states—were unfavorable in many respects. At the beginning of the 1990s, the largest potential host country, the Federal Republic of Germany, slipped into a lengthy recession and a systemic crisis. The welfare state was overburdened by transfer payments to East Germany, and public debt was on the rise, along with the tax burden and unemployment. Deteriorating economic conditions in Germany, in turn, affected its neighbors. The Netherlands and Austria (the latter an especially important transit and host country), along with Sweden, were struggling with economic problems too. Even more unfavorable was the situation in Hungary, which was also located on the flight route to the west, as well as in Slovenia, which had only just achieved its independence.

Because of the recession and the burdens placed on the welfare state by ethnic emigrants from the former Soviet Union, the prevailing mood in Germany was fairly hostile toward taking in more refugees. In September 1991, as the war in Croatia was escalating, Germany's most important news magazine, the left-leaning weekly *Der Spiegel*, had a cover title that ran "Refugees—Ethnic Emigrants—Asylum Seekers: The Onslaught of the Poor" (*"Flüchtlinge—Aussiedler—Asylanten. Der Ansturm der Armen"*).[2] More than ever, conservative media like the daily tabloid *Bild* and the upscale newspaper of record, the *Frankfurter Allgemeine Zeitung*, were staking out the position that the boat was full. In Austria the right-wing populist and nationalist FPÖ exploited the public's anxiety over the many refugees and labor migrants arriving from Eastern Europe for use in its first major xenophobic campaign. The Austrian government accommodated this mood to some extent by imposing a visa obligation on Poles and Romanians. In Germany the conservative-liberal federal government, with the backing of the Social Democrat-led *Länder*, passed the so-called asylum compromise at the end of 1992. This new legislation stipulated that refugees could be turned away if they had entered Germany via a "secure third country." Without a doubt, this meant Austria, from where most of the Croatian and Bosnian refugees had come. By this time, the two most important transit countries, Hungary and Slovenia, had also become democracies and had just ratified the Geneva Refugee Convention. Hungary was the first country in the Eastern Bloc to do so, having already taken this step toward joining the Western community of values in March 1989. At the time, Viktor Orbán, whose rise as a charismatic politician was in its early stages, did not say anything against this initiative.

Taking in refugees from the former Yugoslavia, then, clashed with the legal and political situation at the time in Germany, especially with the asylum compromise. Yet at the beginning of the 1990s the legacy of the Cold War and the revolutions of 1989 still had an impact. Refugees from the GDR during its last year had initially entered the Federal Republic via Hungary, Czechoslovakia, and Austria. Closing off this escape route and erecting a new Iron Curtain in Burgenland (Austria's easternmost province) or in southeastern Bavaria—just three years after the East Germans had fled through the same openings to the West—would have seemed like a betrayal of Germany's own history. Hence, this option did not even come up for discussion in the early 1990s (in contrast to what would happen in 2015).

Furthermore, in the autumn of 1991 and early 1992, the wartime atrocities in the former Yugoslavia were filling the headlines of the international media almost daily. The pictures coming out of Vukovar, from the concentration camps in northern Bosnia, and of the numerous people killed by artillery fire in the siege of Sarajevo shocked the Western public. Such crimes against humanity would have justified a military intervention at any time, but the countries of the EU and NATO hesitated. The member states did not want to risk the lives of their own soldiers and there was no clear war aim. Only when the Bosnian Serb army committed an act of genocide at Srebrenica in the summer of 1995 did NATO at last intervene and bomb Serb positions around Sarajevo and at other strategic locations.

The West wanted at least, as a kind of compensation for their inaction, to offer some help to the suffering civilian population and the refugees. Thus they set up so-called safe havens, security zones established by the UN in Bosnia and Herzegovina that were supplied with food, medicine, and other vital goods (see also Chapter 2.5). For Sarajevo, as in Berlin in 1948, an airlift was organized that made it possible for the capital of Bosnia and Herzegovina to survive a siege that lasted more than three years. In spite of good intentions, these relief actions have left a bitter aftertaste. The peacekeeping troops sent by the UN were so poorly equipped with weapons and military technology that they had to stand by and watch the 1995 genocide in Srebrenica. And the aid deliveries were in part appropriated by customs officials and the Army of the Republika Srpska and only partially reached the many hundreds of thousands of "internally displaced people" in the country.

For victims of war from Bosnia and Herzegovina, it amounted to a blessing in disguise that most of the countries with a sense of obligation to help refugees on humanitarian grounds were not that far away geographically. Many Croats, Bosnians, and Serbs had friends and relatives in Austria, Germany, and other EU states who had migrated there in the 1960s and 1970s as guest workers. Through these networks they could at least find provisional accommodations and then seek assistance with the cooperation of NGOs, churches, and government offices. The early stages of flight often relied on these networks based on family connections or on a common local and national background. That is why in 1992–93, in spite of the huge surge of refugees, there was little need for gymnasiums, schools, and other public buildings to house the newcomers, in contrast to the requirements placed on public spaces in 2015 as refugees were arriving from the Middle East.

As a transit and host country, Austria was the first Western state to be affected by the massive flight out of the former Yugoslavia. As early as the autumn of 1991, 11,000 refugees arrived in Austria fleeing the war in Croatia, and in 1992–93 they were followed by 90,000 people from Bosnia and Herzegovina. Thus, the total number of refugees from the former Yugoslavia (at the end of the 1990s they were joined by about 13,000 people from Kosovo) in Austria significantly exceeded the numbers of Middle Easterners, Asians, and North Africans that would arrive in 2015. Taking in more than a hundred thousand people undoubtedly constituted a burden on the welfare state and labor market, but the refugees were able to register and receive a provisional residence permit without a great deal of bureaucratic fuss, a level of ease that seemed to confirm Austria's self-image as a major Cold War country of asylum. In great part, this was a myth, but it was one that shaped Austria's refugee policy after 1989 and thus the actual course of history. Also playing an important role was a historical connection with Croatia and Bosnia; both regions had been part of the Habsburg Empire prior to 1918.

The next and, on the whole, most important destination in the EU was the Federal Republic of Germany. In spite of the restrictions imposed by the asylum laws of 1992–93 and an unfavorable political climate, Germany did take in around 350,000 people from Croatia and Bosnia-Herzegovina. Sweden, as measured by its population, behaved with even greater generosity, granting asylum to 90,000 people. The Netherlands, Denmark, Switzerland, and Italy also took in their share. The system of international resettlement was likewise set in motion once again. As early as 1992 Canada took in a contingent of 5,000 refugees, and many more over the next several years, while the US allowed 38,000 Bosnians to enter in the 1990s.[3] This was the context in which today's Bosnian community in the US, centered in St. Louis, came into being. That many of the Bosnians were practicing Muslims did not generate suspicion in any of the Western countries taking them in. There was at the time a lingering Cold War dimension to the lineup of friend and foe: the Russian-backed Serbs were perceived as enemies, making their Croat and Bosnian victims putative "allies."

Admitting the Croatians and Bosnians took place, as mentioned, under the premise that the arrivals from the former Yugoslavia were collectively refugees under the terms of the Geneva Convention. Germany even made an exception to its recently concluded asylum compromise and waived the individual case assessment prescribed by its asylum laws. The refugees from the former Yugoslavia were recognized as a group and given a special status. The other EU countries acted in a similar way.

Hungary, Czechoslovakia and its two successor states, and Poland also took in refugees (in contrast to these countries' later behavior in 2015). In Hungary the decision was influenced by the country's geographic location, while the Czech Republic's openness had a historical background. Since the nineteenth century the Czech national movement had maintained close ties to Southeast Europe; in Yugoslavia during the 1990s, moreover, there were still some former Czech and Slovak colonies dating from the time of the Habsburg Empire. Linguistic closeness was an additional argument and would eventually help the refugees integrate into the Czech Republic and Slovakia. Nevertheless, solidarity with the refugees was hardly a given. In 1992 there were cautious voices as well, some even coming from the liberal media, warning that an intake of refugees would financially overburden Czechoslovakia.[4] That "generous impulses" prevailed, in contrast with the much less sympathetic attitudes of 2015, was attributable to the values of 1989 and the advocacy of prominent civil rights activist like Václav Havel, who as Czech president helped shape his country's policies. Like the Western 68ers Havel made moral arguments above all, not utilitarian ones. The latter might also have been persuasive at the time, since a labor shortage in the mid-1990s saw the Czech Republic recruiting more than 100,000 Ukrainian guest workers. Havel was a well-known civil rights leader, yet conservative politicians also agreed to take in refugees because the conflict in the former Yugoslavia still fit the post–Cold War narrative inasmuch as the Communist leader Serbian prime minister Milošević was suppressing nations striving for their independence.[5]

Poland became involved when its first non-Communist prime minister, Tadeusz Mazowiecki, was appointed the UN's "Special Rapporteur" in Bosnia and Herzegovina. (In 1995 he resigned in protest against the genocide in Srebrenica.) During the refugee "crisis" of 2015, by contrast, the EU failed to involve its new East Central European member states, especially Poland, in a similar way (e.g., by appointing a politician from there to a relevant position in refugee affairs).

By admitting refugees from the former Yugoslavia and arranging for their international resettlement, the participating states were agreeing on a de facto expansion of the Geneva Refugee Convention. In the Convention and the Supplementary Protocol of 1967, wars per se were not cited as grounds for flight; instead, the Convention granted refugee status "owing to well-founded fear of being persecuted for reasons of race, religion, nationality, [or] membership of a particular social group or political opinion. . . ."[6] This condition was undoubtedly applied in the case of the Croats, Bosnians, and Serbs who were fleeing in the early 1990s. But in the case of other wars, such as the Iran-Iraq War that lasted from 1980 to 1988, nationalist persecution and violence had not led to refugees from these countries being granted asylum collectively. For the victims of ethnic cleansing in the former Soviet Union, too, it proved very difficult to obtain asylum in one of the EU states. In Poland at the time there was more awareness of the violent conflicts in the former Soviet Union, so that several thousand Chechens who were fleeing from the second Chechen War of 1999 and from the subsequent repressive measures of the Putin regime and its local proxies were at least tolerated in Poland and not immediately turned away at the border. Most of them had come by land through Belarus; in today's Russia, a highly fortified police and surveillance state, this would no longer be possible.

Refugees from the so-called Third World had an even more difficult time, both logistically and legally, in fleeing to Europe and obtaining asylum there. This points once again to the Eurocentrism of Western refugee policy and to a covert bias against non-white refugees in Europe. In recent years the older racism has been superseded by anti-Islamism, which is openly promoted by right-wing populist and nationalist parties. By contrast, the wars in the former Yugoslavia were perceived as a European problem and the refugees as fellow Europeans, which is why 700,000 people were admitted over an extended period of time, with little red tape and hardly any controversy.

None of the receiving states regretted its decision, and they all had good experiences with the refugees from the former Yugoslavia. This is demonstrated by statistics from Sweden and Austria, where most of them were allowed to stay after the war ended and where today they are, as a rule, well integrated in terms of their professional, social, and family life. This success was, however, primarily due to the refugees themselves, who accepted any job, even if it was below their earlier skill level and social position. They aspired to work their way up, however, and this often took a toll, leaving them little time for family, which triggered many intra-family conflicts, and (as was also often the case with earlier cohorts of refugees) discouraged them from speaking about the suffering they had experienced.

Germany, by contrast, followed a more restrictive refugee policy, which ultimately influenced the entire EU more than did the pragmatic and simultaneously more humanitarian position of Austria and Sweden. The government under Chancellor Kohl insisted at the time that the refugees admitted from the former Yugoslavia would have to return home once the war was over. Until then they were to be housed and provided for, but not much more would be done for them. Access to the labor market—again in contrast to Austria and Sweden—required jumping especially high hurdles. If German firms wanted to hire a refugee, they had to prove that there was no suitable German applicant for the available position. Clearly, no permanent integration into the labor market was envisioned. One may therefore characterize German policy as humanitarianism with an expiration date.

If Chancellor Angela Merkel has her way, this scenario will repeat itself in the case of the refugees from Syria and Iraq. At the beginning of 2016, she gave a speech in her East German home state explaining that "we expect that, once there is peace in Syria again, once IS has been defeated in Iraq, that you [will] go back to your home country with the knowledge that you have gained." That Merkel's tone was paternalistic is suggested by her use in German of the pronoun *ihr* (*ihr*—the plural of the familiar *du*, roughly equivalent to "you-all"—is a form of address adults use when speaking to children and persons of the same or lower stature), but in fact her speech was not given before an audience of refugees or at one of the mass facilities where they were housed, but at a regional party congress of the Christian Democratic Union. The clear commitment to returning refugees that she expressed was obviously meant to reassure the conservative wing of her party and potential voters for the right-wing, anti-immigration Alternative for Germany, the AfD.[7] This quote and other statements made by the chancellor demonstrate, incidentally, how exaggerated the attacks made by right-wing populists on Merkel have been. Since 2015 she has been attacked as a smuggler and flight abettor, aspersions also recently cast at French President Emmanuel Macron. These attacks have also had the effect of prompting many liberals and left-wing politicians to overestimate Merkel's humanitarian position on refugees.

But back to history: When the 1995 Peace Accord in Dayton was signed, the German government took the repatriation it prescribed seriously. In the following years most Bosnians really were sent back to their old homeland. Many resisted. They knew that they faced dire prospects: homes and property that had been destroyed, hostile neighbors, and an already impoverished homeland made even more destitute by the war. The tough attitude of the German authorities provoked resistance from civil society groups at the local level as well, where most Bosnians had already become well integrated. Church congregations, NGOs, and German neighbors spoke out, especially for the children who were being pulled out of their schools. And any number of firms would have been only too happy to retain their Bosnian workers and staff. In the end, however, economics decided the day—in 1997 unemployment in Germany exceeded the four million mark for the first time since the 1930s—and repatriation went forward, a process one might view here as disintegration (quite literally, the opposite of integration).

At the same time, the case of the Bosnians also refutes the assertions made by right-wing populists, and curiously echoed by a variety of international observers and writers, that Germany admitted Syrians in 2015 in order to whitewash a conscience soiled by its Nazi past. If that had been the case, the government and society would have adopted a far different line in the mid-1990s, years that marked the apex of intense public debates on coming to terms with the Holocaust, paying reparations to Nazi victims, and restoring stolen Jewish property. Moreover, there was a direct historical link between National Socialism and the Yugoslavian situation. The propaganda of Serbian nationalists had worked most effectively in those regions of Bosnia and Croatia that had suffered the most during the Second World War from the terror of the Germans and their allies, the Croatian Ustaša. Again in 1992, violence in these districts proved especially brutal and repulsive.

Partial closure of the Federal Republic

In addition to the economic and social-policy motives involved, the repatriation of the Bosnians can also be attributed to an altered post–Cold War view of the world. Prior to 1989 neither Western politicians nor refugees could have conceived of a return home to the Eastern Bloc as desirable or even possible. This was as true of Germany as it was of the US, where a caricature of totalitarian rule continued to shape perceptions of the Soviet Union and the Eastern Bloc almost up until their downfall. Refugees indeed had genuine reasons to fear being punished in Communist Europe, especially in the GDR, where eight to ten years in jail awaited anyone who undertook an "illegal border crossing." Owing to these legal sanctions in the countries from which the exiles were escaping, the Federal Republic was very generous to refugees from the Eastern Bloc. Even refugees who were not recognized as such, or whose applications for asylum were rejected, did not have to fear being deported and were allowed to stay in Germany. Sweden, Austria, and other frontline states in the Cold War behaved similarly.

This generous attitude was possible not least because the Warsaw Pact states guarded their borders so strictly. Hence, even in the 1980s, there were few people, with the exception of the Poles, who were able to breach the Iron Curtain on their own initiative. The Western border of the Soviet Union posed a hurdle almost as high. Yet all that changed with perestroika and the fall of the Iron Curtain (which was already riddled with holes even before 1989). East-West migration jumped sharply. As already mentioned, in both 1989 and 1990 nearly 400,000 ethnic German emigrants entered the Federal Republic. In addition, there was a large-scale influx of (post-)Soviet Jews; and in their case, amends for the Nazi past were indeed a major motive. Year for year, the number of asylum applicants also reached a new height; it was 121,000 in 1989 (at the time a record), 193,000 in 1990, more than a quarter million in 1991, and 438,000 in 1992 because of massive flight from the former Soviet Union (see Chapter 3.6). Even more than in the early 1980s, immigration was a campaign issue. The Christian Democrats kept pressing the Social Democrats on this issue until the SPD-governed *Länder* finally caved in to the pressure.

In 1993 the Federal Republic passed a bundle of laws and even a constitutional amendment aimed at stemming the massive flight and immigration.

The initial issue taken up in the so-called asylum compromise was refugees, and the most important innovations in that compromise were provisions about entering via a "secure third state." These new rules allowed authorities, in principle, to deport almost all refugees who came to Germany by land. There were exceptions for Geneva Convention refugees and others in need of protection (these were primarily asylum applicants from the former Yugoslavia), but the goal of sealing off Germany was clear.[8]

In order to provide additional safeguards for these provisions on the foreign policy front, the Federal Republic concluded a series of agreements, starting in 1994, with Poland, the Czech Republic, and other East Central and Southeastern European countries to take back refugees who had passed through their territory on the way to Germany. On this basis it was possible now to return the refugees entering Germany from the East, something practiced frequently especially at the German-Polish border.[9] Moreover, immigration by ethnic German emigrants was also massively restricted, although this did not happen abruptly, as national solidarity apparently counted for more than an unspecific humanitarianism. For the *Aussiedler* there was one more door opener, drawn from the conceptual repertoire of the Geneva Refugee Convention. To the extent that they could prove an "acute pressure of persecution" (*akuter Verfolgungsdruck*), ethnic German emigrants could continue entering the Federal Republic and then immediately receive German citizenship.

The restrictions issued in 1993 did what they were intended to do for domestic political purposes. A year later only 127,000 people applied for asylum, in 1998 applications fell below the 100,000 watermark for the first time in the 1990s, and in 2007 the figure was even lower at 20,000.[10] This meant that the level of the mid-1980s had been reached again. At the same time, chances of achieving recognition in an asylum procedure dropped. In 2006 only four percent of asylum applications were approved in such a way that the applicants were recognized as refugees. Other EU member states watched Germany carefully and took note of what was happening there.

Although the recognition quotient grew again over the next several years, it remained low in comparison with the Cold War era. This shows once again, indirectly, how enmeshed Western humanitarianism was with the Cold War. And it also indirectly confirms Mark Mazower's skeptical theses about Europe's democratization in the period following the Second World War. In his book *Dark Continent: Europe's Twentieth Century*, he concluded that democracy is not embedded in Europe's essence. The expansion of democracy after 1945 and the associated pushback against fascism and Communism were due to a variety of factors, including intensified American involvement in the continent, rising living standards, and now the European Community. That these factors interacted in the way they did was ultimately a matter of luck or contingency. Following the logic of Mazower's argument, we might suggest that the open attitude toward refugees, which lasted through the end of the 1970s and then reappeared in the 1990s, was also a product of political-normative competition between East and West, good overall economic conditions (conditions that were, however, absent in Germany during the unification crisis, which helps to explain that country's partial closure), and of the way in which humanitarianism became universalized and a factor desirable in its own right. By this analysis, the rights of refugees laid down in international law and the Western world's willingness to admit refugees are just as contingent and finite as the constellations of factors behind the postwar European democratization that Mazower cites. To be sure, Germany's partial closure following the asylum compromise was mitigated in part by the actions of civil society groups. Organizations like "pro Asyl" provided free counseling and lawyers, and refugees could also fall back on networks of their compatriots who had already been admitted.

The Dublin Regulations and "Sandcastle" Europe

The marked decline in asylum applications, which continued almost until the Arab Spring, was also linked to Germany's altered geopolitical situation and the Europeanization of its refugee policy. German pressure was especially important in coaxing the then-twelve European Community member states into signing on to the first Dublin Regulation in June 1990. This convention contained a brief regulation stipulating that the state responsible for implementing an asylum procedure should be the state where the applicant first entered the EC. In addition, the twelve signatories agreed to an exchange of data in order to avoid dual and multiple asylum applications. This fell within the logic of the 1985 Schengen Agreement, according to which all intra-European border controls were to be abolished.[11] At the time it was concluded, the Dublin Regulation was not favorable toward recently united Germany, since Bonn (and eventually Berlin) thereby assumed de facto responsibility for all refugees entering from Eastern Europe. In the summer of 1990, however, no one could predict Yugoslavia's violent disintegration, that the Soviet Union's days were numbered, or that the EU and NATO would expand eastward.

In 1997, when the first Dublin Regulation finally went into effect in all the participating countries, as well as in the new EU member states Austria, Finland, and Sweden, the Federal Republic was the largest beneficiary of the agreements. Owing to the revolutions of 1989, the country once on the frontline of the Cold War had now moved to the center of Europe. Austria, as mentioned, now belonged to the EU, and the eventual admittance of the Czech Republic and Poland was foreseeable, since the EU had committed itself to eastern enlargement in 1997 at its Amsterdam summit. This summit is of significance for the history of refugees inasmuch as a catalog of minimum standards for their treatment was concluded there. The EU as a community of states thus made an additional commitment to the Geneva Convention and to humanitarianism.

All the same, the legal provisions about "secure third states" in Germany's asylum compromise and the Dublin Regulation had a completely different relevance than they might have had in the divided Europe of the Cold War. In the course of the European Union's expansion in 1995 and 2004, Germany had surrounded itself with a *cordon sanitaire* that made it almost impossible for refugees to step onto German soil legally and apply for asylum there. Their only legal options were to arrive by ship or air, or they might somehow manage to make their way through to Germany by land without registering in another EU state en route.

In hindsight one has to ask why Italy, Greece, and Spain let themselves be drawn into the Dublin Regulations without simultaneously insisting on some provision for redirecting refugees in cases of acute overload.[12] Critical here is the fact that in the 1990s most conflicts triggering mass flight still occurred in Eastern Europe, while the number of refugees and labor migrants crossing the Mediterranean from North Africa was relatively small. In addition, the Schengen Accord ended controls at most intra-European borders, so that Italy could quietly expect that most migrants landing on her shores would be heading on to France and Germany.

Nonetheless, in order to secure its Mediterranean borders, the Italian government led by Silvio Berlusconi concluded an accord in 2008 with the Libyan dictator Mu'ammer al-Gaddafi that, in addition to provisions for investment and acknowledgment of damages from the colonial era (Libya had been an Italian colony until 1942) included an agreement to curb the influx of refugees.[13] To this extent, then, the much-criticized 2016 "deal" between the EU and Turkey is not substantially new. One difference is that the EU undertook in its treaties to relieve Turkey of its neediest refugees. There was no such humanitarian component in the 2008 Libyan-Italian accord, which was accordingly criticized sharply by the UNHCR and various NGOs.

Within a year the number of arrivals in Italy diminished, as intended, from 37,000 to 9,600, and in 2010 to less than 5,000.[14] Then, with the Arab Spring and the fall of Gaddafi, the accord became obsolete. In 2017 Italy's center-left government concluded a comparable accord with Libya. Although the government in Tripoli controls only part of Libyan territory, the new accord led again to a drastic reduction in flight and migration across the central Mediterranean route. One should not, however, draw the wrong conclusions from these accords. In some years the number of refugees might rise again (as it did after 2010), because ultimately it is not up to the EU how many people decide to head for Europe from the various regional conflicts and poverty zones in Africa, the Middle East, and South Asia.

The fact that Italy—and not the EU—concluded the accord with Gaddafi (farther to the west, Spain and Morocco were the chief actors) shows how limited the Europeanization of refugee policy remained, even after the turn of the millennium. Berlusconi negotiated on his own for Italy not least because of the way that the Dublin Regulation (Dublin II was in effect as of 2003) unloaded one-sided burdens onto states located along the EU's external borders. This burden fell also on the Union's newest member states. On the eastern borders of the EU, however, another constellation has emerged. There the Russian Federation has been pursuing, as in Soviet times, a strict border and visa regime. To this extent, the only refugees traveling through Russia are those that Moscow allows (as, for example, during the refugee crisis in 2015, when several thousand refugees from the Middle East suddenly showed up at the Russian-Norwegian border). With Ukraine the EU negotiated a repatriation accord for refugees in exchange for easing visa and trade restrictions. This entailed some drawbacks; among other things, the accord made tighter controls on Ukraine's borders necessary and so placed a strain on relations with Russia.[15]

In this way the EU has extended the radius of its refugee policy well into the east. Ukraine, like the East-Central European states before it in the 1990s, therefore had little choice but to support the construction of Fortress Europe if it wanted to establish closer relations with the EU. The border and coast guard agency Frontex, founded in the autumn of 2004 shortly after that year's EU expansion, was now supposed to guard this fortress. Yet it was completely ill-equipped for this job. Hence, European refugee policy depended on the stability of neighboring states. On closer examination, the "fortress" looks more like a sandcastle that could collapse at the impact of a single biggish wave.[16]

The choice of Warsaw as Frontex headquarters is yet another indication of the expanded EU's preoccupation with East-West migration. The neighboring Mediterranean regions were neglected—not only when it came to refugee policy but also, and beyond that, to any closer economic and political cooperation for which there might have been an opening after 2011. The EU was not tuned in to any possible chance at exerting stronger influence on the Arab world, where it might actively combat the "root causes of flight." A forward-looking foreign policy on that model has been called for in political soapbox speeches everywhere since 2015.

Another fundamental problem was that the EU states had never agreed on the internal distribution and resettlement of refugees. There certainly were historical prototypes for this, as in 1956, 1968, and 1979 (see Chapter 3.5). At each of those junctures a broad alliance of Western countries, including neutral states such as Switzerland, Austria, and Sweden, had declared their willingness to help those countries in which the refugees initially arrived, albeit only on a voluntary basis and without committing to fixed admittance quotas. To be sure, the third Dublin Regulation of 2014 included a provision on setting up an early warning system in case any country found itself unduly burdened by an influx of refugees. But an intra-European system of resettlements or admittance quotas was not established at that time. One important reason for this lack of international regulation in the EU was the resistance put up by the German government. Two years later Berlin would deeply regret its previous position.

The EU never succeeded, moreover, in harmonizing the asylum laws and procedures. Admittance quotas varied from country to country, which gave refugees an incentive to move to those countries inside the EU where they had the best chances at starting a new life. Conversely, this served to motivate member states to tighten their asylum laws, treat applicants as shabbily as possible, and seal off their borders when they no longer wished to admit refugees. The competition turned negative, and has remained so within the EU since 2016. By no means is there any uniformity about the interpretation of EU asylum laws or of the Geneva Refugee Convention, even in federal states like Germany or the US. For example, refugees have long had better chances of being recognized in New York state than in Republican-governed states.[17] In the Federal Republic, the city-states of Bremen, Hamburg, and Berlin are known to be relatively liberal.

Moreover, even in the 1990s there was already a widespread tendency toward applying more restrictive criteria in deciding refugee status. France, for example, despite its commitment to humanitarianism under Socialist President François Mitterrand, began emulating the Federal Republic's restrictive practices, and Austria severely tightened its regulations in 1999 after the right-wing nationalist FPÖ entered government for the first time.

Because of restrictions tightening asylum laws in Europe, every individual seeking refugee status has had to set forth and prove persuasively that he or she has been persecuted, and how this happened. Invoking an abstract danger or the force of circumstances, as was done during the Cold War, is no longer sufficient. What is now required is some proof of physical violence, imprisonment, or torture. Owing to this higher evidentiary hurdle, the number of positive decisions on asylum applications has declined throughout the EU.

That, in turn, has created a huge problem for refugees who have their asylum applications rejected. Only rarely are they deported back to their countries of origin, and this is not due to insufficient legal foundations for deporting them, but more often simply because deportations are difficult to implement. The logistics of deportation requires either cooperation from the countries of origin and from the migrants themselves or the creation of massive detention facilities (which has happened in all Western countries since the 1980s). The growing discrepancy between the declining number of refugees who are actually recognized as such and the growing number of those migrants who are merely tolerated but still somehow manage to remain is undermining the legitimacy of the entire Western refugee regime. This makes it easier for politicians who coin terms like "pseudo-asylum seekers," "economic refugees," and (most recently) "fake refugees" to spread their message.

Although most of these terms came into being in the 1980s, there were at that time still political and linguistic barriers to mass deportation. The generation of 68ers that had attained political power in the US, England, and Germany during the 1990s brought their humanitarian values along with them. At least on paper, Bill Clinton, Tony Blair, and Gerhard Schröder foregrounded human rights issues and the rights of refugees derived from them. Moreover, these moderate left leaders had more political leeway, since there were no extremely large global refugee movements after 1995 (apart from regional wars in Rwanda, Zaire, and Sudan). As a result, the humanitarian consensus in favor of refugees persisted, though there were early signs that it was weakening.

The countries that wanted to join the EU had to support this consensus. The rejection of refugees by the Visegrád countries (an alliance formed by Poland, Hungary and Czechoslovakia in 1991) since 2015 has shown, however, that this acceptance did not go very deep. Paradoxically, there is a link between negative attitudes and earlier refugee waves out of Hungary, Czechoslovakia, and Poland. Only in isolated cases did the refugees from the Communist crackdowns of 1956, 1968, and 1980–81 return to their homelands, among other reasons because by the 1990s they were well integrated in the West. As a result, Europe's post-Communist societies lacked the insights and public positioning of these (former) refugees, who presumably would have represented and asserted different values than those pushed by Viktor Orbán, Miloš Zeman, or Jarosław Kaczyński. In this regard it is worth noting that the Baltic states did follow the EU's guidelines and admitted refugees. The fact that former Baltic exiles did return to their countries of origin after they gained independence in 1991 and were able to attain high office in their governments may account in part for this difference. Fear of Russia and the desire to prevent a further weakening of the EU also played a role in the Baltic states' positions.

Yet in Western Europe, too (to the extent that we can still divide the world into East and West), the further the Second World War and the Holocaust receded into the past, the fewer boundaries there were on what it was permissible to say about refugees. Especially in Denmark, Austria, and the new EU member states, where right-wing nationalist parties now shared in governing, agitation against migrants and especially against refugees has been going on for some time. The concept of "right-wing populism" insinuates that nationalist and racist positions are genuinely popular. But it is not that clear whether radical anti-immigrant and anti-refugee positions do indeed correspond to the majority view. Hence I prefer to use the term "right-wing nationalism" here. This choice of terminology rests on two observations: First, right-wing nationalism is based on reconstructing the nation around an imagined ethnic core (following this logic, being born in the US might no longer be enough to qualify automatically for US citizenship) and on closing off one's country to the outside. Second, in the eyes of right-wing nationalists, refugees are even worse than other migrants, since they are poor and needy. Yet it would seem that refugees are still arousing compassion in an important segment of the public that adheres to Christian, Jewish, or broader ethical values. This is the deeper reason behind the recent aggressiveness—verbal, legal, and bureaucratic—against refugees in various Western countries.

US refugee policy in comparative perspective

Right-wing nationalists have been governing in the US since 2016, but it would be misleading to equate the historic Republican party with the words and practices of the White House's current occupant. By and large, Ronald Reagan stood by the Refugee Act passed under Jimmy Carter in 1980, the year when the number of resettled refugees reached an all-time high of 200,000. Reagan did restrict the admission of refugees as a result of the Mariel Boat Lift, when 125,000 Cubans were admitted to the US Initially this event was still managed in the Cold War tradition. When it became clear that the Castro government was trying to get rid of jail inmates, however, the Reagan administration put all Cubans without an official host or sponsor (again we see how heavily refugee politics depends on NGOs and civil society activists) into detention centers.[18] Moreover, ships originating in Caribbean countries and carrying "human cargo" (another questionable term popularized in the 1980s) were now increasingly intercepted on the high seas to prevent their passengers from reaching the US. The purpose of these interdictions was to minimize the influx of asylum seekers. So while refugees were still resettled in the US, there was an effort to divert potential asylum seekers on the grounds that they were de facto economic migrants.

Independent of the interdictions, the number of refugees admitted through the mid-1980s fell to around one third of the peak numbers at the beginning of the decade. In comparison to Germany, this decline was not attributable to a generally hostile or defensive attitude toward refugees. The cause was, above all, a number of external factors. Because of the Orderly Departure Program (see Chapter 3.5 for more on this), the mass flight out of Southeast Asia was managed and stemmed. The civil wars in Central America displaced several hundred thousand people, but by and large the global order was more stable than in the 1970s.

Starting in 1989 the number of global refugees rose sharply once again. This was attributable above all to the dissolution of Yugoslavia, the Eastern Bloc, and the Soviet Union. In reaction to this upsurge, the US during the tenure of George H. W. Bush allowed almost half a million refugees to enter the country. Humanitarianism, that is, outlasted the Cold War and accorded with a non-partisan consensus. The goal here was to strengthen American "soft power" as well as to enhance the country's claim to be a moral superpower.

Under Bill Clinton, the Democrats further broadened the reach of human-itarianism. In addition to the de facto recognition of war as one of the legiti-mate grounds for flight, sexual violence and violence committed by gangs found their way into asylum legislation as officially recognized grounds. Above all, these changes affected refugees from Guatemala, Honduras, and El Sal-vador, who were increasingly granted asylum in the US. In addition, within the framework of the international resettlements organized by the UNHCR, the US took in a growing number of refugees from Africa, which in the late 1990s became the world's second largest source of departees (after Europe, where the Bosnians were mostly responsible for the high numbers).

Yet, under the Clinton administration even more potential asylum seekers were turned away before they could reach the US. Ships with migrants, espe-cially Haitians, were stopped on the high seas and returned to their countries of origin. And it was not only the practice of interdiction that was increasing, but also the deportation of illegal migrants from the US. Some of the rejected were asylum seekers. One of the underlying problems was (and still is) the fun-damental difficulty US officials face in distinguishing between refugees and migrants fleeing extreme poverty and distress, especially in the case of those coming from Central America.

Neither the US nor the EU has managed to boost economic development and living standards in their respective "backyards"—that is, in Central Amer-ica and the Middle East. With prosperity so unevenly distributed, migration is almost inevitable, and when violent conflicts are added to the mix, massive flight can result. Mexico has been a positive exception; for nearly a decade, the number of illegal migrants into the US has declined, mainly because Mexico is no longer as poor as it had been before NAFTA.

A deep, yet temporary watershed in US policy toward refugees followed the terror attack on the World Trade Center on September 11, 2001. Over the next two years the US admitted fewer than 30,000 refugees. The reason was fear that terrorists might "stow away" within the framework of international re-settlement programs. This fear was unfounded;[19] and in any event, it was not yet exploited for political purposes in the 2004, 2008, and 2012 presidential elections as it would be in 2016. Indeed from 2004 on, George W. Bush re-turned to the refugee policy of the 1990s. On the whole, Republican presidents cleaved to the refugee policy implemented by the Democrats (both on Capi-tol Hill and occasionally in the White House) and supported by the human rights movement.[20] This can be explained in part by the number of Christian voters (especially mainline Protestants and Catholics) who support Republi-cans and regard help for people in distress, and thus also for refugees, as a good thing. Thus Bush, during his final year in office, actually increased the upper limit for resettlements to 80,000 people, perhaps in order to leave behind him a humanitarian legacy. Eight years later Barack Obama also raised the admit-tance quotas.

All in all, the United States admitted 3.3 million refugees during the more than thirty years from the end of the Vietnam War through the election of Donald Trump.[21] This made America the central harbor of international refugee policy, a haven that indirectly relieved the European Union of refugee burdens. To be sure, Obama took action against labor migration from Central America, as George W. Bush had done before him. During the administration of this Democratic president, the number of deported illegal migrants rose to its historically highest level.[22] Obama also attempted to limit migration from Nicaragua, El Salvador, and Honduras by cooperating with Mexico and the migrants' countries of origin in Central America. Combating the causes of flight did not, however, lead to the desired result. Overall, migration from Central America to the US did not decline under Obama.

The sharp distinction drawn between flight migration and labor migration under Obama led to fundamental contradictions in migration policy. Turning away labor migrants while simultaneously admitting more refugees can only be justified normatively, by conceding a moral right of admittance or asylum to refugees that is refused other migrants. Indeed, this is enshrined in international law. There is a Geneva Convention for Refugees, and since 2018 a Global Compact on Refugees. The United Nation managed to pass a Global Compact on Migration as well, which secured some basic rights of migrants (though not a general right of migration), but the US government has refused to sign it. Moreover, some European countries in which right-wing nationalists share power are now following President Trump's line. Yet many migrants continue to leave their homelands because of extreme poverty and distress. To this extent, the conceptual and legal dividing line between refugees and labor migrants can only be maintained if one ignores the hardships of the latter.

This distinction, moreover, makes little difference to the fact that, following the end of the Cold War, all Western societies have increasingly viewed migrants (of all categories) as competitors for jobs and resources or even as a threat. As recent history in Europe and the US since the 1980s shows, the resulting attitude of hostility and defensiveness has long-term repercussions for refugees, even if they still enjoy a special status in international law and in national laws on asylum. To this extent, the recent victories of right-wing nationalists on both sides of the Atlantic, which were based on the exclusion and defamation of migrants in general and refugees in particular, were already anticipated in the period following the watershed of 1989.

There is, to be sure, an important difference between the US and Europe: the majority of refugees to the United States are admitted within the framework of international resettlements, while the predominant route to Europe was by land and across the Mediterranean, with the result that migrants could apply for asylum in whatever country was their intended destination. This difference has mostly to do with geographic circumstances. The United States can be reached only by land or via straits from Central America and the Caribbean. When the US takes in refugees, it does so primarily of its own accord. By contrast, Europe has no borders predetermined by nature or geography to its east and southeast. Theoretically, then, the US could withdraw into splendid isolation, as it did in the interwar period. Europe, by contrast, cannot reconstruct itself permanently into a fortress. By 2015 the experience of EU member states (which obviously cannot be equated with Europe) more closely resembled life in a sandcastle.

4.2 The Syrian and the European "refugee crisis"

Measured against the volume of refugees Europe has taken in since 2015, it may be an exaggeration (from a historical perspective) to speak of a "refugee crisis" in our times. Following the First World War, and then especially after the Second World War, there were far more people fleeing or expelled from their homelands and forced to start a new life somewhere else. After 1945, thirty million people had to be fed and housed under much less favorable circumstances. Even in proportion to the world population, there were at least twice as many refugees after the Second World War as in 2015.

This historical comparison is not intended, however, to minimize the extent of the catastrophe and the suffering in Syria. So far the war has cost about 500,000 lives, and almost 60 percent of the population, around twelve million people, have been forced to flee. This testifies to the devastation modern weapons can inflict and how ruthlessly the Syrian civil war is being waged. Over the years the international community has tried a variety of diplomatic conventions in hopes of guaranteeing at least some minimal protection for the civilian population. All have failed. As things stand, President Bashar al-Assad and his allies and opponents fully expect to escape prosecution for their war crimes; so far, not even the use of poison gas has been seriously punished. Compared to what happened during the war in Bosnia and Herzegovina, this is a momentous step backward. Assad and his supporters, especially Russia, have a virtual free hand as they continue bombing people out of their homes and cities and driving them into the countries neighboring Syria.

We can expect that the Syrian regime's looming hold on power will result in a situation where most refugees will not be able to return to their homeland. (Historians are not trained to forecast the future, but a historical perspective points toward this conclusion.) Syria's neighboring states and the EU are therefore confronted with a problem whose ramifications are even greater than those of the Palestinian refugee crisis that began in 1948–49. The Nakba, as the Palestinians call their flight and expulsion, is an important point of reference inasmuch as it has brought unremitting destabilization to the entire Middle East. This scenario threatens to repeat itself today. Lebanon and Jordan, the two countries absorbing the largest share of Syrian refugees in proportion to their total populations, are themselves perched on the brink of collapse. In Lebanon an already fragile political order is in dire peril. In Jordan "only" the government's budget is immediately threatened, but there, too, an initial revolt against austerity measures erupted in 2018, and the budget cuts responsible for the unrest are attributable to the unsustainable costs of housing and feeding the Syrian refugees. So this is clearly a real refugee crisis, especially when compared with the EU. In the fragile European Union, it is domestic conflicts over refugee and migration policy that are the problem, not the refugees themselves, which a community of states with more than five hundred million inhabitants can obviously afford to house and feed.

The Syrian civil war

The Syrian civil war began in the spring of 2011 when the regime reacted to what was actually a rather harmless youth protest in the city of Daraa, south of Damascus, by arresting and abusing the protesters. A few days later special units of the police shot at the demonstrators, who were protesting against the state's excessive use of force in the earlier protest. In the following months the protests and violence spread to additional sites and finally across almost the entire country. Like other civil wars, this one had deep-seated social and economic causes, including a high birth rate, rising unemployment, a growing gap between rich and poor, and the Syrian regime's blatant corruption.[23]

Occasionally, international media and professional journals have also cited climate change as one of the causes of the civil war and the global increase in refugee waves.[24] The behavior of so-called climate refugees better fits the pattern of labor migrants, however, than that of refugees. Refugees from drought, desertification, and rising sea water levels typically move at first from the countryside to cities in their respective home countries. They might migrate to other countries at some point, but this is again a pattern far more similar to labor migration than to mass flight. While violence can occur, it is not a decisive factor. Moreover, to the extent that climate flight is not triggered by a natural catastrophe, it is a long-term migration. To call it "flight" is a misleading dramatization. Strong and persistent migration into cities can, of course, increase social tensions. But the outbreak of the civil war in Syria is attributable to a genuine political conflict, specifically to the inability of the Assad regime to handle criticism and protest.

The escalation of violence and the destruction of most of Syria also have external political causes. The civil war in Syria turned into a proxy war between Shiite Iran, along with its regional allies, and the Sunni Gulf states, most prominently Saudi Arabia. Both sides sent weapons, while the Lebanese Hezbollah and Iran added military advisers and soldiers who protected Assad from an impending military defeat in 2013. The US held back after the failure of its intervention in Iraq, but Russia exploited the power vacuum that ensued and pushed back against the influence of the West and Turkey's inept intervention.

Another actor responsible for massive flight in the Syrian civil war was the so-called Islamic State. IS (the abbreviation in Arabic transcription is "Daesh") recruited fighters for the radicalizing Sunni opposition while also exploiting the chaos of the civil war. At times IS occupied large parts of Syria and neighboring Iraq, where it persecuted religious minorities like Yazidis, Christians, Alawites, and the Druze with extreme brutality. In order to intimidate the population, IS staged and celebrated mass public executions and beheadings. Behind closed doors women were enslaved and raped. In a countermove, government troops fought Sunni rebels with barrel bombs and poison gas. At the local and regional levels this escalation of violence led to the complete removal of religious minorities, to the extent that they had not already fled.

In 2016 and 2017 denominational homogenization was even pursued by agreement between the parties to the civil war. The population in besieged enclaves was given free passage into the area controlled by the government, with reciprocity granted to the rebels. Since IS chiefly mobilized its followers among Arabs, the conflict with the Kurds in the north of Syria and Iraq acquired an ethno-national component: there the warring parties attempted to secure territories in part through ethnic cleansing.

At the beginning of the civil war, Syrians were primarily fleeing within their own country. After the civil war's first year, in the autumn of 2012, there were 4.2 million internally displaced persons (IDPs) according to the UNHCR. About 600,000 succeeded in reaching safety in the states neighboring Syria. As hostilities expanded to envelop almost the entire country and IS temporarily gained ground, the number of people fleeing abroad kept growing. At first it doubled with each new year of the war; then, by the end of 2014, it crossed the three million mark.[25] It was at this point that flight to Europe increased significantly. According to the most recent update, by the end of 2018, more than five and a half million people had fled to safety abroad, including 3.5 million to Turkey, barely a million to Lebanon, and 670,000 to Jordan. (Since then, Jordan has closed its overstrained borders.) About a quarter million people took refuge in neighboring Iraq, overwhelmingly in the Kurdish-controlled regions of the country's north. One hundred thirty thousand Syrians have made it through to Egypt. Some refugees were indeed able to return to their old homeland, especially after the defeat of IS, but later offensives launched by government troops south of Damascus and in Idlib in Syria's north, the last major province held by the rebels, caused the total number of refugees to climb in 2018 as well.

An additional 6.5 million Syrians have taken flight inside their own country. As a rule, these IDPs (internally displaced persons) are much worse off than international refugees, since they are frequently unprotected and can easily get caught between military frontlines.[26] Overall, twelve million inhabitants were uprooted in this way; only nine million Syrians of a total population of around twenty-one million still live in their former houses and apartments. From a comparative historical perspective, these proportions are unusual and shocking. In Bosnia and Herzegovina, where the war's violence was also deliberately directed against the civilian population due to efforts at ethnic cleansing, there were not nearly as many refugees, either in absolute numbers or as a percentage of the population, and certainly not if one includes all of Yugoslavia (which in 1991 had roughly the same number of inhabitants as did Syria in 2011).

The inadequate response of the international community

The response of the international community to the humanitarian catastrophe in Syria has been inadequate from the outset, failing both at the levels of diplomacy and humanitarian assistance. All efforts at mediating between the parties to the conflict were fruitless, and the UN and UNHCR also failed at delivering needed emergency relief. The United Nations cannot be held responsible, as it is dependent on the commitment and financial support of its member states. In December 2014, the UN's World Food Programme had to call off its food aid to 1.7 million Syrian refugees for lack of money. In spite of the steep rise in the number of refugees, donors either did not meet their obligations or did not increase payments in spite of additional need. In the spring and summer of 2015, the UN warned that food rations in the refugee camps would soon have to be cut. Several times the UNHCR pleaded for more funds, again almost always without results.[27] Hardly any international resettlements got off the ground, although these too might have alleviated the situation of the refugees on site. Against this background of desperation and shortfalls, the great exodus to Europe in the autumn of 2015 was entirely predictable, born out of sheer distress. Here I would like to add a personal observation: I encountered the first refugees from the Middle East on my numerous train rides from Budapest to Vienna at the beginning of 2015, when I had a guest professorship at the Central European University. As a historian one could already suspect that, owing to the situation in Syria and Iraq, many more people would soon be coming to Europe. This was the immediate catalyst for the writing of this book.

Since the outbreak of the civil war, according to the UNHCR, about one million Syrians have fled to Europe, of whom more than half have gone to Germany, 110,000 to Sweden, and 50,000 to Austria.[28] Thirty-two thousand have been accommodated in the EU within the framework of international resettlements. Seen this way, and measured against earlier international programs for redirecting refugees from the Cold War era, the EU has made a small contribution to coping with the consequences of the Syrian civil war—no more than that.

It should be mentioned that Russia, Saudi Arabia, and the other Gulf states so far have not taken in any refugees.[29] In light of their participation in the war through the supply and financing of weapons, not to mention Russia's military intervention, terms like "inhuman" or "lacking in solidarity" ring downright euphemistic. Above all, this attitude is irresponsible. We shall look more closely into the role of the US below. There other conditions must be taken into account, if only inasmuch as the United States is hardly reachable from the Middle East by land or sea. Hence, Syrian refugees have been admitted only within the framework of international resettlements. Through the end of 2014, only 172 Syrians had this rare good fortune.[30] On the western side of the Atlantic, too, the plight of the refugees in Syria was sadly underestimated.

Explaining the mass departure for Europe

Until 2015, no one in Europe was expecting that hundreds of thousands of people would be making their way into the EU on their own. Syria seemed so far away, as far away as Palestine after 1948 or Lebanon during the civil wars from 1975 to 1991. Back then refugees stayed in the Middle East. The members of some wealthier families or merchants might have reached the West, where they would have been especially welcome if they wanted to invest or stash their money. In 2015 is went largely unnoticed how effectively social media had brought the seemingly distant continent of Europe closer than ever before to the Middle East. Since the invention of Google Street View in 2007, a (sufficiently wealthy) Syrian or Iraqi could use the internet service to take a virtual stroll through Berlin, Paris, or London. As Europe and the Middle East moved media-wise ever closer to one another, their mutual awareness grew as well. The impact of this high-tech convergence is just as hard to measure, however, as the impact of the selfies showing Angela Merkel with refugees in the autumn of 2015.

In Turkey the Syrians were initially accommodated in reception camps in the country's southeast. Over the course of time many of them then set off into the west of the country, to Istanbul or Izmir, where it was easier to find work. Once there, they had already covered about half of the distance from Aleppo or the Turkish-Syrian border to Central Europe. Istanbul was a dead end. The land border between Turkey and Bulgaria and Greece has long been heavily guarded because of the Cold War and the tense relations between NATO partners Turkey and Greece. Yet the Aegean sea could not be controlled as tightly, and thus became once again a bridge for refugees. The first time, after the Balkan Wars of 1912–13, it was a bridge leading southeast; the second time, before and after the Turkish War of Independence, it led westward; and then in 2015 again toward Greece and farther into the EU. Here, too, geography played an important role: in some places Greek islands in the eastern Aegean are within view of the Asia Minor coast and can be quickly reached with a sturdy dinghy.

After the outbreak of the Syrian civil war, Turkey had no interest in controlling its coasts with more vigor than before. There had been an agreement with Greece on stemming illegal border crossings and repatriating migrants since 2002, but until 2016 the EU had not transferred so much as a cent to help defray the costs that Turkey had incurred for housing and feeding the refugees. By the summer and autumn of 2014, the number of Syrians arriving in Europe via sea had doubled to almost 70,000. By the time winter was over, this massive exodus was moving rapidly into third states beyond the Mediterranean. In the first half of 2015 alone, according to figures from the UNHCR, 137,000 Middle East refugees and other migrants arrived in the EU by sea. (The doubling of refugee numbers thus followed almost exactly developments transpiring in Syria, with about a year's delay.)

Sitting on one of the numerous boats that traveled from the Turkish seaside resort of Bodrum to the Greek island of Kos in the summer of 2015 was the family of Alan Kurdi. Besides Alan himself, there was his father, mother, and five-year-old brother. The outlines of the story were told at the very beginning of this book: the boat capsized and all the family members drowned, except the father who was able to save himself. Alan's body washed up on a nearby Turkish beach. A photograph of the small child's body moved the world. And it had political consequences as well. Refugee children have always had a special status. Even at the end of the 1930s, when the doors were shut to refugees all over the world, children still had a chance of being taken in.

By the time Alan Kurdi drowned in the Aegean, the first refugee columns had already arrived in Hungary. After the Dublin Regulations (since 2013 Dublin III was already in force), Hungary was responsible for the initial admittance, accommodation, and asylum proceedings for refugees, to the extent they had not already been registered in Greece. Indirectly, this worked as an incentive for Greece to refrain from registering refugees, a chore the Greeks were only too willing to forgo. Severe austerity measures had been imposed on Greece after its economy was bailed out in the euro crisis, and its coffers were bled dry. Meanwhile, a backup of refugees was forming in Hungary at the Keleti train station, Budapest's main terminal, because the Hungarian State Railways authority had canceled train traffic heading toward Austria and finally had blocked access to the station altogether. This was followed by an announcement that one train would after all be allowed to travel in the direction of Austria. Refugees thereupon stormed the railway station, but the train they boarded changed directions after forty kilometers and headed toward an interim camp. In the end the refugees took taxis or set out on foot, blocking the motorway between Budapest and Vienna.[31]

As the refugees approached the Austrian border, the government in Vienna was forced to act. Closing the border would have required a massive deployment of the military and police, and possibly even orders to shoot. Austria, which had never secured its neutral status by massive military armament (unlike Sweden and Switzerland), was not prepared for measures that extreme. What is more, closing the border would not have fit in with Austria's tradition of openness dating back to 1956, 1968, and 1992. And it would have been much more difficult logistically in 2015 than in the postwar era because, following the EU's enlargement in 2004, all border installations had been taken down in line with the Schengen Agreement.

In this increasingly acute situation, Austrian chancellor Werner Faymann made a call to his German colleague, seeking a consultation. The decision that ensued will live in the pages of history books for years to come. Despite all claims to the contrary, assertions disseminated even by respected newspapers like the *New York Times*, we now know that Angela Merkel did not *open* the borders.[32] The borders of Europe were already open owing to the advanced state of European integration. What Faymann and Merkel agreed to do on that September 4th in 2018 was merely to not close the borders.

On every day of the following week, between 6,000 and 10,000 refugees entered Germany from Austria. The German Interior Ministry briefly debated refusing entry to refugees.[33] The head of the Federal Police and senior civil servants also made this suggestion, but Angela Merkel refused to seal the border. There were logistical reasons for not doing so; the longest foreign border of the Federal Republic runs largely through hill country and the Alps and could be kept under surveillance only with difficulty. Turning away refugees would have meant stranding more than two hundred thousand people, who at this point were already en route through Austria, Hungary, and Southeastern Europe. This would have triggered a chain reaction of border closings, creating enormous chaos and no doubt sparking protests in Salzburg and at other German-Austrian border crossings. Moreover, Merkel was concerned about the stability of the Balkan states and debt-ridden Greece, especially because a glance at the map indicated that the refugees could easily circumvent Austria and enter Germany by way of other countries. Last but not least, the chancellor had personal reasons for her aversion to walls and border fortifications. Merkel, who had grown up in the walled-in GDR as the daughter of a Protestant pastor, knew the Bible and its passages about refugees better than most Christian Democratic politicians. Another factor may well have been public opinion. In the summer of 2015 a clear majority of Germans was against closing the border; twenty-five years after the fall of the Berlin Wall, this was hardly surprising.[34] Even more Germans would have opposed a robust police and military deployment along the border.

Merkel's non-decision was possibly the most consequential of her tenure in office. This was offset, however, by the bad job she made of communicating and selling the admission of refugees as a political program—except for a few catchy slogans like her upbeat "Wir schaffen das" [We can handle this]. Apart from her phone conversation with Faymann, her decision to admit the refugees to Germany was not cleared either with the CDU's Bavarian sister party in her governing coalition, the Christian Social Union, or with the other European heads of government. To this extent, this looked like Germany going it alone or at least with Austria as its only partner.

There was one country that greatly benefited from Merkel's decision. The redirection of the Middle East refugees to Germany and Austria relieved Hungary of a huge humanitarian burden. On top of that, Faymann and Merkel were ignoring the Dublin Regulation, which obligated Hungary to register these refugees and to implement asylum proceedings. Yet at this very critical moment in the first weeks of September 2015, Hungarian prime minister Viktor Orbán threw a monkey wrench into the works. Reacting to Merkel's and Faymann's decision, Orbán announced that from now on the refugees were a German problem. He did not mention that his government's attempt at massive internment had just failed.

At the same time, Orbán saw to it that the refugees became a problem also for Croatia and Slovenia. In the summer of 2015 he had a four-meter-high, barbed wire–fortified fence erected along Hungary's border with Serbia and then with Croatia. It was finished by mid-September, and the official opening featured water cannons: when a group of refugees attempted to run along the railroad track from Serbia to Hungary and protest at the border, they were hosed down and beaten away. The message of these ugly pictures was clear: refugees were not welcome in Hungary. Orbán offered a legal argument to the effect that he was dealing with illegal migrants—after all they were coming from countries like Turkey where they were no longer directly threatened. By following that same argument all of Hungary's 1956 refugees would have had to stay put in Austria. It is also an argument that ignores the Geneva Refugee Convention. The Federal Republic of Germany, by contrast, continued to adhere to the Convention and to uphold one of its iron precepts, the prohibition against sending refugees back (non-refoulement). To be sure, Germany's Federal Border Guard introduced passport and personal screening at the German-Austrian border in mid-September 2015; and train traffic from Salzburg to Munich was stopped. This led to speculation that the Federal Republic might one day close the borders.

The approaching refugees—on some days they numbered up to 10,000— were exhausted from the long journey, and they had basic needs. Above all, they needed food and a roof over their heads. After some initial difficulties, the authorities managed to cope with the challenge. No one had to sleep on the street as they had on their escape routes through Anatolia and Southeast Europe, and there were no outbreaks of famine or epidemics. This was no small feat, as measured against earlier flight waves. Indeed the incessant complaints since 2015 about a "refugee crisis" have eclipsed awareness of the considerable humanitarian progress made before that watershed year. In Turkey and in Europe—apart from tragic deaths on the Mediterranean—there have been no massive casualties among the refugees like the fatalities that occurred during the interwar and early postwar period.

For this humanitarian progress the refugees and the governments in Europe owe a debt of gratitude in particular to the hands-on assistance of NGOs and church parishioners, and to the spontaneous helpfulness of the public. According to a comprehensive study carried out by the Lutheran Church in Germany, about every sixth German participated actively in refugee assistance during the autumn of 2015, and a third donated goods in kind.[35] If so many people commit themselves to a common cause, their joint achievement is sufficient that a name must be created to describe it. The German language, with its nearly inimitable facility for forming compound words (though, in his famous essay "The Awful German Language," Mark Twain overlooked the fact that Slavic languages work in much the same way), generated a special term for this brand of communal hospitality: *Willkommenskultur* (a culture of welcoming). The term probably originated in the administrative lexicon of the Interior Ministry, which as of 2011 was promoting labor migration to Germany in the face a growing shortage of skilled workers. Many well-educated immigrants decided not to remain in the Federal Republic because they in fact did not feel welcomed and integrated.[36] In order to keep these workers, government officials issued a plea for a *Willkommenskultur*, and eventually the term became as familiar an expression in the summer and autumn of 2015 as Chancellor Merkel's emboldening, "We can handle this."

Whether there really was a welcoming culture—an attitude of welcome embedded in a majority of the German people—is rather questionable upon closer examination. The impressive numbers emerging from the Lutheran Church's survey on the commitment of civic groups also reveal that two thirds of the population was *not* reaching out to refugees in the autumn of 2015. Whether they were holding back for lack of time, due to indifference, or because they fundamentally rejected Merkel's refugee policy is a question the historian cannot easily answer.

Yet the bottom line remains: in the autumn of 2015, about fifteen million volunteers became active in Germany. In Austria, which was doubly burdened both as a transit country to Germany and a destination, there were also many volunteers relative to the total population. Even in Hungary the refugees who were camping out around the Keleti railway station during the summer owed most of the care they received to donations and community relief services. The government quickly choked off these initiatives; and since 2018, giving aid to migrants is a criminal offense in Hungary.

If *Willkommenskultur* has a false ring in other languages, one can always substitute plainer terms like "hospitality" or "helpfulness." Whatever it is called, one should not confuse willingness to aid a stranger with acquiescence to that stranger's permanent settlement (see Jenny Erpenbeck's novel *Gehen, ging, gegangen* or Jacob Preuss's film *When Paul Came Over the* Sea). In the new member states of the EU, civil society's sense of commitment to refugees was limited from the outset. Each society had its own resources and priorities; moreover charitable commitment requires time and money that is not available in equal measure to all persons, classes, or countries.

As the examples of Hungary and Poland demonstrate, however, the decisive factor was not a country's particular set of social preconditions; what mattered most was how the political elite dealt with the "refugee crisis." Even in democracies, structures of civil society can quickly weaken and shatter if the government in power moves against them. Many local refugee initiatives in the US found this out after 2016, when their funding was cut.

When the number of refugees arriving in Germany climbed to over 200,000 in October 2015, with over a million more expected, the federal government began to get cold feet. At the time, the conservative daily paper *Die Welt* was even predicting as many as three million more arrivals, an instance of panic-mongering that shows again how fluid the boundaries often are between conservatives and right-wing nationalists.[37] In Sweden, too, where 163,000 people had been taken in, almost twice as many as in Germany in relation to the total population, there were increasing demands to shut the borders. In both countries local governments, which had the ultimate responsibility for organizing the refugees' accommodations and meals and for making athletic halls and other spaces available to house them, ran up against capacity limits. There were undoubtedly serious practical problems.

By the autumn of 2018, these difficulties were reflected in public opinion. Surveys by the Bertelsmann Foundation, a liberal think tank and promoter of civil society initiatives, revealed that the public was anxious about the future. Depending on how the question was posed, between one third and a half of the German population expressed a positive view of the "welcoming culture"; nonetheless, three fourths of those surveyed feared additional burdens on the welfare state and growing conflict between native Germans and immigrants. About two thirds expected problems in the schools and a housing shortage in Germany's cities.[38] The Bertelsmann Foundation thus unintentionally confirmed a disconnect between the short-term spirit of helpfulness and any long-term enthusiasm for the admittance of refugees.

Even more critical are the views that have been expressed in social media since 2015. According to a study by the Internet data research firm Bakamo Social, carried out between the start of 2015 and March 2016 (that is, before and during the "refugee crisis"), online discussions increasingly revolved around fears. Hateful statements were also on the rise. An evaluation of more than five million communications in social media like Facebook, Twitter, Internet forums, and blogs yielded a picture of the growing rejection of refugees over time.[39] The main reason appears to have been a general fear of change. Specifically, 70 percent of Germans (that is, of those who took a position on this in the Internet) feared a loss of welfare and social cohesion and of values such as equality between men and women, and an increase in religious extremism.[40]

The biggest mistake made by Germany in the autumn of 2015 was to frame debate over its affirmative refugee policy in predominantly normative terms—with moral arguments, rather than pragmatically. This was in tune with the temper of Western humanitarianism since the 1970s, but it was also useful to the opponents of admitting refugees, who also made mostly normative arguments. Right-wing nationalists such as Viktor Orbán rejected assistance to refugees in Europe on principle. The chair of the Polish governing party PiS, Jarosław Kaczyński, even went so far as to call them carriers of dangerous diseases and warn against a "social catastrophe."[41] The only constructive point that right-wing nationalists in Europe have conceded in the public debate is that developed countries should do more on site in the Middle East. Yet one only needs to look at the budgets for supporting Middle Eastern victims of war put together in Hungary, Poland, and (since 2017) by the coalition of conservatives and right-wing nationalists governing Austria to recognize that any proposals to increase foreign aid were at best lip service.

In fact, the dispute over taking in refugees actually began before the so-called refugee crisis in the spring and summer of 2015, when the German government made several preemptive attempts at convincing the EU to implement a fixed formula for distributing refugees throughout the European Union. Such uniform regulation of asylum and migration policy was rejected most resolutely by the Visegrád states, but also by countries like Denmark, in which a minority center-right government was backed by right-wing nationalists. On the surface, the debate was about the refugees, but the conflict was really about national sovereignty, and it related to the fundamental question of how much power individual nation-states were willing to concede to Brussels and to Germany as the EU's undeclared hegemon. The federal government in Berlin could have advocated more persuasively for its cause had it not voted against a fixed distribution system in 2013 when the Dublin III Regulation was decided.

But in the summer of 2015 the frontline positions in the debate over refugee policy were not yet completely immobile. Poland was still governed by a liberal-conservative Civic Platform (the Platforma Obywatelska) that advocated, in principle, deeper European integration. (Then, in October 2015, it lost Poland's parliamentary elections, due primarily to its neglect of social welfare policy.) In September 2015, the Civic Platform, already under pressure from the election campaign, did at least undertake to admit 7,500 refugees on a voluntary basis. Local and regional church initiatives advocated an even more generous opening, as did NGOs who calculated that Poland could accommodate 20,000 to 30,000 refugees without much difficulty. The right-wing nationalist PiS won the election, however, and refused to admit even a single refugee from the Middle East.

Although Czech business associations, facing an almost completely dry labor pool, expressed an interest in recruiting a few thousand refugees, the government in Prague, like its Polish counterpart, advocated a hard line. One of the arguments cited was that refugees were going to move on to Germany anyway, which of course implied that there would be little downside to finding accommodations for Syrians as an interim solution. Slovakia, which also refused to absorb refugees, was nonetheless simultaneously renting out empty prefabricated buildings in the town of Gabčikovo (which had attracted attention at the end of the 1980s because of protests against a gigantic hydropower station nearby) to the Austrian government, which housed more than five hundred refugees there in order to unburden its transit camp in Traiskirchen. The unbounded cynicism surrounding the debate on how to deal with refugees was also demonstrated by the erection, in 2016, of one of the largest refugee camps in Hungary. It was not built on the southern or eastern border (close to where refugees were entering Hungary), but rather in the west of the country. The geography was perfect for slipping over the border into Austria at night.[42]

In retrospect, one might ask whether the German government had handled its relations with the Visegrád states adroitly in the summer and autumn of 2015. In those countries, Germany's constant emphasis on moral arguments came across as lecturing. Orbán and like-minded politicians criticized the call for an EU-wide refugee quota as an infringement on their national sovereignty, already diminished (according to right-wing nationalists) by Brussels' edicts and German dominance. The Federal Republic might well have had more success with its eastern neighbors had it reached out to their civil society organizations, which favored the limited admittance of refugees. Another possibility would have been to follow the approach taken in 1992, when representatives of these countries had been included in decision-making at the highest level. Yet by the autumn of 2015, because of domestic politics in the four Visegrád states, nothing more could be done. The different political parties—by no means only the so-called right-wing populists—were engaged in a competition to see who could talk in the most derogatory and dismissive terms about refugees and Muslims. The rhetoric about these two groups was usually interchangeable, even though in 2015 almost one in seven of the Syrian refugees arriving in Europe was a Christian, and there were also numerous Yazidis fleeing the Middle East.[43] Syria, furthermore, was a secular state, and not every Sunni-born person was a practicing Muslim. The country's secular and Western character was reflected not least in the values of the refugees, which large-scale empirical studies have shown to be overwhelmingly democratic and secular. In fact, male refugees also stated that they did not oppose their wives practicing a profession.[44]

However, the Islamist terror attacks in Europe in 2015 and 2016 played into the hands of the right-wing nationalists. They quickly seized on the attacks in Paris, Nice, Brussels, Berlin, London, Stockholm, Manchester, and Barcelona to link the issues of flight and terror. Given the chaos of the massive flight taking place during the autumn and winter of 2015, it really was impossible to know whether followers of IS might be reaching Europe along with the rest. The assassins of Paris and Brussels, however, turned out to be not refugees but French or Belgian citizens. Islamist terrorism proved to be predominantly a homemade problem, but this was of little comfort inasmuch as it drew attention to the difficulties of the older EU countries in integrating some of their Muslim fellow citizens.

As of the autumn of 2015, the Visegrád states were pursuing a hard line against refugees, even beyond the borders of the EU. Led by Hungary, they sent military and police units to Macedonia, ostensibly in order to help with the surveillance of the border with Greece. Included in the equipment these units brought along was a field hospital in which people wounded after a future border closing could be treated. Austria's then foreign minister (later its chancellor) Sebastian Kurz recognized the potential in these issues of flight and migration for his upcoming election campaign. He initially conducted secret talks with the heads of state and government in different Southeast European states and then, in February 2016, summoned a conference in Vienna of the so-called West Balkan states (a term that makes no sense geographically, since the Balkans are only one of many southeast European mountain ranges passing through northern Bulgaria). Not invited was the German chancellor, nor was—and at first glance this is rather surprising—Viktor Orbán.

At this conference, standing before the imperial Habsburg backdrop of Vienna, Sebastian Kurz was then able to proclaim his aspiration to close the so-called Balkan route. This designation makes no sense either, as there was no such route in any literal sense of the word. The refugees from the Middle East made their way to Central Europe along different pathways, and none of them came anywhere near the aforementioned Balkan Mountains. At the same time Angela Merkel had succeeded in extracting an agreement between Turkey and the EU on guarding the coast of Asia Minor and taking back refugees arriving on the Greek isles. In return, the EU finally provided Ankara financial assistance and promised Turkey, within the framework of resettlements, to admit especially needy persons for every refugee intercepted in the Aegean. This model has a humanitarian component inasmuch as it has afforded more women and children a chance for asylum.

In 2015 the situation had been exactly the reverse, since at that time it was overwhelmingly men who got through to the EU; in the age cohort between sixteen and thirty, men predominated by up to three fourths of the total.[45] A secondary set of criteria for selection was educational level (according to Betts and Collier, every second Syrian with a university degree is currently in the EU).

Wealth was also in play, since the median cost of flight to Germany in 2015–16 came to about 5,000 euros per person.[46] Later we will discuss the questions this social selection raises for advocates of a humanitarian refugee policy. Although well-educated people usually have a much easier time finding a job and learning the language, it is not exactly humanitarian if they prevail over poorer or uneducated refugees.

The closure of the Macedonian border meant that at least 50,000 refugees were stuck in Greece. Some of them attempted to storm the border near the Greek village of Idomeni but were repulsed by police and military units. For Austrian foreign minister Sebastian Kurz "these ugly pictures" were definitely welcome, since they deterred additional refugees and (something Kurz was less candid in admitting) appealed to voters in his Alpine homeland.[47] These measures brought the massive flight toward Europe to a halt within about a year.

The humanitarian and political price paid was, however, high. Flight became more dangerous and more expensive. In 2016 alone, more than 5,000 people died crossing the Mediterranean. They shared the fate of Alan Kurdi, whose death does not seem to upset anyone today, at least not the international media. The new conditions also give a boost to social selection, while leaving behind defenseless women and children—excepting those who have the rare good fortune of receiving assistance within the framework of international resettlements.

Moreover, freedom of movement in Europe, especially as facilitated by the Schengen Agreement, has been massively curtailed. Since the autumn of 2015 controls have been reintroduced at a number of intra-European borders, including between Denmark and Sweden, and between Austria and Germany. This was justified by invoking an overburdened border control system during the refugee crisis, by the need to defend against the dangers of terrorism, and by an alleged craving for security on the part of the population living at the Austrian border. (Indeed, in the parliamentary elections of 2016 southeastern Bavaria voted disproportionally for the right-wing nationalist AfD). Yet this was security policy in appearance only. Inspections were carried out only on the Autobahn and on trains, since local border traffic otherwise would have broken down, seriously damaging the economy of the border regions. It should be pointed out, however, that switching to smaller border crossings and regional trains would now be enough for anyone trying to reach Germany with evil intentions. A second paradox is that passport inspections only affect those states that were initially acting in a humanitarian way in 2015, thus indirectly rewarding those countries that have erected fences and walls on their borders. These contradictions, however, cannot be charged to the right-wing nationalists, but rather to those parties and politicians who are located somewhere in the center of the political spectrum but no longer know how to justify a liberal and humanitarian refugee policy.

It is a testament to the shortcomings of the EU in 2015 that this community of nations could not agree on any common line. In 1956, 1968, and 1979, by contrast, a much looser alliance of Western states was able to parcel out refugees among themselves. To be sure, resettlements during the postwar era were based on voluntary undertakings and not on fixed quotas established by one seemingly dominant central authority.

The dispute about refugees from the Middle East and the constant shifting of responsibility back and forth also expose what it is that today's Europe lacks: there is insufficient religious and denominational solidarity. The US and other Western countries do not have a great track record here either, for otherwise there would have long existed a special program for Christians, who were unquestionably being persecuted in the war zones of Syria and Iraq. There is apparently greater Christian solidarity closer to home in the Middle East. Tiny Armenia, measured against the size of its population, has taken in the third largest contingent of refugees from Syria. Here, admittedly, we are chiefly dealing with members of the Armenian-Orthodox Church, so that both denominational and national ties come into play. In Europe a comparable kind of national solidarity would be impossible, except for some sympathy from Arabs, Kurds, or other groups that had immigrated or fled earlier.

By contrast, solidarity toward the Syrians by the Arab states, similar to what they had already shown the Palestinians in 1948–49 and 1967, is weak or nonexistent. So far only neighboring Lebanon, Jordan, and Iraq have taken in refugees from Syria, while Arab states farther away have not (with the exception of Egypt). Nor have there been any major aid operations in other Islamic states outside the region.

Even political solidarity has been limited, although the vast majority of the Syrians fled from the violent regime of Bashar al-Assad and the even more violent IS. One could ask the counterfactual question, how many Syrian refugees would have been admitted to the West had the Syrian civil war started in 1976, like the war in Lebanon? At that time Syria was a close ally of the Soviet Union, and the Baath Party of Hafiz al-Assad (father of the current dictator) was an advocate of Syrian socialism. In February 1982 Assad had at least 10,000 people from the opposition killed in Hama, so there was a reason to flee but no opportunity, since Assad besieged and sealed off Hama. Seen this way, Syrian refugees under the aegis of the Cold War and Western humanitarianism could have hoped for sympathetic treatment similar to that given the Vietnamese boat people. But challenging this assumption is the fact that Europe has always kept its distance from the major humanitarian crises and refugee problems of the Middle East. This is demonstrated above all by the case of the Palestinians, whose plight may have been lamented, and who may have been offered verbal and even substantial financial support (also a good opportunity for anti-Semites to point a finger at the Jewish state), but who have never benefited from any international resettlement program.

In the summer of 2015 there was a brief moment, especially after the death of Alan Kurdi, when a positive attitude toward Syrian refugees prevailed in most European countries. There was a consensus reaching from the Greens and Social Democrats to the Christian Democrats that the Syrians fleeing to Europe were victims of persecution and a gruesome war. This attitude, however, was short-lived, if only because the Syrians represented only about half of the refugees arriving in 2015–16, followed by Afghans and Iraqis, as well as labor migrants from numerous other countries.

Universal humanitarianism is apparently no substitute for the kind of religious, national, and political solidarity that has so greatly eased the hardships of massive flight since the late seventeenth century, and especially in the period following the Second World War. The limits of humanitarianism, the overburdening of the states immediately adjoining Syria, and the (attempted) closing off of the Western world renders the victims of the Syrian civil war who have not yet managed to escape abroad extremely vulnerable. Those suffering the most are children, who later in life will be unable to make up for long periods of hunger and missed school. Even in the darkest hours in the long history of refugees, on the eve of the Second World War, a limited number of children were able to take refuge in safe countries like Great Britain. Yet today there is not even consensus supporting a children-friendly refugee policy in Europe or the US. The separation of asylum seekers' children from their parents in the United States in the spring of 2018 is perhaps the most telling and embarrassing example of this ideational change. Even in Sweden and Germany, unaccompanied minors have come under increasing suspicion and scrutiny. This is connected to horrible cases of rape and even murder committed by refugees in their late teens, some of whom had falsified their age. These criminals are valuable fodder for right-wing social media campaigns not unlike early-twentieth-century antisemitic libels against Jews accused of abusing Christian women. To be sure, a rape is far more insidious than a hate crime, but one has to wonder what made some parts of Western societies so receptive to hate messages.

Is this lack of consensus a reaction to the perhaps naïve advocates of open borders, or to the ways in which Germany and Sweden have been acting with a good heart but poor reasoning, as Betts and Collier maintain? Or are the refugees themselves to blame because they came to Europe in so short a time and in such great numbers? In the history of massive flight waves, changes of mood are nothing new. Initial helpfulness has often turned into skepticism and rejection. But in 2015 and 2016 the mood reached a tipping point, because the refugees could so easily become a screen on which to project a variety of fears and ready targets for a resurgent and partially racist nationalism.

The (attempted) closing off of Europe and the US signals a profound change in direction. Perhaps the long legacy of the civil rights and student movements from the 1960s and the political normativity they represent has reached an end. Was this solely the fault of humanitarianism's opponents, or of humanitarianism's built-in contradictions?

Regardless of how one answers these questions, bad times dawned for refugees in 2015. This is regrettable in many respects, both in normative and utilitarian terms, since refugees almost always contribute to the welfare of the countries that take them in. Yet the increasingly defensive advocates of human rights should not lose heart. The stakes in the public and political debates since 2015–16 are, ultimately, greater than the future of flight and migration; the basic values of the West and its democracies are at issue. Yet this reengagement will only be possible if the limits of humanitarianism are acknowledged and openly debated.

4.3 The limits of humanitarianism

Since the long history of refugees and their absorption began, very different and mixed motives have come into play. As we saw in Chapters One through Three, religious (denominational), national, and political ties matter. They create bonds of solidarity between refugees and their hosts and are of benefit to both. There has always been, however, a second principal argument for accepting refugees, which has receded into the background since the 1970s: namely, the enrichment, cultural and even more so economic, that refugees bring to the societies that take them in. From the perspective of the right-wing nationalists who are gaining strength as they push for closed, ethnically homogenous societies, both species of argument are irrelevant and damaging. Yet for the advocates of open societies it is useful to discuss both perspectives on refugee policy, the humanitarian and the utilitarian. In the end, what is at stake here is one of humanity's highest values, the protection of human life. Refugees are especially reliant on upholding this value because, by definition, they are defenseless.

In a long-term historical analysis, sometimes humanitarianism has the upper hand, at other times utilitarianism. Of course, one must make distinctions not only according to time, but also by country and based on the social and cultural context, something that these few pages in a final chapter can only accomplish to a limited extent. Pondering the tradeoffs between humanitarian and utilitarian motives, moreover, is complicated by the way in which political leaders, from early modern monarchs to democratic statesmen, have used both kinds of arguments as a pretext for getting society to approve whatever refugee policy (be it inclusionary or exclusionary) they seek to achieve. To what extent such consent is even necessary depends, in turn, on the political system: Absolutist rulers and dictators can order the refugees to be admitted by decree, while in democracies that is not possible. In democratic systems policy toward all forms of migration is a more delicate subject, for it ultimately turns on how the particular *demos* on which the democracy rests is configured. However, it is also very clear that the taking in of refugees has a longer history than that of their rejection and deportation. In spite of all the tragedies depicted in this book's biographical case studies, overall these stories transmit more light than darkness.

In the early modern era, with which this book began, economic arguments and considerations played an important role. Taking in refugees was supposed to benefit the host country—increasing the population and thereby stimulating growth and development. Of course there was also a moral component: the Huguenots presented themselves as "religious refugees," victims of religious intolerance, while the countries taking them in improved their image as a refuge of tolerance and liberty. Yet on the whole utilitarian motives predominated; it was deemed economically useful to take in refugees (and other migrants). There also was a feedback effect on the countries of origin; over time Austria and other Catholic states came to understand that intolerance toward Protestants and other religious minorities harmed the countries expelling them.

At the time of the French Revolution and in the nineteenth century, by contrast, the decision to admit or reject refugees depended on secular political convictions and forms of solidarity. From a financial viewpoint it was not terribly difficult to show solidarity, since in 1831 and 1848 there were not a great many political refugees. However small they were in numbers, though, the "Forty-Eighters" did manage to inscribe themselves into the history of the US and to impart a political meaning to German labor migration there. The long era of peace that prevailed in large parts of Europe between 1871 and 1914 brought about an overall decline in massive flight.

Nonetheless, the wars against the Ottoman Empire, the radical nationalism and anti-Islamic sentiment of the Southeast European national movements, and the antisemitism and pogroms in the Russian Empire uprooted several million people. The Ottomans, evoking the concept of *muhacir* (see Chapter 1.5), appealed to religious solidarity, but at a practical level this appeal to an international Muslim community failed as a political rationale for integrating refugees. Russian and Polish Jews emigrated above all to North America; but there, as well as in Western and Central Europe, migration due to flight was not common, vastly outpaced by massive rates of labor migration. Because of major trans-Atlantic wanderings back and forth (for a long time, migration experts underestimated remigration to Europe) and the invention of the steamship, the US moved closer to Europe and became a major destination for European refugees. The American value system was affected by this change; in the US and Europe, diaspora communities and emerging NGOs began to advocate for humanitarian concerns and, as early as the late nineteenth century, were active on both continents.

Owing to the catastrophe of the "long" First World War, humanitarianism acquired a new relevance and an expanded reach at the international level through the League of Nations and the activities of transnational NGOs. Within this framework, new principles of refugee policy emerged, such as the prohibition on extraditing migrants back to their countries of origin and, with the Nansen passports, the first rudiments of international resettlement. A weak link in this nascent Western refugee regime, from the outset, was American isolationism. With the Immigration Act of 1924, the United States implanted a utilitarianism oriented entirely toward the country of immigration and its needs; and America's increasingly prosperous society regarded destitute refugees chiefly as a burden and not as an enrichment. The global economic crisis of the Great Depression then led to a sealing off of both European destinations and of all the traditional emigration countries overseas that, like the US, Canada, Brazil, Argentina, and Australia, acted and thought about migration primarily in utilitarian terms. This one-sided utilitarianism made it impossible to react appropriately to the humanitarian challenges of the 1930s—with well-known and too often tragic implications for Jewish refugees and Spanish Republicans.

Redirecting and admitting DPs, establishing the UNHCR, and passing the Geneva Refugee Convention are among the few instances where the international community learned from the mistakes of the past. It took another two decades, however, before humanitarianism gained the upper hand. While refugee policy after 1956 and 1968 was still strongly affected by the Cold War—in the context of East-West conflict it was politically useful for the West to take in refugees, especially as there was at the time a high demand for skilled labor—the Indochina refugees were not "useful" to any of the countries that received them after 1978. The brief time prior to the second oil crisis was the high point for humanitarianism within the entire lengthy period analyzed in this book. At the same time, international resettlement, along with emergency assistance in conflict zones and repatriation after conflicts ended, became the third main instrument of international refugee policy.

When the postwar economic boom ended and unemployment rose in the 1980s, openness toward refugees declined. This was one current in the broader context of migration policy. Because of the first oil crisis, Western Europe had already begun severely restricting labor migration from countries in its near neighborhood—Turkey, the Middle East, and North Africa. The US, in a parallel move, cut labor migration from Mexico, Central America, and the Caribbean. Not only labor migrants but, with something of a delay, also refugees came to be regarded as a burden. Sometimes sooner, sometimes later (depending on the country), their motives became suspect. The anti-immigration mood gave rise to terms like "pseudo asylum seekers," "economic refugees," and more recently the "fake refugee."

The liberal revolutions of 1989 gave humanitarianism another boost. The new era's ostensible "triumph of human rights" resulted in an expansion of refugee rights. For the first time, the West took in war victims without examining each individual case, and new grounds for persecution were added into asylum legislation, for example gang criminality and violence originating in civil wars.

This broadening of the grounds recognized as legitimate for flight was not, however, matched by a corresponding readiness to admit refugees permanently. Various European countries, the newly unified Germany in particular, tightened asylum law at the beginning of the 1990s. In the US the number of resettlements rose not at all under Bill Clinton (compared to his predecessor's numbers), nor did Barack Obama act as a savior of the world's displaced (a fact that did not prevent Trump from pillorying the Democrats as flight abettors). For a long time the discrepancy between humanitarianism in the abstract and actual willingness to admit refugees was not apparent, because the number of international refugees worldwide declined from barely fifteen million in 1989 to eight and a half million (not counting the IDPs) in 2005. Moreover, almost all refugees in the conflict zones of the Third World stayed put; only a few reached Europe and the US.

Then, in the refugee crisis of 2015, the limits of humanitarianism came starkly to light. The spirit of helpfulness that originally prevailed in some European countries gave way to a growing skepticism as incoming aliens increasingly triggered fear rather than compassion. This was related to one of the immediate motives for flight; namely, the spread of radical Islamism in the civil war zones of the Middle East. Flight and terror were lumped together, especially in social media. This linkage is not entirely new; even in earlier times there were cases of refugees being suspected of harboring the very ideologies they were in fact fleeing. This was the experience of refugees from the Russian Civil War who were suspected of being Bolsheviks, and of Jews fleeing the Third Reich who were suspected of being German agents.

The negative stereotypes of refugees also reflect the primal fear of strangers described by sociologist Georg Simmel.[48] Until recently, rising prosperity in Western societies facilitated the expression of solidarity with the oppressed. Today, on the other hand, the surge of impoverished refugees and labor migrants has already triggered fears that national prosperity might have to be shared, at least to some extent. It is well known that the current world order rests on a very unequal division of power, wealth, and resources. When the very poorest arrive, whether from the Middle East or Central America, the world's misery stands revealed at the doorstep of Western societies (if not already with its foot in the door). This is probably the deeper reason behind the defensive reactions against refugees and the underlying fearful and hostile attitudes we have witnessed throughout the history of humankind. What is new is the shamelessness with which right-wing nationalists have exploited these fears and used them in the conduct of their election campaigns.

I would now like to set aside my moral and normative judgment on this most recent turn against refugees and ask the (seemingly) simple question: Is it really in the interest of Western societies to keep refugees at bay by building fences and walls?

Normativism and utilitarianism

These prefatory remarks establish the parameters for the concluding debate. In this debate, normativism and utilitarianism will be juxtaposed. And at the same time, I shall ask whether and how these two principles might be tied together. Moral philosophers and ethicists are probably better qualified to seek an answer to this ambiguous question. As an historian I will restrict myself to the answers I can derive from the state of research and from my own historical knowledge. I am well aware of the political obstacles that stand in the way of my efforts. Right-wing nationalists are currently setting the tone of the debate, and with them neither normative nor humanitarian arguments are of any avail. Both seem fruitless because these nationalists are fundamentally opposed to refugees, along with other migrants. Morever, they use them to leverage more radical changes in their countries' political discourses and systems. Yet it is important to understand why right-wing nationalists have succeeded in taking the offensive in this way. Their assault on established norms indirectly exposes the limits and hidden contradictions of humanitarianism or (to put this another way) of a refugee policy that is purely normative in orientation.

The kind of normativism I am discussing here (with the accent on humanitarianism) does have one advantage, though: it is easier to build persuasive and conclusive value systems using humanitarian norms than by means of utilitarian arguments, which inevitably lead to the transactional question—*cui bono*? The answer, it turns out, can vary greatly, depending on whether it comes from the perspective of the host states and societies, the refugees, or the countries of origin (countries that should not be completely neglected in these discussions). The drawback to this normativism is that value systems are always open to attack, and that they change. The rise of right-wing nationalism since the financial and economic crisis of 2008–9 is just one example of many.

Moreover, in their much-discussed book, Alexander Betts and Paul Collier of Oxford's Refugee Study Center have asserted that there has always been a gap between the good intentions embedded in refugee policy and the possibilities for implementing them. No country in this world can take in, house, and feed twelve million Syrian refugees and IDPs. Certainly this would not be possible for highly developed welfare states that have minimum standards for social assistance and living space in addition to relatively high living costs. Help for refugees must, accordingly, be limited, both with respect to the level of support for each individual recipient and the number of people receiving assistance. These unavoidable limits on humanitarianism raise hard-to-solve ethical dilemmas. Furthermore, democracies must configure support for refugees in a way that the majority of the population will approve or at least accept it.

Does admitting refugees lend itself to a utilitarian justification? This question may well be an uncomfortable one, as the first order of business in international refugee policy is to help people who have been persecuted and are in distress. We have seen in this book's chapter on the Jews and the refugees from the Spanish Civil War how the exclusive utilitarianism of the 1930s led to refugees being turned away and consequently losing their lives. Isn't it cynical then to judge refugees according to whether they might or might not be useful to the country that takes them in? These objections are valid, but the question nevertheless merits a closer look, first with a view toward the democratic majorities that are necessary in the long run for an active humanitarianism, and second because there are historical examples of utilitarian refugee policies that are by no means unethical.

One reason that traditional immigration countries are designated as such is because this is how they see themselves. Most citizens of the US, Canada, Australia, and New Zealand would certainly agree that their prosperity has been built on the hard work of immigrants, including in the mix some refugees. In the US this consensus is integral to the national iconography; the poem by Emma Lazarus inscribed on the Statue of Liberty quite literally engraves it in stone (though at the time the wording was controversial and has been attacked again and again ever since). Agreement about the value of past immigration is, however, no guarantee of equally high support for future immigrants. In fact there has always been debate about how extensive this immigration should be, and where the country's new fellow citizens should come from. For a long time, selection was based on national origins, in the end a policy dictated by racism. Owing to distributive conflicts and competition on the labor market, social consensus in favor of immigration almost vanished in the traditional receiving countries in the mid-1920s. The Great Depression then further tipped the political balance against the admission of refugees and general immigration. Already at that time, refugees and other destitute migrants found themselves singled out for scaremongering by right-wing nationalists and racists. But after the Second World War these nations reclaimed their self-identification as immigration countries, and that identity has endured, until recently.

Economic and labor migration should not, of course, be equated with migration based on flight; each type requires a different set of regulations. Because they have experienced violence and material losses, it is as a rule harder for refugees to start a new life than for labor migrants. To be sure, the latter also face many hardships, which is why many potential migrants do decide *not* to migrate but to stay where they are. When have-nots arrive in large numbers, this triggers fears in the societies taking them in. After 1923 Greeks wondered how their country, poor and overwhelmingly agrarian, could possibly accommodate all their fellow Greeks and other Christians who had been driven out of Asia Minor. How could Germany, destroyed by the Second World War, absorb twelve million refugees? How was Poland going to take in more than two million "repatriates" in addition to the roughly three million people displaced during the war? Yet even in such seemingly impossible situations, where the admitting countries were at first cruelly overburdened, the outcomes were positive in the long run. After 1923, Greece, with the aid of outside loans earmarked for mitigating the country's emergency as a whole and helping the refugees in particular, underwent major urbanization and a boost to development.[49] In Germany the gigantic reservoir of labor provided by the refugees was one of the foundations on which the German Economic Miracle was built. Postwar Polish society was so dynamic because there were so many people who had lost everything and who were therefore highly mobile geographically, occupationally, and in terms of their private lives.[50] One of the reasons Israel—to cite an additional example—has been so successful economically is that millions of refugees immigrating in successive waves constructed whole new livelihoods for themselves. In the US, too, the arrival of 3.4 million resettled refugees since 1980 has certainly benefited both the newcomers and society at large; this mutual advantage was the result of the US taking in immigrants whose motivation was especially high. These arguments are not new. Refugees themselves have helped to develop them, as over the centuries they have written themselves into the history of their host countries as industrious workers, skilled laborers, and carriers of modernization processes.

This image of accomplishment stands in conspicuous contrast to the way refugees are depicted by NGOs and international organizations, such as the UNHCR. In their appeals for donations, they portray refugees almost exclusively as weak and needy. Pictures of emaciated and exhausted people certainly do correspond to the terrible reality of countries afflicted by civil war, such as Syria and Yemen, where millions of people suffer from hunger. These images also effectively encourage the worthy humanitarian goal of soliciting more international support and donations. But at the same time they turn refugees into the passive objects rather than active subjects of history. This is not what these organizations intend; and yet it is what happens, and it illustrates one of the disadvantages of viewing refugees exclusively through the lens of humanitarianism.

Very often refugees perceive their arrival in the receiving country as a moment of relief. But it would be wrong to overlook the privations they experience *after* their arrival. They are subject to economic, social, and cultural pressures, often forced to accept jobs for which they are overqualified, and required to adapt themselves linguistically and culturally. Yet it still seems possible, based on these very experiences, to develop a utilitarian argument for taking in refugees. It is only under unfavorable circumstances that refugees destabilize countries and societies, as happened in the late nineteenth century in the Ottoman Empire and after 1948 with Israel's Arab neighbors. In the former case this can be ascribed to systemic corruption in public administration and to the feudal order in the countryside, in the latter to the fact that the countries neighboring Israel, with the exception of Jordan, refused to integrate the Palestinian refugees.

The answer as to why refugees almost always benefit the countries taking them in is one that may be found, among other places, in their social profile. In most cases flight goes hand in hand with some kind of social selection, although this overlap is not always easy to recognize because it is often obscured by the refugees' impoverished condition. As was already the case with the Huguenots, political refugees in the nineteenth century as well as those fleeing the Russian Revolution and later from National Socialism were overwhelmingly members of the middle class and an intellectual elite. The recent flight from Syria to the EU is an excellent example, as it has rested on especially intense social selection. This is presumably one of the reasons why integration into the labor market of the EU's major admitting countries has gone well so far for the Syrians, and even somewhat better than expected in Germany.[51] But for the society where the refugees originated (to switch perspective briefly for a moment), this same development is likely fraught with disadvantage. Syria will need these elite members and their energy one day to rebuild their country.

Moreover, there is the question of what to do with those refugees who have found a job but have not been recognized within the asylum procedure. From a utilitarian standpoint, they should not be deported, which is also the argument their employers make. But in the debate now ongoing in Germany and other European countries over "changing lanes" from one category of immigration status to another, right-wing nationalists and conservative politicians have advocated a normative position to the effect that no failed asylum applicant should ever be redefined as a labor migrant, both because this would violate asylum law and because one cannot retrospectively grant access to the labor market for those rejected as refugees. From a historical perspective the utilitarian and pragmatic way of thinking has stood the test. This has been demonstrated by recent history in Austria, which made a good and reasonable decision in allowing Bosnians to stay, under certain conditions, after the Dayton peace agreement had cleared the way for their return home. The coalition of conservatives and right-wing nationalists that governed Austria after 2017, however, vehemently rejected any attempts at "changing lanes"—a good example of how it is possible *not* to learn from history. Austria's pragmatic policy toward the end of the 1990s is a case in which a normative or humanitarian approach—taking in refugees—led ultimately to a utilitarian decision, permitting them to stay.

Due to their experiences of violence, trauma, and loss of property, most refugees tend to be less prepared for starting their proverbial new life than labor migrants. However, the aforementioned social selection works in their favor. From a humanitarian perspective this poses an ethical dilemma. If one were to admit refugees on the principle of "women and children first" that is followed after shipwrecks or natural catastrophes, this would have the effect of diluting or even reversing the benefits of social (and gender) selection. Somewhat surprisingly, however, there is a strong utilitarian argument on behalf of helping women, children, and families. Children have less trouble with integration, especially when it comes to language, and women from Muslim countries cope better than men with the loss of social status caused by flight, and they are more accepting of the differences between Western gender roles and those in their homelands.

As mentioned, three quarters of the refugees aged between 16 and 30 who arrived in Germany from the Middle East in 2015 were men. One may assume that they will have just as hard a time finding partners among German women as the guest workers from Turkey did in earlier years (and one may safely suppose that the situation is not much different in Austria, the Netherlands, Sweden, or other European countries). This gender imbalance means, at least in purely statistical terms, that only one out of three young male refugees has a decent chance of marrying within his own group. All the others would have to remain single, which, in light of the value placed on family in their countries of origin, would place a heavy future burden on them and on the societies taking them in. This predicament is a strong argument for using the international resettlements program to bring privileged women and young families to Europe.

In the European debate about the 2015 refugee policy, the high cost refugees incurred in fleeing their countries is frequently overlooked. By their own accounts, the Syrians admitted into Germany spent on average more than 7,000 euros for their escape, and the median figure for their costs (a more meaningful number in this case) was 5,000 euros (as mentioned earlier). This means that the roughly one million Syrians who came from a country that was poor to begin with and rendered even poorer by the civil war spent at least five million euros in order to get to Europe. About 30 percent of these expenditures went to smugglers. Viewed both from a normative and utilitarian point of view, this was very deleterious: the Syrians could better have used the capital they lost on hazardous travel to take language courses, or maybe to start a businesses or embark on some other career path.

Betts and Collier make an additional calculation. They contrast the high costs for housing and feeding refugees in the EU with the lower sum it would take to assist them on the ground back home.[52] Indeed, offering a meal, providing housing, or operating a school in Lebanon or Jordan would cost a fraction of what it takes to fund these services in Western Europe. Even in more affluent Turkey, which since 2016 has finally received reasonable compensation from the EU to support its efforts on behalf of Syrian refugees, the costs would be much lower than in Europe. Yet in making this calculation Betts and Collier potentially disregard an important political factor: how much assistance would the West provide to Syria, its neighboring states, and to the UNHCR if the Syrians had not set out on their long and arduous trek to Europe? A glance at Yemen, where another civil and proxy war is also claiming many victims, does not give cause for optimism. Yemenite refugees are starving and sickened by cholera epidemics (something Europe also experienced earlier, for example in Greece in 1923), and yet in spite of these appalling conditions, they receive hardly any Western aid. One reason for this paltry assistance is that Yeminis have almost no hope of reaching the EU. Geography and their great poverty work against them.

The old principle "out of sight, out of mind" still seems to guide international refugee policy and conflict resolution. Recently 490 Yemenite refugees found their way via Kuala Lumpur to the South Korean vacation island Jeju because there is no visa requirement there for travelers from Malaysia, their interim destination.[53] This is evidence yet again of the ingenuity of refugees in plotting new and completely unexpected flight routes when they can see no other way out. In this case the role played by social selection is even more obvious than in the case of the Syrians who went to the EU using ships, buses, and their own feet. But, at the same time, the Yemenites illustrate an ethical dilemma: they would hardly have qualified for a UNHCR resettlement program because they were almost all men, and apparently from a prosperous social class. They therefore had to take their fate into their own hands if they were going to escape the humanitarian catastrophe in their homeland.

Much like the regulations protecting refugees in the Geneva Convention, the rules about redirecting refugees to third states willing to admit them go back to the interwar period, when the League of Nations invented the Nansen passports that refugees could use to travel farther on their own. As we have seen, 90 percent of the refugees from Hungary in 1956–57 were dispatched to countries other than their initial place of refuge (which was typically Austria). Years later, this machinery was given a second chance to work on behalf of the Czechs, Slovaks, and "Indochina refugees" of the late 1960s and 1970s. Not only did these resettlements have normative justification; they also had a utilitarian dimension in that they proved useful in helping defuse tensions in international trouble spots. Moreover, they spared the refugees a prolonged odyssey and saved them a lot of money that would otherwise have had to be spent on the remaining legs of their journey or, as in 2015, on paying smugglers.

In the postwar period and after 1989, the US served as an anchor for this system of international resettlements. One reason was its geographical location, another the normative conviction that the wealthier countries of the world should contribute more to solving its acute problems. Taking a longer view, it is possible to add also a utilitarian argument: without this American commitment the problems of the so-called Third World would sooner or later backfire on the West, perhaps in the form of massive flight. To this extent it was also reasonable, and not just a good deed, for the US to take in so many people by way of international settlements since the passage of the Refugee Act in 1980.

Admitting refugees was, as indicated, justified above all on humanitarian grounds, but it was simultaneously useful for the society taking them in. Resettled refugees often felt a lifelong debt of gratitude to the United States. For the helpers, usually representatives of local NGOs and religious congregations, their humanitarian engagement also brought with it a sense of fulfillment. Even those groups among the Indochina refugees less well-equipped for integration into the labor market and other areas of American life, groups like the Hmong from Laos, experienced upward social mobility.

Moreover, on the basis of its refugee policy the US has been able to present itself on the international stage as a moral superpower. One can agree with this picture or not—especially given the Cold War, or the 2003 invasion of Iraq in violation of international law. But the amount of rhetoric lavished on America's moral hegemony—and the rage heaped on the United States by adversaries such as Russian President Vladimir Putin—provides indirect confirmation of how relevant a high moral status was in terms of power politics. (We have to say "was" because developments since 2017 have certainly pushed America's claim to moral leadership into the past tense.)

The West's "soft power" during the Cold War era and its hegemony in the period after 1989 rested in particular on the normative and political allure of human rights. Without the special rights accorded refugees, without the Geneva Refugee Convention that is their foundation (however deserving of criticism some aspects of the Convention may be), the West would have lost a great deal and been forced to withdraw to the arena of pure power politics, occasionally dressed up as Realpolitik, an odd choice of word, for it suggests that values somehow cannot also be regarded as *realia*. To the contrary, values are not only real but they have real utility, above all, as a way of communicating to recently arrived refugees what it is that the societies taking them in stand for and pointing the direction in which the newcomers should be headed (or toward the goals they can aim to achieve) as they make the effort to integrate themselves.

Immediately following his inauguration in January 2017, Donald Trump announced a moratorium on admitting refugees. This "refugee ban" was given less media attention because the simultaneous "Muslim country ban" featured more prominently in the news as a topic of immediate relevance to domestic politics. In the summer of 2017, to be sure, the Trump administration partly rescinded this admission restriction under court orders. Pressure from the Christian base of the Republican party may also have played a role. But the government lowered the annual quota for resettlements in two steps, first to

45,000, and then 30,000 people. In 2018 the actual number of admissions was even below the level of 2002, that is, right after the shock of 9–11. One is tempted to pose the question: who attacked the US this time? What is more, the admissions halt did remain in force for refugees from predominantly Muslim countries. Syrians in particular have no chance of admission to the US, which has indirectly increased refugee pressure on the EU.

That indirect intensification of pressure on the European Union could already be felt in the period leading up to 2015. During the first four years of the Syrian civil war, the United States accepted fewer than 1,900 Syrians.[54] A more generous attitude would surely have had an impact on the EU, especially on Poland and the Czech Republic, countries that traditionally see themselves as close allies of the US. Germany, Sweden, and Austria would not have been so isolated by their generous refugee policies. Now America's erstwhile leadership in welcoming refugees has shifted into reverse; today it is by sealing off its borders that the US is setting international standards.

The EU has reacted to the US's eliminating itself as an anchor of international resettlements, even if the response has been hesitant and limited. In the autumn of 2017, and then again early in 2018, twenty member states announced that they were willing to take in 50,000 refugees for resettlement in the course of a year. To what extent this resolution will be implemented remains to be seen. As is well known, in the EU-internal redistribution of refugees from Greece and Italy, only about 10 percent of the pledges made have been fulfilled (13,500 of 120,000 for the year 2016). Nonetheless, the door was opened slightly for families, single mothers, children, and other people in need of special protection. As a rule, it was the UNHCR that made the selection of beneficiaries, and that organization has been indirectly strengthened as a result.

As discussed earlier, transporting refugees from crisis regions directly into the countries accepting them would prove useful in that a direct path to the EU would frustrate smugglers, save refugees a lot of money, and bring into the European Union's aging societies new citizens who would be grateful to their host societies. But should these "humanitarian corridors," as the refugee resettlement program has been called for the past several years, be regarded as an exclusively good deed? Or must one reckon with side effects that miss the mark of the program's original goal?[55]

One initial objection to humanitarian corridors is that they force democracies to cooperate with governments and authoritarian rulers, involvements that democratic states normally avoid. This obvious objection was frequently raised in 2016. The agreement between Brussels and Ankara, for example, that contained a promise of six billion euros in assistance really did elevate the status of Turkish President Erdoğan. It contributed to his victory in the constitutional referendum that followed and to Turkey's conversion into an authoritarian system. This was due, however, to the timing of the accord and could have been avoided if Angela Merkel, owing to the pressure of public opinion in Germany, had not been in such a hurry to reach an agreement. (In Germany, the events on New Year's Eve before 2016 constituted a turning point. During the festivities at Cologne's main railway station, numerous women were sexually harassed and robbed by Mediterranean-looking men, although it turned out that the great majority of the perpetrators were migrants from the Maghreb and not refugees from the Middle East.) In principle, however, the normative objection to the "deal" between the EU and Turkey (based on worries about rewarding authoritarian rulers) is invalid, inasmuch as emergency assistance in war zones has often depended on cooperation with warring parties, warlords, and even people later sentenced as criminals, as in the former Yugoslavia. (One drawback to the Dayton peace accords and the negotiations leading up to them was that Milošević, one of the perpetrators of the war, was elevated in status.)

Another, more fundamental objection may be raised against the concept of the corridor. It is useful, once again, to refer to the EU-Turkey agreement for a better understanding of the problem. According to the terms of that agreement, the only legal flight path to Europe resides in the quota of refugees the EU agrees to take from Turkey. (How generously or parsimoniously the treaty may be interpreted is another question entirely.) Outside of this humanitarian corridor there commences, by definition, a gray area of irregular or illegal migration.[56] Is it even possible to channel migration from the Middle East (and Africa), whether due to flight or labor markets, on such a vast scale? Or is the very effort to steer this unruly process setting up a bureaucratic mirage that can only lead to disappointments later and create vulnerable new targets for right-wing nationalists to attack?

These questions take on even greater urgency when one ponders the relatively small numbers of those who have been resettled versus the millions of people currently stuck in refugee camps all over the world. According to figures from the UNHCR, in 2017 6.2 million people were living in camps, and of these more than a million were housed in improvised, self-built camps, most of which were not connected to an electricity grid and did not have access to running water.[57] The 50,000 resettlements agreed to by the 20 EU states, accordingly, offered the global camp population a less than one percent chance of reaching Europe. The chances for Syrians to get to the EU legally were even worse. In the first two years after the signing of this agreement, the EU took 12,500 refugees off Turkey's hands.[58] That amounts to four tenths of a percent of the Syrians living there, which puts their prospects for success lower than their chances of winning a lottery. Is that defensible from a humanitarian point of view? Or, one could equally well ask: Does that make sense? Won't it lead desperate refugees, examining their chances, to entrust themselves once again to smugglers, with all the aforementioned consequences?

As of the spring of 2016, sealing off the Aegean led to an outcome that migration experts had predicted: flight and migration via the central Mediterranean sea route increased dramatically, and pressure shifted from southeast Europe to Italy, where the center left Italian government now had to cope with the flight wave. Patterning its own negotiations on the model of the EU-Turkey accord, the Rome government at the beginning of 2017 concluded an agreement with Libya. Indirectly, Silvio Berlusconi figured as the godfather, since in 2008 he had (as mentioned earlier) concluded a similar agreement with the Libyan dictator Gaddafi to hold back refugees and migrants in Northern Africa. Like the earlier Turkish case, this "deal" involved getting the government in the country of exit to promise, in return for a large payment, to stop boats from taking off with refugees and other migrants.

The current Libyan government, however, is not in control of the whole of Libya. The East of the country and parts of the coast are controlled by warlords who share responsibility for the horrific conditions in the camps for refugees and labor migrants and who make decisions based on figuring out whether they can earn more from cooperating with the smugglers or taking funds from Europe to stop the mass migration. Therefore, apart from the normative dubiousness of Italy's deal with Libya, there is also the question as to whether in the end the agreement will have the desired utilitarian effect. In order to soften criticism from aid and human rights organizations, the Italian government adopted an initiative crafted by Catholic lay organizations, who in 2017 had started to fly in Syrian refugees directly from Lebanon to Italy. This was a good deed. Its influence radiated to Brussels and inspired the previously mentioned twenty-state EU resolution authorizing a resettlement quota of 50,000 people per year. But it did nothing to stop the alliance of left-wing populists and right-wing nationalists promising an end to every kind of immigration into Italy from winning the 2018 national election.

Accordingly, the new Italian government immediately abandoned these humanitarian corridors. It is now demanding, like other European governments where right-wing nationalists either share power or lead, that asylum procedures be outsourced to countries on the other side of the Mediterranean. Austrian Chancellor Sebastian Kurz has even added humanitarian arguments, to the effect that fewer people would then risk a dangerous Mediterranean crossing and drown. Even if one were to take this argument at face value and not as a pretext, it is highly doubtful whether Kurz's assumption holds. If the chance of reaching Europe stands at four tenths of a percentage point, as is currently the case with Turkey, over the long run refugees are certainly going to try other ways.

Moreover, we can expect that the number of genuine refugees as a share of total migration to Europe will fall, as already happened in 2017, since refugees will be less able to afford the long journey along a flight route and less able to make the necessary payments to smugglers compared with labor migrants, who count on having to meet these costs. This may be exactly what the right-wing nationalists in Europe are calculating will happen. They are also pushing a strategy of delegitimization at the level of language. In the programs of the right-wing nationalist parties in Europe, whether the Lega in Italy, the Front National in France, the Alternative für Deutschland in Germany, or the FPÖ in Austria, there are no longer any refugees, just illegal migrants. Donald Trump is proceeding along the same path in the US. In his rhetoric, people in distress or refugees from Central America no longer exist; illegal migrants are all there is.

When we think in humanitarian terms, of course, we are apt to criticize strategies like this at a normative level and inquire into the status of human rights, the rights of refugees derived from human rights, or simply basic values like Christian compassion. For purposes of political debate, however, it might conceivably be more useful to counter the sealing off of borders advocated by these strategies with pragmatic and therefore utilitarian questions. Would it be possible to run asylum centers for the EU in Libya and other African countries? What concrete steps would the participating European states and governments have to take? Should embassy grounds be expanded in order to process asylum applications, or should the asylum centers operate under the direction of the Libyan government? And, to take note of the question frequently posed by Austrian chancellor Sebastian Kurz: What part does Austria want to play in these asylum centers in Africa, and will it order Austrian civil servants to Libya to this end?

In the US one would have to ask: Is it a proportionate and sensible response to station 15,000 soldiers along the border to ward off past and future "migration caravans" headed toward the United States from Honduras and Guatemala via Mexico?[59] Would we expect these soldiers, should the occasion arise, to shoot at these people as they approach the border? The latter question may sound too cynical to set down in writing, but in the last midterm election campaign the incumbent president really did call for something like this, as did the leader of the AfD in Germany two years earlier.[60] To this extent, the questions posed here are ones that must be seriously asked of all politicians currently advocating the militarization of borders and the sealing off of the US and Europe by all means necessary. The separation of parents and children in the spring of 2018 ordered by President Trump and invented by one of his closest advisers, Stephen Miller, was, quite apart from its ethics, expensive and senseless. When a court order ended the separation program, authorities faced the nightmarish task of trying to locate the parents of more than 1,600 children. As of November 2018 the search has failed to reunite upwards of 300 of these children with their parents; it is also an extremely expensive undertaking. If things go the way the right-wing radical ideologues in the Trump government want, the problem would be solved in the future by closing the border completely. Yet even here it has to be asked: How high are the financial and political costs? Should it be taken into account that a wall can only be built on land, and not in the Pacific or the Atlantic ocean? If "illegal migrants" could bypass the barrier by sea, might such a wall simply give rise to new "boat people," and rising expenses for the coast guard?

Perhaps discussions like this will bring attention also to the consequences that a rejection of Western values would have for us. To what extent would human rights still count for citizens of our own countries if they were deliberately violated in our dealings with foreigners? What happens to our societies when poverty becomes grounds for exclusion? How will soldiers from border patrol units behave when they are ordered to shoot at refugees and other migrants? One could extend this catalog of questions even further, but the answers always remain the same: sealing off Europe and the US from the outside, as demanded by nationalists, makes no sense either from a normative or a utilitarian standpoint.

The right-wing nationalists who claim to speak for the—ethnically redefined—nation are not acting in the national interest. In all the years I have spent studying nationalism and violent conflicts, I have avoided the term "national interest" because it has been so widely abused by nationalists. But perhaps there is only a need to change its definition, so that national interest comes to include decency, a sense of proportion, and a rational approach in dealing with mass flight, its causes, and its consequences.

4.4 Experiences of flight: A summary

So far this book has focused on the main causes of population displacement, the patterns of flight with often lengthy escape routes, and the refugee politics of the receiving countries. For the sake of a systematic overview, this way of proceeding makes sense, but it can also have the unintended effect that the refugees themselves are overlooked. Hence, by way of conclusion here, the motives and existential experiences of refugees will be foregrounded once again. In so doing, we will revisit the biographical case studies used throughout this book.

Because it does not make sense to retell the individual life stories here, they will have to be conceived abstractly. The drawback of generalizations based on a bird's-eye perspective can be that they are very remote from individual experiences, actions, and values. Nevertheless, four types of individual flight experiences and motives will be distinguished here. We are dealing again with ideal types in Max Weber's sense, with a lot of overlap between the categories, even within individual biographies. Yet I am convinced that historical scholarship informed by social science requires dismantling historical processes in order to reassemble them anew. With this in mind, the overlaps often reveal more than the seemingly clear-cut cases.

A first category in this typology may be called existential flight. To people in truly desperate situations, it represents the only opportunity to save themselves from the worst kinds of mistreatment and often even from certain death. Examples of this are the life stories of Ruth Klüger and her mother. It is highly likely that both these women, like so many concentration camp inmates, would have died on one of the death marches in 1945 had they not run away at a favorable moment and disguised themselves as German refugees. Existential flight was always marked by a very high level of risk. Hannah Arendt also escaped at the last moment, just before she risked falling into the hands of the National Socialists. Much the same can be said about Manès Sperber although, because of the time he spent in a German prison in 1933, he would have known in 1942 what was in store for him. Hence he took to flight just in time, before coming as perilously close to danger as the two Klügers later were. The fate of the Dublon family and of Manuel Alarcón Navarro, by contrast, shows the consequences of failed existential flight. The German-Jewish family and the Spanish Republican died in the concentrations camps of the National Socialists and Spanish Fascists, respectively.

Precisely because it was fundamentally a matter of life and death to them, survivors frequently saw flight as rescue and liberation, not punishment and fate. This is reflected in the numerous individual narratives of flight that live off a dialectical contradiction between stories of persecution (including detailed description of the perpetrators) and of rescue. In this dialectic between evil and good there is usually little room for the rest of the refugees' lives, which as a rule proceeded with much less drama than their stories of survival. We usually know much less, for example, about the later chapters of Holocaust survivors' lives, unless they dedicated themselves to the prevention of future genocides by writing books or making films about the worst crime in the history of humanity. At the same time, one learns from their works or from the autobiographical writings of Manès Sperber that there is a fate worse than flight, namely death.

A second type of flight can be designated as predetermined, because in these cases government authorities did not allow for any exceptions and applied massive physical violence. In contrast to a genocide in the narrower sense (as defined by the International Criminal Court in The Hague since the war in the former Yugoslavia), however, the aim in these cases was not the mass killing of members of a particular group but rather their total removal from a specific region or country. There are many examples of this: early ones like the expulsion of Muslims and Jews after the Reconquista in Spain, and later ones such as the ethnic cleansings in the twentieth century, and most recently in the former Yugoslavia.

The term "predetermined" refers to the narrow room for maneuver available to refugees. One example would be the Germans remaining in the Reich's eastern territories toward the end of the Second World War. Either they had already fled from the Red Army in the winter of 1944–45, were driven across the Oder and Neiße rivers early in 1945, or were subjected to forced resettlement following the Potsdam Agreement. The populations defined as German were collectively punished for the crimes committed by the Nazis (though it should not be forgotten that there were Nazis among the refugees as well) and they were completely removed. While in religious wars there was always a chance that Protestants could convert to Catholicism or vice versa, a "national conversion" was almost impossible (with just a few exceptions, to be noted below).

The Palestinian family of the woman who would later become Jordan's Queen Rania also had little room for maneuver when it was forced to leave its homeland twice, first in 1967 and then again in 1991. That the expulsion from Palestine has taken such a prominent place in memory compared to the persecution the same Palestinians suffered at the hands of other Arabs is not, by contrast, something predetermined. This second variant of flight, which is frequently called expulsion, was almost always associated with large material losses, and personal memories of the old homeland are often later affixed to these traumas, such as a lost house or stolen family jewels.

The defenselessness of refugees, moreover, is often exploited to humiliate or mistreat them, either in full public view as an act of deterrence or behind closed doors, as their tormenters act on sadistic instincts. Since time immemorial women in particular have suffered from these kinds of violence; one need only think of the mass rapes toward the end of the Second World War and in the former Yugoslavia. The variant of predetermined flight has often led also to serious traumatization or even death. Thus, although the family of Alan Kurdi was indeed able to escape from Kobane, a Syrian city besieged for months by ISIS, the mother and her two children subsequently drowned on their flight across the Aegean.

Predetermined flight is often preceded in time by proactive flight. Proactive in this context means that people try to reach safety in anticipation of an approaching army, a regime change, or other immediate dangers. As a rule, this third variant of flight depends on greater self-initiative, the kind of effort that makes it possible, at a minimum, to take along a suitcase, some personal documents, money, and smaller valuables. These meager rescued possessions then serve to jump-start a new life, regardless of whether they are clothes for official occasions, seeds for agriculture, or tools to build a workshop. There are cases in which flight was even forbidden, whether for economic reasons (as with the Huguenots in France) or because a nearly defeated regime is taking a last stand against a hostile invading army (as, for example, the Nazis in the winter of 1945 in East Prussia). This increased the risks associated with flight. However, as in the case of the Robillard family, it could also result in a risky flight being experienced as something more than a fate that had to be endured passively.

The Huguenots especially, but also other political refugees, often presented their life stories as the outcome of conscious decisions against injustice, oppression, and persecution. In this way they justified the decision they had made to themselves and their families. Also, in retrospect, the refugees wanted to give some meaning to their sacrifices and losses that might to some degree compensate for the property, homeland, and social position they left behind. This construction of meaning was a powerful tool for positioning themselves in the receiving societies as well. Dramatic and sometimes celebratory heroic narratives often served to underpin demands for government services, social solidarity, and their own political demands. In the most favorable case, the proactive refugees arrived at their different destinations exhausted yet outwardly safe and sound. In the worst case, proactive flight devolved into something more like the predetermined kind, as might happen when enemy armies overran refugees or there was an unanticipated regime change. Finding the right time to flee is ultimately a question of luck, which one can only recognize in hindsight.

The best escapes were managed by those proactive refugees who belonged to a social and economic elite, such as Tadeusz Kościuszko or Giuseppe Mazzini. Here, in some cases, one may even speak of a privileged flight that opened up favorable opportunities in the host country to start a new professional and social life abroad. Sometimes flight and permanent accommodation in the host country were directly related to each other, as in the case of the Huguenots who managed to get to England, the Netherlands, Prussia, Hesse-Kassel, and the smaller states of the Holy Roman Empire in Germany. Things were much the same for the refugees of 1956 and 1968, whose transition from exodus to exile was relatively seamless. They were welcomed so warmly not because of their own past and convictions, but because they helped to lift the moral and political status of the receiving countries. This shortened both the time it took to flee and the length of the escape routes. It is one of the achievements of the twentieth century (an era usually held in ill repute) that fewer refugees died en route over the course of time, especially as measured against the steep increase in their overall numbers. Since 2016 this has changed everywhere in the West—if indeed the West still exists as a normative and political community. Now proactive refugees are no longer portrayed as heroes but are placed on the same level with economic migrants and seen more as a danger than an asset. This means that proactive refugees are more likely to be stuck somewhere in between the country of departure and prospective countries of arrival, draining their resources and turning into passive recipients of help.

Fourth, there were numerous cases of optional flight—situations where other solutions besides leaving the homeland were conceivable. This was especially the case when religious or national conversion was possible or even desired. It was the situation faced, for example by the Huguenots, who had stayed somewhat longer in France due to a lack of financial resources or for a variety of other reasons. Similar constellations arose in the twentieth century in certain regions of Europe where, parallel to the ethnic cleansings taking place, there was the option to change one's nationality. Upper Silesia is a good case in point. There, after 1945, about a million citizens of the defeated and dismembered German Reich stayed on and, for various reasons, declared their support (at least outwardly) for the Polish nation, thus escaping deportation and the loss of house and home. Their social integration failed, however, and so in order to keep open the door to emigration, most members of this group defined themselves over the course of the postwar period as part of a German minority. In these and other cases, flight did not take place at one fell swoop, but instead stretched out across years and decades.

Political flight was also optional, as a rule, since (except in the heyday of the Stalinism) dissidents in the Eastern Bloc countries (and also in earlier dictatorships) had the opportunity to go into "inner emigration"—a term coined by German intellectuals who chose to remain in Nazi Germany despite their opposition to the dictatorship—or to make some other arrangement with an oppressive regime. Many refused to take advantage of this option, however, because of their convictions, as in the case of Jerzy Giedroyc, the parents of Madeleine Albright, and other refugees of the Cold War. They did not necessarily have to flee, but in retrospect it was one of the best decisions of their lives. Some people decided rather spontaneously to flee—this would apply to Conrad Schumann, whose biography contradicts the notion that all optional refugees were ultimately happy with their decision to leave their homelands. Though they may have lacked for nothing materially, many were plagued by guilt about family members left behind, and even more of them suffered from terrible homesickness.

In some biographies, one flight is followed by another. This was the case, for example, with Manès Sperber, and also with Tadeusz Kosciuszko, who in a later phrase of his life could have returned to his homeland but rejected that course on political grounds. When it comes to optional flight, therefore, mixed motives come into play, which sometimes make for fluid boundaries between flight and other forms of migration. The extent of compulsion and violence, the things that allow us to distinguish flight from labor migration in the first place, have always varied in historical flight waves. Age and social position play a role in each individual decision; older people and families tend to be tied to a locality more than young people who may come to feel that they can no longer endure an oppressive and corrupt government. This was how many Poles felt who left for the West after martial law was proclaimed in 1981. The younger generation in particular could no longer abide political censorship, the rationing of almost all food as if their country's economy were on a wartime footing, being forced to stand in line every day, and the breakdown in social solidarity that all this triggered. Similar frustrations motivated many Cubans to cross the strait to Florida, and more recently people from the Central American triangle to escape from gang violence, and of course, dismal living conditions.

If one were to classify all of these people as "fake refugees," it would betray a noble Cold War tradition. If one were to condemn "false asylum seekers," as has so often happened in Germany since the 1980s, to be consistent one would also have to condemn those refugees who fled across the Iron Curtain and the Berlin Wall. They had good reasons for abandoning the GDR and other Eastern Bloc countries, but it was not as if all of them had to do so. Ultimately, when it comes to classifying this or that kind of "outsider," one ends up facing fundamental philosophical questions about what makes a life worth living, or at least what makes it bearable. Optional refugees were not necessarily fleeing from raw, physical violence or some immediate threat; instead, they might be fleeing from the pressure of unbearable living conditions.

In spite of these differences, there is one defining constant of all four variants of flight—the existential, the predetermined, the proactive, and the optional. Leaving one's homeland has massive economic and social consequences. Flight is almost always accompanied by a loss of wealth, property, professional position, and social contacts. After arriving at their destination, refugees have to start a new life. The full weight of this challenge may well be something that only people who have experienced it can fully understand.

ACKNOWLEDGMENTS

I edited the translation of this book and wrote new chapters for the English version during a stay at New York University in the academic year 2018/19. I am deeply grateful to Larry Wolff and the provost of NYU for their generous invitation; under the regular working conditions at the University of Vienna it would have taken much longer to finish the work. I also would like to thank the students in my NYU-seminar on refugee history for their feedback. I cannot mention everybody by name, but I learned especially from Anne Schult, Giulio Salvati, and Marc Dorpema. I also feel indebted to a second foreign institution, Sciences Po, especially to Jakob Vogel and Marc Lazar. The invitation to Paris in February and March 2017 helped me to explore the indispensable French literature and to finish the original German manuscript.

In Vienna I am deeply grateful to a number of colleagues at my institute, particularly Manuel Neubauer. In the years 2014–17 he found a great amount of literature and original sources. Iris Engemann and her company Berlin-Text have provided excellent data and literature compilations on integration processes in various European countries. Fabian Stegmayer, Pauli Aro, Andreea Petruescu, Iurii Chainskyi, and Hülya Çelik wrote excellent synopses about various countries which guided my further reading. Matthias Kaltenbrunner and Mojmir Stransky supported my teaching so that I could spare extra time for writing. Anita Biricz provided administrative and technical support, as did Mizanur Khan.

I also have received excellent hints on literature and theory from Aga Pasieka, Machteld Venken, Piotr Filipkowski, Fredrik Stöcker, Ulrich Hofmeister, and Konrad Petrovszky. My colleagues Sepp Ehmer and Peter Becker provided excellent feedback on a very early book prospectus; Peter's idea on how to structure the book rescued me from an impasse. Kerstin Jobst helped me to find literature on the Crimea, Vladimir Hamed-Troyansky greatly enriched my knowledge of the Ottoman Empire. Daniel Fazekas and his data research company Bakamo Social in Budapest have taught me a lot about social media communication and the creation of big data. I would also like to thank Constantin Goschler at the University of Bochum and the German Historical Institute in Washington D.C. (in particular Jan Jansen) for their invitation to present early versions of my book. I owe sincere thanks for the invitations and excellent feedback provided by Belinda Davis, Melissa

Feinberg, and Paul Hanebrink at Rutgers University, Paul Kramer, Alexander Joskowicz, Helmut Smith, and David Blackbourn at Vanderbild University, John Connelly and the members of his Kroužek at Berkeley, Małgorzata Mazurek at Columbia University, Howard Louthan and Gary Cohen at the University of Minnesota, and Ke Chin Hsia and Padraic Kenney at Indiana University. I am also very grateful to Dominique Arel for organizing and chairing a book panel at the 2019 convention of the Association for the Study of Nationalism, and to Daniel Naujoks, Lisa Koryushkina, and Lenni Benson for their great comments. You all have greatly helped me to refine my arguments and to bring my manuscript into its final shape. Xosé Manoel Núñez Seixas (University of Santiago de Compostela), Kiran Patel (University of Maastricht), Daniel Stone (U.S. Naval War College), Peter Holquist (University of Pennsylvania), and Jochen Oltmer (IMIS), Nancy Green, and Catherine de Wenden (Sciences Po) all gave me good advice on various research issues. My sister Friederike Ther (University of Almería) has explored the family archive of her Spanish in-laws.

This book is based on research about refugees and integration history that has kept me busy since the 1990s. So it is a good opportunity to pay tribute to the mentors who supported my research and gave me the freedom to carry it out. In 1993 Andrzej S. Kamiński (Georgetown University) inspired me to undertake my first comparative study on refugees. Klaus Zernack (†) was a wonderful PhD in Berlin, Jürgen Kocka was a great mentor in my years at the Berlin Center for Comparative History. I always ask a friend to be the first reader of my draft manuscripts; this time I owe thanks to Florian Oberhuber for his intellectual (and musical) inspiration. Heinrich Geiselberger was, as usual, a wonderful editor at Suhrkamp, my German publisher. The manuscript has tremendously profited from his questions and editing, and I am happy that we could realize my idea about the drawings for the analytical portraits.

I will finish my acknowledgments by offering thanks for the wonderful support I received here in the United States. First and foremost, I would like to thank the staff of Princeton University Press. Brigitta van Rheinberg, you have been a great history editor, and I wish you all the best now as Director of Global Development and Associate Director of the Press. At a time when the world seems to be informed primarily by Twitter, it is all the more important to publish excellent academic books that are able to reach a wider audience. I am also very indebted to my two peer reviewers, who have provided very many pages of detailed advice and helped me to structure the argument and the English version of this book in a new way. The new fourth chapter was almost entirely inspired by my second reviewer. Carole Fink then read and carefully edited that chapter. Eric Crahan took over the editing of history books and the production of my manuscript in the fall of 2018, and cooperation went on as smoothly as before. I am also grateful for Pamela Weidman's and James

Schneider's support. Eva Jaunzems has been a great copy editor, who helped me a lot to improve the quality of the manuscript. The German booktraders' association is owed my thanks for its generous translation grant.

Jeremiah Riemer is named as translator, but he has been much more than that. He has provided information on historical and recent debates in American academia, on US immigration policy, integration history, and the specificities of the English language. It is also to his credit that we could produce an American version of my book rather than merely an English translation. Finally, I would like to thank my family, my kids for preventing me from being even more overworked, and my wife, Martina, for her love and intellectual input. I hope that my book will remain relevant for a number of years and be of some service to future refugees.

NOTES

Introduction: Flight and refugees in historical perspective

1. Cited according to Greek Refugee Settlement Commission: *Greek Refugee Settlement* (Geneva: Publications of the League of Nations, 1926), xv.
2. The article from *Foreign Affairs* is cited in Onur Yıldırım, *Diplomacy and Displacement: Reconsidering the Turco-Greek Exchange of Populations, 1922–1934* (New York: Routledge, 2006), 55.
3. Roth was reporting for the *Neue Berliner Zeitung*; the German quotation here is from Anne-Christin Saß, *Berliner Luftmenschen: Osteuropäisch-jüdische Migranten in der Weimarer Republik* (Göttingen: Wallstein, 2012), 130; the slightly altered translation used here is from Joseph Roth, *What I Saw: Reports from Berlin*, translated with an introduction by Michael Hofmann, German selection by Michael Bienert (New York: W.W. Norton), 37.
4. On the housing shortage for refugees in Vienna, cf. Beatrix Hoffmann-Holter, *"Abreisendmachung": Jüdische Kriegsflüchtlinge in Wien, 1914 bis 1923* (Vienna: Böhlau, 1995), 176. In Berlin physicians were also reporting that families of eight to ten members were often housed in one- or two-room apartments; see Saß, *Berliner Luftmenschen*, 100.
5. On the number of deaths in Greece, cf. Renée Hirschon, *Heirs of the Greek Catastrophe: The Social Life of Asia Minor Refugees in Piraeus* (Oxford: Clarendon Press, 1989), 37.
6. On his official title (in the secondary literature it is usually overlooked that the official title initially applied only to his work on Russian refugees), see Fridtjof Nansen, "Russian Refugees: General Report of the Work accomplished up to March 15th, 1922, by Dr. Fridtjof Nansen, the High Commissioner of the League," *League of Nations: Official Journal* (May 1922): 385 (2). In 1920 Nansen had already assumed responsibility for the repatriation of foreign troops stranded in the Russian Empire following the First World War.
7. In 1922, in light of new refugee flows, the adjective "Russian" was omitted in Greece and Turkey, and Nansen, under the pressure of circumstances, was made into a general High Commissioner for Refugees; on this, see again the files of the League of Nations in the archive of the United Nations. *Records of the Third Assembly: Minutes of the Fifth Committee* (Geneva: League of Nations, 1922).
8. On the Treaty of Lausanne, see Philipp Ther, *The Dark Side of Nation States: Ethnic Cleansing in Modern Europe* (New York: Berghahn, 2014), 74–81. The only exceptions made were for Istanbul and Western Thrace.
9. See Peter Gatrell, *The Making of the Modern Refugee* (Oxford: Oxford University Press, 2013), 32–35, 109–115. On displaced persons (DPs) and their influence on international law, in particular on the creation of both the UNHCR and the Geneva Refugee Convention, see Gerard Daniel Cohen, *In War's Wake: Europe's Displaced Persons in the Postwar Order* (Oxford: Oxford University Press, 2012).
10. On the definition of refugees in the nineteenth century, see Delphine Diaz, *Un asile pour tous les peuples? Exilés et réfugiés étrangers en France au cours du premier XIXe siècle* (Paris: Armand Colin, 2014), 30–42.

11. See Atle Grahl-Madsen, *The Status of Refugees in International Law* (Leyden: Sijthoff, 1966, 1972), vol. 1, 12.
12. The original text of the Convention (the official title is the "Convention relating to the Status of Refugees") may be found on the website of the UNCR, accessible online at http://www.unhcr.org/3b66c2aa10.pdf (accessed 27 December 2017).
13. Cf. Articles 17–19 of the Convention.
14. Integration has long been a major topic for German sociologists. It is defined and debated by Richard Münch, among others, in his "Elemente einer Theorie der Integration moderner Gesellschaften," in Wilhelm Heitmeyer, ed., *Bundesrepublik Deutschland: Auf dem Weg von der Konsens- zur Konfliktgesellschaft*, vol. 2: *Was hält die Gesellschaft zusammen?* (Frankfurt am Main: Suhrkamp, 1997), 66–109. On different approaches to integration, see also the knowledgeable lexicon entry by Wilhelm Heitmeyer and Sandra Hüpping in Sina Farzin and Stefen Jordan, eds., *Lexikon Soziologie und Sozialtheorie: Hundert Grundbegriffe* (Stuttgart: Reclam, 2008), 126–129. A groundbreaking book for the field of "integration history" (although focused on labor migrants, not on refugees) is Leo Lucassen, David Feldman, and Jochen Oltmer, eds., *Paths of Integration: Migrants in Western Europe, 1880–2004* (Amsterdam: Amsterdam University Press, 2006).
15. On the field of migration history, see, inter alia, the magnum opus by Dirk Hoerder, *Cultures in Contact: World Migrations in the Second Millennium* (Durham: Duke University Press, 2002), as well as the publications of the Dutch migration historian Leo Lucassen; see, among a wide variety of works, Leo Lucassen and Jan Lucassen, eds., *Migration, Migration History, History: Old Paradigms and New Perspectives*, 3rd ed. (Frankfurt am Main: Peter Lang, 2005). Among German-language migration historians, see, inter alia, Klaus Bade, *Migration in European History*, trans. Allison Brown (Malden: Blackwell, 2003), ix; Jochen Oltmer, *Migration im 19. und 20. Jahrhundert*, 2nd ed. (Munich: Oldenbourg, 2013). Social science research on migration was also of central importance to this book. It would fill too many pages to list a complete bibliography, so a volume that is already a bit older but still very much worth reading may stand in for this literature: Heinz Fassmann and Rainer Münz, eds., *Migration in Europa: Historische Entwicklungen, aktuelle Trends, politische Reaktionen* (Frankfurt am Main: Campus, 1996). A great many books and essays were published within the framework of the European research network IMISCOE and are accessible via its website https://www.imiscoe.org/ (accessed April 2017). Additional literature is cited in this book's individual chapters.
16. See Carl Bon Tempo, *Americans at the Gate: The United States and Refugees during the Cold War* (Princeton: Princeton University Press, 2008). For the period after 1989, see María Cristina García, *The Refugee Challenge in Post-Cold War America* (Oxford: Oxford University Press, 2017).
17. Simmel's essay is accessible online at https://www.infoamerica.org/documentos_pdf/simmel01.pdf (accessed December 2018). See the essay's very first paragraph.
18. Simmel's theory of power is developed in Georg Simmel, *Soziologie: Untersuchungen über die Formen der Vergesellschaftung*, vol. 11, *Gesamtausgabe*, Otthein Rammstedt, ed. (Frankfurt a.M.: Suhrkamp, 1992). Unfortunately, this volume (or rather chapter) was not included in the most recent English translation of his major works published by Brill. On Simmel's relevance to the study of refugees, see Bettina Severin-Barboutie and Nikola Tietze, "Umkämpfte Interaktionen: Flucht als Handlungszusammenhang in asymmetrischen Machtverhältnissen," *Zeithistorische Forschungen/Studies in Contemporary History*, online edition 15 (2018), no. 3, http://www.zeithistorische-forschungen.de/3-2018/id=5611 (accessed December 2018). See esp. part 2 of the article dealing with "conceptual considerations."
19. See http://www.ushistory.org/paine/commonsense/sense4.htm (accessed January 2018); the citation is taken from chapter 4, "Thoughts on the Present State of American Affairs."

20. See Gatrell, *The Making*; Cohen, *In War's Wake*. Some older books are also still worth reading; this is particularly true of Michael Marrus's *The Unwanted: European Refugees in the Twentieth Century* (New York: Oxford University Press, 1985). When dealing with the history of America I confess to concentrating on the US and slighting Canada and Mexico. I hope the reader will forgive me. A more even coverage would have entailed additional reading and processing of secondary literature beyond what was possible for me, and the result would have exceeded the length limits of a single volume. In dealing with Europe, I also had to focus of specific areas and countries to the neglect of others. Although the word "refugees" is not in the title, the following dictionary deals with all major refugee movements in twentieth century Europe: Detlef Brandes, Holm Sundhaussen, and Stefan Troebst, eds., *Lexikon der Vertreibungen: Deportation, Zwangsaussiedlung und ethnische Säuberung im Europa des 20. Jahrhunderts* (Vienna: Böhlau, 2010).

21. See Bon Tempo, *Americans at the Gate*; García, *The Refugee Challenge*; and Stephen R. Porter, *Benevolent Empire: U.S. Power, Humanitarianism and the World's Dispossessed* (Philadelphia: University of Pennsylvania Press, 2017). The subchapters and paragraphs in which I deal with American refugee politics are based mostly on these books and some additional literature and data.

22. On the First World War, see, inter alia, Peter Gatrell, *A Whole Empire Walking: Refugees in Russia during World War I* (Bloomington: Indiana University Press, 2005); a special issue of *Contemporary European History* 16/4 (2007). In addition, online publications are becoming more important, see e.g., the survey article by Peter Gatrell, "Refugees," in *1914–1918 Online: International Encyclopedia of the First World War* (8 Oct. 2014), accessible online at http://encyclopedia.1914–1918-online.net/article/refugees (accessed April 2017). On the interwar period, see Claudena Skran, *Refugees in Inter-War Europe: The Emergence of a Regime* (Oxford: Clarendon Press, 1995); Nick Baron and Peter Gatrell, eds., *Homelands: War, Population and Statehood in Eastern Europe and Russia, 1918–1924* (London: Anthem Press, 2004). The literature on individual countries will be cited in the appropriate chapters of this book.

23. This is also true for my own book on ethnic cleansing. See Ther, *The Dark Side of Nation States*. A great deal of data and statistics are taken from this book. I also collected many archival sources for my dissertation, a comparative history on the integration of refugees in postwar Poland and Germany, published as Philipp Ther, *Deutsche und polnische Vertriebene: Gesellschaft und Vertriebenenpolitik in der SBZ/DDR und in Polen, 1945–1956* (Göttingen: Vandenhoeck & Ruprecht, 1998). For this book and later publications I accessed archives in Germany, Poland, Ukraine (also for covering the western Soviet Union), and the Czech Republic, and records from the League of Nations, the United Nations, and several NGOs (in particular from the collections of the Open Society Archive in Budapest).

24. This part of refugee history is available for the US in Stephen Porter, *Benevolent Empire: U.S. Power, Humanitarianism, and the World's Dispossessed* (Philadelphia: University of Pennsylvania Press, 2017). See especially chapters 5 through 7 (pp. 128–204), where he covers the (mostly negative) individual and group experiences of Hungarians and Cubans who had been admitted to the US.

25. See Rogers Brubaker, *Ethnicity without Groups* (Cambridge: Harvard University Press, 2004).

26. On this, see the seminal anthology by Joachim Bahlcke, ed., *Glaubensflüchtlinge: Ursachen, Formen und Auswirkungen frühneuzeitlicher Konfessionsmigration in Europa* (Münster: LIT, 2008).

27. The radicalization of nationalism and the social and intellectual history of its foundations are treated, with reference to the standard literature, in my earlier book, *The Dark Side of Nation States* (see 17–56 of that publication).

28. There is a burgeoning literature on exile and émigrés, although for the most part it has not focused on their cultural production. Some recent studies also take into account everyday lives and living environments. From among these many books I would like to single out Yossi Shain's *The Frontier of Loyalty: Political Exiles in the Age of the Nation State*, 2nd ed. (Ann Arbor: University of Michigan Press, 2005). For German émigrés, see, inter alia, Claus-Dieter Krohn et al., eds., *Handbuch der deutschsprachigen Emigration, 1933–1945* (Darmstadt: Wissenschaftliche Buchgesellschaft, 1998).
29. See Cohen, *In War's Wake*, 150.
30. See e.g., the comparative book by political scientist Rebecca Hamlin, *Let Me Be a Refugee. Administrative Justice and the Politics of Asylum in the United States, Canada, and Australia* (Oxford: Oxford University Press, 2014).
31. Cf. Stéphane Dufoix, *Politiques d'exil: Hongrois, Polonais et Tchécoslovaques en France après 1945* (Paris: Presses Universitaires de France, 2002), 50, cited here by Diaz, *Un asile pour tous les peuples*, 9.
32. My notion of citizenship is a broad one, as defined in T. H. Marshall's classic study *Citizenship and Social Class* (Cambridge: Cambridge University Press, 1950).
33. See again Münch and Heitmeyer, n. 14 above.
34. See Elizabeth Anderson, *The Imperative of Integration* (Princeton: Princeton University Press, 2010). It could be noted, however, that Anderson writes about racial integration and the US.
35. See, among many volumes, Nathan Glazer and Patrick Moynihan, *Beyond the Melting Pot: The Negroes, Puerto Ricans, Jews, Italians, and Irish of New York City*, 2nd ed. (Cambridge: MIT Press, 1970). See, with a dose of self-historicization, Michael Novak, *Unmeltable Ethnics: Politics and Culture in American Life* (New Brunswick: Transaction Publishers, 1996).
36. I am very grateful to Jeremiah Riemer's insights into these American debates. His analysis of ethnic pluralism as a consensus encompassing both multiculturalism on the left and melting pot assimilation on the right was articulated in a lecture delivered in 2001 for the Heinrich Böll Foundation in Germany. A brief summary of the talk—"Streitkultur als Leitkultur: Amerikanische Juden als Außenseiter und Insider der Einwanderungsgesellschaft"—was later published in the newsletter *Informationsdienst Soziokultur*, 1–2002 (47), 5–7.
37. See Marlou Schrover, "Integration and Gender," in Marco Martiniello and Jan Rath, eds., *An Introduction to Immigrant Incorporation Studies: European Perspectives* (Amsterdam: Amsterdam University Press, 2014), 117–142.
38. Very interesting in this regard is the comparative study by Susanne Lachenicht, *Hugenotten in Europa und Nordamerika: Migration und Integration in der Frühen Neuzeit* (Frankfurt am Main: Campus, 2010).
39. Joseph Roth, *Juden auf Wanderschaft*, Karl-Maria Guth, ed. [a completely new edition] (Berlin: Hofenberg, 2015), 41; Anton Kaes, Martin Jay, and Edward Dimendberg, eds.,*The Weimar Republic Sourcebook* [English trans.] (Berkeley: University of California Press, 1995), 263.
40. On the distinction between direct and indirect coercion (which rests, in turn, on the reflections of Krystyna Kersten, a Polish historian who died in 2008), cf. Ther, *Deutsche und polnische Vertriebene*, 96.
41. See the introduction to Lucassen, *Migration, Migration History, History*.
42. Occasionally it is asserted that there are more refugees in relation to the global population than ever before; see e.g., Alexander Betts and Paul Collier, *Refuge: Rethinking Refugee Policy in a Changing World* (New York: Oxford University Press, 2017), 15. That is, however, incorrect; between 1945 and 1948 at least 2 percent of the world's population at the time was in flight (whereas today it is barely 1 percent).
43. Norman Davies, *Europe: A History* (Oxford: Oxford University Press), 9.

44. On Europe's changing borders, see Maria Todorova, *Imagining the Balkans*, 2nd ed. (Oxford: Oxford University Press, 2009).

45. Some historians of southeastern Europe continue to advocate excluding Turkey and the Ottoman Empire from the field of European history; see Konrad Clewing, "Staatensystem und innerstaatliches Agieren im multiethnischen Raum: Südosteuropa im langen 19. Jahrhundert," in Konrad Clewing and Oliver Schmitt, eds., *Geschichte Südosteuropas: Vom frühen Mittelalter bis zur Gegenwart* (Regensburg: Pustet, 2011), 438, 529. A major argument against this is the experience of the postwar era, when Turkey became a NATO member and, like other European states, received Marshall Plan funds. It should also not be forgotten that Turkey, especially after 1848, became a country of exile for refugees from Poland and Hungary. For these references I wish to thank Jared Manasek (Fordham University), who is currently researching exile in the Ottoman Empire.

46. I did so in my book on ethnic cleansing, which to my knowledge was the first monograph on that topic that included a comparative chapter on the Indian partition. I also went to India on a lecture trip in 2007, where I was sometimes confronted with a phenomenon that could be labeled as "Indocentrism." But I refrain from doing so, because I learned a lot from the discussion with Indian and Bangladeshi colleagues and their knowledge of their respective national and Southern Asian history. I understand the discourse about "Eurocentrism" in the US as an emancipation agenda against what was once upon a time taught as "European civilization." I sometimes sympathize with that agenda, though I believe, as aforementioned, that the intellectually more challenging and rewarding agenda might be a critique of Occidentalism.

47. This encountered criticism when the Refugee Convention was adopted and the "universalists" were unable to prevail; on this, see Cohen, *In War's Wake*, 152–154.

48. On the delayed integration of other refugees as well, see Hirschon, *Heirs of the Greek Catastrophe*, 5.

49. On the number of people drowned in flight, cf. International Organization for Migration, "Mediterranean Migrant Arrivals in 2016: 204.311; Deaths 2.443" (31 May 2016), accessible online at https://www.iom.int/news/mediterranean-migrant-arrivals-2016–204311 -deaths-2443 (accessed April 2017).

50. The truth of this is, however, disputed among migration researchers. Leo Lucassen has advanced a well-founded thesis arguing that the present is often viewed too pessimistically, while integration's historical achievements are idealized; on this point, see the introduction to the seminal anthology by Leo Lucassen, David Feldman, and Jochen Oltmer, eds., *Paths of Integration: Migrants in Western Europe, 1880–2004* (Amsterdam: Amsterdam University Press, 2006).

Chapter 1. The roots of intolerance: Religious conflicts and religious refugees

1. On the rebellion and forced conversion in the former kingdom of Granada, see Leonard Harvey, *Muslims in Spain: 1500 to 1614* (Chicago: University of Chicago Press, 2005), 24–37.

2. In 1500 the city of Andarax had been the site of a similar massacre; see Harvey, *Muslims in Spain*, 225, 36.

3. According to Harvey, who in turn refers to calculations by Henri Lapeyre, 116,022 Moriscos were evacuated from the ports of Valencia, about 20,000 were deported to France, and 41,600 departed via other ports; cf. Harvey, *Muslims in Spain*, 316–319.

4. On this figure, see Simon Dubnow, *Weltgeschichte des jüdischen Volkes: Von seinen Uranfängen bis zur Gegenwart*, vol. 5: *Die Geschichte des jüdischen Volkes in Europa: Vom XIII. bis zum XV. Jahrhundert* (Berlin: Jüdischer Verlag, 1927), 405.

5. On the population losses caused by the Ottoman conquest, see Grigor Boykov, "The Human Cost of Warfare: Population Loss during the Ottoman Conquest and the

Demographic History of Bulgaria in the Late Middle Ages and Early Modern Era," in Oliver Schmitt, ed., *The Ottoman Conquest of the Balkans: Interpretations and Research Debates* (Vienna: Verlag der Österreichischen Akademie der Wissenschaften, 2016), 103–166. For alerting me to this essay and additional literature, I thank Dr. Konrad Petrovszky.

6. On the development of the millet system, see Clewing, "Staatensystem und innerstaatliches Agieren im multiethnischen Raum," 506–510 and 516–519.

7. On this, see Mark Mazower, *Salonica, City of Ghosts: Christians, Muslims, and Jews, 1430–1950* (New York: Vintage Books, 2006).

8. In 2006 the German Historical Museum in Berlin even used the Huguenots as the point of departure for an exhibition about 500 years of immigration to Germany; see the exhibition catalog edited by Sabine Beneke and Hans Ottomeyer, *Zuwanderungsland Deutschland: Die Hugenotten* (Wolfratshausen: Edition Minerva, 2005).

9. On the etymology of *réfugié*, see the entry in the *Encyclopédie Universelle*, accessible online at http://encyclopedie_universelle.fracademic.com/65285 (accessed February 2018); also Ernest Klein, *A Comprehensive Etymological Dictionary of the English Language: Dealing with the Origin of Words and Their Sense Development thus Illustrating the History of Civilization and Culture* (Amsterdam: Elsevier, 1971).

10. The way migration is guided by emigration countries has lately become an important topic in the historical study of migration, whereas earlier the focus was above all on the immigrant countries; for a model of this change in perspective, see Tara Zahra, *The Great Departure: Mass Migration from Eastern Europe and the Making of the Free World* (New York: Norton, 2016).

11. On this, see inter alia Philip Benedict et al., eds., *Reformation, Revolt and Civil War in France and the Netherlands, 1555–1585* (Amsterdam: Koninklijke Nederlandse Akademie van Wetenschappen, 1999); Guido Marnef, "Multiconfessionalism in a Commercial Metropolis: The Case of Sixteenth-century Antwerp," in Thomas Max Safley, ed., *A Companion to Multiconfessionalism in the Early Modern World* (Leiden: Brill, 2011), 96.

12. Conversely, of course, the question as to whether all of the Huguenots and Salzburgers were really fleeing religious persecution—or whether other motives played a role in their flight—is an issue that we should subject to critical scrutiny. The Berlin historian Alexander Schunka has doubts about the concept of the religious refugee; see Alexander Schunka, "Konfession und Migrationsregime in der Frühen Neuzeit," *Geschichte und Gesellschaft* 35 (2009), 28–63.

13. Both narratives were stored for several generations in two separate family archives. Toward the end of the nineteenth century, the mother's story was the first to be published in the Preußische Jahrbücher; the style of the translation was somewhat exaggerated so as to capture the attention of the general reader. Both memoirs have been reproduced in their original French, along with a good English translation and an excellent introduction in Carolyn Lougee Chappell, "'The Pains I Took to Save My/His Family': Escape Accounts by a Huguenot Mother and Daughter after the Revocation of the Edict of Nantes," *French Historical Studies* 22/1 (1999), 1–64.

14. The daughter gave her age as seventeen. But, according to the critical evaluation of sources undertaken by Lougee Chappell, Suzanne must have been nineteen at the time.

15. The illustration does not show the historic Robillards, of whom no likenesses have come down to us. All other illustrations in this book show the original persons.

16. On the aforementioned numbers of refugees and victims among the Hutterites, cf. Thomas Winkelbauer, "Die Vertreibung der Hutterer aus Mähren 1622: Massenexodus oder Abzug der letzten Standhaften?" in Joachim Bahlcke, ed., *Glaubensflüchtlinge: Ursachen, Formen und Auswirkungen frühneuzeitlicher Konfessionsmigration in Europa* (Münster: LIT, 2008), 215, 232.

17. On Frankfurt and on the initial reception and additional travels of the Huguenots, see Michelle Magdelaine, "Francfort-sur-le-Main et le réfugiés huguenots," in Guido Braun

and Susanne Lachenicht, eds., *Hugenotten und deutsche Territorialstaaten: Immigrations-politik und Integrationsprozesse* (Munich: Oldenbourg, 2007), 35–50; Barbara Döle-meyer, *Die Hugenotten* (Stuttgart: Kohlhammer, 2006), 38–49. According to Magdelaine, more than half of Frankfurt's residents at the time were migrants. Her essay also provides information about the fundraising conducted on behalf of the refugees.

18. For an international comparative perspective on these privileges, see Barbara Dölemeyer, "Rechtliche Aspekte konfessioneller Migration im frühneuzeitlichen Europa am Beispiel der Hugenottenaufnahme," in Bahlcke, *Glaubensflüchtlinge*, 1–26; see too the brief overview by Heinz Schilling, "Die frühneuzeitliche Konfessionsmigration," *IMIS-Beiträge* 20 (2002), 67–90.

19. On these compulsory services and the protest against them, cf. Ulrich Niggemann, "Konflikte um Immigration als 'antietatistische' Proteste? Eine Revision der Auseinandersetzung bei der Hugenotteneinwanderung," *Historische Zeitschrift* 286/1 (2008), 37–61, esp. 46; on the resistance to these obligations and to refugees, see also Lachenicht, *Hugenotten in Europa und Nordamerika*, 118–123.

20. On these institutions, see Dölemeyer, "Rechtliche Aspekte," 10 f.

21. See Lachenicht, *Hugenotten in Europa und Nordamerika*.

22. On marriage behavior, see ibid., 152, with reference to Berlin; the state of research for other places where immigrants settled, is usually poor.

23. On the political function served by this narrative of integration, see Alexander Schunka, "No Return? Temporary Exile and Permanent Immigration among Confessional Migrants in the Early Modern Era," in Jason Coy, Jared Poley, and Alexander Schunka, eds., *Migrations in the German Lands, 1500–2000* (New York: Berghahn, 2016), 67–87.

24. 1785 was also the anniversary of the Edict of Potsdam, which had encouraged Huguenots to resettle in Prussia.

25. On the Salzburger exiles, see Mack Walker, *The Salzburg Transaction: Expulsion and Redemption in 18th Century Germany* (Ithaca: Cornell University Press, 1992). Prussian tolerance was not always what it was cracked up to be; for example, in the eighteenth century between 800 and 1,000 Mennonites had to leave Prussia; see too Hans-Jürgen Bömelburg, "Konfession und Migration zwischen Brandenburg-Preußen und Polen-Litauen 1640–1772," in Bahlcke, *Glaubensflüchtlinge*, 143.

26. For drawing my attention to this group, I thank Andrzej S. Kamiński; on the exiles, see Michał Kulecki, *Wygnańcy ze Wschodu: Egzulanci w Rzeczypospolitej w ostatnich latach panowania Jana Kazimierza i za panowania Michała Korybuta Wiśniowieckiego* (Warsaw: DIG, 1997). An additional reason for their flight lay in the fact that the czar had confiscated the estates of the exiles because the aristocrats did not fit in with the political system of Russian autocracy.

27. Owing to the border shifts of 1945, most of these villages and towns are now located in Lithuania and Ukraine.

28. See the case of Timişoara in Andreas Helmedach, "Bevölkerungspolitik im Zeichen der Aufklärung: Zwangsumsiedlung und Zwangsassimilierung im Habsburgerreich des 18. Jahrhunderts—eine noch ungelöste Forschungsaufgabe," *Comparativ* 6/1 (1996), 53. It frequently happened that Jews, who were also regarded as undesirables, emigrated along with the Muslims.

29. See Hannes Grandits and Karl Kaser, "Familie und Gesellschaft an der habsburgischen Militärgrenze: Lika und Krbava zu Beginn des 18. Jahrhunderts," in Drago Roksandić, ed., *Microhistory of the Triplex Confinium* (Budapest: Institute on Southeastern Europe, 1996), 27–68.

30. Justin McCarthy even puts the number of Turks killed at 25,000; cf. Justin McCarthy, *Death and Exile: The Ethnic Cleansing of Ottoman Muslims, 1821–1922* (Princeton: Darwin Press, 1995), 12. However, McCarthy intends a narrative of Turkish victimhood. On the deeper roots of this Christian violence, see Philippe Buc, *Heiliger Krieg: Gewalt im Namen des Christentums* (Darmstadt: Zabern, 2014).

31. As an example we may take the war epic *Bergkranz*, which the prince-bishop of Monte-negro, Petar II, Petrović-Njegoš, published in 1847. To this day, this is a work regarded as a magnum opus of Serbian literature. The text celebrates the expulsion, mass killing, and extermination of "the Turks," and numerous examples of such actions are given. Njegoš also called for the killing of the "Turkified"; on this writing and the Serbian my-thology surrounding it, see Holm Sundhaussen, *Geschichte Serbiens: 19.–21. Jahrhundert* (Vienna: Böhlau, 2007), 104–107; on the renewed dissemination of this work in the 1980s, see Sundhaussen, 409, as well as Slobodan Drakulic, "Anti-Turkish Obsession and the Exodus of Balkan Muslims," *Patterns of Prejudice* 43/3–4 (2009), 233–249.

32. Nevertheless, there was also great admiration for the Serbs, who (for example) motivated Leopold von Ranke, one of the founders of modern historical scholarship, to write a his-tory of Serbia, which he published in 1829, with a revised edition in 1844.

33. See Sundhaussen, *Geschichte Serbiens*, 130. The Ottoman garrison was dissolved in 1867.

34. Holquist puts the number at 400,000 to 480,000. Peter Holquist, "To Count, to Extract and to Exterminate: Population Statistics and Population Politics in Late Imperial and Soviet Russia," in Ronald Suny, Grigor Roland, and Terry Martin, eds., *A State of Na-tions: Empire and Nation Making in the Age of Lenin and Stalin* (Oxford: Oxford Uni-versity Press, 2001), 113–119; for higher estimates, see Kemal Karpat, *Ottoman Popula-tion, 1830–1914: Demographic and Social Characteristics* (Madison: University of Wisconsin Press, 1985), 68–70. Karpat puts the total at about two million refugees from the Caucasus. Vladimir Hamed-Troyansky estimates that around one million Muslims from the North Caucasus arrived in the Ottoman Empire: Vladimir Hamed-Troyansky, "Imperial Refugee: Resettlement of Muslims from Russia in the Ottoman Empire, 1860–1914" (Ph.D. diss., Stanford University, 2018), 2. Part of the quantitative difference might be explained by the fact that the Ottoman Refugee Commission did not manage to count every arriving refugee, and by the simple fact that many people died en route.

35. Karpat provides a figure of 227,627 refugees from the Crimea (based on Ottoman ar-chives). Cf. Karpat, *Ottoman Population*, 66; on mortality rates among the refugees, see ibid., 69. In her most recent book on the Crimean war, Mara Kozelsky estimates the num-ber of Tatar refugees and emigrants (based on Russian archives) at 192,360. See Mara Kozelsky, *Crimea in War and Transformation* (Oxford: Oxford University Press, 2019), 202. On the previous deportations carried out by the military, 131.

36. See Dawn Chatty, "Integration without Assimilation in an Impermanent Landscape: Dis-possession and Forced Migration in the Arab Middle East," in Panikos Panayi and Pippa Virdee, eds., *Refugees and the End of Empire: Imperial Collapse and Forced Migra-tion in the Twentieth Century* (Basingstoke: Palgrave Macmillan, 2011), 145.

37. See Alexandre Toumarkine, *Les migrations des populations musulmanes balkaniques en Anatolie, 1876–1913* (Istanbul: Les éditions Isis, 1995), 29. Later in then nineteenth century, the commission was renamed the "Islamic Refugee Commission." In this way the authorities stressed once more the relevance of religious bonds and solidarity.

38. These numbers also come from Toumarkine, *Les migrations*, 29, who refers to calcula-tions by Kemal Karpat.

39. Later the commission was renamed the Idare-i Umumiye-i Muhacirin Komisyonu.

40. Isa Blumi, *Ottoman Refugees, 1878–1939: Migration in a Post-Imperial World* (London: Bloomsbury, 2013), 51. The murder victim was the governor of the Ottoman vilâyet of Kosovo, whose territory was much larger than today's state of the same name.

41. Cf. Hamed-Troyansky, "Imperial Refugee," v and, in more detail, 33–53.

42. On the settlement of the Circassians in Lebanon, see Chatty: "Integration without As-similation," 134.

43. Usually, the regions in question did not profit from the change in rule; for an example, see the regional study by Ulf Brunnbauer, "Abgebrochene Entwicklung? Die Rhodopen

als regionale Fallstudie für die wirtschaftlichen Folgen des Zerfalls des Osmanischen Reiches," *Südost-Forschungen* 59/60 (2000–2001), 324–350.

44. On this controversy, see Wolfgang Höpken, "Flucht vor dem Kreuz? Muslimische Emigration aus Südosteuropa nach dem Ende der Osmanischen Herrschaft (19./20. Jahrhundert)," *Comparativ* 6/1 (1996), 1–24.

45. John Klier and Shlomo Lambroza, eds., *Pogroms: Anti-Jewish Violence in Modern Russian History* (Cambridge: Cambridge University Press, 1992).

46. See Börries Kuzmany, "Jüdische Pogromflüchtlinge in Österreich 1881/82 und die Professionalisierung der internationalen Hilfe," in Börries Kuzmany and Rita Garstenauer, eds., *Aufnahmeland Österreich: Über den Umgang mit Massenflucht seit dem 18. Jahrhundert* (Vienna: Mandelbaum, 2017), 94–125.

47. For a good overview of Jewish emigration out of Europe, see Tobias Brinkmann, "Jüdische Migration," *Europäische Geschichte Online (EGO)*, edited by the Institut für Europäische Geschichte (3 December 2010), accessible online at http://ieg-ego.eu/de/threads/europa-unterwegs/juedische-migration/tobias-brinkmann-juedische-migration (accessed February 2018). Brinkmann estimates the number of East European Jews who emigrated as high as three million, of whom about two million arrived in the United States.

48. The gains in prosperity attributable to emigration are the focus of the book by Livi-Bacci, who concentrates above all on agriculture (or rural settlement); see Massimo Livi-Bacci, *A Short History of Migration* (Cambridge: Polity Press, 2010). Better occupational opportunities were provided by industrialization, which was just taking hold at this time in the United States. By the same logic in reverse, however, this would mean that the occupational integration of refugees and other migrants today is a more difficult challenge, given the Western world's recent inclination toward deindustrialization.

49. On social welfare assistance for Muslim refugees, see Chatty, "Integration without Assimilation," 146.

50. On the population figures, see Toumarkine, *Les migrations*, 73.

51. On all the movements of refugees resulting from the Balkan Wars, see Ther, *The Dark Side*, 61.

52. The original purpose of this analytical portrait was also to make Talaat better known to a wider Western public. When I wrote the original German version of this book, no serious biography of him had yet been published. Talaat's autobiography, which I hoped to use, was an effort to legitimize the Armenian genocide, for which he is revered by Turkish right-wing nationalists, but does not refer to his experience of displacement as a young man. By the time this English-language edition of the book was in preparation, a scholarly biography had finally become available: Hans-Lukas Kieser, *Talaat Pasha: Father of Modern Turkey, Architect of Genocide* (Princeton: Princeton University Press, 2018). My case study here is based on Kieser's lengthy political biography, and on additional readings where I was assisted by Hülya Çelik from the Institute of Oriental Studies at the University of Vienna. On Talaat's autobiography and its posthumous career in Turkey, see Hülya Adak, "Identifying the 'Internal Tumors' of World War I: Talat Paşa'nın Hatıraları [Talat Paşa's Memoirs], or the Travels of a Unionist Apologia into History," in Andreas Bähr et al., eds., *Räume des Selbst: Selbstzeugnisforschung transkulturell* (Vienna: Böhlau, 2007), 151–169.

53. It does not seem to be entirely certain where Talaat was born; according to Kieser (p. 41) it was Edirne, but his family came from the aforementioned Kırcaali, another possible birthplace. See Allama Tabatabai, "Talat Pascha," in *Enzyklopädie des Islam*, online accessible under http://www.eslam.de/begriffe/t/talat_pascha.htm (accessed April 2017).

54. See Kieser, *Talaat Pasha*, 232–283. On the resettlement of refugees from the Balkans, see 254.

55. On the Armenian genocide, see inter alia Vahakn Dadrian, *The History of the Armenian Genocide: Ethnic Conflict from the Balkans to Anatolia to the Caucasus* (New York: Berghahn, 2004); on Turkey's violent nation-building from a longer time perspective, see Uğur Ümit Üngör, *The Making of Modern Turkey: Nation and State in Eastern Anatolia, 1913–50* (New York: Oxford University Press, 2011).
56. On the impact of these traumas, see Erik Jan Zürcher, "The Balkan Wars and the Refugee Leadership of the Early Turkish Republic," in M. Hakan Yavuz and Isa Blumi, eds., *War & Nationalism: The Balkan Wars, 1912–1913, and Their Sociopolitical Implications* (Salt Lake City: University of Utah Press, 2013), 665–678.
57. See again Zürcher, "The Balkan Wars." On the involvement of Turks from southeastern Europe in the leadership of the Young Turks, see also Kieser, *Talaat Pasha*, 55.
58. Of these Muslims, close to six million live in the Balkan states and about ten million in the European part of Turkey. These figures come from Eurostat statistics, the World Factbook (accessible online at https://www.cia.gov/library/publications/the-world-factbook/geos/kv.html), as well as the Statistical Office of Turkey; on the (it goes without saying) controversial 2013 census in Bosnia and Herzegovina, see Ivo Mijnssen, "Eine Volkszählung mit Sprengkraft," *Neue Zürcher Zeitung* (4 July 2016), accessible online at https://www.nzz.ch/international/europa/bosniens-muslime-sind-in-der-mehrheit-eine-volkszaehlung-mit-sprengkraft-ld.103781 (both accessed February 2018).
59. For this, see again Porter, *The Benevolent Empire*.

Chapter 2. The two faces of nationalism: Ethnic cleansing and national solidarity

1. On the origins of modern nationalism, see, inter alia, Miroslav Hroch, *Das Europa der Nationen: Die moderne Nationsbildung im europäischen Vergleich* (Göttingen: Vandenhoeck & Ruprecht, 2005); Eric J. Hobsbawm, *Nations and Nationalism since 1780: Programme, Myth, Reality*, 2nd ed. (Cambridge: Cambridge University Press, 1992).
2. An English translation of the Constitution of 1793 (which was in effect only for a brief period) may be found online at http://oll.libertyfund.org/pages/1793-french-republic-constitution-of-1793 (accessed 24 July 2018). The translation comes from the appendix to Francis Lieber, *On Civil Liberty and Self-Government*, 3rd rev. ed., Theodore D. Woolsey, ed. (Philadelphia: J.B. Lippincott, 1883).
3. Translation (slightly modified here) by R. Anthony Lodge, *French: From Dialect to Standard* (London & New York: Routledge, 1993), 214. The original formulation can be found in Louis-Jean Calvet, *Les langues véhiculaires* (Paris: P.U.F., 1981).
4. On Barère and the decree, cf. Delphine Diaz, *Un asile pour tous les peuples? Exilés et réfugiés étrangers en France au cours du premier XIXe siècle* (Paris: Armand Colin, 2014), 78.
5. The quotes are from a letter by Stein to the governor of Berg, Privy Councilor Justus Gruner; see Freiherr vom Stein, *Briefe und amtliche Schriften*, vol. 5: *Stein in Westfalen, Monumenta Germaniae Historica, Verfassungsfragen (Januar 1819-Mai 1826)*, Erich Botzenhart, ed., newly issued by Walter Hubatsch (Stuttgart: Kohlhammer, 1964), 1–3.
6. On this, see again Maria Todorova, *Imagining the Balkans*, 2nd ed. (Oxford: Oxford University Press, 2009)—a book that is just as relevant today as when it was first published twenty years ago.
7. See for this number and a good first overview, Peter Gatrell, "Refugees," in *1914–1918 Online: International Encyclopedia of the First World War* (8 October 2014), accessible online at http://encyclopedia.1914-1918-online.net/article/refugees (as of April 2017).
8. A German translation of the monumental work by these two Polish colleagues has already appeared (Włodzimierz Borodziej and Maciej Górny, *Der vergessene Weltkrieg: Europas Osten 1912–1923*, 2 vols. [Darmstadt: WBG, 2018]); an English translation is in the making.
9. The Soviet demographer Yevgeniy Volkov calculated as many as 7.4 million Russian refugees, but recent Russian research is more cautious in its estimates; see, inter alia, Irina

Belova, *Vynuždennye migranty: Bežency i Voennoplennye Pervoj mirovoj voiny v Rossii. 1914–1925 gg.* (Moscow, AIRO-XXI: 2014), 10–13. So probably Gatrell is just right. See on the wartime deportations of Germans and Jews, Eric Lohr, *Nationalizing the Russian Empire: The Campaign against Enemy Aliens during World War I* (Cambridge, MA: Harvard University Press, 2003.)

10. These figures are based on Gatrell, "Refugees," and additional data from Julie Thorpe, "Displacing Empire: Refugee Welfare, National Activism and State Legitimacy in Austria-Hungary in the First World War," in Panikos Panayi and Pippa Virdee, eds., *Refugees and the End of Empire. Imperial Collapse and Forced Migration in the Twentieth Century* (Basingstoke: Palgrave Macmillan, 2011), 102–126. The figures on the Ottoman Empire are divided up into 250,000 Armenians who found their way to Russian Armenia and about 150,000 Greeks, many of them recruits. There were unfortunately no reliable data that could be obtained about the flight from Arab regions of the Ottoman Empire.

11. Sperber's autobiography, on which this portrait is largely based, spans three separate books that should long ago have been published in a single volume. The individual citations are Manès Sperber, *Die Wasserträger Gottes: All das Vergangene . . .* (Vienna: Europa-Verlag, 1974) [vol. 1]; Manès Sperber, *Die vergebliche Warnung: All das Vergangene . . .* (Vienna: Europa-Verlag, 1975) [vol. 2]; Manès Sperber, *Bis man mir Scherben auf die Augen legt: All das Vergangene . . .* (Vienna: Europa-Verlag, 1977) [vol. 3]. The quote here about the miserable conditons in Vienna is taken from page 168 of vol. 1, English translation by Joachim Neugroschel from Sperber, *God's Water Carriers* (New York: Holmes & Meier, 1987) [vol. 1], 104. The other volumes in English transation are: *The Unheeded Warning, 1918–1933*, trans. Harry Zohn (New York Holmes & Meier, 1991) [vol. 2] and *Until My Eyes Are Closed with Shards*, trans. Harry Zohn (New York: Holmes & Meier, 1994 [vol. 3]. There is a long list of studies in literary criticism dealing with Sperber's works. For this sketch I have relied above all on the outstanding literary biography by Mirjana Stančić, *Manès Sperber: Leben und Werk* (Frankfurt am Main: Stroemfeld Verlag, 2003); see, in addition, Anne-Marie Corbin, *Manès Sperber: Un combat contre la tyranie (1934–1960)* (Bern: Peter Lang, 1996).

12. On his adolescent years in Vienna, see Stančić, *Manès Sperber*, 72–87.

13. On the arrest and the conditions of detention, cf. ibid., 224–231.

14. Cf. ibid., 354.

15. Sperber, *Bis man mir Scherben auf die Augen legt*, 105 (English edition: Sperber, *Until My Eyes Are Closed with Shards*, 70).

16. Sperber wrote about his internment in the camp in his autobiography: "The people interned in such camps had no rights whatever, but they were strictly forbidden even to complain, as if a complaint were an act of mutiny. Those who planned and operated the camps in this fashion were acting in the spirit of Adolf Hitler." (From Sperber, *Bis man mir Scherben auf die Augen legt*, 298—English translation by Harry Zohn from *Until My Eyes Are Closed with Shards*, 208). For his positive experiences in the parsonage, by contrast, see his account a few pages later (301–302 of the original German memoir, and p. 211 in the English translation).

17. Quoted by Stančić, *Manès Sperber*, 407. Translation here, from the French, in Jennifer Aileen Orth-Veillon, "Ignazio Silone, Albert Camus, and Manès Sperber: Writing between Stalinism and Fascism" (Ph.D. dissertation, Emory University 2011), 203, endnote 6 ([original French wording on page 10]); the dissertation may be downloaded at https://legacy-etd.library.emory.edu/file/view/pid/emory:94m8j/etd/emory:94m7d/orth-veillon_dissertation.pdf (accessed 25 July 2018).

18. Oltmer assumes that there were almost ten million; this estimate is also plausible; cf. Jochen Oltmer, "Flucht, Vertreibung und Asyl im 19. und 20. Jahrhundert," *IMIS Beiträge* 20 (2002), 113.

19. On these numbers, cf. ibid. and Philipp Ther, *The Dark Side*, 67.

20. Carole Fink, *Defending the Rights of Others: The Great Powers, the Jews, and International Minority Protection, 1878–1938* (Cambridge: Cambridge University Press, 2004), 236–264.
21. A German minority that included all of Poland and the different German-speaking groups there, and that also self-identified as German in an ethno-nationalist sense, actually arose only as a result of nation-state formation; on this, see Winson Chu, *The German Minority in Interwar Poland* (Cambridge: Cambridge University Press, 2012). On analogous processes of nation-building among other national minorities, see Ther, *The Dark Side*, 26.
22. The Treaty of Neuilly is reprinted in, among other books, Harold William Vazeille Temperley, ed., *A History of the Peace Conference of Paris*, vol. 5: *Economic Reconstruction and Protection of Minorities*, reprint (London: Oxford University Press, 1969), 305–358; on paragraph 56, see 317.
23. On this commission, see Ther, *The Dark Side*, 73. On the disturbances that preceded it, see Elisabeth Kontogiorgi, *Population Exchange in Greek Macedonia: The Rural Settlement of Refugees 1922–1930* (New York: Oxford University Press, 2006); this book is also the most important study of the problems encountered by Greeks from Asia Minor in their efforts to integrate.
24. On this, cf. the counts based on government documents in Žečo Čankov, *Naselenieto na Bulgariia* (Sofia: Knigoizdvo Kazanluška dolina, 1935), 220. (I thank Dimitar Dimitrov from the International Institute for Peace in Vienna for referring me to this and additional literature on Bulgaria.)
25. On the IMRO, see Stefan Troebst, *Zwischen Arktis, Adria und Armenien: Das östliche Europa und seine Ränder* (Cologne: Böhlau, 2017), 123–132 and 137–144.
26. The quotation in full has Curzon saying that "he deeply regretted that the solution now being worked out should be the compulsory exchange of populations—a thoroughly bad and vicious solution, for which the world will pay a heavy penalty for a hundred years to come"—quoted according to the minutes of the proceedings from the Conference on Near Eastern Affairs, *Lausanne Conference on Near Eastern Affairs, 1922–1923: Records of Proceedings and Draft Terms of Peace* (London: Her Majesty's Stationery Office, 1923), 212.
27. Cf. Wanatowicz, Maria, *Historia społeczno-polityczna Górnego Śląska i Śląska Cieszyńskiego w latach 1918/1945* (Katowice: Wydawnictwo Uniwersytetu Śląskiego, 1994), 147.
28. On this, see Kontogiorgi, *Population Exchange in Greek Macedonia*, 174–175, 182, and 187.
29. Grzegorz Berendt, *Żydzi na terenie Wolnego Miasta Gdańska w latach, 1920–1945 (Działalność kulturalna, polityczna i socjalna)* (Gdańsk: Gdańskie Towarzystwo Naukowe, 1997), 56–57. Between 1926 and 1928, however, citizenship was assigned to 600,000 Jews who had immigrated from Russia following the First World War; on this, see Włodzimierz Borodziej, *Geschichte Polens im 20. Jahrhundert* (Munich: C. H. Beck, 2010), 165.
30. The figures on Romania vary widely. While contemporary observers like John Hope Simpson put the number at around 40,000 Russian Jews, the Romanian historian Vadim Guzun has calculated, on the basis of his archival studies, a number between 60,000 and 100,000; see Vadim Guzun, *Indezirabilii: aspecte mediatice, umanitare și de securitate privind emigrația din Uniunea Sovietică în România interbelică* (Cluj-Napoca: Editura Argonaut, 2013), 30–32. Lower figures are provided by the Russian historian Miroslav Jovanovich, *Russkaya emigraciya na Balkanach, 1920–1940* (Moscow: Russkii puť, 2005).
31. See Tobias Brinkmann, "Ort des Übergangs—Berlin als Schnittstelle der jüdischen Migration aus Osteuropa nach 1918," in Verena Dohrn and Gertrud Pickhan, eds., *Transit*

und Transformation: Osteuropäisch-jüdische Migranten in Berlin, 1918–1939 (Göttingen: Wallstein, 2010), 25–44.

32. See Berendt, *Żydzi na terenie*, 60.
33. See Norman Naimark, *Fires of Hatred: Ethnic Cleansing in Twentieth-Century Europe* (Cambridge, MA: Harvard University Press, 2001), 57–84.
34. See Sperber, *Bis man mir Scherben auf die Augen legt*, 106 (English translation by Harry Zohn in Sperber, *Until My Eyes Are Closed with Shards*, 71).
35. All the figures about flight from Nazi Germany come from Claudena Skran, *Refugees in Inter-War Europe: The Emergence of a Regime* (Oxford: Clarendon Press, 1995), 48–54. This book, well over twenty years old, is among the most important foundations for the book presented here.
36. On this, see ibid., 197–200.
37. On this, see ibid., 201.
38. On this, see ibid., 206.
39. The commission was named after its chair, the Earl William Peel, an elder statesman who had served as a minister in the cabinets of various British governments.
40. Writing in the *Frankfurter Allgemeine Zeitung*, the distinguished historian of Russia Jörg Baberowski (of all people) made an early contribution to criminalizing refugees by speaking of "illegal migrants"; see id., "Europa ist gar keine Wertegemeinschaft," *Frankfurter Allgemeine Zeitung* (14 September 2015), accessible online at http://www.faz.net/aktuell /feuilleton/debatten/joerg-baberowski-ueber-ungesteuerte-einwanderung-13800909 .html (accessed April 2017). Further details on the policies of European and non-European states toward refugees from Germany may be found in Claus-Dieter Krohn, et al. (eds.), *Handbuch der deutschsprachigen Emigration 1933–1945* (Darmstadt: Wissenschaftliche Buchgesellschaft, 1998), 129–468. For an overview, see also Skran, *Refugees in Inter-War Europe*, 216.
41. The history of immigration to Canada and of the rejection of refugees in the 1930s is well documented on the website "Canada—A Country by Consent," http://www .canadahistoryproject.ca/1930s/1930s-07-intolerance.html (accessed April 2017).
42. The wanderings of the *St. Louis* are well documented on the webpage of the United States Holocaust Memorial Museum, https://www.ushmm.org/wlc/en/article.php?ModuleId =10005267 (accessed April 2017).
43. Cf. Sarah A. Ogilvie and Scott Miller, *Refuge Denied: The St. Louis Passengers and the Holocaust* (Madison: University of Wisconsin Press, 2006). On the Dublons, see ibid., 102–104.
44. There is also a German-language publication about the *St. Louis*, with an appendix reprinting the complete diary of Erich Dublon; cf. Georg Reinfelder, *MS 'St. Louis': Die Irrfahrt nach Kuba. Frühjahr 1939* (Teetz: Hentrich & Hentrich, 2002), 125f., 218–234. The diary conveys an almost casual and optimistic atmosphere among the passengers on their way to the US and their subsequent anxiety when the ship was turned back.
45. By June 2017, the manifesto (or the Twitter account under this name) had already attracted more than 70,000 followers: https://twitter.com/stl_manifest?lang=de.
46. On the "Refugee Children Movement," see Wolfgang Benz, Claudia Curio, and Andrea Hammel, eds., *Die Kindertransporte 1938/39: Rettung und Integration* (Frankfurt am Main: Fischer, 2003).
47. On these numbers, see Wolfgang Benz, "Die jüdische Emigration," in Krohn et al., eds., *Handbuch der deutschsprachigen Emigration, 1933–1945*, 6, 9, and 11.
48. Hannah Arendt, "We Refugees," *Menorah Journal* 31, no. 1 (January 1943), 70. The text is available online at http://www.documenta14.de/de/south/35_we_refugees (accessed April 2017). The full article is also reprinted in Arendt, *The Jew as Pariah*, ed. Ron H. Feldman (New York: Grove, 1978), 55–66. (In the original text, Arendt writes about "a new kind of human beings" [sic].

49. See *Menorah Journal*, ibid., 74.
50. Ibid., 69, 73, 77.
51. On the Second Vienna Arbitration, the Treaty of Craiova, and concrete details of their implementation, see Ther, *The Dark Side*, 106–109.
52. See Michael Marrus, *The Unwanted: European Refugees in the Twentieth Century* (New York: Oxford University Press, 1985), 201. In addition, there were 70,000 refugees from Luxemburg and 50,000 from the Netherlands.
53. See ibid., 297. Gatrell puts the number at 40 million civilians forced to flee as a result of the Second World War; cf. Peter Gatrell, *The Making of the Modern Refugee* (Oxford: Oxford University Press, 2013), 89.
54. On this, see the foundational work by Jozo Tomasevich, *War and Revolution in Yugoslavia, 1941–1945: Occupation and Collaboration* (Stanford: Stanford University Press, 2001), 738.
55. The best book on the Polish-Ukrainian "war within the war" remains Grzegorz Motyka's *Tak było w Bieszczadach: Walki polsko-ukraińskie, 1943–1848* (Warsaw: Oficyna Wydawnicza Volumen), 1999.
56. On the expulsions from Nazi-occupied territories, cf. Ther, *The Dark Side*, 95–104.
57. There is now a secondary literature on this subject, which for a long time had hardly been researched because it was overshadowed by crimes of the German occupation that were even more gruesome; on the expulsion from Poland and the Warthegau, see Maria Rutowska, *Wysiedlenia ludności polskiej z Kraju Warty do Generalnego Gubernatorstwa, 1939–1941* (Poznań: Instytut Zachodni, 2003). There is also a very detailed and impressive diary from the Zamość district: Zygmunt Klukowski, *Zamojszczyzna*, vol. 1: *1918–1943* (Warsaw, Karta, 2008); in that book, see 126–127, 177–179, and 197.
58. Quotation from Winston S. Churchill, *His Complete Speeches, 1897–1963*, vol. 7: *1943–1949*, Robert Rhodes James (New York: Chelsea House Publishers, 1974), 7069.
59. On this, see Rüdiger Overmans, "Personelle Verluste der deutschen Bevölkerung durch Flucht und Vertreibung," *Dzieje Najnowsze* 26/2 (1994), 60.
60. Estimates vary in the literature. According to Stedingk, it was 1.83 million refugees, of whom a good half were not German speakers. According to Helczmanowski, the number was 1.43 million, of whom about 800,000 were not German-speaking. See Yvonne von Stedingk, *Die Organisation des Flüchtlingswesens in Österreich seit dem Zweiten Weltkrieg: Treatises on Refugee Problems* (Vienna: Braumüller, 1970), 27.
61. Exceptions were made only for refugees who had close family members in Austria. In the end, therefore, about 350,000 refugees, most of them from areas near the Czech-Austrian border in southern Moravia and Bohemia, were able to remain in Austria. For more information about Austrian refugee politics, there is a good collection of articles in *Mitteilungen des oberösterreichischen Landesarchivs* 19 (2000), which shows the situation of the refugees in postwar Upper Austria and conveys the official stance of Austrian historiography. For a more critical approach and a detailed survey about the situation in Lower Austria in 1945/46, see Niklas Perzi, "Aufnahme und Abschub. Die Sudetendeutschen in Niederösterreich 1945/46," *Jahrbuch für Landeskunde von Niederösterreich*, NF 82 (2016), 135–233.
62. On the Jewish DPs, see (inter alia) Michael Brenner, *After the Holocaust: Rebuilding Jewish Lives in Postwar Germany*, trans. Barbara Harshav (Princeton: Princeton University Press, 1997), 7–41, as well as the contemporary witness accounts from the DP camps on pages 77–99. The maximum number of Jewish DPs reached 182,000 in the summer of 1947, but before that there had been several hundred thousand refugees who had already fled onward to third countries or been taken in there. See on the DPs also Angelika Königseder and Juliane Wetzel, *Lebensmut im Wartesaal: Die jüdischen DPs (Diplaced Persons) im Nachkriegsdeutschland* (Frankfurt am Main: Fischer Taschenbuch, 1994).
63. See Ruth Klüger, *Still Alive: A Holocaust Girlhood Remembered* (New York: Feminist Press at the City University of New York, 2001), 138. The entire flight is treated on

pages 135–149. The quote about the "jumble of requirements and quotas" for her American entry visa is on p. 158. The German original of the book was published as Ruth Klüger, *Weiter leben: eine Jugend* (Göttingen: Wallstein, 1992).

64. Klüger, *Still Alive*, 145.

65. On this, see a conversation between Stalin and Gheorghe Gheorghiu-Dej, general secretary of the Romanian Communist Party, in Tatiana V. Volokitina et al., eds., *Vostočnaja Evropa v dokumentach rossijskich archivov, 1944–1953 gg.*, vol. 1: *1944–1948 gg.* (Novosibirsk: Sibirskii chronograf, 1997), 582. On the conflict surrounding Transylvania, see Holly Case, *Between States: The Transylvanian Question and the European Idea during World War II* (Stanford: Stanford University Press, 2009). Former soldiers in the Hungarian army were, however, exempted from this repatriation.

66. On the sequence of events in this repatriation, see Philipp Ther, *Deutsche und polnische Vertriebene: Gesellschaft und Vertriebenenpolitik in der SBZ/DDR und in Polen, 1945–1956* (Göttingen: Vandenhoeck & Ruprecht, 1998), as well as the extensive documentation of sources in Stanislaw Ciesielski, ed., *Umsiedlung der Polen aus den ehemaligen polnischen Ostgebieten nach Polen in den Jahren 1944–1947* (Marburg: Herder Institut, 2006).

67. On the "exodus" of the Italians from Istria and Dalmatia, see Marina Cattaruzza, *L'Italia e il confine orientale, 1866–2006* (Bologna: Il Mulino, 2007), as well as the regional study by Piero Purini, *Metamorfosi etniche: I cambiamenti di popolazione a Trieste, Gorizia, Fiume e in Istria: 1914–1975* (Udine: Kappa Vu, 2010).

68. I dedicated a chapter to the "British Track of Ethnic Cleansing" in my previous book. See Ther, *The Dark Side of Nation States*, 247–249.

69. For a good overview, see Silvia Salvatici, "Between National and International Mandates: Displaced Persons and Refugees in Postwar Italy," *Journal of Contemporary History* 49 (2014), 514–536. This special issue of the JCH is devoted to "Refugees and the Nation-State in Europe, 1919–59."

70. On the Italians in Libya, see the comprehensive study by Angelo Del Boca, *Gli italiani in Libia*, 2 vols. (Milan: Mondadori, 1993/94).

71. For more details on Saxony, see my earlier book: Ther, *Deutsche und polnische Vertriebene*, 116–135. On Hamburg, see Evelyn Glensk, Rita Bake, and Oliver von Wrochem, eds., *Die Flüchtlinge kommen: Ankunft und Aufnahme in Hamburg nach Kriegsende* (Hamburg: Ergebnisse Verlag, 1998).

72. See Michael Schwartz, *Vertriebene und 'Umsiedlerpolitik': Integrationskonflikte in den deutschen Nachkriegs-Gesellschaften und die Assimilationsstrategien in der SBZ/DDR, 1945 bis 1961* (Munich: Oldenbourg, 2004).

73. Several years later the subject received more extensive book-length treatment by the same author in Paul Lüttinger, *Integration der Vertriebenen: Eine empirische Analyse* (Frankfurt am Main: Campus, 1989).

74. See Andreas Kossert, *Kalte Heimat: Die Geschichte der deutschen Vertriebenen nach 1945* (Berlin: Siedler, 2008).

75. See Eugen Lemberg and Friedrich Edding, *Die Vertriebenen in Westdeutschland: Ihre Eingliederung und ihr Einfluss auf Gesellschaft, Wirtschaft, Politik und Geistesleben*, 3 vols. (Kiel: Ferdinand Hirt, 1959).

76. The latter, however, applies only to men; women expellees did not work as frequently as natives, which was attributable to more traditional values and above all to the availability of jobs; on unemployment and employment among expellees, see ibid., 111 and 136.

77. On the border closing, see Brunhilde Scheuringer, "Die Situation der sudetendeutschen Flüchtlinge in Oberösterreich seit 1945," *Mitteilungen des Oberösterreichischen Landesarchivs*, vol. 19 (Linz: Oberösterreichisches Landesarchiv, 2000), 145–146. On the discussion concerning the Gablonzers, some of whom ended up in Upper Austria during their flight, see Gertrude Enderle-Burcel and Rudolf Jeřábek, eds., *Protokolle des Ministerrates der Zweiten Republik: Kabinett Leopold Figl I: 20. Dezember 1945 bis 8.*

November 1949, vol. 1: *20. Dezember 1945 bis 9. April 1946* (Vienna: Verlag Österreich, 2004), 82. I thank Pauli Aro for this reference.

78. On the "refugee industries," see two relevant essays in Lemberg and Edding, *Die Vertriebenen in Westdeutschland*, vol. 2, 166–374, esp. 334.

79. Ibid., vol. 1, 105. On the convergence and dissolution of old milieus, see also the essay by Alfred Karasek-Langer in the same volume (especially 682–683). It is not entirely a coincidence that the essay's title "Nationhood in a State of Flux" (the word is *Volkstum* in the original German—"Volkstum im Umbruch"—and it imparts an ethno-national connotation to "nationhood") sounds like something out of German history before 1945. Karasek-Langer was a specialist on German settlement enclaves in Eastern Europe, as an SS Obersturmführer (first lieutenant in the Nazi paramilitary force that included the Gestapo) he was responsible for the resettlement of the Volhynian and Bessarabian Germans during the war, and later for the plundering of Soviet universities and art collections.

80. This statement about the Polish-German border is documented in a short biographical sketch of Steinbach that appears on the website of the public radio station RBB (Rundfunk Berlin-Brandenburg): http://www.deutscheundpolen.de/personen/person_jsp/key=erika_steinbach.html (accessed April 2017).

81. Cf. Philipp Ther, "Zentrum gegen Vertreibungen," in Detlef Brandes, Holm Sundhaussen, and Stefan Troebst, eds., *Lexikon der Vertreibungen: Deportation, Zwangsaussiedlung und ethnische Säuberung im Europa des 20. Jahrhunderts* (Vienna: Böhlau, 2010), 736–739.

82. Cf. the letter of resignation on her website, http://www.erika-steinbach.de/erklaerung.html (accessed April 2017).

83. There is an excellent English language book about the refugee politics of the postwar German governments and how this priority shaped their foreign policy. See Pertti Ahonen, *After the Expulsion: West Germany and Eastern Europe, 1945–1990* (New York: Oxford University Press, 2003).

84. See "League of Nations: Mandates Palestine report of the Palestine Royal Commission, presented by the Secretary of State for the colonies to the United Kingdom Parliament by Command of His Britannic Majesty (July 1937)," *Jewish Virtual Library*, accessible online at http://www.jewishvirtuallibrary.org/jsource/History/peel1.html (accessed April 2017).

85. The additional sequence of events for this flight (through September 1948) and the distribution of refugees are recorded with considerable detail in a report to the UN Security Council; see United Nations, *Progress Report of the United Nations Mediator on Palestine (16 September 1948)*, accessible online at https://digitallibrary.un.org/record/703168/files/A_648-EN.pdf (accessed April 2019).

86. Cited by Ilan Pappé, *The Ethnic Cleansing of Palestine* (Oxford: Oneworld, 2006), 49. Pappé's thesis of ethnic cleansing planned well in advance, however, is controversial. In his own study, Benny Morris stresses the military components and the short-term nature of the planning; see Benny Morris, *1948: A History of the First Arab-Israeli War* (New Haven: Yale University Press, 2008). By contrast, the historian Nur Masalha, who teaches in England (and is of Palestinian descent), advocates a longue-durée thesis; see his *Expulsion of the Palestinians: The Concept of 'Transfer' in Zionist Political Thought, 1882–1948* (Washington, DC: Institute for Palestine Studies, 1992). He emphasizes a broader pattern of European thinking about the Balkans and the Near East that was evidently shaped by Orientalism and colonialism. And, indeed, as early as the beginning of the twentieth century, British, French, German, and Swiss sociologists and ethnologists were proposing extensive population shifts for this part of the world; on these intellectual architects of ethnic cleansing, see Ther, *The Dark Side*, 33.

87. See, too, the fundamental critique offered by Didier Fassin, *Humanitarian Reason: A Moral History of the Present* (Berkeley: University of California Press, 2012).

88. Quoted from an original document in Pappé, *The Ethnic Cleansing of Palestine*, 166.

89. For an overview, see Malka Hillel Shulewitz, ed., *The Forgotten Millions: The Modern Jewish Exodus from Arab Lands* (London: Bloomsbury, 2001). In addition, there are numerous detailed studies on the individual countries of origin that, for reasons of space, cannot be cited here.

90. See Yfaat Weiss, *A Confiscated Memory: Wadi Salib and Haifa's Lost Heritage*, Avner Greenberg, trans. (New York: Columbia University Press, 2011). On Tiberias, see the research of the Palestinian historian Mustafa Abbasi, "The War on the Mixed Cities: The Depopulation of Arab Tiberias and the Destruction of its Old, 'Sacred' City (1948–9)," *Holy Land Studies* 7/1 (2008), 45–80. The findings treated here are largely derived from a 2005–2008 research project of the German-Israeli-Foundation entitled "Out of Place: Ethnic Migration, Nation State Formation, and Property Regimes in Poland, Czechoslovakia and Israel," in which the author was a participant, and which included conferences and research visits in Israel. On Jaffa, see Daniel Monterescu, *Jaffa Shared and Shattered: Contrived Coexistence in Israel/Palestine* (Bloomington: University of Indiana Press, 2015).

91. See again, by way of example, Lüttinger's study on the integration of German expellees.

92. The Israeli writer Amos Oz has captured this beautifully in his autobiographical novel *Eine Geschichte von Liebe und Finsternis* (Berlin: Suhrkamp, 2008); see, inter alia, 112–113. See also the American edition: *A Tale of Love and Darkness* (Orlando: Harcourt, 2004).

93. On this (from a postcolonial perspective that is pertinent here), see Yehouda Shenhav, *The Arab Jews: A Postcolonial Reading of Nationalism, Religion, and Ethnicity* (Stanford: Stanford University Press, 2006).

94. One poignant example is the story of Charlotte Knobloch, for many years the chair of the Central Council of Jews in Germany. Her mother, who had initially converted to Judaism yet was regarded as "Aryan," divorced her Jewish father in 1936. The father managed, however, to keep the little girl hidden with acquaintances who passed her off as their own daughter; on this, see Philipp Gessler, "Eine hartnäckige Deutsche," *taz* (6 June 2006), accessible online at http://www.taz.de/Archiv-Suche/!423039&s=&SuchRahmen =Print/ (accessed April 2017).

95. On these estimates, see Nadine Picaudou, "The Historiography of the 1948 Wars," *Online Encyclopedia of Mass Violence* (1 November 2008), accessible online at http://www .sciencespo.fr/mass-violence-war-massacre-resistance/en/document/historiography -1948-wars (accessed April 2017).

96. See Avi Shlaim, *The Politics of Partition: King Abdullah, the Zionists, and Palestine, 1921–1951* (Oxford: Oxford University Press, 1998). This version of partition, which prevented the Palestinians from getting their own state, was supported by Great Britain. In this way, London hoped to build up an ally in the Near East, which it succeeded in doing; on this, cf. ibid., 111.

97. See Jalal Al Husseini and Riccardo Bocco, "The Status of the Palestinian Refugees in the Near East: The Right of Return and UNRWA in Perspective," *Refugee Survey Quarterly* 28/2–3 (2010), 263, fn. 9. Jordanian policy toward the Palestinians is also treated extensively in Shaul Mishal, *West Bank/East Bank—The Palestinians in Jordan, 1949–1967* (New Haven: Yale University Press, 1978).

98. See Abbas Shiblak, "Residency Status and Civil Rights of Palestinian Refugees in Arab Countries," *Journal of Palestine Studies* 25/3 (1996), 38; on this, see also Khalil, "Socioeconomic Rights."

99. This misleading metaphor is much used by Western media outlets to this day. A quick Internet search will yield a long list of hits.

100. On this, and on the problems of the Palestinians, see Dorothée Klaus, "Palästinenser im Libanon zwischen Ghetto und Integration," in Stefan Wild and Hartmut Schild, eds., *Akten des 27. Deutschen Orientalistentages (Bonn—28. September bis 2. Oktober 1998): Norm und Abweichung* (Würzburg: Ergon, 2001), 499–509; see also the study—suffused with a tone of Palestinian nation-building, nevertheless worth reading—by Rosemary

Sayigh, *Too Many Enemies: The Palestinian Experience in Lebanon* (London: Zed Books, 1994).

101. Currently there is, unfortunately, only one foreign-language book (bound in a mauve cover) about Queen Rania, but its thirty-two pages do contain the most important biographical details: Mary Englar, *Queen Rania of Jordan* (Mankato: Capstone Press, 2009).

102. See Asem Khalil, "Socioeconomic Rights of Palestinian Refugees in Arab countries," *International Journal of Refugee Law* 23/4 (2011), 701.

103. Cf. Maya Sela, "Jordan's Queen Rania Rejects Offer to Publish Hebrew Edition of Her Children's Book," *Haaretz* (14 July 2010), accessible online at http://www.haaretz.com /jordan-s-queen-rania-rejects-offer-to-publish-hebrew-edition-of-her-children-s-book -1.301791 (accessed April 2017). The queen, however, soon disputed that an offer had been made.

104. Quoted in Kayleigh Lewis, "Jordan's Queen Rania Visits Child Refugees in Lesbos and Calls for 'Exceptional Response'," *The Independent* (25 April 2016), accessible online at http://www.independent.co.uk/news/world/europe/refugee-crisis-jordan-queen-rania -visits-refugees-lesbos-calls-for-exceptional-response-a7000596.html (accessed April 2017).

105. See Klaus, "Palästinenser im Libanon zwischen Ghetto und Integration," 505.

106. Nevertheless, in 2010—a good sixty years after Palestinian refugees started arriving in Lebanon—access to the labor market was eased. Since then Palestinians can receive services in return for the contributions they pay into social insurance funds. They remain ineligible to vote, and access to public schools and universities remains restricted, as in Egypt; see Khalil, "Socioeconomic rights," 698–701.

107. On the Gaza Strip and Egypt's policy toward the Palestinians, see Oroub El-Abed, *Unprotected: Palestinians in Egypt since 1948* (Washington, DC: Institute for Palestine Studies/Ottawa: International Development Research Centre, 2009), 22.

108. On this, see Howard Adelman and Elazar Barkan, *No Return, No Refuge: Rites and Rights in Minority Repatriation* (New York: Columbia University Press, 2011). This astute analysis shows how much the perpetuation of refugee status and the "right of return" have shaped Palestinian national identity. The book would be even more persuasive if it had reviewed the state of research on the ethnic cleansing of Palestinians, which is relativized and played down in some passages.

109. On the relevant document, Resolution 194 (III) of the UN General Assembly from December 1948, see Adelman and Barkan, *No Return, No Refuge*, 190.

110. Journalists' coverage of this problem at the time is discussed in detail by Matthew Frank, *Expelling the Germans: British Opinion and Post-1945 Population Transfer in Context* (Oxford: Oxford University Press, 2007), 122–163. According to Frank, Victor Gollancz, a British publisher from a Polish-Jewish family, played a key role in changing public opinion. Unfortunately, he failed to do so during wartime, although he did draw broad public attention to the mass murder of Jews in concentration camps as early as 1943.

111. The official designations for these conventions are accessible on the website of the UN; see the original texts at http://www.un.org/en/universal-declaration-human-rights/index .html and http://www.un-documents.net/a3r260.htm (both accessed April 2017). Due to lack of space, we are using abbreviated designations here.

112. However, this irresponsibility is not restricted to Putin's Russia. It also exists in the US, e.g., when John Bolton, the (already former) US ambassador to the United Nations, stated in 2007 that there was no connection between the US invasion of Iraq and the later mass flight out of that country. See García, *The Refugee Challenge*, 145–146. The Obama administration thought differently: up to 2013, 85,000 refugees from Iraq had been allowed to enter the US.

113. This section and the following remarks on the flight from Algeria are based on the foundational French literature that I reviewed for a 2012 lecture in Paris comparing refugees in Germany, France, and Poland; see, inter alia, Benjamin Stora, *Histoire de l'Algérie*

coloniale (1830–1954), 2nd ed. (Paris: La Découverte, 2004); Marco Ferro, ed., *Le livre noir du colonialisme: XVIe-XXIe siècle: De l'extermination à la repentance* (Paris: Robert Laffont, 2003); Benjamin Stora, *Histoire de la guerre d'Algérie (1954–1962)*, 4th ed. (Paris: La Découverte, 2004); Daniel Lefeuvre, "Les pieds-noirs," in Mohammed Harbi and Benjamin Stora, eds., *La guerre d'Algérie* (Paris: Robert Laffont, 2004), 381–410; see also, in German, Christiane Kohser-Spohn and Frank Renken, eds., *Trauma Algerienkrieg: Zur Geschichte und Aufarbeitung eines tabuisierten Konflikts* (Frankfurt am Main: Campus, 2006).

114. On this, see Gil Loescher, "The UNHCR and World Politics: State Interests vs. Institutional Autonomy," *International Migration Review* 35/1 (2001), 35 f. (This volume also contains a number of other essays about the UNHCR that are worth reading but cannot all be cited here for lack of space.) In conducting this literature search and research on the UNCHR, I was aided by Pauli Aro, now a doctoral candidate at the EUI in Florence, whom I wish to thank once more for his assistance.

115. See ibid., 36–38; Michael Barnett, "Humanitarianism with a Sovereign Face: UNHCR in the Global Undertow," *International Migration Review* 35/1 (2001), 255–259.

116. On this critique, see Loescher, "The UNHCR and World Politics," 46–53; Betts and Collier, *Refuge: Rethinking Refugee Policy*, 227–236. On the problem of the IDPs, see Young Hoon Song, "International Humanitarianism and Refugee Protection: Consequences of Labeling and politicization," *Journal of International and Area Studies* 20/2 (2013), 1–19.

117. See Eric Savarèse, *L'invention des Pieds-Noirs* (Paris: Séguier, 2002).

118. There is a growing literature on the Harkis; for a first overview in English with further references, see Abderahmen Moumen, "Housing the Harkis: Long-term Segregation," accessible at https://www.metropolitiques.eu/IMG/pdf/MET-Moumen-en.pdf (accessed December 2018).

119. On the absorption and integration of the "repatriés," see Yann Scioldo-Zürcher, *Devenir métropolitain: Politique d'intégration et parcours de rapatriés d'Algérie en metropole (1954–2005)* (Paris: Éditions de l'École des hautes études en sciences sociales, 2010), as well as an English-language summary of his book in Yann Scioldo-Zürcher, "The Postcolonial Repatriations of the French of Algeria in 1962: An Emblematic Case of a Public Integration Policy," in Manuel Borutta and Jan C. Jansen, eds., *Vertriebene and Pieds-Noirs in Postwar Germany and France: Comparative Perspectives* (Basingstoke: Palgrave Macmillan, 2016), 95–114.

120. On the reception of the "repatriés" (from their perspective as well), see Jean-Jacques Jordi, *1962: L'arrivée Des Pieds-Noirs* (Paris: Autrement, 1995), 27 and 49–50.

121. The re-calculation and computation of purchasing power can be undertaken on the website of the French Institut national de la statistique et des études économiques: https://www.insee.fr/fr/information/2417794 (accessed April 2017); for research on this, I again thank Manuel Neubauer from the IOG. One consequence of the restitution payments for land and other property, however, was that the very unequal colonial social order was reproduced in France.

122. Etemad estimates the number of postcolonial migrants through 1990 at a minimum of 1.75 to a maximum of 2.2 million people; see Bouda Etemad, "Europe and Migration after Decolonisation," *Journal of European Economic History* 27/3 (1998), 465.

123. See Dominique Schnapper, "L'échec du 'modèle républicain'? Réflexion d'une sociologue," *Annales: Histoire, Sciences Sociales* 61/4 (2006), 759–776. In this article, moreover, Schnapper draws interesting comparisons with Great Britain and Germany. While political integration was much more successful in France (among other reasons because of its citizenship law), the economic situation of postcolonial immigrants and their descendants ranks worst there.

124. On the pieds-noirs and their involvement in the Front National (which until today has its bastions in communities with a high proportion of Algerian French and their

descendants), see Emmanuelle Comtat, *Les pieds-noirs et la politique: quarante ans après le retour* (Paris: Presses de Sciences Po, 2009), 237–266.

125. A good overview is provided by Jean-Louis Miège and Colette Dubois, eds., *L'Europe retrouvée: Les migrations de la décolonisation* (Paris: L'Harmattan, 1994), where the compulsive character of postcolonial remigration is emphasized (see the book's introduction [10]), as well as (in abbreviated form) Etemad, "Europe and Migration after Decolonisation."

126. Cf. Guno Jones, *Tussen onderdanen, rijksgenoten en Nederlanders: Nederlandse politici over burgers uit Oost en West en Nederland, 1945–2005* (Amsterdam: Rozenberg, 2007), 85–86, 369–370.

127. Cf. Guy Vanthemsche, *Belgium and the Congo, 1885–1980* (New York: Cambridge University Press, 2012), 208–209.

128. On colonial remigration to Portugal, see Norrie MacQueen, *The Decolonization of Portuguese Africa: Metropolitan Revolution and the Dissolution of Empire* (London: Longman, 1997).

129. In France this context of flight from postcolonial wars entered into legislative language favoring the French from Algeria and other colonies. In that legislation the compulsive character of remigration was explicitly emphasized; cf. Scioldo-Zürcher, "The Postcolonial Repatriations of the French of Algeria in 1962," 97.

130. See varying estimates in Colette Dubois and Jean-Louis Miège, "Introduction," in Jean-Louis Miège and Colette Dubois, eds., *L'Europe retrouvée: Les migrations de la décolonisation* (Paris: L'Harmattan, 1994), 18. Etemad estimates the number of postcolonial refugees and remigrants at between 3.3 and 4 million people.

131. On the history of Cyprus, see the comprehensive, four-volume series by Heinz A. Richter, above all *Geschichte der Insel Zypern*, vol. 4 (1 + 2): *1965–1977* (Mainz: Rutzen, 2009).

132. On this, see United Nations Security Council, S/11789 (5 August 1975), "Interim Report of the Secretary General pursuant to Security Council Resolution 370 (1975)." The accords are accessible online at https://documents-dds-ny.un.org/doc/UNDOC/GEN/N75/151/45/PDF/N7515145.pdf?OpenElement (September 2016 and April 2017; unfortunately, the link is not always reliable).

133. On flight from Bulgaria, see Brandes, Sundhaussen, and Troebst, eds., *Lexikon der Vertreibungen*, 662–667.

134. On the collapse of Yugoslavia and the ensuing wars, see Holm Sundhaussen, *Jugoslawien und seine Nachfolgestaaten 1943–2011: Eine ungewöhnliche Geschichte des Gewöhnlichen* (Vienna, Böhlau, 2012). Of course, there is also a lot of English literature on the violent dissolution of Yugoslavia. See, inter alia, Susan Woodward, *Balkan Tragedy: Chaos and Dissolution after the Cold War* (Washington, DC: Brookings Institution, 1995); Steven L. Burg and Paul S. Shoup, *The War in Bosnia-Hercegovina: Ethnic Conflict and International Intervention* (Armonk, NY: M.E. Sharpe, 1999).

135. These incidents are documented in the court records of the International Criminal Tribunal for the former Yugoslavia (ICTY). On this, see the "Vukovar Hospital" trial in Den Haag at http://www.icty.org/case/mrksic/4 (accessed April 2017).

136. The best analysis of the conflict's military dimension is still Central Intelligence Agency/Office of Russian and European Analysis, *Balkan Battlegrounds: A Military History of the Yugoslav Conflict, 1990–1995*, vol. 1 (Washington, DC: CIA, 2002).

137. Everyday life in the Serbian ethnocracy is penetratingly analyzed by Armina Galijaš, *Eine bosnische Stadt im Zeichen des Krieges: Ethnopolitik und Alltag in Banja Luka (1990–1995)*, (Munich: Oldenbourg, 2011).

138. On Austria, see Rainer Münz, Peter Zuser, and Josef Kytir, "Grenzüberschreitende Wanderungen und ausländische Wohnbevölkerung: Struktur und Entwicklung," in Heinz Fassmann and Irene Stacher, eds., *Österreichischer Migrations- und Integrationsbericht: Demographische Entwicklungen—sozioökonomische Strukturen—rechtliche Rahmenbedingungen* (Vienna: Drava Verlag, 2003), 26–27. In the case of the Federal Republic of

Germany, nobody at the time was circulating an account of the "refugee crisis" (as they do today) attributing Germany's acceptance of displaced persons to guilt feelings about the country's Nazi past.

139. Numerous reports are recorded in the Open Society Archive in Budapest and were already examined by the author in preparing earlier publications; see the collections deposited there: HU OSA, 304-0-2 (International Human Rights Law Institute, Interim and Supplementary Reports of the UN Special Rapporteur); see further HU OSA 304-0-6 (International Human Rights Law Institute, Materials on Ethnic Cleansing); HU OSA 304-0-4 (International Human Rights Law Institute, United Nations, International Red Cross Committee, International Court of Justice).

140. The first case in which mass rapes were attested and punished by the ICTY concerned the Bosnian Serb commander Dragoljub Kunarać, who commanded a VRS unit that was made up overwhelmingly of volunteers and that maintained a house near the East Bosnian city of Foča in which numerous women were held captive and raped. The incidents there are documented in the court records of the ICTY. The files are accessible only at http://www.icty.org/x/cases/kunarac/ind/en/kun-iii991108e.pdf (accessed April 2017).

141. Recent studies like Miriam Gebhardt's book show that numerous rapes also took place as the US Army invaded; see Miriam Gebhardt, *Crimes Unspoken: The Rape of German Women at the End of the Second World War* (Cambridge: Polity, 2017). Gebhardt's estimates of 190,000 rapes by GIs are, however, disputed.

142. See Naimark, *Fires of Hatred*, 167–170.

143. The legal foundation for the refugees' absorption was the Bund-Länder-Aktion für bosnische Kriegsvertriebene (Federal-State Action for Bosnian War Expellees), which ceased operations in 1998. On repatriation and the option to stay, see the European comparison undertaken by Annegret Bendiek, *Der Konflikt im ehemaligen Jugoslawien und die Europäische Integration: Eine Analyse ausgewählter Politikfelder* (Wiesbaden: VS Verlag für Sozialwissenschaften, 2004), 79–85. On the percentage of Bosnians who remained in Austria, see Münz, Zuser, and Kytir, "Grenzüberschreitende Wanderungen und ausländische Wohnbevölkerung," 26–27.

144. On the guest workers, see Ulf Brunnbauer, "Labour Emigration from the Yugoslav Area from the Late 19th Century until the End of Socialism: Continuities and Changes," in id., ed., *Transnational Societies: Transterritorial Politics: Migrations in the (Post-)Yugoslav Region, 19th–21st Century* (Munich: Oldenbourg, 2009), 17–50.

145. See the study by Heinz Fassmann, Josef Kohlbacher, and Ursula Reeger, *Integration durch berufliche Mobilität? Eine empirische Analyse der beruflichen Mobilität ausländischer Arbeitskräfte in Wien* (Vienna: Verlag der Österreichischen Akademie der Wissenschaften, 2001).

146. On the data about occupational branches, see the chapter "Arbeit und Beruf" in the report issued by Statistik Austria/Kommission für Migrations- und Integrationsforschung [Austrian Statistics/Commission for Migration and Integration Research], *Migration & Integration: Zahlen. Daten. Indikatoren 2013* (Vienna: Statistik Austria, 2013). On the data about de-skilling, see Bettina Stadler and Beatrix Wiedenhofer-Galik, "Dequalifizierung von Migrantinnen und Migranten am österreichischen Arbeitsmarkt," *Statistische Nachrichten* 5 (2011), 383–399, as well as Martina Stadlmayr, *Arbeitsmarktintegration und Dequalifizierung von Menschen mit Migrationshintergrund* (Universität Linz: unpublished dissertation, 2012), an abbreviated version of which is accessible at http://www.ibe.co.at/fileadmin/AblageBox/TEAM/Stadlmayr/Kurzfassung_Diss_Stadlmayr.pdf (accessed April 2017).

147. These were also the findings of the studies for the aforementioned research seminars at the University of Vienna, although these works were not, as a rule, published. Here I refer to a study by Karin Weißinger and Mersiha Zukorlic about the integration of Bosnian refugees into the Austrian labor market (prepared in the summer semester of 2014); the

authors, in addition to evaluating social science studies of the subject, conducted oral history interviews.

148. Labor market integration was delayed in countries where refugees were not allowed to work right after their arrival. Hence, openness to refugees saves social expenditure and pays off economically. See for this conclusion the comparative study by Mikkel Barslund, Matthias Busse, Karolien Lenaerts, Lars Ludolph, and Vilde Renman, "Integration of Refugees: Lessons from Bosnians in Five EU Countries," *Intereconomics* 5 (2017), 257–263.

149. Carolin Leutloff-Grandits, "Post-Dayton Ethnic Engineering in Croatia through the Lenses of Property Issues and Social Transformations," *Journal of Genocide Research* 18/4 (2016), 485–502.

150. On the practice of deportation, see "Bosnien-Flüchtlinge: Vor die Hunde," *Der Spiegel* 15 (1997), 36–37, accessible at http://www.spiegel.de/spiegel/print/d-8693231.html (accessed April 2017).

151. Cf. Naimark, *Fires of Hatred*, 167–170.

152. On this, cf. Brandes, Sundhaussen, and Troebst, eds., *Lexikon der Vertreibungen*, 50–51, 58–59, 266–267.

153. On the Kosovo conflict and its prehistory, see, inter alia, Noel Malcolm, *Kosovo: A Short History* (London: Macmillan, 1998); Wolfgang Petritsch, Robert Pichler, and Karl Kaser, *Kosovo/Kosova: Mythen, Daten, Fakten* (Klagenfurt: Wieser, 1999). UÇK stands for Ushtria Çlirimtare e Kosovës.

154. These historical analogies and arguments were already being made, to some extent, at the beginning of the war in Croatia and Bosnia. The French intellectual Alain Finkielkraut was especially active making arguments of this kind; see his book *Dispatches from the Balkan War and Other Writings* (Lincoln: University of Nebraska Press, 1999).

155. On this, see the diverse (and, in part, questionable) case studies in Alex J. Bellamy and Tim Dunne, *The Oxford Handbook of the Responsibility to Protect* (Oxford: Oxford University Press, 2016).

156. On these incidents and the entire Western mission in Kosovo, see Helmut Kramer and Vedran Džihić, *Die Kosovo-Bilanz—Scheitert die internationale Gemeinschaft?*, 2nd ed., updated and corrected (Vienna: LIT, 2006). Next to KFOR, the EU mission EULEX, entrusted with setting up constitutional structures, was especially important.

157. On this, see, inter alia, Shaun Walker, "The Ukrainians Starting a New Life—in Russia," *Guardian* (5 January 2016), accessible at https://www.theguardian.com/world/2016/jan/05/ukrainian-russia-refugee-conflict (accessed April 2017).

Chapter 3. Political refugees and the emergence of an international refugee policy

1. In addition, there were about 15,000 slaves who were taken along by their owners; see Maya Jasanoff, *Liberty's Exiles: American Loyalists in the Revolutionary World* (New York: Knopf, 2011).

2. On the number of refugees from the revolution, see Massimo Boffa, "Die Emigranten," in vol. 1 of François Furet and Mona Ozouf, eds., *Kritisches Wörterbuch der Französischen Revolution: Ereignisse, Akteure* (Frankfurt am Main: Suhrkamp, 1996), 546–564, as well as Klaus Bade, *Europa in Bewegung: Migration vom späten 18. Jahrhundert bis zur Gegenwart* (Munich: C. H. Beck, 2000), 189 f. On their reception in the host countries, see Joachim Bahlcke, "Zwischen offener Zurückweisung und praktischer Solidarität: Vom Umgang mit französischen Revolutionsemigranten in Deutschland während des ausgehenden 18. Jahrhunderts," in Joachim Bahlcke, Rainer Leng, and Peter Scholz, eds., *Migration als soziale Herausforderung: Historische Formen solidarischen Handelns von der Antike bis zum 20. Jahrhundert* (Stuttgart: Steiner, 2011),

255–272. On various cases of flight and the motives for fleeing, see Friedemann Pestel, *Kosmopoliten wider Willen: Die 'monarchiens' als Revolutionsmigranten* (Berlin: de Gruyter, 2015), 101–103, 107–118.

3. See "Merkel dankt Syrer für Mithilfe," *Die Zeit* (10 Oct. 2016), accessible online at http://www.zeit.de/politik/deutschland/2016-10/verdaechtiger-von-chemnitz-festgenommen (accessed April 2017).

4. On this, see Radmila Slabáková, *Le destin d'une famille noble émigrée d'origine française dans l'empire des Habsbourg et en Tchécoslovaquie de la fin du XVIIIe aux années trente du XXe siècle: les Mensdorff-Pouilly* (PhD diss., University of Grenoble 1999). Accessible online at https://www.academia.edu/8544653/Le_destin_dune_famille_noble_émigrée_dorigine_française_dans_lempire_des_Habsbourg_et_en_Tchécoslovaquie_de_la_fin_du_XVIIIe_aux_années_trente_du_XXe_siècle_les_Mensdorff-Pouilly (accessed April 2017). For drawing attention to these two families, I again thank the aforementioned research seminar on refugees held during the summer semester of 2016, and in particular the seminar paper (using numerous sources) by Susanne Zenker. One of the family's given names, Emmanuel, was also Germanized, and "Baron" Pouilly became a "Count" in German (a "*Graf* . . . zu Mensdorf"); later the family resumed using its double name.

5. On Kościuszko's life, see the detailed entry by Stanisław Herbst, "Kościuszko Andrzej Tadeusz Bonawentura (1746–1817)," in Polska Akademia Nauk/Instytut Historii, *Polski Słownik Biograficzny*, vol. 14: *Kopernicki Izydor—Kozłowska Maria* (Wrocław: Zakład Narodowy Imienia Ossolińskich, 1968/69), 430–440. According to some other sources, Kościuszko's studies in France (discussed below) might have been formally confined to engineering and to auditing classes at the French Military Academy, where foreigners were not officially allowed to enroll.

6. On the enthusiasm for Poland, see the written and visual sources in the exhibition catalog by Anna Kuśmidrowicz-Król et al., eds., *Solidarność 1830: Niemcy i Polacy po powstaniu listopadowym/Polenbegeisterung: Deutsche und Polen nach dem Novemberaufstand 1830* (Warsaw: Zamek Królewski, 2005).

7. See Herbert Reiter, *Politisches Asyl im 19. Jahrhundert: Die deutschen politischen Flüchtlinge des Vormärz und der Revolution von 1848/49 in Europa und den USA* (Berlin: Duncker & Humblot, 1992), 41.

8. On this term, cf. Delphine Diaz, *Un asile pour tous les peuples? Exilés et réfugiés étrangers en France au cours du premier XIXe siècle* (Paris: Armand Colin, 2014), 98. On the subsidies for refugees, which in 1833 fell into five classes, overall, see ibid., 306.

9. There are, however, different versions of this picture, including one showing only black-red-gold flags.

10. In 1829 Ranke had published a book about the Serbian revolution, and a revised edition came out in 1844; see Holm Sundhaussen, *Geschichte Serbiens: 19.-21. Jahrhundert* (Vienna: Böhlau, 2007), 54.

11. The number of women was five. On this compilation, see Reiter, *Politisches Asyl im 19. Jahrhundert*, 101.

12. See ibid., 112.

13. See Reiter, *Politisches Asyl im 19. Jahrhundert*, 123.

14. Various biographies have been published about Mazzini; one introduction that can be recommended is the comprehensive entry in the *Dizionario biografico degli italiani*, accessible online at http://www.treccani.it/enciclopedia/giuseppe-mazzini_(Dizionario-Biografico)/ (accessed April 2017); for further reading, see the political biography by Denis Mack Smith, *Mazzini* (New Haven: Yale University Press, 1994).

15. See Reiter, *Politisches Asyl im 19. Jahrhundert*, 105.

16. See Giuseppe Mazzini, *Filosofia della Musica*, ed. by Marcello de Angelis (Florence: Guaraldi, 1977), 33–77.

17. See, inter alia, Rudolf Jaworski, "Völkerfrühling 1848," in Dieter Langewiesche, ed., *Demokratiebewegung und Revolution 1847 bis 1849: Internationale Aspekte und europäische Verbindungen* (Berlin: Springer, 1998), 36–51.
18. At the height of the refugee wave, Switzerland recorded about 12,000 refugees, France fewer than 1,000, while Belgium counted 2,400 refugees, although most of them first arrived after Napoleon III's coup d'état in 1851, and in 1853 England registered its highest level of refugees at 4,386; for these figures, see Reiter, *Politisches Asyl im 19. Jahrhundert*, 203, 226, 261. But since many of these refugees returned home or moved to another country relatively soon, the estimate of about 12,000 people is certainly not too high.
19. For a comprehensive treatment of this, see Reiter, *Politisches Asyl im 19. Jahrhundert*, 164–170.
20. See the original quote, ibid., 205: "parce qu'ils croient y'trouver l'occasion, qu'ils cherchent de porter le dernier coup à l'ordre européen et en particulier à l'ordre social actuel en France."
21. These numbers refer only to those refugees who were fleeing to Belgium; on this, see ibid., 210. Overall, there were certainly more.
22. To be sure, this mostly applied to well-known aristocratic families, who were able to afford hiring Polish private tutors and to bear the entire expense of cultivating their national traditions; for an overview of Polish exile in the wake of the Grande Émigration, see Jerzy Borejsza, "Polnische politische Flüchtlinge in Mittel- und Westeuropa im 19. Jahrhundert," in Klaus Bade et al., eds., *Enzyklopädie Migration in Europa: Vom 17. Jahrhundert bis zur Gegenwart* (Paderborn: Schöningh, 2007), 885–889; see too the monograph by Jerzy Borejsza, *Emigracja polska po powstaniu styczniowym* (Warsaw: PWN, 1966).
23. On attitudes toward refugees, see Reiter, *Politisches Asyl im 19. Jahrhundert*, 234.
24. See the chapter "Asyl in der Schweiz," in Reiter, *Politisches Asyl im 19. Jahrhundert*, especially 225; for the following numbers, ibid., 226.
25. On English refugee policy and attitudes toward refugees, see ibid., 258–274.
26. On this committee, see Sabine Freitag, "Introduction," in Freitag, ed., *Exiles from European Revolutions: Refugees in Mid-Victorian England* (New York: Berghahn, 2003), 6; at almost the same time another committee, the Comité Révolutionnaire des Démocrates Socialistes Réfugiés, was founded on the isle of Jersey; both organizations, however, lasted only a few years.
27. This episode is discussed at the beginning of the outstanding book by Diaz, *Un asile pour tous les peuples*, 7.
28. Paine's polemical treatise is accessible online at http://www.ushistory.org/paine /commonsense/sense4.htm (accessed April 2017); in that pamphlet, see the chapter "Thoughts on the Present State of American Affairs."
29. See on German-American politics at the time Andrew Zimmerman, "From the Rhine to the Mississippi: Property, Democracy, and Socialism in the American Civil War." *Journal of the Civil War Era* 5 (2015), 3–37.
30. See the calculations made by Reiter, *Politisches Asyl im 19. Jahrhundert*, 254 f.
31. On this, see Carole Fink, *Defending the Rights of Others: The Great Powers, the Jews, and International Minority Protection, 1878–1938* (Cambridge: Cambridge University Press, 2004).
32. The lawsuits against the "Muslim country ban" and the "refugee ban" were interrelated. While Trump could eventually uphold the Muslim country ban by expanding visa restrictions to include North Korea and Venezuela, he partially lost the legal battle about the admission of refugees. The courts first rejected the 120-day moratorium and later insisted that refugees already admitted to the US had the right to be united with their families (a decision based on *Doe vs Trump*). However, the Supreme Court did not reject the restrictions imposed on admitting newly arriving refugees. Hence, the ACLU achieved at most a partial victory.

33. On these figures (and the estimate of a total of ten million Russian Civil War dead), see the concise essay by David R. Stone, "The Russian Civil War, 1917–1921," in Robin Higham and Frederick W. Kagan, eds., *The Military History of the Soviet Union* (New York: Palgrave, 2002), 13–33. Siegelbaum and Moch distinguish between wartime, civil war and famine refugees (there was a famine in 1921–22 from which around 1.8 million refugees fled and as many as three million people may have died). Cf. Lewis H. Siegelbaum and Leslie Page Moch, *Broad Is My Native Land: Repertoires and Regimes of Migration in Russia's Twentieth Century* (Ithaca: Cornell University Press, 2014), 237. For the massive displacement, see also Peter Holquist, *Making War, Forging Revolution: Russia's Continuum of Crisis, 1914–1921* (Cambridge: Harvard University Press, 2002).
34. For the perspective of a contemporary, see John Hope Simpson, *The Refugee Problem: Report of a Survey* (London: Oxford University Press, 1939), 82.
35. See Mark Mazower, *What You Did Not Tell: A Russian Past and the Journey Home* (New York: Other Press, 2017), 63–65. Unfortunately, there are not many individual accounts like this, nor are there enough broader studies about the flight out of Russia after the Bolsheviks seized power.
36. About 100,000 Russian and Jewish refugees came to Romania in the course of the interwar period; on this estimate and Romanian refugee policy, see Vadim Guzun, *Indezirabilii: aspecte mediatice, umanitare şi de securitate privind emigraţia din Uniunea Sovietică în România interbelică* (Cluj-Napoca: Editura Argonaut, 2013), 30–32.
37. On this, see Dorota Sula, *Powrót ludności polskiej z byłego Imperium Rosyjskiego w latach 1918–1937* (Warsaw: Trio, 2013), 219; see also Włodzimierz Borodziej, *Geschichte Polens im 20. Jahrhundert* (Munich: C. H. Beck, 2010), 99.
38. See Peter Gatrell, *The Making of the Modern Refugee* (Oxford: Oxford University Press, 2013), 57.
39. Emilian Wiszka, *Emigracja ukraińska w Polsce, 1920–1939* (Toruń: Mado, 2004), 653.
40. See on flight and labor migration from Ukraine and the networks of the migrants, Matthias Kaltenbrunner, *Das global vernetzte Dorf. Eine Migrationsgeschichte* (Campus: Frankfurt am Main, 2017). An English version of this book is in the making.
41. See Tobias Brinkmann, "Ort des Übergangs—Berlin als Schnittstelle der jüdischen Migration aus Osteuropa nach 1918," in Verena Dohrn and Gertrud Pickhan, eds., *Transit und Transformation: Osteuropäisch-jüdische Migranten in Berlin, 1918–1939* (Göttingen: Wallstein, 2010), 25–44.
42. On the different flight waves out of Spain, see Geneviève Dreyfus-Armand, *L'exil des républicains Espagnols en France: De la Guerre civile à la mort de Franco* (Paris: Albin Michel, 1999), 33–55 (for referring me to the literature in French, I thank Nancy Green of the EHESS in Paris). On the flight out of northern Spain, see also Alicia Alted, *La voz de los vencidos: El exilio republicano de 1939* (Madrid: Aguilar, 2005), 38–40.
43. See a variety of quotes like this from the French media in Alted, *La voz de los vencidos,* 64.
44. Dreyfus-Armand, *L'exil des républicains espagnols en France,* 39.
45. Ibid.
46. On the Kindertransports, see Alted, *La voz de los vencidos,* 40.
47. On the history of the camps and how they were labeled, see Dreyfus-Armand, *L'exil des républicains espagnols en France,* 63–72.
48. See Alted, *La voz de los vencidos,* 63. For a critical account of French policy toward the Spanish refugees, see an older book: Louis Stein, *Beyond Death and Exile: The Spanish Republicans in France, 1939–1955* (Cambridge: Harvard University Press, 1979).
49. On this, with Belgium as an example, see Frank Caestecker and Sarah Eloy, eds., *Los Niños. Tien vluchtelingen-kinderen uit de Spaanse Burgeroorlog vertellen* (Antwerp: EPO, 2007).
50. One hundred and twelve thousand Spanish refugees were counted in France in 1951; more than 10,000 lost their lives during the Second World War serving in the French

army and in Nazi concentration camps following the surrender of France; on these figures, see Marrus, *The Unwanted*, 193.

51. On the flight of the Austrian National Socialists and the Austrian Legion, see the comprehensive study by Hans Schafranek, *Söldner für den Anschluss: Die Österreichische Legion, 1933–1938* (Vienna: Czernin, 2011).

52. From this archive I learned, by way of my sister who is married to a Spaniard, that Manuel Alarcón Navarro was the grandfather of my brother-in-law.

53. Almería was the scene of numerous German war crimes. Early in 1937 the Luftwaffe bombed the city, wantonly targeting refugees fleeing from the defeated city of Malaga and camping in the harbor district and on the streets along "La Rambla."

54. The camp in Miranda was one of the largest Spanish concentration camps and is relatively well known because, among other reasons, many international combatants were interned there. The camp was built and managed on the German model and only closed in 1947 as the last of the Spanish concentration camps; on Miranda del Ebro and additional Spanish concentration camps, see "Los campos de concentración franquistas en el contexto europeo," *Ayer* 57/1 (2005), as well as the studies by the Madrid research group of 2000, accessible online at http://web.archive.org/web/20120616210917/http:/www.cefid.uab.es/files/comunicII-3.pdf; on the camp in Vernet, which served during the war as an internment camp for "undesirable foreigners" and for Jews, see the information available online at http://www.campduvernet.eu/ (both sites accessed April 2017); Vernet became known, among other reasons, because of his part in Arthur Koestler's bestselling novel *Scum of the Earth*, published in London in 1941.

55. On the Sudeten German "refugees" and Freikorps formed by Sudeten Germans in Germany, see Werner Röhr, "Der 'Fall Grün' und das Sudetendeutsche Freikorps," in Hans-Henning Hahn, ed., *Hundert Jahre sudetendeutsche Geschichte. Eine völkische Bewegung in drei Staaten* (Frankfurt am Main: Peter Lang, 2007), 243–258.

56. On this, see Jan Gebhart, "Migrationsbewegungen der tschechischen Bevölkerung in den Jahren 1938–39: Forschungsstand und offene Fragen," in Detlef Brandes et al., eds., *Erzwungene Trennung: Vertreibungen und Aussiedlungen in und aus der Tschechoslowakei 1938–1947 im Vergleich mit Polen, Ungarn und Jugoslawien* (Essen: Klartext, 1999), 11–22.

57. Cf. Hanna Diamond, "La France en 1940: images des réfugiés," in Stefan Martens and Steffen Prauser, eds., *La guerre de 1940: Se battre, subir, se souvenir* (Villeneuve: Presses Universitaires du Septentrion), 196.

58. Her biography can be regarded as one more example of a failed flight. Némirovsky was descended from a Russian Jewish family. Her first flight as a teenager from the Bolsheviks to France had worked out well, but she was caught by the Germans in 1942 and then murdered in Auschwitz. As if she had presaged her fate, Némirovsky complained in her novel about French society's lack of solidarity with the refugees (see esp. p. 94 of the original French edition). Her novel is available in English translation: Irène Némirovsky, *Suite Française*, Sandra Smith, trans. (New York: Alfred A. Knopf, 2006). The book was not published until sixty-two years after her death, because it was hidden in her personal papers and only belatedly discovered by her daughter, who survived the war and the Holocaust.

59. Already in his inaugural speech as prime minister, Pétain had explicitly mentioned the fate of the refugees. In subsequent statements he also used them to legitimize the severe terms of the armistice on June 25. The speech given that day can be accessed online under http://pages.livresdeguerre.net/pages/sujet.php?id=docddp&su=48&np=97 (accessed November 2018).

60. On the different dates given for the start of the Cold War, and by way of introduction to the basic literature, see inter alia Georges-Henri Soutou, *La Guerre froide: 1943–1990* (Paris: Fayard, 2010); Bernd Stöver, *Der Kalte Krieg: Geschichte eines radikalen*

Zeitalters, 1947–1991 (Munich: C. H. Beck, 2007); Melvyn Leffler and Odd Arne Westad, eds., *The Cambridge History of the Cold War*, 3 vols. (New York: Cambridge University Press, 2010).

61. On the figures for refugees, see Swedish press accounts and government sources of the time, cited by Fredrik Stöcker, *Bridging the Baltic Sea: Networks of Resistance and Opposition during the Cold War Era* (Lanham, MD: Lexington Books, 2018), 10.

62. See examples in Stöcker, *Bridging the Baltic Sea*, 10.

63. See Stöcker, *Bridging the Baltic Sea*, 42.

64. On the postwar history of Greece and the civil war there, see Mark Mazower, ed., *After the War Was Over: Reconstructing the Family, Nation and State in Greece, 1943–1960* (Princeton: Princeton University Press, 2000).

65. See Michael Fleming, "Greek 'heroes' in the Polish People's Republic and the Geopolitics of the Cold War, 1948–1956," *Nationalities Papers* 36/3 (2008), 379.

66. On the change of attitude toward children, see the pathbreaking book by Tara Zahra, *The Lost Children: Reconstructing Europe's Families after World War II* (Cambridge, MA: Harvard University Press, 2011); see also Machteld Venken and Maren Röger, eds., "Growing Up in the Shadow of the Second World War: European Perspectives," *European Review of History/Revue européenne d'histoire* 22/2 (2015), 199–220.

67. On the history of the Greek civil war refugees in the Soviet Union, see Kostis Karpozilos, "The Defeated of the Greek Civil War: From Fighters to Political Refugees in the Cold War," *Journal of Cold War Studies* 16/3 (2014), 62–87.

68. On the Greek civil war refugees in the GDR, see Stefan Troebst, "Schwierige Gäste: Politische Emigranten aus Griechenland in der DDR 1949–1989," *Deutschland-Archiv* 38/1 (2005), 93–101.

69. On the expulsion and forced evacuation from Görlitz, see Franz Scholz, *Wächter, wie tief die Nacht? Görlitzer Tagebuch 1945/46*, 2nd ed. (Eltville: Walter, 1984). This book is among the most impressive (and not at all revanchist) eyewitness accounts published in the Federal Republic. On the Greeks in Zgorzelec, see Stefan Troebst, *Zwischen Arktis, Adria und Armenien: Das östliche Europa und seine Ränder* (Cologne: Böhlau, 2017), 144–153. For an overview on the Greeks in Poland, see Kazimierz Pudło, "Uchodźcy polityczni z Grecji w Polsce (1948–1995)," in Zbigniew Kurcz, ed., *Mniejszości narodowe w Polsce* (Wrocław: Wydawnictwo Uniwersytetu Wrocławskiego, 1997), 149–152.

70. On these figures, see Marrus, *The Unwanted*, 310.

71. On this, see Marcin Zaremba, *Wielka Trwoga: Polska, 1944–1947* (Kraków: Znak, 2012). A German translation appeared in 2016.

72. On the DPS and these figures, see Gerard Daniel Cohen, *In War's Wake: Europe's Displaced Persons in the Postwar Order* (Oxford: Oxford University Press, 2012), 5.

73. On the attitude of the US, see Jason Kendall Moore, "Between Expediency and Principle: U.S. Repatriation Policy towards Russian Nationals, 1944–1949," *Diplomatic History* 24/3 (2000), 381–404.

74. Ibid., 388–392.

75. Ibid., 398.

76. On repatriation from Austria, see the comprehensive anthology by Peter Ruggenthaler and Walter M. Iber, eds., *Hitlers Sklaven—Stalins "Verräter": Aspekte der Repression an Zwangsarbeitern und Kriegsgefangenen: Eine Zwischenbilanz* (Innsbruck: Studienverlag, 2010), 284; on resistance to repatriation in Germany, see Ulrike Goeken-Haidl, *Der Weg zurück: Die Repatriierung sowjetischer Kriegsgefangener und Zwangsarbeiter während und nach dem Zweiten Weltkrieg* (Essen: Klartext, 2006), 332–338.

77. The reference to this film comes from Susan L. Carruthers, "Between Camps: Eastern Bloc 'Escapees' and Cold War Borderlands," *American Quarterly* 57/3 (2005), 915.

78. On these numbers, see Gatrell, *The Making of the Modern Refugee*, 97; Marrus, *The Unwanted*, 323. For West Germany, Goeken-Haidl cites a figure showing 323,000 Soviet

citizens who did not want to be repatriated (80 percent of them came from the Baltic
states and the eastern regions of Poland occupied and annexed by the Soviet Union);
see Goeken-Haidl, *Der Weg zurück*, 291.

79. Carruthers, 'Between Camps," 919–921.
80. Quoted in Susan L. Carruthers, *Cold War Captives: Imprisonment, Escape, and Brain-washing* (Berkeley: University of California Press, 2009), 74.
81. See Edward Shils, "Social and Psychological Aspects of Displacement and Repatriation," *Journal of Social Issues* 2/3 (1946), 3–18; quoted by Gatrell, *The Making of the Modern Refugee*, 104; see also Cohen, *In War's Wake*, 155.
82. On this incident, see Dariusz Stola, *Kraj bez wyjścia? Migracji z Polski, 1949–1989*, (Warschau: PAN ISP, 2010), 43.
83. Overall, there were as many people who died at the Czech-Austrian border as along the Berlin Wall; 129 lost their lives to firearms, in the minefields, or on the electrified fences; see Stefan Karner, *Halt! Tragödien am Eisernen Vorhang: Die Verschlussakten* (Salzburg: Ecowin, 2013).
84. See Carruthers, "Between Camps," 921.
85. On this fundraising effort, see the memoirs of Jerzy Giedroyc, *Autobiografia na cztery ręce: Opracował i posłowiem opatrzył Krzysztof Pomian* (Warsaw: Czytelnik, 1994), 153. For alerting me to this I thank Łukasz Mikołajewski, a former doctoral candidate from my time at the EUI in Florence (his thesis has now appeared under the title *Disenchanted Europeans: Polish Émigré Writers from Kultura and Postwar Reformulations of the West* [Frankfurt: Peter Lang, 2018]. The biggest individual donor was a French diplomat and Polish-Jewish entrepreneur, Edward Berenbaum, who came from Bielsko-Biała in the Polish part of Silesia and opened a textile factory in Montevideo.
86. Quoted in ibid., 929.
87. These figures come from Marrus, *The Unwanted*, 345.
88. On these figures, see ibid., 338f.
89. On this, see Gatrell, *The Making of the Modern Refugee*, 159–166.
90. On the composition of the first flight wave and the reactions in Austria, see the very detailed essay by Peter Haslinger, "Flüchtlingskrise 1956—die Ungarische Revolution und Österreich," in Jerzy Kochanowski and Joachim von Puttkamer, eds., *1956. (Nieco) inne spojrzenie: Eine (etwas) andere Perspektive* (Warsaw: Neriton, 2016), 129 f.
91. See Haslinger, "Flüchtlingskrise 1956," 129.
92. See Anton Bayer, "Die ungarischen Flüchtlingslager in Österreich," *Integration. Bulletin International* 5/2 (1957), 107.
93. See on the support offered to Soviet Jews in the US, Porter, *Benevolent Empire*, 212–213.
94. Quoted in Haslinger, "Flüchtlingskrise 1956," 148.
95. See ibid., 142.
96. The figures are based on data from the Hungarian Refugee Relief Association of the League of Red Cross Societies, quoted in Andreas Wenninger, "Ungarische Emigration 1956" (MA thesis, Institut für Osteuropäische Geschichte, Vienna, 1997).
97. On these regional differences among refugees, see Zoltán Dövényi and Gabriella Vukovich, "Ungarn und die internationale Migration," in Heinz Fassmann and Rainer Münz, eds., *Migration in Europa: Historische Entwicklungen, aktuelle Trends, politische Reaktionen* (Frankfurt am Main: Campus, 1996), 272.
98. Cf. Stéphane Dufoix, *Politiques d'exil: Hongrois, Polonais et Tchécoslovaques en France après 1945* (Paris: Presses Universitaires de France, 2002), 50.
99. Quoted in Haslinger, "Flüchtlingskrise," 147. See on the poor conditions in the refugee camps and after arrival in the US, see also Porter, *Benevolent Empire*, 164.
100. Cf. István Szépfalus, "A legújabb felismeresek az 1956/57-es magyar menekülthullámról" [Latest findings about the Hungarian refugee wave, 1956/57], *Limes* 1 (1998), 115. Porter reports on Hungarians who even wanted to return from the US (see Porter,

Benevolent Empire, 165), but apparently they stayed because their return would certainly have been exploited as Communist proganda.

101. See Haslinger, "Flüchtlingskrise," 151.

102. See on these cases, Porter, *Benevolent Empire*, 118–125.

103. On World Refugee Year and its initiator, see Gatrell, *The Making of the Modern Refugee*, 113 f.

104. On the system competition between East and West, see Christoph Kleßmann, *Zwei Staaten, eine Nation: Deutsche Geschichte, 1955–1970* (Bonn: Bundeszentrale für politische Bildung, 1997).

105. The definitive monograph on this topic remains Helge Heidemeyer, *Flucht und Zuwanderung aus der SBZ/DDR, 1945/49–1961: Die Flüchtlingspolitik der Bundesrepublik Deutschland bis zum Bau der Berliner Mauer* (Düsseldorf: Droste Verlag, 1994); in addition, see the comprehensive account by Frank Wolff, "Deutsch-deutsche Migrationsverhältnisse: Strategien staatlicher Regulierung, 1945–1989," in Jochen Oltmer, ed., *Handbuch Staat und Migration in Deutschland seit dem 17. Jahrhundert* (Berlin: de Gruyter, 2016), 773–814.

106. On this regulation and the discussions leading up to it, see Heidemeyer, *Flucht und Zuwanderung aus der SBZ/DDR, 1945/46–1961*, 98 f.

107. On the (West) German redistribution of the refugees, see ibid., 133. In 1953 an agreement was reached on a new distribution formula, which significantly relieved the state of North Rhine-Westphalia of its burden.

108. Even the United Nations offered to build a housing development; see ibid., 162.

109. See ibid., 96–106, 124.

110. See the statistics on the countries of origin for the evacuees resettled in Germany, accessible online at http://www.bund-der-vertriebenen.de/information-statistik-und -dokumentation/spaetaussiedler/aktuelle-aussiedlerstatistik.html (accessed April 2017).

111. See Philipp Ther, "Die einheimische Bevölkerung des Oppelner Schlesiens nach dem Zweiten Weltkrieg: Die Entstehung einer deutschen Minderheit," *Geschichte und Gesellschaft* 26 (2000), 407–438.

112. See Philipp Ther, *Deutsche und polnische Vertriebene: Gesellschaft und Vertriebenenpolitik in der SBZ/DDR und in Polen, 1945–1956* (Göttingen: Vandenhoeck & Ruprecht, 1998), 342.

113. On the legal details or special status of the refugees and expellees who fled the GDR, see Heidemeyer, *Flucht und Zuwanderung aus der SBZ/DDR, 1945/46–1961*, 39–45.

114. Klaus Bade and Jochen Oltmer, "Einführung: Aussiedlerzuwanderung und Aussiedlerintegration: Historische Entwicklung und aktuelle Probleme," in Klaus Bade and Jochen Oltmer, eds., *Aussiedler: deutsche Einwanderer aus Osteuropa* (Osnabrück: Universitätsverlag Rasch, 1999), 20. On German policy toward the evacuees and changing social attitudes, see in addition a more up-to-date essay by Jannis Panagiotidis, "Staat, Zivilgesellschaft und Aussiedlermigration, 1950–1989," in Oltmer, ed., *Handbuch Staat und Migration in Deutschland seit dem 17. Jahrhundert*, 895–930.

115. See the unemployment and detailed labor statistics in Eugen Lemberg and Friedrich Edding, *Die Vertriebenen in Westdeutschland: Ihre Eingliederung und ihr Einfluss auf Gesellschaft, Wirtschaft, Politik und Geistesleben* (Kiel: Ferdinand Hirt, 1959), vol. 1, 129.

116. I have gathered these gender statistics from Gerhard Reichling, *Die Heimatvertriebenen im Spiegel der Statistik* (Berlin: Duncker & Humblot, 1958), 51.

117. This subject is treated comprehensively in Andrea Schmelz, *Migration und Politik im geteilten Deutschland während des Kalten Krieges: Die West-Ost-Migration in die DDR in den 1950er und 1960er Jahren* (Opladen: Leske + Budrich, 2002).

118. On the treatment of the KPD, see Josef Foschepoth, "Rolle und Bedeutung der KPD im deutsch-deutschen Systemkonflikt," *Zeitschrift für Geschichtswissenschaft* 56/11 (2008), 901.

119. The information from the Stasi files was used for an article in the *Augsburger Allgemeine Zeitung*. Strangely enough, this is currently the most comprehensive writing about Conrad Schumann one can find; see Stefan Küpper, "Der Sprung seines Lebens," *Augsburger Allgemeine Zeitung* (6 May 2010), accessible online at http://www.augsburger -allgemeine.de/panorama/Der-Sprung-seines-Lebens-id7791041.html; see also the entry in the "Chronik der Mauer" compiled by the Bundeszentrale für politische Bildung, accessible online at http://www.chronik-der-mauer.de/fluchten/180921/sprung-in-die -freiheit-die-flucht-des-ddr-grenzpolizisten-conrad-schumann-15-august-1961 (both accessed April 2017).

120. On these figures, see Dušan Šimko, "Tschechoslowakische Flüchtlinge in West-, Mittel- und Nordeuropa seit 1968," in Klaus Bade et al., eds., *Enzyklopädie Migration in Europa: Vom 17. Jahrhundert bis zur Gegenwart* (Paderborn: Schöningh, 2007), 1050–1053.

121. Vlasta Valeš, "Die tschechoslowakischen Flüchtlinge, 1968–1989," in Gernot Heiss and Oliver Rathkolb, eds., *Asylland wider Willen: Flüchtlinge in Österreich im europäischen Kontext seit 1914* (Vienna: Dachs, 1995), 172–181.

122. See Patrice G. Poutros, "Spannungen und Dynamiken: Asylgewährung in der Bundesrepublik Deutschland von den frühen 1950ern bis zur Mitte der 1970er Jahre," in Maria Mesner and Gernot Heiss, eds., *Asyl: Das lange 20. Jahrhundert* (Vienna: Löcker, 2012), 131.

123. The number of asylum applications was 27,622 according to the encyclopedia *Migration in Europa*, cf. Šimko, "Tschechoslowakische Flüchtlinge." This number may be a rather low estimate, since in 1971 the Federal Republic registered six times as many (53,000) asylum applications as in 1970; here there is an obvious connection with the suppression of the Prague Spring uprising. Two thousand three hundred Czechs and Slovaks went to Sweden, 1,750 to France.

124. See Renate Rendl, "Die Integration der Flüchtlinge aus der Tschechoslowakei in der Schweiz seit 1968," in Monika Bankowski et al., eds., *Asyl und Aufenthalt: Die Schweiz als Zuflucht und Wirkungsstätte von Slaven im 19. und 20. Jahrhundert* (Basel: Helbing und Lichtenhahn, 1994), 244.

125. On this, see the article "Der letzte 'Bote' aus der ČSSR war ein Lastzug," *Passauer Neue Presse* (23 August 1968); this and additional articles are accessible online at http://www .begegnungsraum-geschichte.uni-passau.de/unterrichtsmaterialien/eiserner-vorhang /unterricht-materialien/schriftquellen/zeitungsartikel-zum-prager-fruehling/artikel -vom-23-08-1968/ (accessed June 2017). Numerous articles from the Austrian press are documented in a 1994 master's thesis: Andrea Fasching, "Die Berichterstattung über Flüchtlinge in den österreichischen Tageszeitungen 'AZ', 'Kurier' und 'Die Presse': Ein Vergleich der Jahre 1968 (CSSR-Krise) und 1991 (Jugoslawien-Krise)" (MA thesis, University of Vienna, 1994).

126. See Valeš, "Die tschechoslowakischen Flüchtlinge, 1968–1989," 176.

127. See Christine Banki and Christoph Späti, "Ungarn, Tibeter, Tschechen und Slowaken: Bedingungen ihrer Akzeptanz in der Schweiz der Nachkriegszeit," in Carsten Goehrke and Werner G. Zimmermann, eds., *"Zuflucht Schweiz": Der Umgang mit Asylproblemen im 19. und 20. Jahrhundert* (Zurich: Hans Rohr, 1994), 370.

128. See Gatrell, *The Making of the Modern Refugee*, 205; Bouda Etemad, "Europe and Migration after Decolonisation," *Journal of European Economic History* 27/3 (1998), 465.

129. For these figures, see Carl Bon Tempo, *Americans at the Gate: The United States and Refugees during the Cold War* (Princeton: Princeton University, 2008), 145.

130. The numbers for Cambodia are taken from Ben Kiernan, *Pol Pot Regime: Race, Power, and Genocide in Cambodia under the Khmer Rouge, 1975–79* (New Haven: Yale University Press, 2008); W. Courtland Robinson, *Terms of Refuge: The Indochinese Exodus & the International Response* (London: Zed Books, 2000), 294–296. On the repatriation efforts and the (rare) international resettlement of Cambodian refugees, see Evan

Gottesman, *Cambodia after the Khmer Rouge: Inside the Politics of Nation Building* (New Haven: Yale University Press, 2004).

131. On taking in the Vietnamese refugees, see Bon Tempo, *Americans at the Gate,* 146–162.

132. Cited in Astri Suhrke and Frank Klink, "Contrasting Patterns of Asian Refugee Movements: The Vietnamese and Afghan Syndromes," in James T. Fawcett and Benjamin V. Carino, eds., *Pacific Bridges: The New Immigration from Asia and the Pacific Islands* (New York: Center for Migrations Studies, 1987), 92, fn. 5.

133. On these numbers and the reception of the boat people, see Olaf Beuchling, "Vietnamesische Flüchtlinge in West-, Mittel- und Nordeuropa seit den 1970er Jahren," in Klaus Bade et al., eds., *Enzyklopädie Migration in Europa: Vom 17. Jahrhundert bis zur Gegenwart* (Paderborn: Schöningh, 2007), 1072–1076.

134. See Gatrell, *The Making of the Modern Refugee*, 208.

135. On the founding of the Committee, see the entry in the online archive of the WDR, the West German public broadcasting station for the North Rhine-Westphalia region based in Cologne, http://www1.wdr.de/stichtag8090.html (accessed April 2017).

136. See Felix A. Jiménez Botta, "The Foreign Policy of State Terrorism: West Germany, the Military Juntas in Chile and Argentina and the Latin American Refugee Crisis of the 1970s," *Contemporary European History* 27 (2018), 627–650.

137. Formally, "Convention for the Unification of Certain Rules of Law with Respect to Collisions between Vessels," concluded in Brussels 23 September 1910. On the stand of the German Foreign Office, see "Vietnam-Flüchtlinge," *Der Spiegel* (5 November 1979), accessible online at http://www.spiegel.de/spiegel/print/d-39868686.html (accessed April 2017).

138. On taking in and integrating the Vietnamese in the Federal Republic of Germany, see Fukimo Kosaka-Isleif, *Integration südostasiatischer Flüchtlinge in der Bundesrepublik Deutschland und in Japan: eine international vergleichende Studie zur Lage einer neuen Minderheit* (Saarbrücken: Breitenbach, 1991). On the Tamils, see Kurt Salentin, *Tamilische Flüchtlinge in der Bundesrepublik* (Frankfurt: Verlag für Interkulturelle Kommunikation, 2002).

139. For a similar measure that was passed in the US in 1996, see Chapter 4.1.

140. These numbers from the Statistisches Bundesamt (Federal Statistical Office of Germany) are cited by Münz, Seifert, and Ulrich, *Zuwanderung nach Deutschland*, 58. The decline in applications was also related to the Asylum Procedure Act of July 1982, not mentioned in that book.

141. See on welfare provision for refugees (or the lack of it), Porter, *Benevolent Empire*, 188–190 pertaining to the destitution of Cuban refugees, 194–196 to the later expansion of refugee welfare under the Kennedy administration. For social policies directed at refugees in the Carter years, see also García, *The Refugee Challenge*, 5.

142. These cultural differences are dealt with in Chan, Sucheng: *Hmong Means Free: Life in Laos and America* (Philadelphia, Temple University Press, 1994). Part of my findings and reading of this are based on a review essay written by Marc Dorpema for my class on refugee history taught at NYU in the fall of 2018 and on earlier student feedback at the Diplomatic Academy in Vienna. On the history of the Hmong, see also Keith Quincy, *Hmong: History of a People* (Seattle: University of Washington Press, 1997).

143. See Kinzer, Stephen, "Hunter Tells Police He Was Threatened," *New York Times*, 24 Nov. 2004, online https://www.nytimes.com/2004/11/24/us/hunter-tells-police-he-was-threatened.html. On the court trial, see also Neil Karlen, "Man Accused of Killing 6 Hunters Says He Feared for His Life," *New York Times*, 16 Sept. 2005, online https://www.nytimes.com/2005/09/16/us/man-accused-of-killing-6-hunters-says-he-feared-for-his-life.html. The perpetrator was eventually found guilty of murder and sentenced to a mandatory life prison term. On the final verdict, see Bob Kelleher, "Vang Found Guilty on All Counts," *Minnesota Public Radio*, 16 Sept. 2005, online http://news.minnesota.publicradio.org/features/2005/09/16_kelleherb_vangverdict/ (all accessed December

2018). See also, on the conflicts about property and hunting, David N. Bengston et al., "Listening to Neglected Voices: Hmong and Public Lands in Minnesota and Wisconsin," *Society and Natural Resources* 21 (2008), 876–90.

144. See Hein, *Ethnic Origins*, 100.

145. Miles McNall, Timothy Dunnigan, and Jeylan T. Mortimer, "The Educational Achievement of the St. Paul Hmong," *Anthropology and Educational Quarterly* 25 (March 1994), 44–65.

146. See MayKao Yangblongsua Hang, "Growing Up Hmong American: Truancy Policy and Girls," *Hmong Studies Journal* 1 (Spring 1997), 1–54.

147. On this, see chapter 4 in the German version of my book, where I write amply about the integration record of the former guest workers and their children, and where newly created statistical series are consulted. For the history of the guest workers, see also the fundamental work by Karin Hunn, *"Nächstes Jahr kehren wir zurück . . .": Die Geschichte der türkischen "Gastarbeiter in der Bundesrepublik"* (Göttingen: Wallstein, 2005).

148. See on these cutbacks, Porter, *Benevolent Empire*, 215.

149. There used to be a journal with the name *Zeitschrift für Türkeistudien*, published from 1988 until 2007, but there are no equivalent publications on Poles living in Germany or on guest workers such as the Italians, Yugoslavs, etc.

150. On Solidarność and the coup of 1981, see Borodziej, *Geschichte Polens im 20. Jahrhundert*, 360–372.

151. See Stola, *Kraj bez wyjścia*, 312.

152. See Eugen Antalovsky, "Polenflüchtlinge in Österreich—neue Dimensionen, neue Aspekte," *AWR-Bulletin* 21/30, 2–3 (1983).

153. See Stola, *Kraj bez wyjścia*, 310.

154. The letter, which was disseminated via Radio Free Europe, is extensively documented in Stola, *Kraj bez wyjścia*, 321. In the end, only 2,119 of the Poles who were interned and could have emigrated availed themselves of this opportunity. On the comparison to the French Revolution, see Diaz, *Un asile pour tous les peuples*, 24.

155. See the economic data in Borodziej, *Geschichte Polens im 20. Jahrhundert*, 359. On martial law emigration, see Stola, *Kraj bez wyjścia*, 323.

156. See Hans-Peter Meister, "Polen in der Bundesrepublik Deutschland," in Berliner Institut für Vergleichende Sozialforschung, ed., *Ethnische Minderheiten in Deutschland: Arbeitsmigranten, Asylbewerber, Ausländer, Flüchtlinge, regionale und religiöse Minderheiten, Vertriebene, Zwangsarbeiter* (Berlin: Edition Parabolis, 1992), accessible online at http://www.expolis.de/polen_in_der_bundesrepublik_deutschland.html (accessed April 2017), the sentence about a "Polenflut" prior to footnote 25. Meister does, however, also refer to sympathetic attitudes toward the country of Poland, especially in 1982.

157. According to Stola, American estimates had it that about 150,000 Poles actually remained in the US in the 1980s after their visas had expired. Most of them were eventually able to obtain a legal residency status; see Stola, *Kraj bez wyjścia*, 358.

158. On this count, see ibid., 352.

159. Ibid., 337.

160. On this milieu, see Sven Reichardt, *Authentizität und Gemeinschaft: Linksalternatives Leben in den siebziger und frühen achtziger Jahren* (Berlin: Suhrkamp, 2014).

161. The term *Aussiedler* is almost impossible to translate into English. The prefix "Aus-" can mean "from" or "ex-" (as in "expat"), or also "dis-" (as in displaced), while "Siedler" is the equivalent of "settler." Of course, there is no noun like "ex-settler" or "dis-settler" in English, so the most common translation is "ethnic emigrant" or "ethnic German emigrant." This translation conveys the political and legal premise accepted by postwar West German governments, to the effect that these emigrants from Eastern Europe were indeed ethnic Germans. In later official usage, the government has sometimes used the term "resettler" in English-language translations of documents (in which the relevant

German term would be *Umsiedler*)—but, again, this is not a noun found in any standard English-language dictionary (such as Merriam-Webster or Oxford).

162. See the wittily written family memoir and autobiography by Emilia Smechowski, *Wir Strebermigranten* (Berlin: Hanser, 2018). A work argued at a scholarly level is Peter Oliver Loew, *Wir Unsichtbaren: Geschichte der Polen in Deutschland* (Munich: Beck, 2014).

163. See the statistics accessible online at http://www.bund-der-vertriebenen.de/information -statistik-und-dokumentation/spaetaussiedler/aktuelle-aussiedlerstatistik.html (accessed April 2017).

164. Along with the ethnic German emigrants, there were also numerous Russians who left the successor states of the Soviet Union; between 1990 and 1994 alone, they numbered 1.7 million. See Anatoli Vishnevsky and Zhanna Zayonchkovskaya, "Auswanderung aus der früheren Sowjetunion und den GUS-Staaten," in Heinz Fassmann and Rainer Münz, eds., *Migration in Europa: Historische Entwicklungen, aktuelle Trends, politische Reaktionen* (Frankfurt am Main: Campus, 1996), 377–378.

165. Quoted in Bade and Oltmer, "Einführung," 27.

166. Ibid., 32–34; see also additional chapters in this anthology, which is already old but still relevant.

167. On this, see inter alia Barbara Dietz, "Jugendliche Aussiedler in Deutschland: Risiken und Chancen der Integration," in Klaus Bade and Jochen Oltmer, eds., *Aussiedler: deutsche Einwanderer aus Osteuropa* (Osnabrück: Universitätsverlag Rasch, 1999), 153–176; see also the study based on interviews and participant observation by Roland Eckert, Christa Reis, and Thomas A. Wetzstein, "Bilder und Begegnungen: Konflikte zwischen einheimischen und Aussiedlerjugendlichen," in Bade and Oltmer, *Aussiedler*, 191–206.

168. See the excellent summary in Ulrich Herbert, "Flucht und Asyl: Zeithistorische Bemerkungen zu einem aktuellen Problem," *Zeitgeschichte online* (December 2015), accessible online at http://www.zeitgeschichte-online.de/thema/flucht-und-asyl (accessed April 2017); see also Münz, Seifert, and Ulrich, *Zuwanderung nach Deutschland*, 57.

169. The agreements are presented with commentary in a study by BAMF (the Federal Office for Migration and Refugees); see Axel Kreienbrink, "Freiwillige und zwangsweise Rückkehr von Drittstaatsangehörigen aus Deutschland," accessible online at http://ec.europa .eu/dgs/home-affairs/what-we-do/networks/european_migration_network/reports /docs/emn-studies/return-migration/4b._de_emn_ncp_return_country_study_final _april2007de_version_de.pdf (accessed April 2017).

170. See on this legislation García, *The Refugee Challenge*, 199–120.

171. See ibid. 7.

172. This question is addressed by political scientist Rebecca Hamlin, *Let Me Be a Refugee*, 21–25 (nevertheless, Hamlin argues broadly for taking in refugees).

173. See the very detailed book by Emmanuel Comte, *The History of the European Migration Regime: Germany's Strategic Hegemony* (London: Routledge, 2018).

174. Of course then the actual treatment of the refugees differed substantially from US ideals. This is how the title of Stephen Porter's book *The Benevolent Empire* must be understood (and not misunderstood, as in some critical reviews).

175. See Cohen, *In War's Wake*, 150.

176. The connection was already recognized by researchers on German expellees at the end of the 1950s; see again Lemberg and Edding, *Die Vertriebenen in Westdeutschland*.

Chapter 4. Refugee politics after the Cold War

1. This was the subject of my latest book, *Europe since 1989: A History* (Princeton: Princeton University Press, 2016).

2. See "'Soldaten an die Grenzen'," *Der Spiegel* 37 (9 September 1991), accessible online at http://www.spiegel.de/spiegel/print/d-13491284.html (accessed April 2017).
3. See the information on the US available online at https://www.revolvy.com/topic /Bosnian%20American&item_etype=topic. On Canada, see the official government web site "Canada: A History of Refuge," available online at http://www.cic.gc.ca/english /refugees/timeline.asp (both accessed April 2017).
4. See, e.g., the article entitled "The Refugees Bring Fear" in the liberal weekly *Respekt* by Jindřich Šídlo, "Uprchlíky Žene Strach," *Respekt*, 3 May 1993, accessible online at https:// www.respekt.cz/tydenik/1993/17/uprchliky-zene-strach (accessed December 2018, although there is a paywall lifted only for subscribers).
5. In 1990 Milošević had the League of Communists, which he dominated, renamed as the Socialist Party of Serbia, but this did nothing to change how it was perceived from the outside.
6. This is stated in Article 1 of the Genera Refugee Convention. See https://www.ohchr.org /en/professionalinterest/pages/statusofrefugees.aspx (accessed 28 October 2018).
7. See the quote in "Merkel: Flüchtlinge müssen nach dem Krieg wieder in ihre Heimat gehen," *Frankfurter Allgemeine Zeitung* (1 February 2016), 1. As early as the autumn of 2015, the same newspaper (the *FAZ*) was calling for a reversal in refugee policy. An English version is accessible at https://www.reuters.com/article/us-europe-migrants -germany-refugees-idUSKCN0V80IH (accessed November 2018).
8. See Karen Schönwälder, "Migration, Refugees and Ethnic Plurality as Issues of Public and Political Debates in (West) Germany," in David Sesarani and Mary Fulbrook, eds., *Citizenship, Nationality and Migration in Europe* (London: Routledge, 1996), 159–178. See on the changes in the 1980s, 166–169.
9. The agreements are listed along with commentary in a study from the Federal Office for Migration and Refugees (BAMF); see Axel Kreienbrink, "Freiwillige und zwangsweise Rückkehr von Drittstaatsangehörigen aus Deutschland," accesssible online at http://ec .europa.eu/dgs/home-affairs/what-we-do/networks/european_migration_network /reports/docs/emn-studies/return-migration/4b._de_emn_ncp_return_country_study _final_april2007de_version_de.pdf (accessed April 2017).
10. These numbers refer to the initial applications (not to follow-up applications or applications for renewal); the relevant figures are accessible online at https://www.bpb.de/politik /innenpolitik/flucht/218788/zahlen-zu-asyl-in-deutschland (accessed April 2017); this website from the Federal Agency for Civil Education (Bundeszentrale für politische Bildung) also lists the rates of recognition and rejection.
11. On the genesis of the Schengen Agreement and European migration policy, see Emmanuel Comte, *The History of the European Migration Regime: Germany's Strategic Hegemony* (London: Routledge, 2018)—especially ch. 5.
12. In the third Dublin Regulation from 2014, an early warning system was introduced, but the attempt to create a system for redirecting refugees using admittance quotas for different countries foundered (not least) on the resistance put up by the Federal Republic. The official view of the EU regarding a "Common European Asylum System" (CEAS) and about the Dublin Regulation can be seen online at https://ec.europa.eu/home-affairs /sites/homeaffairs/files/e-library/docs/ceas-fact-sheets/ceas_factsheet_en.pdf (accessed October 2018).
13. On the accord, see "Berlusconi da Gheddafi, siglato l'accordo: 'Uniti sull'immigrazione'," *Corriere della Sera*, 30 Aug. 2008, online at https://www.corriere.it/esteri/08_agosto_30 /berlusconi_libia_gheddafi_bengasi_478ee3f4-767e-11dd-9747-00144f02aabc.shtml (accessed September 2018).
14. For the statistics on flight and migration to Italy across the Mediterranean, see the website of the Istituto Nazionale di Statistica (ISTAT): https://de.slideshare.net/slideistat /laccoglienza-dei-profughi-il-modello-organizzativo-regionale-e-i-dati-statistici -disponibili-sabina-giampaolo-54907275 (accessed October 2018).

15. See Tatiana Zhurzhenko, "Regional Cooperation in the Ukrainian-Russian Borderlands: Wider Europe or Post-Soviet Integration?" in Imre Nagy and James Scott, eds., *EU Enlargement, Region-Building and Shifting Borders of Inclusion and Exclusion* (Aldershot: Ashgate, 2006), 95–111.

16. Originally, Frontex had the awkward name "European Agency for the Management of Operational Cooperation at the External Borders of the Member States of the European Union." In 2016 it was renamed as the "European Border and Coast Guard Agency." On the history of its foundation, see, inter alia, https://frontex.europa.eu/about-frontex /origin-tasks/ (accessed October 2018).

17. See on the divergence between countries and within states Hamlin, *Let Me Be a Refugee*, 7.

18. This probably did mark the beginning of mass detention for refugees and illegal migrants. See Ana Raquel Minian, "America Didn't Always Lock Up Immigrants," in the *New York Times*, 2 December 2018, Sunday Review, 1 and 6. However, DPs from the Soviet Union had also been detained both during and immediately after the Second World War.

19. There were however, earlier cases of terrorists who exploited US asylum laws to remain and hide in the country to prepare attacks. This was, for example, true for one of the main perpetrators of the first World Trade Center bombing in 1993, Ramzi Yousef. See García, *The Refugee Challenge*, 114.

20. Bon Tempo puts greater emphasis on the differences between Republicans and Democrats, especially the latter's left wing (see especially chapter 7, 167–196, on the 1980s). Yet, compared to Germany, in the United States admitting refugees through resettlement and legal procedures for granting asylum was less contested. In the US after 1989, there was also no turning point as sharp as Germany's "asylum compromise." Porter, *The Benevolent Empire* (213–215) stresses cuts in welfare provisions for refugees. However, cuts in social services were a more general trend and introduced not only by Republican presidents but also by the Clinton administration in 1996.

21. The exact figure (always updated to represent the latest finding) surveyed by the US State Department are accessible on the website of the Refugee Processing Center (RPC). See http://www.wrapsnet.org/admissions-and-arrivals/ and the link found there to the "Arrivals Graph by Region." According to these statistics, 3,337,517 refugees arrived in the United States between 1975 and 2016.

22. Cf. Garcia, *The Refugee Challenge*, 133.

23. On the long-term causes, see Alice Bonfatti, "The Socio-economic Roots of Syria's Uprising," *Al-Jumhuriya* (21 Sept. 2016), online at https://www.aljumhuriya.net/en/content /socio-economic-roots-syria's-uprising (accessed October 2018).

24. See, inter alia, the Special Report, "Syria's Climate Refugees," *Scientific American*, 17 Dec. 2015 (accessed October 2018). It is correct, of course, to assume that global climate change is leading to severe social and political conflicts worldwide. But debates about the impact of climate change should not be mixed up with issues related to fleeing violence and war, since confusing the two strengthens the impression that it is pointless even to try coping with worldwide movements of refugees. General panic about uncontrollable migration is an important factor behind the attempt of the West to seal itself off from the rest of the world, and it is grist for the mill of right-wing nationalists.

25. See once again the data from UNHCR, accessible online at http://data.unhcr.org /syrianrefugees/regional.php (accessed April 2017).

26. On these statistics, see the (continually updated) figures of the UNHCR, accessible online at https://data2.unhcr.org/en/situations/syria (accessed Oct. 2018).

27. See "UNO stellt Hungerhilfe für 1,7 Millionen syrische Flüchtlinge ein," *Der Standard* (1 Dec. 2014), available online at http://derstandard.at/2000008848109/UNO-stellt -Hungerhilfe-fuer-17-Millionen-syrischen-Fluechtlinge-ein. The cuts in food rations from 2015 are listed in Ruth Eisenreich, "Was Merkel übersehen hat," *Süddeutsche*

Zeitung (24 Sept. 2015), accessible online at http://www.sueddeutsche.de/politik /syrien-fluechtlinge-was-merkel-uebersehen-hat-1.2662655 (both links accessed April 2017).

28. See, too, the data from UNHCR, accessible online at http://data.unhcr.org/syrianrefugees /asylum.php (accessed April 2017). These statistics include Norway and Switzerland; values are rounded off to the nearest thousand here.

29. This, at any rate, is what Amnesty International claims with reference to the relocation programs of the UNHCR; see Amnesty International, "Syria's Refugee Crisis in Numbers" (4 Sept. 2015), accessible online at https://www.amnesty.org/en/latest/news/2015 /09/syrias-refugee-crisis-in-numbers/ (accessed April 2017).

30. For a full picture of Syrian refugees admitted to the US, see https://www.migrationpolicy .org/article/syrian-refugees-united-states (accessed October 2018).

31. For a chronology of the events, see Georg Blume et al., "Grenzöffnung für Flüchtlinge: Was geschah wirklich?" *Die Zeit* (18 August 2016), accessible online at http://www.zeit .de/2016/35/grenzoeffnung-fluechtlinge-september-2015-wochenende-angela-merkel -ungarn-oesterreich (accessed April 2017).

32. *New York Times* columnist Ross Douthat most likely misunderstood this when he called for the resignation of Angela Merkel (see https://www.nytimes.com/2016/01/10/opinion /sunday/germany-on-the-brink.html). Merkel-bashing might produce media headlines, but neither her demonization nor her idealization are well informed.

33. See Robin Alexander, *Die Getriebenen: Merkel und die Flüchtlingspolitik: Report aus dem Inneren der Macht* (Berlin: Siedler, 2017), 51–66. Even before writing this book, it should be noted, Alexander (an investigative journalist reporting for the conservative daily paper *Die Welt*) was regarded as a Merkel critic. His attitude is easy to recognize from the derogatory tone of his remarks about the chancellor.

34. Ibid., 49, 67–69.

35. Dispensing meals and gifts in kind, among other services, were included in this statistic. The study can be accessed online at https://www.ekd.de/Studie-SI-der-EKD-Skepsis -und-Zuversicht-22058.htm (accessed April 2017). See too Matthias Kamann, "EKD-Studie: Jeder zehnte Deutsche in der Flüchtlingshilfe aktiv," *Die Welt* (21 Dec. 2015), accessible online at https://www.welt.de/politik/deutschland/article150200411/Viele -Deutsche-helfen-haben-aber-auch-Angst.html (accessed April 2017).

36. "Willkommenskultur" has only been an entry in Duden (the German equivalent of *Merriam-Webster* or the *Oxford English Dictionary*) since 2017. On the origins of the term in administrative lingo, see an article published by the consulting firm Hauff before the refugee crisis, found online at https://www.haufe.de/oeffentlicher-dienst/haushalt -finanzen/willkommenskultur-in-der-oeffentlichen-verwaltung/ursprung-der -willkommmenskultur_146_304046.html (accessed October 2018).

37. On this completely inflated prediction, and as evidence of the conservative rejection of Merkel, see Stefan Aust et al., "Herbst der Kanzlerin: Geschichte eines Staatsversagens," *Die Welt* (9 Nov. 2015), accessible online at https://www.welt.de/politik/deutschland /article148588383/Herbst-der-Kanzlerin-Geschichte-eines-Staatsversagens.html (accessed October 2018).

38. Cf. Bertelsmann Stiftung, *Willkommenskultur im "Stresstest": Einstellungen in der Bevölkerung 2017 und Entwicklungen und Trends seit 2011/12* (Gütersloh: Bertelsmann Stiftung, 2017), accessible online at https://www.bertelsmann-stiftung.de/fileadmin/files /Projekte/28_Einwanderung_und_Vielfalt/IB_Umfrage_Willkommenskultur_2017 .pdf (accessed April 2017), 8 and 16. The Bertelsmann Foundation did conclude, however, that German society had withstood the "stress test" of 2015. It was not explained how the authors of the study were using this concept, which they borrowed from the financial world, and how it might be interpreted in any greater depth. Significantly lower approval values emerged from a social psychology investigation commissioned by the Mercator-Stiftung; see "Zustimmung zur Willkommenskultur ist deutlich gesunken,"

Frankfurter Allgemeine Zeitung (7 July 2016), accessible online at http://www.faz.net
/aktuell/politik/fluechtlingskrise/studie-zustimmung-zur-willkommenskultur-ist
-deutlich-gesunken-14328870.html. Both foundations, in turn, are represented in a
larger umbrella foundation established in 2008 under the name Sachverständigenrat
deutscher Stiftungen für Migration und Integration (acronym SVR—the English name
of the council is the "Expert Council of German Foundations on Integration and Migration"), whose assessments are available for viewing on the internet at https://www
.svr-migration.de/ (links mentioned here accessed April 2017).

39. Of these five million communications, 50,000 were manually evaluated for content, and
then a sample of 500 was quantified. The study is not currently accessible on the internet,
but it can be acquired from the research firm by directing a request to dani@bakamo
social.com by E-mail.

40. 38 percent expressed attitudes of rejection toward refugees, 32 percent were hate-filled,
and only 24 percent positive. The last value is, however, relatively high compared with
other European countries.

41. See these quotes in, inter alia, Adam Leczyński, "Kaczyński straszy 'katastrofami
społecznymi' w Polsce po przyjęciu uchodźców," *Oko Press* (22 May 2017), accessible online at https://oko.press/kaczynski-straszy-katastri-spolecznymi-przyjeciu-uchodzcow
-innych-krajach-nastapily/ (accessed Oct. 2018).

42. On this practice, cf. Jürgen Strelhammer, "Ungarn verlegt Flüchtlinge an Österreichs
Grenze," *Die Presse* (2 May 2016), accessible online at http://diepresse.com/home/ausland
/aussenpolitik/4980532/Ungarn-verlegt-Fluechtlinge-an-Oesterreichs-Grenze; see also
"Grenzübertritt: Ungarn wollte Flüchtlinge nicht zurücknehmen, *Der Standard* (16
January 2017), accessible online at http://derstandard.at/2000050794716/Fluechtlinge
-stundenlang-im-Niemandsland-an-Grenze-zu-Ungarn (both accessed April 2017).

43. Unfortunately, even while they were housed in German refugee accommodations, these
Christians were subjected to discrimination and persecution. See "Gewalt gegen christ-
liche Flüchtlinge," *Frankfurter Allgemeine Zeitung* (10 May 2016), 1, 5, as well as another article in the arts and culture feature pages (Feuilleton) of the same edition
(p. 11).

44. Cf. Herbert Brücker, Nina Rother, and Jürgen Schupp, eds., *IAB-BAMF-SOEP-Befragung
von Geflüchteten: Überblick und erste Ergebnisse* (Nuremberg: IAB, 2016), 78 and 82. Accessible online at http://doku.iab.de/forschungsbericht/2016/fb1416.pdf (accessed
April 2017).

45. These figures are for the Federal Republic of Germany. On the share of men and women,
cf. Bundesamt für Migration und Flüchtlinge, *Das Bundesamt in Zahlen 2016: Asyl* (Berlin: Bamf, 2017), 20. Overall the share of men among all refugees who came to the Federal Republic, based on asylum applications from 2016 made by the three largest groups
(Syrians, Afghanis, and Iraqis), came to barely two thirds.

46. On the costs of flight, see Brücker, Rother, and Schupp, eds., *IAB-BAMF-SOEP-Befragung
von Geflüchteten*, 29 (table 3.2). Average costs were even higher, at more than 7,000 euros
(including flight from Syria to the first country of admittance). On the education of the
Syrian refugees, see Betts and Collier, *Refuge: Rethinking Refugee Policy*, 199.

47. On this quote (expressed on several occasions), see (inter alios) Silke Mühlherr, "Es wird
nicht ohne hässliche Bilder gehen," *Die Welt* (13 January 2016), accessible online at https://
www.welt.de/politik/ausland/article150933461/Es-wird-nicht-ohne-haessliche-Bilder
-gehen.html (accessed April 2017).

48. An English translation of the text is online accessible under https://www.infoamerica
.org/documentos_pdf/simmel01.pdf (accessed April 2019).

49. This is emphasized above all by historians of the 1960s and 1970s, when modernization
theories were still among the leading ideas of historical scholarship, especially in social
history. See the work by Dimitri Pentzopoulos that has acquired an almost paradigmatic
status, *The Balkan Exchange of Minorities and Its Impact upon Greece* (Paris: Mouton,

1962). (A new edition of this work, published in London in 2002, is still in stock.) Of course, this success story also calls for critical scrutiny; the imperfect integration of refugees from Asia Minor provided the Communists with additional supporters and can thus be viewed as one of the deeper causes of the civil war after 1945.

50. See my dissertation, which is based on archival studies that have also entered into this book indirectly: Ther, "Deutsche und Polnische Vertriebene," 188–203, 216–225, and 330–346.

51. On professional integration in Germany, see Nadine Oberhuber, "Flüchtlinge und Arbeitsmarkt: Besser als gedacht," *Die Zeit* (9 August 2018), accessible online at https://www .zeit.de/wirtschaft/2018–08/fluechtlinge-arbeitsmarkt-integration-ausbildung -arbeitsplatz (accessed September 2018). The employment rate, accordingly, climbed to 27 percent.

52. See again Betts and Collier, *Refuge: Rethinking Refugee Policy*, 156–181.

53. See Choe Sang-Hun, "Migrants Expected Warm Welcome on Korean Resort Island. They Were Wrong," *New York Times* (12 September 2018), online at https://www.nytimes.com /2018/09/12/world/asia/south-korea-jeju-yemen-refugees.html (accessed Oct. 2018).

54. See the data of the US State Department at https://www.migrationpolicy.org/article /syrian-refugees-united-states (accessed November 2018). Only in 2016 did the USA act more generously by then taking in 12,500 Syrians.

55. On this and other initiatives in Italy, see Luca Liverani, "Comunità di Sant'Egidio: Un anno di corridoi umanitari, altri 50 profughi a Fiumicino," *Avvenire* (27 February 2017), accessible online at https://www.avvenire.it/attualita/pagine/corridoi-umanitari-arrivo -a-fiumicino (accessed April 2017).

56. Massive flight across the Aegean was called "irregular migration" in the EU-Turkey accord. On the text of the agreement, see https://www.consilium.europa.eu/de/press/press -releases/2016/03/18/eu-turkey-statement/ (accessed November 2018).

57. On these numbers, see UNHCR, *Global Trends: Forced Migration in 2017* (Geneva: UNHCR, 2018), 60 or table 5 on that page. Accessible online at http://www.unhcr.org /en-us/statistics/unhcrstats/5b27be547/unhcr-global-trends-2017.html (accessed October 2018).

58. On these numbers, see "The EU-Turkey Refugee Agreement: A Review," *Deutsche Welle* (18 March 2018), accessible online at https://www.dw.com/en/the-eu-turkey-refugee -agreement-a-review/a-43028295 (accessed October 2018).

59. See Kirk Semple, "What Is the Migration Caravan and Why Does It Matter to Trump?" *New York Times* (19 October 2019), A13, accessible online at https://www.nytimes.com /2018/10/18/world/americas/trump-migrant-caravan.html (accessed October 2018).

60. Needless to say, this proposal aroused public outrage. See "Empörung über Petrys Forderung," *Die Zeit* (30 January 2016), accessible online at https://www.zeit.de/politik /deutschland/2016–01/afd-frauke-petry-schusswaffen-fluechtlinge-reaktionen (accessed December 2018). The outrage was certainly part of a broader media strategy that has worked very well. The amount of attention the AfD has received, including from liberal and mainstream media, is out of proportion to the party's share of the electorate.

ARCHIVAL RESOURCES

Poland

Archiwum Akt Nowych
- Ministerstwo Ziem Odzyskanyh
- Ministerstwo Administracji Publicznej
- Generalny Pełnomocnik Rządu RP do spraw Repatriacji w Warszawie
- Zarząd Centralny PUR

Archiwum Panstwowy w Opolu
- Panstwowy Urząd Repatriacyjny

Archiwum Panstwowy w Katowicach
- Panstwowy Urząd Repatriacyjny w Województwie Śląsko-Dąbrowskim
- Urząd Województwa Śląsko-Dąbrowskiego, Wydział Osiedleńczy

Archiwum Instytutu Zachodniego, Poznań
- Pamiętniki osadników, 1957
- Pamiętniki młodzieży urodzonej na ziemiach zachodnich, 1966
- Pamiętniki mieskańców ziem zachodnich, 1970

Archiwum Instytutu Śląskiego, Opole
- Pamiętniki trzech pokoleń mieszkańców Ziem Odzyskanych, 1986
- Pierwsze lata władzy ludowej we wspomnieniach Opolan, 1982

Centralny Archiwum Ministerstwa Spraw Wewnętrznych
- Ministerstwo Administracji Publicznej

Germany

Bundesarchiv Lichterfelde
- DO 2 Zentralverwaltung für deutsche Umsiedler

Brandenburgisches Landeshauptarchiv
- Ld. Br. Rep. 203 (Ministerium des Innern)
- Ld. Br. Rep. 206 (Ministerium für Wirtschaft)
- Ld. Br. Rep. 208 (Ministerium für Landwirtschaft und Forsten)
- Ld. Br. Rep. 250 (Landratsämter Calau/Senftenberg, Cottbus und Lübben)

Sächsisches Hauptstaatsarchiv Dresden
- MdI (Ministerium des Innern)
- MinAS (Ministerium für Arbeit und Soziales)
- Landeskreis/Kreistag Bautzen und Hoyerswerda

Hungary

Open Society Archive, Budapest
- HU OSA 304-0-2 (International Human Rights Law Institute, Interim and Supplementary Reports of the UN Special Rapporteur)

- HU OSA 304-0-6 (International Human Rights Law Institute, Materials on Ethnic Cleansing)
- HU OSA 304-0-4 (International Human Rights Law Institute, United Nations, International Red Cross Committee, International Court of Justice)

USA

AGUSA (The Armenian Genocide in the U. S. Archives, 1915–1918), Mikrofiche 337.

BIBLIOGRAPHY

Abbasi, Mustafa. "The War on the Mixed Cities: The Depopulation of Arab Tiberias and the Destruction of Its Old, 'Sacred' City (1948-9)," *Holy Land Studies* 7/ 1 (2008), 45-80.

Adida, Claire L., David D. Laitin, and Marie-Anne Valfort. *Why Muslim Integration Fails in Christian-Heritage Societies*. Cambridge: Harvard University Press, 2016.

Alexander, Robin. *Die Getriebenen: Merkel und die Flüchtlingspolitik: Report aus dem Inneren der Macht*. Berlin: Siedler, 2017.

Anderson, Elizabeth. *The Imperative of Integration*. Princeton: Princeton University Press, 2010.

Arendt, Hannah. *The Jew as Pariah*, Ron H. Feldman, ed. New York: Grove, 1978.

———. *Wir Flüchtlinge*. Stuttgart: Reclam, 2016. English original: "We Refugees," *Menorah Journal* 31, no. 1 (January 1943). Also accessible online at http://www.documenta14.de/de /south/35_we_refugees (accessed April 2017) and reprinted in Arendt, *The Jew as Pariah*.

Bade, Klaus J. *Migration in European History*, trans. Allison Brown. Malden: Blackwell, 2003.

Bade, Klaus, and Jochen Oltmer. "Einführung: Aussiedlerzuwanderung und Aussiedlerintegration: Historische Entwicklung und aktuelle Probleme," in Klaus Bade and Jochen Oltmer, eds., *Aussiedler*, 9-54.

Bade, Klaus, and Jochen Oltmer, eds. *Aussiedler: deutsche Einwanderer aus Osteuropa*. Osnabrück: Universitätsverlag Rasch, 1999.

Bahlcke, Joachim, ed. *Glaubensflüchtlinge. Ursachen, Formen und Auswirkungen frühneuzeitlicher Konfessionsmigration in Europa*. Münster: LIT, 2008.

Bahlcke, Joachim, Rainer Leng, and Peter Scholz, eds. *Migration als soziale Herausforderung: Historische Formen solidarischen Handelns von der Antike bis zum 20. Jahrhundert*. Stuttgart: Steiner, 2011.

Banki, Christine, and Christoph Späti. "Ungarn, Tibeter, Tschechen und Slowaken: Bedingungen ihrer Akzeptanz in der Schweiz der Nachkriegszeit," in Carsten Goehrke and Werner G. Zimmermann, eds., *"Zuflucht Schweiz": Der Umgang mit Asylproblemen im 19. und 20. Jahrhundert*. Zurich: Hans Rohr, 1994, 369-416.

Barnett, Michael. "Humanitarianism with a Sovereign Face: UNHCR in the Global Undertow," *International Migration Review* 35/1 (2001), 255-259.

Baron, Nick, and Peter Gatrell, eds. *Homelands: War, Population and Statehood in Eastern Europe and Russia, 1918-1924*. London: Anthem Press, 2004.

Bellamy, Alex J., and Tim Dunne. *The Oxford Handbook of the Responsibility to Protect*. Oxford: Oxford University Press, 2016.

Belova, Irina. *Vynuždennye migranty: Bežency i voennoplennye Pervoj mirovoj vojny v Rossii, 1914-1925 gg.* Moscow: AIRO-XXI, 2014.

Benedict, Philip, et al., eds. *Reformation, Revolt and Civil War in France and the Netherlands, 1555-1585*. Amsterdam: Koninklijke Nederlandse Akademie van Wetenschappen, 1999.

Benz, Wolfgang, Claudia Curio, and Andrea Hummel, eds. *Die Kindertransporte, 1938/39: Rettung und Integration*. Frankfurt am Main: Fischer, 2003.

Berendt, Grzegorz. *Żydzi na terenie Wolnego Miasta Gdańska w latach, 1920–1945 (Działalność kulturalna, polityczna i socjalna)*. Gdańsk: Gdańskie Towarzystwo Naukowe, 1997.

Betts, Alexander, and Paul Collier. *Refuge: Rethinking Refugee Policy in a Changing World*. New York, Oxford University Press, 2017.

Blume, Georg et al. "Grenzöffnung für Flüchtlinge. Was geschah wirklich?" in *Die Zeit* (18 August 2016), accessible online at http://www.zeit.de/2016/35/grenzoeffnung-fluechtlinge -september-2015-wochenende-angela-merkel-ungarn-oesterreich (accessed April 2017).

Blumi, Isa. *Ottoman Refugees, 1878–1939: Migration in a Post-Imperial World*. London: Bloomsbury, 2013.

Boffa, Massimo. "Die Emigranten," in François Furet and Mona Ozouf, eds., *Kritisches Wörter- buch der Französischen Revolution*, vol. 1: *Ereignisse, Akteure*, 546–564. Frankfurt am Main: Suhrkamp, 1996.

Bon Tempo, Carl. *Americans at the Gate: The United States and Refugees during the Cold War*. Princeton: Princeton University Press, 2008.

Borejsza, Jerzy. *Emigracja polska po powstaniu styczniowym*. Warsaw: PWN, 1966.

Borodziej, Włodzimierz. *Geschichte Polens im 20. Jahrhundert*. Munich: C. H. Beck, 2010.

Borodziej, Włodzimierz, and Maciej Górny. *Der vergessene Weltkrieg: Europas Osten, 1912– 1923*, 2 vols. Darmstadt: WBG, 2018.

Boykov, Grigor. "The Human Cost of Warfare: Population Loss during the Ottoman Con- quest and the Demographic History of Bulgaria in the Late Middle Ages and Early Mod- ern Era," in Oliver Schmitt, ed., *The Ottoman Conquest of the Balkans: Interpretations and Research Debates*, 103–166. Vienna: Verlag der Österreichischen Akademie der Wissen- schaften, 2016.

Brandes, Detlef, Holm Sundhaussen, and Stefan Troebst, eds. *Lexikon der Vertreibungen: De- portation, Zwangsaussiedlung und ethnische Säuberung im Europa des 20. Jahrhunderts*. Vienna: Böhlau, 2010.

Brinkmann, Tobias. "Jüdische Migration," in *Europäische Geschichte Online (EGO)* (3 Decem- ber 2010), accessible online at http://ieg-ego.eu/de/threads/europa-unterwegs/juedische -migration/tobias-brinkmann-juedische-migration (accessed April 2017).

Brunnbauer, Ulf. "Labour Emigration from the Yugoslav Area from the Late 19th Century until the End of Socialism: Continuities and Changes," in Brunnbauer, ed., *Transnational Societies, Transterritorial Politics: Migrations in the (Post-)Yugoslav Region, 19th– 21st Century*, 17–50. Munich: Oldenbourg, 2009.

Bundeszentrale für Politische Bildung. *"Zahlen zu Asyl in Deutschland"* (10 April 2017), ac- cessible online at https://www.bpb.de/politik/innenpolitik/flucht/218788/zahlen-zu-asyl-in -deutschland (accessed April 2017).

Caestecker, Frank, and Sarah Eloy, eds. *Los Niños. Tien vluchtelingenkinderen uit de Spaanse Burgeroorlog vertellen*. Antwerp: EPO, 2007.

Carruthers, Susan L. "Between Camps: Eastern Bloc 'Escapees' and Cold War Borderlands," *American Quarterly* 57/3 (2005), 911–942.

Cattaruzza, Marina. *L'Italia e il confine orientale, 1866–2006*. Bologna: Il Mulino, 2007.

Chappell, Carolyn Lougee. "'The Pains I Took to Save My/His Family': Escape Accounts by a Huguenot Mother and Daughter after the Revocation of the Edict of Nantes," *French His- torical Studies* 22/1 (1999), 1–64.

Chatty, Dawn. "Integration without Assimilation in an Impermanent Landscape: Dispossess- sion and Forced Migration in the Arab Middle East," in Panikos Panayi and Pippa Virdee, eds., *Refugees and the End of Empire: Imperial Collapse and Forced Migration in the Twen- tieth Century*, 127–151. Basingstoke: Palgrave Macmillan, 2011.

Chu, Winson. *The German Minority in Interwar Poland*. Cambridge: Cambridge University Press, 2012.

Ciesielski, Stanislaw, ed. *Umsiedlung der Polen aus den ehemaligen polnischen Ostgebieten nach Polen in den Jahren 1944–1947*. Marburg: Herder Institut, 2006.

Cohen, Gerard Daniel. *In War's Wake: Europe's Displaced Persons in the Postwar Order*. Oxford: Oxford University Press, 2012.

Comte, Emmanuel. *The History of the European Migration Regime: Germany's Strategic Hegemony*. London: Routledge, 2018.

Comtat, Emmanuelle. *Les pieds-noirs et la politique: quarante ans après le retour*. Paris: Presses de Sciences Po, 2009.

Conference on Near Eastern Affairs. *Lausanne Conference on Near Eastern Affairs 1922–1923, Records of Proceedings and Draft Terms of Peace*. London: Her Majesty's Stationery Office, 1923.

Diaz, Delphine. *Un asile pour tous les peuples? Exilés et réfugiés étrangers en France au cours du premier XIXe siècle*. Paris: Armand Colin, 2014.

Dietz, Barbara. "Jugendliche Aussiedler in Deutschland: Risiken und Chancen der Integration," in Klaus Bade and Jochen Oltmer, eds., *Aussiedler: deutsche Einwanderer aus Osteuropa*, 153–176. Osnabrück: Universitätsverlag Rasch, 1999.

Dölemeyer, Barbara. *Die Hugenotten*. Stuttgart: Kohlhammer 2006.

Dövényi, Zoltán, and Gabriella Vukovich. "Ungarn und die internationale Migration," in Heinz Fassmann and Rainer Münz, eds., *Migration in Europa: Historische Entwicklungen, aktuelle Trends, politische Reaktionen*. Frankfurt am Main: Campus, 1996, 263–284.

Dreyfus-Armand, Geneviève. *L'exil des républicains espagnols en France: De la Guerre civile à la mort de Franco*. Paris: Albin Michel, 1999.

Dufoix, Stéphane. *Politiques d'exil: Hongrois, Polonais et Tchécoslovaques en France après 1945*. Paris: Presses Universitaires de France, 2002.

Etemad, Bouda. "Europe and Migration after Decolonisation," *Journal of European Economic History* 27/3 (Winter 1998), 457–470.

Fassin, Didier. *Humanitarian Reason: A Moral History of the Present*. Berkeley: University of California Press, 2012.

Fassmann, Heinz, and Rainer Münz, eds. *Migration in Europa: Historische Entwicklungen, aktuelle Trends, politische Reaktionen*. Frankfurt am Main: Campus, 1996.

Fink, Carole. *Defending the Rights of Others: The Great Powers, the Jews, and International Minority Protection, 1878–1938*. Cambridge: Cambridge University Press, 2004.

Fleming, Michael. "Greek 'Heroes' in the Polish People's Republic and the Geopolitics of the Cold War, 1948–1956," *Nationalities Papers* 36/3 (July 2008), 375–397.

Foschepoth, Josef. "Rolle und Bedeutung der KPD im deutsch-deutschen Systemkonflikt," *Zeitschrift für Geschichtswissenschaft* 56/11 (2008), 889–909.

Frank, Matthew. *Expelling the Germans: British Opinion and Post-1945 Population Transfer in Context*. Oxford: Oxford University Press, 2007.

Freitag, Sabine, ed. *Exiles from European Revolutions: Refugees in Mid-Victorian England*. New York: Berghahn, 2003.

Galijaš, Armina. *Eine bosnische Stadt im Zeichen des Krieges: Ethnopolitik und Alltag in Banja Luka (1990–1995)*. Munich: Oldenbourg, 2011.

García, María Cristina. *The Refugee Challenge in Post-Cold War America*. Oxford: Oxford University Press, 2017.

Gatrell, Peter. *The Making of the Modern Refugee*. Oxford: Oxford University Press, 2013.

———. "Refugees," in *1914–1918 Online. International Encyclopedia of the First World War* (8 October 2014), accessible online at http://encyclopedia.1914-1918-online.net/article /refugees (accessed April 2017).

———. *A Whole Empire Walking: Refugees in Russia during World War I*. Bloomington: Indiana University Press, 2005.

Goeken-Haidl, Ulrike. *Der Weg zurück. Die Repatriierung sowjetischer Kriegsgefangener und Zwangsarbeiter während und nach dem Zweiten Weltkrieg*. Essen: Klartext, 2006.

Grahl-Madsen, Atle. *The Status of Refugees in International Law*, 2 vols. Leyden: Sijthoff, 1966, 1972.

Grandits, Hannes, and Karl Kaser. "Familie und Gesellschaft in der habsburgischen Militärgrenze: Lika und Krbava zu Beginn des 18. Jahrhunderts," in Drago Roksandić, ed., *Microhistory of the Triplex Confinium*, 27–68. Budapest: Institute on Southeastern Europe, 1998,

"Greek" Refugee Settlement Commission. *Greek Refugee Settlement*. Geneva: Publications of the League of Nations, 1926.

Guzun, Vadim. *Indezirabilii: aspecte mediatice, umanitare și de securitate privind emigrația din Uniunea Sovietică în România interbelică*. Cluj-Napoca: Editura Argonaut, 2013.

Hamed-Troyansky, Vladimir. *Imperial Refugee: Resettlement of Muslims from Russia in the Ottoman Empire, 1860–1914*. Ph.D. diss., Stanford University, Department of History, July 2018.

Hamlin, Rebecca. *Let Me Be a Refugee. Administrative Justice and the Politics of Asylum in the United States, Canada, and Australia*. Oxford: Oxford University Press, 2014.

Harvey, Leonard. *Muslims in Spain, 1500 to 1614*. Chicago: University of Chicago Press, 2005.

Haslinger, Peter. "Flüchtlingskrise 1956—die Ungarische Revolution und Österreich," in Jerzy Kochanowski and Joachim von Puttkamer, eds., *1956. (Nieco) inne spojrzenie. Eine (etwas) andere Perspektive*, 125–156. Warsaw: Neriton, 2016.

Heidemeyer, Helge. *Flucht und Zuwanderung aus der SBZ/DDR, 1945/49–1961: Die Flüchtlingspolitik der Bundesrepublik Deutschland bis zum Bau der Berliner Mauer*. Düsseldorf: Droste Verlag, 1994.

Heitmeyer, Wilhelm. ed., *Bundesrepublik Deutschland: Auf dem Weg von der Konsens- zur Konfliktgesellschaft*, vol. 2: *Was hält die Gesellschaft zusammen?* Frankfurt am Main: Suhrkamp, 1997.

Helmedach, Andreas. "Bevölkerungspolitik im Zeichen der Aufklärung: Zwangsumsiedlung und Zwangsassimilierung im Habsburgerreich des 18. Jahrhunderts—eine noch ungelöste Forschungsaufgabe," *Comparativ* 6/1 (1996), 41–62.

Herbert, Ulrich. "Flucht und Asyl: Zeithistorische Bemerkungen zu einem aktuellen Problem," in *Zeitgeschichte Online* (December 2015), accessible online at http://www.zeitgeschichte-online.de/thema/flucht-und-asyl (accessed April 2017).

———. *Geschichte der Ausländerpolitik in Deutschland. Saisonarbeiter, Zwangsarbeiter, Gastarbeiter, Flüchtlinge*. Munich: C. H. Beck, 2001.

Hirschon, Renée. *Heirs of the Greek Catastrophe: The Social Life of Asia Minor Refugees in Piraeus*. Oxford: Clarendon Press, 1989.

Hoerder, Dirk. *Geschichte der deutschen Migration: vom Mittelalter bis heute*. Munich: C. H. Beck, 2010.

———. *Cultures in Contact: World Migrations in the Second Millennium*. Durham: Duke University Press, 2002.

Hoffmann-Holter, Beatrix. *"Abreisendmachung": Jüdische Kriegsflüchtlinge in Vienna, 1914 bis 1923*. Vienna: Böhlau, 1995.

Holquist, Peter. *Making War, Forging Revolution: Russia's Continuum of Crisis, 1914–1921*. Cambridge: Harvard University Press, 2002.

———. "To Count, to Extract and to Exterminate: Population Statistics and Population Politics in Late Imperial and Soviet Russia," in Roland Suny, Grigor Ronald, and Terry Martin, eds., *A State of Nations: Empire and Nation Making in the Age of Lenin and Stalin*, 111–144. Oxford: Oxford University Press, 2001.

Höpken, Wolfgang. "Flucht vor dem Kreuz? Muslimische Emigration aus Südosteuropa nach dem Ende der Osmanischen Herrschaft (19./20. Jahrhundert)," *Comparativ* 6/1 (1996), 1–24.

Hroch, Miroslav. *Das Europa der Nationen: Die moderne Nationsbildung im europäischen Vergleich.* Göttingen: Vandenhoeck & Ruprecht, 2005.

Hunn, Karin. *"Nächstes Jahr kehren wir zurück . . .": Die Geschichte der türkischen "Gastarbeiter" in der Bundesrepublik.* Göttingen: Wallstein, 2005.

The International Criminal Tribunal for the Former Yugoslavia. "Case No.: IT-96-23-PT. The Prosecutor of the Tribunal against Dragoljub Kunarac and Radomir Kovac" (November 8, 1999), accessible online at http://www.icty.org/x/cases/kunarac/ind/en/kun-iii991108e.pdf (accessed April 2017).

The International Criminal Tribunal for the Former Yugoslavia. "Mrkšić et al. (IT-95-13/1)," accessible online at http://www.icty.org/case/mrksic/4 (accessed April 2017).

The International Organization for Migration. "Mediterranean Migrant Arrivals in 2016: 204,311; Deaths 2,443," May 31, 2016, accessible online at https://www.iom.int/news /mediterranean-migrant-arrivals-2016-204311-deaths-2443 (accessed April 2017).

Jasanoff, Maya. *Liberty's Exiles: American Loyalists in the Revolutionary World.* New York: Alfred A. Knopf, 2011.

Jones, Guno. *Tussen onderdanen, rijksgenoten en Nederlanders: Nederlandse politici over burgers uit Oost en West en Nederland, 1945–2005.* Amsterdam: Rozenberg, 2007.

Jordi, Jean-Jacques. *1962: L'arrivée Des Pieds-Noirs.* Paris: Autrement, 1995.

Jovanovich, Miroslav. *Russkaja emigracija na Balkanach, 1920–1940.* Moscow: Russkii puť, 2005.

Kaes, Anton, Martin Jay, and Edward Dimendberg, eds. *The Weimar Republic Sourcebook* [English trans.]. Berkeley: University of California Press, 1995.

Karpat, Kemal. *Ottoman Population, 1830–1914: Demographic and Social Characteristics.* Madison: University of Wisconsin Press, 1985.

Karpozilos, Kostis. "The Defeated of the Greek Civil War: From Fighters to Political Refugees in the Cold War," *Journal of Cold War Studies* 16/3 (2014), 62–87.

Khalil, Asem. "Socioeconomic Rights of Palestinian Refugees in Arab Countries," *International Journal of Refugee Law* 23/4 (2011), 680–719.

Kieser, Hans-Lukas. *Talaat Pasha: Father of Modern Turkey, Architect of Genocide.* Princeton: Princeton University Press, 2018.

Kleßmann, Christoph. *Polnische Bergarbeiter im Ruhrgebiet, 1870–1945: Soziale Integration und nationale Subkultur einer Minderheit in der deutschen Industriegesellschaft.* Göttingen: Vandenhoeck & Ruprecht, 1978.

Klier, John, and Shlomo Lambroza, eds. *Pogroms: Anti-Jewish Violence in Modern Russian History.* Cambridge: Cambridge University Press, 1992.

Klüger, Ruth. *Weiter leben: eine Jugend.* Göttingen: Wallstein, 1992. English ed.: *Still Alive: A Holocaust Girlhood Remembered.* New York: Feminist Press at the City University of New York, 2001.

Kohser-Spohn, Christiane, and Frank Renken, eds. *Trauma Algerienkrieg: Zur Geschichte und Aufarbeitung eines tabuisierten Konflikts.* Frankfurt am Main: Campus, 2006.

Königseder, Angelika, and Juliane Wetzel. *Lebensmut im Wartesaal: Die jüdischen DPs (Displaced Persons) im Nachkriegsdeutschland.* Frankfurt am Main: Fischer Taschenbuch, 1994.

Kontogiorgi, Elisabeth. *Population Exchange in Greek Macedonia: The Rural Settlement of Refugees, 1922–1930.* New York: Oxford University Press, 2006.

Kossert, Andreas. *Kalte Heimat. Die Geschichte der deutschen Vertriebenen nach 1945.* Berlin: Siedler, 2008.

Kozelsky, Mara: *Crimea in War and Transformation*. Oxford: Oxford University Press, 2019.

Krohn, Claus-Dieter, et al., eds. *Handbuch der deutschsprachigen Emigration, 1933–1945*. Darmstadt: Wissenschaftliche Buchgesellschaft, 1998.

Kulecki, Michał. *Wygnańcy ze Wschodu: Egzulanci w Rzeczypospolitej w ostatnich latach panowania Jana Kazimierza i za panowania Michała Korybuta Wiśniowieckiego*. Warsaw: DiG, 1997.

Labrador Juarros, Román-Fernando. "Campos de concentración en la provincial de Burgos, 1936–1939," accessible online at http://web.archive.org/web/20120616210917/http:/www.cefid.uab.es/files/comunicII-3.pdf (accessed April 2017).

Lachenicht, Susanne. *Hugenotten in Europa und Nordamerika: Migration und Integration in der Frühen Neuzeit*. Frankfurt am Main: Campus, 2010.

Lausanne Conference on Near Eastern Affairs 1922–1923, Records of Proceedings and Draft Terms of Peace. London: Her Majesty's Stationery Office, 1923. Also accessible online at https://archive.org/details/recordsofproceed00confuoft (accessed April 2017).

Lefeuvre, Daniel. "Les pieds-noirs," in Mohammed Harbi and Benjamin Stora, eds., *La guerre d'Algérie*, 381–410. Paris: Robert Laffont, 2004.

Leffler, Melvyn, and Odd Arne Westad, eds. *The Cambridge History of the Cold War*, 3 vols. New York: Cambridge University Press, 2010.

Lemberg, Eugen, and Friedrich Edding, eds. *Die Vertriebenen in Westdeutschland: Ihre Eingliederung und ihr Einfluss auf Gesellschaft, Wirtschaft, Politik und Geistesleben*, 3 vols. Kiel: Ferdinand Hirt, 1959.

Liverani, Luca. "Comunità di Sant'Egidio: Un anno di corridoi umanitari, altri 50 profughi a Fiumicino," *Avvenire* (February 27, 2017), accessible online at https://www.avvenire.it/attualita/pagine/corridoi-umanitari-arrivo-a-fiumicino (accessed April 2017).

Loescher, Gil. "The UNHCR and World Politics: State Interests vs. Institutional Autonomy," *International Migration Review* 35/1 (2001), 33–65.

Lohr, Eric. *Nationalizing the Russian Empire: The Campaign against Enemy Aliens during World War I*. Cambridge: Harvard University Press, 2003.

Lougee Chappell, Carolyn. "'The Pains I Took to Save My/His Family': Escape Accounts by a Huguenot Mother and Daughter after the Revocation of the Edict of Nantes," *French Historical Studies* 22/1 (Winter 1999), 1–64.

Lucassen, Leo. "Poles and Turks in the German Ruhr area: Similarities and differences," in Leo Lucassen, David Feldman, and Jochen Oltmer, eds., *Paths of Integration: Migrants in Western Europe (1880–2004)*. Amsterdam: Amsterdam University Press, 2006, 27–45.

Lucassen, Leo, David Feldman, and Jochen Oltmer, eds. *Paths of Integration: Migrants in Western Europe, 1880–2004*. Amsterdam: Amsterdam University Press, 2006.

Lucassen, Leo, and Jan Lucassen, eds. *Migration, Migration History, History: Old Paradigms and New Perspectives*, 3rd. ed. Frankfurt am Main: Peter Lang, 2005.

MacQueen, Norrie. *The Decolonization of Portuguese Africa: Metropolitan Revolution and the Dissolution of Empire*. London: Longman, 1997.

Magdelaine, Michelle. "Francfort-sur-le-Main et le réfugiés huguenots," in Guido Braun and Susanne Lachenicht, eds. *Hugenotten und deutsche Territorialstaaten: Immigrationspolitik und Integrationsprozesse*, 35–50. Munich: Oldenbourg, 2007.

Malcolm, Noel. *Kosovo: A Short History*. London: Macmillan, 1998.

Marrus, Michael. *The Unwanted: European Refugees in the Twentieth Century*. New York: Oxford University Press, 1985.

Marshall, T. H. *Citizenship and Social Class and Other Essays*. Cambridge: Cambridge University Press, 1950.

Masalha, Nur. *Expulsion of the Palestinians: The Concept of "Transfer" in Zionist Political Thought, 1882–1948*. Washington, DC: Institute for Palestine Studies, 1992.

Mazower, Mark. *Dark Continent: Europe's Twentieth Century.* New York, Alfred A. Knopf, 1999.

Mazower, Mark, ed. *After the War Was Over: Reconstructing the Family, Nation, and State in Greece, 1943–1960.* Princeton: Princeton University Press, 2000.

Miège, Jean-Louis, and Colette Dubois, eds. *L'Europe retrouvée: Les migrations de la décolonisation.* Paris: L'Harmattan, 1994.

Monsagrati, Giuseppe. "Mazzini, Giuseppe," in *Dizionario biografico degli italiani*, vol. 72: *Massimo-Mechetti* (2008), accessible online at http://www.treccani.it/enciclopedia /giuseppe-mazzini_(Dizionario-Biografico)/ (accessed April 2017).

Moore, Jason Kendall. "Between Expediency and Principle: U.S. Repatriation Policy towards Russian Nationals, 1944–1949," *Diplomatic History* 24/3 (2000), 381–404.

Morris, Benny. *1948: A History of the First Arab-Israeli War.* New Haven: Yale University Press, 2008.

Motyka, Grzegorz. *Tak było w Bieszczadach: Walki polsko-ukraińskie, 1943–1948.* Warsaw: Oficyna Wydawnicza Volumen, 1999.

Münch, Richard. "Elemente einer Theorie der Integration moderner Gesellschaften," in Wilhelm Heitmeyer, ed., *Bundesrepublik Deutschland: Auf dem Weg von der Konsens- zur Konfliktgesellschaft*, vol. 2: *Was hält die Gesellschaft zusammen?* 66–109. Frankfurt am Main: Suhrkamp, 1997.

Münz, Rainer, Wolfgang Seifert, and Ralf Ulrich, eds. *Zuwanderung nach Deutschland: Strukturen, Wirkungen, Perspektiven*, 2nd ed. Frankfurt am Main: Campus, 1999.

Nansen, Fridtjof. "Russian Refugees: General Report of the Work Accomplished Up to March 15th, 1922, by Dr. Fridtjof Nansen, the High Commissioner of the League," *League of Nations: Official Journal* (May 1922), 385–395.

Niggemann, Ulrich. "Konflikte um Immigration als 'antietatistische' Proteste? Eine Revision der Auseinandersetzung bei der Hugenotteneinwanderung," *Historische Zeitschrift* 286/1 (2008), 37–61.

Ogilvie, Sarah A., and Scott Miller. *Refuge Denied: The St. Louis Passengers and the Holocaust.* Madison: University of Wisconsin Press, 2006.

Oltmer, Jochen. "Flucht, Vertreibung und Asyl im 19. und 20. Jahrhundert," *IMIS Beiträge* 20 (2002), 107–134.

———. *Migration im 19. und 20. Jahrhundert*, 2nd ed. Munich: Oldenbourg, 2013.

Palestine Royal Commission. "League of Nations: Mandates Palestine Report of the Palestine Royal Commission, presented by the Secretary of State for the Colonies to the United Kingdom Parliament by Command of His Britannic Majesty (July 1937)," in the *Jewish Virtual Library*, accessible online at http://www.jewishvirtuallibrary.org/jsource/History /peel1.html (accessed April 2017).

Panagiotidis, Jannis. "Staat, Zivilgesellschaft und Aussiedlermigration, 1950–1989," in Jochen Oltmer, ed., *Handbuch Staat und Migration in Deutschland seit dem 17. Jahrhundert*, 895–930. Berlin: De Gruyter, 2016.

Pappé, Ilan. *The Ethnic Cleansing of Palestine.* Oxford: Oneworld, 2006.

Porter, Stephen R. *Benevolent Empire: U.S. Power, Humanitarianism and the World's Dispossessed.* Philadelphia: University of Pennsylvania Press, 2017.

Poutros, Patrice G. "Spannungen und Dynamiken: Asylgewährung in der Bundesrepublik Deutschland von den frühen 1950ern bis zur Mitte der 1970er Jahre," in Maria Mesner and Gernot Heiss, eds., *Asyl: Das lange 20. Jahrhundert.* Vienna: Löcker, 2012, 126–145.

Reiter, Herbert. *Politisches Asyl im 19. Jahrhundert. Die deutschen politischen Flüchtlinge des Vormärz und der Revolution von 1848/49 in Europa und den USA.* Berlin: Duncker & Humblot, 1992.

Rendl, Renate. "Die Integration der Flüchtlinge aus der Tschechoslowakei in der Schweiz seit 1968," in Monika Bankowski et al., eds., *Asyl und Aufenthalt: Die Schweiz als Zuflucht und*

Wirkungsstätte von Slaven im 19. und 20. Jahrhundert, 239–252. Basel: Helbing und Lichtenhahn, 1994.

Richter, Heinz A. *Geschichte der Insel Zypern*, vol. 4 (1 + 2): *1965–1977*. Mainz: Rutzen, 2009.

Röhr, Werner: "Der 'Fall Grün' und das Sudetendeutsche Freikorps," in Hans-Hennig Hahn, ed., *Hundert Jahre sudetendeutsche Geschichte: Eine völkische Bewegung in drei Staaten*, 243–258. Frankfurt am Main: Peter Lang, 2007.

Roth, Joseph. *What I Saw: Reports from Berlin*, trans. with an introduction by Michael Hofmann. New York: W.W. Norton.

Salentin, Kurt. *Tamilische Flüchtlinge in der Bundesrepublik*. Frankfurt am Main: Verlag für Interkulturelle Kommunikation, 2002.

Salvatici, Silvia. "Between National and International Mandates: Displaced Persons and Refugees in Postwar Italy," *Journal of Contemporary History* 49 (2014), 514–536.

Saß, Anne-Christin. *Berliner Luftmenschen: Osteuropäisch-jüdische Migranten in der Weimarer Republik*. Göttingen: Wallstein, 2012.

Sayigh, Rosemary. *Too Many Enemies: The Palestinian Experience in Lebanon*. London: Zed Books, 1994.

Schafranek, Hans. *Söldner für den Anschluss: Die Österreichische Legion, 1933–1938*. Vienna: Czernin-Verlag, 2011.

Schnapper, Dominique: "L'échec du ›modèle républicain? Réflexion d'une sociologue," *Annales: Histoire, Sciences Sociales* 61/4 (2006), 759–776.

Schunka, Alexander. "Konfession und Migrationsregime in der Frühen Neuzeit," *Geschichte und Gesellschaft* 35 (2009), 28–63.

Scioldo-Zürcher, Yann. *Devenir métropolitain: Politique d'intégration et parcours de rapatriés d'Algérie en métropole (1954–2005)*. Paris: Éditions de l'École des hautes études en sciences sociales, 2010.

Shain, Yossi. *The Frontier of Loyalty: Political Exiles in the Age of the Nation State*, 2nd ed. Ann Arbor: University of Michigan Press, 2005.

Shenhav, Yehouda. *The Arab Jews: A Postcolonial Reading of Nationalism, Religion, and Ethnicity*. Stanford: Stanford University Press, 2006.

Shiblak, Abbas. "Residency Status and Civil Rights of Palestinian Refugees in Arab Countries," *Journal of Palestine Studies* 25/3 (Spring 1996), 36–45.

Shlaim, Avi. *The Politics of Partition: King Abdullah, the Zionists, and Palestine 1921–1951*. Oxford: Oxford University Press, 1998.

Shulewitz, Malka Hillel. *The Forgotten Millions: The Modern Jewish Exodus from Arab Lands*. London: Bloomsbury, 2001.

Siegelbaum, Lewis H., and Leslie Page Moch. *Broad Is My Native Land: Repertoires and Regimes of Migration in Russia's Twentieth Century*. Ithaca: Cornell University Press, 2014.

Simmel, Georg. *Soziologie: Untersuchungen über die Formen der Vergesellschaftung. Gesamtausgabe*, vol. 11, Otthein Rammstedt, ed. Frankfurt a.M.: Suhrkamp, 1992.

Skran, Claudena. *Refugees in Inter-War Europe: The Emergence of a Regime*. Oxford: Clarendon Press, 1995.

Soutou, Georges-Henri. *La Guerre froide: 1943–1990*. Paris: Fayard, 2010.

Sperber, Manès. *Bis man mir Scherben auf die Augen legt: All das Vergangene. . . .* Vienna: Europa-Verlag, 1977. English trans. (vol. 3) Harry Zohn, *Until My Eyes Are Closed with Shards*, New York: Holmes & Meier, 1994.

———. *Die vergebliche Warnung. All das Vergangene. . . .* Vienna: Europa-Verlag, 1975. English trans. (vol. 2) Harry Zohn, *The Unheeded Warning, 1918–1933*, New York: Holmes & Meier, 1991.

———. *Die Wasserträger Gottes: All das Vergangene. . . .* Vienna: Europa-Verlag, 1974. English trans. (vol. 1) Joachim Neugroschel, *God's Water Carriers*, New York: Holmes & Meier, 1987.

Stadler, Bettina, and Beatrix Wiedenhofer-Galik. "Dequalifizierung von Migrantinnen und Migranten am österreichischen Arbeitsmarkt," *Statistische Nachrichten* 5 (2011), 383–399.

Stančić, Mirjana. *Manès Sperber: Leben und Werk.* Frankfurt am Main: Stroemfeld Verlag, 2003.

Statistisches Bundesamt. *Bevölkerung und Erwerbstätigkeit: Bevölkerung mit Migrationshintergrund—Ergebnisse des Mikrozensus 2014* (Fachserie 1 Reihe 2.2), 2017, accessible online at https://www.destatis.de/DE/Publikationen/Thematisch/Bevoelkerung/Migration Integration/Migrationshintergrund2010220147004.pdf?__blob=publicationFile (accessed April 2017).

Statistisches Bundesamt. *Datenreport 2016: Ein Sozialbericht für die Bundesrepublik Deutschland.* Bonn: Bundeszentrale für politische Bildung, 2016.

Stöcker, Fredrik. *Bridging the Baltic Sea: Networks of Resistance and Opposition during the Cold War Era.* Lanham, MD: Lexington Books, 2018.

Stola, Dariusz. *Kraj bez wyjścia? Migracji z Polski, 1949–1989.* Warsaw: PAN ISP, 2010.

Stora, Benjamin. *Histoire de la guerre d'Algérie (1830–1954),* 4th ed. Paris: La Découverte, 2004.

———. *Histoire de la guerre d'Algérie (1954–1962),* 4th ed. Paris: La Découverte, 2004.

Sula, Dorota. *Powrót ludności polskiej z byłego Imperium Rosyjskiego w latach 1918–1937.* Warsaw: Trio, 2013.

Sundhaussen, Holm. *Geschichte Serbiens: 19.-21. Jahrhundert.* Vienna: Böhlau, 2007.

———. *Jugoslawien und seine Nachfolgestaaten, 1943–2011: Eine ungewöhnliche Geschichte des Gewöhnlichen.* Vienna: Böhlau, 2012.

Temperley, Harold William Vazeille, ed. *A History of the Peace Conference of Paris,* vol. 5: *Economic Reconstruction and Protection of Minorities.* Neudruck, London: Oxford University Press, 1969.

Ther, Philipp. *The Dark Side of Nation States: Ethnic Cleansing in Modern Europe.* New York: Berghahn, 2014.

———. *Deutsche und polnische Vertriebene: Gesellschaft und Vertriebenenpolitik in der SBZ/DDR und in Polen, 1945–1956.* Göttingen: Vandenhoeck & Ruprecht, 1998.

Thorpe, Julie. "Displacing Empire: Refugee Welfare, National Activism, and State Legitimacy in Austria-Hungary in the First World War," in Panikos Panayi and Pippa Virdee, eds., *Refugees and the End of Empire: Imperial Collapse and Forced Migration in the Twentieth Century,* 102–126. Basingstoke: Palgrave Macmillan, 2011.

Todorova, Maria. *Imagining the Balkans,* 2nd ed. Oxford: Oxford University Press, 2009.

Tomasevich, Jozo. *War and Revolution in Yugoslavia, 1941–1945: Occupation and Collaboration.* Stanford: Stanford University Press, 2001.

Toumarkine, Alexandre. *Les migrations des populations musulmanes balkaniques en Anatolie, 1876–1913.* Istanbul: Les éditions Isis, 1995.

Troebst, Stefan. *Zwischen Arktis, Adria und Armenien: Das östliche Europa und seine Ränder.* Köln: Böhlau, 2017.

Üngör, Uğur Ümit: *The Making of Modern Turkey: Nation and State in Eastern Anatolia, 1913–50.* New York: Oxford University Press, 2011.

UNHCR. "Europe: Syrian Asylum Applications," accessible online at http://data.unhcr.org/syrianrefugees/asylum.php (accessed April 2017).

UNHCR. "Internally Displaced People (July 7, 2016)," accessible online at http://www.unhcr.org/sy/29-internally-displaced-people.html (accessed April 2017).

UNHCR. "Syria Regional Refugee Response," accessible online at http://data.unhcr.org/syrianrefugees/regional.php (accessed April 2017).

United Nations. Progress Report of the United Nations Mediator on Palestine. Submitted to the Secretary-General for Transmission to the Members of the United Nations (1948), accessible online at https://digitallibrary.un.org/record/703168/files/A_648-EN.pdf (accessed April 2017).

Valeš, Vlasta. "Die tschechoslowakischen Flüchtlinge, 1968–1989," in Gernot Heiss and Oliver Rathkolb, eds., *Asylland wider Willen. Flüchtlinge in Österreich im europäischen Kontext seit 1914*, 172–181. Vienna: Dachs, 1995.

Vanthemsche, Guy. *Belgium and the Congo, 1885–1980*. New York: Cambridge University Press, 2012.

Vishnevsky, Anatoli, and Zhanna Zayonchkovskaya. "Auswanderung aus der früheren Sowjetunion und den GUS-Staaten," in Heinz Fassmann and Rainer Münz, eds., *Migration in Europa: Historische Entwicklungen, aktuelle Trends, politische Reaktionen*, 365–390. Frankfurt am Main: Campus, 1996.

Walker, Mack. *The Salzburg Transaction: Expulsion and Redemption in 18th Century Germany*. Ithaca: Cornell University Press, 1992.

Weichselbaumer, Doris. "Discrimination against Migrants in Austria: An Experimental Study," *German Economic Review* 18/2 (2017), 237–265.

Weiss, Yfaat. *A Confiscated Memory: Wadi Salib and Haifa's Lost Heritage*, Avner Greenberg, trans. New York: Columbia University Press, 2011.

Wieder, Rosalie: "Who Are the Vietnamese Americans?" in Susan Gall and Irene Natividad, eds., *Asian American Almanac: A Reference Work on Asians in the United States*, 165–174. Detroit: Gale Research, 1995.

Winkelbauer, Thomas. "Die Vertreibung der Hutterer aus Mähren, 1622: Massenexodus oder Abzug der letzten Standhaften?" in Joachim Bahlcke, ed., *Glaubensflüchtlinge. Ursachen, Formen und Auswirkungen frühneuzeitlicher Konfessionsmigration in Europa*, 207–233. Münster: LIT, 2008.

Wolff, Frank. "Deutsch-deutsche Migrationsverhältnisse: Strategien staatlicher Regulierung, 1945–1989," in Jochen Oltmer, ed., *Handbuch Staat und Migration in Deutschland seit dem 17. Jahrhundert*, 773–814. Berlin: de Gruyter, 2016.

Yıldırım, Onur. *Diplomacy and Displacement: Reconsidering the Turco-Greek Exchange of Populations, 1922–1934*. New York: Routledge, 2006.

Zahra, Tara. *The Great Departure: Mass Migration from Eastern Europe and the Making of the Free World*. New York: Norton, 2016.

———. *The Lost Children: Reconstructing Europe's Families after World War II*. Cambridge: Harvard University Press, 2011.

Zaremba, Marcin. *Wielka Trwoga: Polska, 1944–1947*. Kraków: Znak, 2012.

Zürcher, Erik Jan. "The Balkan Wars and the Refugee Leadership of the Early Turkish Republic," in M. Hakan Yavuz and Isa Blumi, eds., *War and Nationalism: The Balkan Wars, 1912–1913, and Their Sociopolitical Implications*, 665–678. Salt Lake City: University of Utah Press, 2013.

INDEX—PEOPLE, PLACE NAMES, SUBJECTS